PELICAN BOOKS

ROOTS OF WAR

Richard J. Barnet is cofounder and codirector of The Institute for Policy Studies. During the Kennedy Administration he served as an official of the State Department and the U.S. Arms Control and Disarmament Agency, and as a consultant to the Department of Defense. Articles by him have appeared in major magazines and newspapers across the country. In addition to *Roots of War*, books to his credit include *The Economy of Death*, *Intervention and Revolution*, and *Who Wants Disarmament?*

Richard J. Barnet

ROOTS
OF WAR

Penguin Books Inc   CATALOGUED
Baltimore · Maryland

Penguin Books Inc
7110 Ambassador Road
Baltimore, Maryland 21207, U.S.A.

First published by Atheneum Publishers, New York 1972
Published in Pelican Books 1973

Printed in the United States of America by
Kingsport Press, Inc., Kingsport, Tennessee 37662

For Ann

Acknowledgments

B ECAUSE this book attempts a synthesis of many aspects of American life my intellectual debt to writers in many fields cannot be adequately acknowledged. Among the thinkers who have been most influential in helping me to formulate the questions of this book are Hannah Arendt, Elias Canetti, Sigmund Freud, Erich Fromm, Vladimir Lenin, Walter Lippmann, Niccolò Machiavelli, Karl Mannheim, Karl Marx, C. Wright Mills, Lewis Mumford, Gunnar Myrdal, Franz Neumann, Marcus Raskin, Joseph Schumpeter, Max Weber, and William Appleman Williams. As is obvious from the list, my answers, such as they are, would certainly not be accepted by all of such a group and perhaps by none of them. To absolve any of them for responsibility for the results of their teaching would be gratuitous.

This book is an attempt to record my personal education in the meaning and operation of American foreign policy and its domestic roots. Thus it is also based on endless conversations with patient people over a number of years. Some of the people who most contributed to that education include Carl J. Barnet, Robert Borosage, Robb Burlage, Noam Chomsky, Clark Clifford, Benjamin V. Cohen, Joe Collins, Richard Falk, Gabriel Kolko, Milton Kotler, Terence McCarthy, Michael Maccoby, David Morris, Earl Ravenal, Leonard Rodberg, Franz Schurmann, Ralph Stavins, Hugo Valadares, Paul Kattenberg, Gene La Rocque, and Stanley Weiss.

All of the people who have been involved in the production of this book have also left their imprint on it. The list includes Simon Michael Bessie and Tony Clark, of Atheneum, and Marie Nahikian, Janice Carroll, Jan Hackman, Bethany Weidner, and Tina Smith, of the Institute for Policy Studies. My debt to all of them is gratefully acknowledged.

Contents

INTRODUCTION *In Search of the National Interest* **3**

PART I THE BUREAUCRATIC REVOLUTION
AND ITS CONSEQUENCES

CHAPTER 1 *Bureaucratic Homicide and Imperial Expansion* 13

CHAPTER 2 *The Bureaucratic Revolution* 23

CHAPTER 3 *The Education of a Governing Class* 48

CHAPTER 4 *The National Security Managers and the President* 76

CHAPTER 5 *The Operational Code of the National Security Managers* 95

PART II THE POLITICAL ECONOMY
OF EXPANSIONISM

CHAPTER 6 *The American Business Creed and the National Interest* 137

CHAPTER 7 *The Government-Business Partnership in Foreign Affairs* 176

CHAPTER 8 *Changing Patterns of Imperialism: Capitalism, Expansionism, and War* 206

PART III IMPERIAL DEMOCRACY

CHAPTER 9 *The Public Mood: Isolationism Old and New* 241

CHAPTER 10 *The Manipulation of Public Opinion* 266

CHAPTER 11 *Foreign Policy and Electoral Politics* 307

CHAPTER 12 *A Generation of Peace?* 333

ROOTS OF WAR

Introduction:

In Search of the National Interest

WE ARE THE number one nation," President Lyndon B. Johnson told the National Foreign Policy Conference at the State Department at a crucial moment in the Vietnam War, "and we are going to stay the number one nation." * There has never been a more succinct definition of the American national interest. This book is an examination of our national interest—who decides how American power is to be used in the world, and why.

Staying number one is a struggle for permanent victory. One failure of will, President Nixon has warned, will expose the United States to the world as a "pitiful helpless giant." In the pursuit of permanent victory the United States has engaged in a form of permanent war. Since 1940 this country has mobilized and maintained the most powerful military force in the world. In this period American forces have waged a global war and two large land wars (Korea and Vietnam). Since 1945 the United States has also conducted a major military compaign or a paramilitary CIA operation in a former colonial or dependent country on an average of once every eighteen months—Greece (1948), Iran (1953), Guatemala (1954), Indo-

* Lyndon Johnson is quoted in Townsend Hoopes, *The Limits of Intervention* (New York: David McKay and Co., 1969), p. 206.

nesia (1958), Lebanon (1958), Laos (1960), Cuba (1961), Congo (1964), British Guiana (1964), Dominican Republic (1965), and, of course, Vietnam (1950–present).* An American flotilla dominates the Mediterranean and the Far Pacific. American bombers loaded with hydrogen bombs and missiles concealed in concrete are poised to annihilate within minutes any society in the world. The American nuclear arsenal holds the equivalent of ten thousand tons of TNT for every man, woman, and child on earth. To pay for this the American economy has been on a war footing since 1940. Each year between fifty and seventy cents of every tax dollar goes to support this military establishment.

Until the Vietnam War most Americans accepted the militarization of America as a necessary and natural response to a dangerous world. A generation of war was forced upon America by a world that would not accept peace. Summing up that generation, Charles E. Bohlen, former Ambassador to the Soviet Union, asserts that the United States had "no sinister design, no hidden purpose, certainly no imperialist ambitions, in our policy, but simply moved in answer to a challenge. . . ." † It is, of course, as convenient for retired officeholders to apply the doctrine of inevitability to the past as it is for revolutionary propagandists to apply it to the future. Nevertheless Bohlen's characterization of America's defensive posture and pure motives has been accepted by most Americans for a generation. It has been the heart of the foreign policy consensus.

But that consensus has begun to crack as a result of the monumental defeat which the number one nation has suffered in Indochina. After spending more than fifty thousand lives and $150 billion, the United States could not achieve the modest imperial objective of establishing a stable, subservient government in South Vietnam. In its frustration the United States showed itself to be a homicidal menace for millions of innocent people of Indochina. As a consequence of its dropping the equivalent of three Hiroshima-strength bombs a month on the Indochinese for more than six years, hundreds of thousands have died, millions more have been maimed, and about one-fourth of the population of Vietnam are refugees in their own land. Although still admired and envied for its technological prowess and standard of living, the number one nation is surpassed by none in the fear and hatred it has inspired around the world.

Because these facts have begun to seep into the American consciousness, much more has been lost than positions of privilege in Southeast Asia. The Vietnam War has brought America to a spiritual

---

* For CIA operations abroad see Richard J. Barnet, *Intervention and Revolution* (New York: New American Library, 1968), chapters 9 and 10.

† Charles E. Bohlen, *The Transformation of American Foreign Policy* (New York: W. W. Norton and Co., Inc., 1969), p. 124.

crisis in which the values of our civilization and the very legitimacy of our system are under attack. One can see the signs in all sorts of places. Soldiers refuse to fight. A majority of the public, according to a succession of public-opinion polls, think the government lies. Draft-card burning, bombings, frenetic displays of the American flag, growing contempt for public officials, creeping cynicism about the American way of life, and pessimism about the nation's future all suggest that the citizens of the number one nation no longer feel like winners. Among the managers of American institutions there is a growing incapacity to cope with the problems of government and even a failure of will to rule. Mayors, college presidents, corporation executives, even a President of the United States, voluntarily renounce their offices. The pursuit of the national interest through permanent war has left the American people confused as to what the national interest really is.

This book is not about the Vietnam War but about the roots of a generation of war. What is there about mid-century America that has led her to pursue the national interest by spreading death, terror, and destruction? This analysis has grown out of a conviction that the United States has committed monumental crimes in Indochina and that these crimes are likely to be repeated unless we gain a much deeper understanding of what we have done as a nation and why we have done it.

The thesis of this book is that war is a social institution, that America's permanent war can be explained primarily by looking at American society, and that America's wars will cease only if that society is changed. It must be said that each of these propositions runs counter to much popular wisdom. The UNESCO constitution states that wars are made in the minds of men and it is in the minds of men that the defenses of peace must be constructed. In one sense, of course, the statement is undebatable. War is sparked by the passions of men. If the hatred of war were absolute and universal, there would be no war. Human nature makes war possible, but it is not its cause. Despite efforts of the apologists of American policy to justify permanent war by invoking pop anthropology, the view that militarism is a biologically determined aspect of the human condition cannot stand serious scrutiny. War, which we shall define as the organized killing for a community objective, is unknown among some of the most primitive men—the Great Basin Shoshone Indians, for example, who are about as close to a biological "state of nature" as one can find. Individual murder is almost universal, but group killing for social purposes appears to vary greatly according to the organization and experiences of a society. The descendants of the ferocious Swedes who terrorized northern Europe in the eighteenth century are now professional peacemakers.

Books such as Konrad Lorenz's *On Aggression* * have enjoyed wide popularity in part because they have been misread to mean that man is a hopeless predator who cannot help fighting wars against his fellow man. In fact, the book really lends some support for the proposition that social organization is at least as important as instinct in driving men, unlike other animals, to fight in groups against their own kind for abstract principles and remote goals. The dismal view of man as a natural warrior offers a certain bizarre comfort because it absolves individuals of responsibility of identifying, much less removing, the specific political, organizational, and economic causes of militarism and war. If human beings, males particularly, have biological urges to slaughter their own species at regular intervals, there is nothing to be done. Remorse is as useless as reform.

This book argues that the struggle of domestic political, economic, and social forces within a nation is the primary determinant of the national interest. In short, despite what statesmen say and many citizens believe, foreign policy is more an expression of our own society than a programmed response to what other nations do. Obviously, outside events play a role in the shaping of the national interest, but these events are filtered through American prisms. The policies that evolve in response to what goes on in Russia, China, Cuba, or anywhere else are primarily a reflection of American habits of mind, American fears, American hopes, and American values. There is nothing "inevitable" about the way a nation responds to the outside world. The world offers an infinite variety of plausible threats. Why do some become obsessions and why are others ignored? Is not the explanation to be found in the internal processes by which a society perceives and handles threats?

This book will concentrate upon the domestic sources of American foreign policy. Specifically, it will seek to explain why those who have been in charge of defining and meeting the threats facing the United States have determined that the national interest must be pursued by war and preparation for war. It will trace the roots of war within various elements of American society—the state, the economy, the political process, and the public. In one sense this book is a search for the elusive word "we" so often invoked in state papers during the past generation. "We" had "commitments" to forty-two countries. "We" gave our word to a clique of generals and politicians in Saigon and millions of Americans were conscripted to redeem that pledge. "We" can be safe, the Pentagon tells us, only if we are prepared to fight two and a half (recently reduced to one and a half) wars simultaneously.† It is now time to have a hard look at who "we" is.

---

* New York: Bantam, 1967.

† Carl Kaysen, "Military Strategies, Military Forces, and Arms Control," in *genda for the Nation*, Kermit Gordon, ed. (Washington, D.C.: Brookings Institution, 1968), pp. 549–580.

The proposition that foreign policy cannot change significantly without structural change in our society is exceedingly threatening to many Americans. Although our society likes the idea of change in the abstract, and "revolutionary" is a favorite term of Madison Avenue copy writers, no one likes to give up either old habits of mind or established privilege. For this reason most analyses of American foreign policy consider how to make the outside world safe for America as it is rather than how to make America safe for the world. The official and semiofficial post-mortems on the Vietnam war, which began to be performed somewhat prematurely in the seventeenth year of active American involvement in the conflict, have all emphasized that the war is a "mistake" of tragic proportions. To call a policy a "mistake" is comforting, because it implies that it is merely a bad choice which need not be repeated if we learn the right lessons. Of course the Indochina policy was a "mistake" in the sense that it did not turn out as American war planners intended or hoped. Any lost war is a mistake in that sense. But the evidence that has come to light about the planning of the war, particularly the Pentagon papers, reveals that America's leaders were not misled about the consequences of their decisions. What happened in Vietnam was not desired, but it was amply predicted within the foreign policy establishment.

When, in 1966, the Chairman of the Joint Chiefs of Staff told President Johnson, at a time when there were fewer than two hundred thousand American men in Vietnam, that it would take seven hundred thousand U.S. troops at least five years to achieve victory, the President told the general he was crazy and walked out of the room. Before the crucial decisions to land an expeditionary force in Vietnam and to commence bombing of North Vietnam, detailed intelligence estimates were prepared which came up with exceedingly pessimistic conclusions. On the basis of mathematical calculations about bombing damage the CIA deduced that North Vietnam could not be bombed into submission. Nor could the ground war in the South be won quickly, the intelligence experts argued, because the NLF was an authentic nationalist movement despite its aid from Hanoi. The high-ranking officers who played the "Sigma" war games at the Pentagon in 1964 were also forced into the view that it would be a long and inconclusive war. Yet something kept driving American policymakers deeper and deeper into the quagmire.

The Vietnam War was certainly a mistake. But it was not an accident. The Vietnam policy arose from the same analysis of the national interest, from the same theories of statecraft and human behavior, from the same technological impetus, and from the same economic pressures that have been the driving forces behind America's successful wars. The Vietnam War has had a unique result not because American policy has been fundamentally different from what it was when the American military effort smashed the Greek guerrilla movement in 1949 or suppressed the Dominican revolution in 1965 but because the Vietnamese exacted a price for American victory that the United States was unwilling to pay.

It is tempting to accept the "mistake" theory because it suggests that avoidance of future Vietnams will be easy. After all, what government within living memory would fight another land war in Asia? But such a view pushes one into the familiar trap that has snared so many hapless generals: thinking about the next war as if it were the last one. The "future Vietnams" have already begun. In Brazil, Greece, South Africa, and many other countries the United States continues to support forces of repression and to fear the forces of liberation and change. The scale and instruments of warfare will no doubt be different, but disengagement from Indochina will not in itself mean the end of America's generation of war.

Because nations are mystical entities, they resist serious self-analysis. The temptations to pin the blame for the Vietnam War on everything but the structures of our own society are overwhelming. A variety of ancient psychological devices are available. The Air Force already has its version of the "stab in the back" myth: The civilian leaders were unwilling to kill enough people fast enough to win the war. The civilian leaders resist all analysis of their readiness to order or to condone provocative acts of war, mass deportation, terror bombardment, torture of prisoners, and wanton destruction of land and crops—acts for which their predecessors a generation ago tried Nazi leaders—by pointing out that they are honorable men. The frustrations of the war have also inspired a new breed of American imperialist, who, like Pericles in fifth-century Athens, argue that the fate of greatness is to be feared and hated. The United States suffered a failure of will in Vietnam, they say, because the war planners were not tough enough to take the criticism of the world. Then there is the reaction of self-hate. Young Americans reared on liberal rhetoric about world law, United Nations, building a world of diversity, and struggling for freedom, have experienced feelings of betrayal, cynicism, or, simply, numbness, as they watched the deepening horror of the war. Many of them stood official orthodoxy on its head and sought to explain U.S. foreign policy in terms of America's unique corruption just as their fathers explained it in terms of her unique virtue. Finally, there is the related myth of mass guilt which denies the connection between power and responsibility and proclaims that the American people as a whole are all equally responsible.

This book starts from the premise that we must probe beyond these traditional responses of recrimination, denial, easy absolution, self-hatred, or immobilizing guilt. If we are to recover our sanity as a nation and to earn again the decent opinion of those with whom we share the planet, including our own children, Americans must engage in serious self-examination of those drives within our society that impel us toward destruction. The chapters that follow offer a framework for such a social self-analysis, which, it is hoped, may lead to concrete acts of political and social reconstruction. Our inquiry will center on three basic sets of questions.

In Part I we will consider these related issues: Who are the men who make the decisions? Why do they act as they do? What is the effect of bureaucratic structures such as the Pentagon and the CIA on foreign policy decisions? What kind of men become foreign policy planners and what is the operational code that governs their behavior while they occupy their offices?

Part II deals with the relationship of foreign policy and the economy: What are the economic roots of foreign policy? What role does business play in determining the national interest? Can America stop expansionism and war within the framework of the present economic system?

Part III examines the domestic politics of foreign policy: What is the impact of public opinion on foreign policy decisions? What does foreign policy mean to the ordinary citizen? How is public opinion manipulated and to what ends? What role does foreign policy play in electoral politics? Is a democratic foreign policy possible?

I

THE BUREAUCRATIC
REVOLUTION AND
ITS CONSEQUENCES

I

Bureaucratic Homicide and
Imperial Expansion

THINKERS with as different a view of the world as Sigmund Freud and Mikhail Bakunin have been struck by the fact that the role of the state is to assert a monopoly on crime. Individuals get medals, promotions, and honors by committing the same acts for the state for which they would be hanged or imprisoned in any other circumstance. "If we did for ourselves what we did for our country," Cavour once observed, "what rascals we should all be." The very meaning of sovereignty which states guard so jealously is the magical power to decide what is or is not a crime. The "state" is of course an abstraction to describe the activities of thousands of human beings organized into bureaucratic structures.

There is nothing new, to be sure, about government-ordered slaughters. Since man first built cities, from the Assyrians to Genghis Khan, from the Crusades to the Indian Wars, war has been an instrument of policy. No age has escaped the passion and fury of the professional killer. It is not homicide in the line of duty that is new, but the incredibly sophisticated organization of homicidal activities and techniques.

The essential characteristic of bureaucratic homicide is division of labor. In general, those who plan do not kill and those who kill do not plan. The scene is familiar. Men in blue, green, and khaki tunics and others in three-button business suits sit in pastel offices and plan complex operations in which thousands of distant human beings will die. The men who planned the saturation bombings, free fire zones, defoliation, crop destruction, and assassination programs in the Vietnam War never personally killed anyone.

The bureaucratization of homicide is responsible for the routine character of modern war, the absence of passion, and the efficiency of mass-produced death. Those who do the killing are following standing orders. As Frank Harvey has described it in *Air War: Vietnam,** a pilot with orders not to come back with bombs "lawnmowers" an area, "killing or maiming anybody on a path several hundred feet wide and many yards long." An American lieutenant following his instruction at Fort Benning's Officers' Candidate School extracts information from prisoners by means of the "water cure" or the "half a chopper ride." (In the first instance the victim is slowly drowned, in the other he is pushed out of a helicopter.) An infantryman, aware that even old men, women, and little children will shoot or lay booby traps for foreigners who burn their village, sprays machine-gun fire randomly into a crowd of cowering "Vietcong sympathizers." In each case the man who does the killing or terrorizing on behalf of the United States has been sent by others—usually men he has never seen and over whom he has no control.

The complexity and vastness of modern bureaucratic government complicates the issue of personal responsibility. At every level of government the classic defense of the bureaucratic killer is available: "I was just doing my job!" The essence of bureaucratic government is emotional coolness, orderliness, implacable momentum, and a dedication to abstract principle. Each cog in the bureaucratic machine does what it is supposed to do.

The Green Machine, as the soldiers in Vietnam call the military establishment, kills cleanly, and usually at a distance. America's highly developed technology makes it possible to increase the distance between killer and victim and hence to preserve the crucial psychological fiction that the objects of America's lethal attention are less than human. For the bureaucratic killer destruction is almost hygienic provided one does not have to lay hands on his victim. A U.S. diplomat in Laos, a tiny nation which the United States has given the distinction of being the most heavily bombed place on earth, told the French correspondent Jacques DeCornoy, "To make progress in this country, it is necessary to level everything. The inhabitants must go back to zero, lose their traditional culture, for it blocks everything."

* Quoted in Philip Slater, *The Pursuit of Loneliness* (Boston: Beacon Press, 1970), pp. 37 ff. These descriptions of tortures were given in testimony of Vietnam Veterans Against the War before the House Foreign Affairs Committee, April, 1971.

This American ambassador prided himself on his knowledge and affection for Laotian culture and wrote admiringly of the Laotians as a gentle people as he presided over their liquidation, much as the Nazi specialists in Jewish culture drew up elaborate plans for a museum in Prague to commemorate the race their leader hoped to make extinct.

Bureaucratic homicide is the monster child of technology and expansionism. The slow tentative progress human beings have made in the direction of civilization has been overwhelmed by the phenomenal advances in lethal technology. Not many people today believe with the Prussian militarists of a hundred years ago that war is the health of the state, and fewer dare to say so publicly. Twentieth-century man demonstrates in law and political propaganda a sensitivity to human suffering which did not trouble fifteenth-century man. But the modest advances in civilization have been more than wiped out by technological developments which make it possible to kill without exertion, without passion, and without guilt. The airplane enables the cool contemporary killer to set his victims on fire without ever laying eyes on them. The mass air raid and the repeated air strike which long ago were rationalized as conventional warfare by the prophets of airpower, such as General Billy Mitchell and the Italian General Douhet, make destruction "systematic" in a quite literal sense. Americans, along with Germans and British to a lesser degree, have been engaged in this form of bureaucratic homicide for almost thirty years, since the decision in 1942 to bomb Germany into submission. A milestone was the fire raid on Tokyo in 1944, when fire bombs incinerated one hundred eighty thousand residents of the city. Along with new developments in lethal technology have come new ideologies and organizational structures which offer absolution to honorable men when they plan homicide in behalf of the state.

Bureaucracy by nature finds it easy to accept an assigned homicidal role. On January 20, 1942, Reinhard Heydrich, the chief of the SS, called a meeting of fifteen high-ranking representatives of various ministries to the lovely Berlin suburb of Wannsee "to clear up the fundamental problems" of getting rid of all the Jews of Europe. Plans were carefully and coolly discussed and implemented. Although there was serious discussion of the transportation problems connected with the "final solution," no one questioned the project. Adolph Eichmann was a dispassionate long-range killer who, according to testimony at his trial, hated to visit the camps. His pleasure was in designing virtuoso solutions to complicated logistical problems. The psychiatrist who visited him in an Israeli jail reported that his tests revealed an "insatiable killing intention," but his record suggests that he would do any job of disposal well. The bureaucratic killer looks at an assigned homicidal task as a technical operation much like any other. He does not question its moral purpose. Indeed, he is not even interested in such questions.

It would be reassuring if pathological personality were a necessary ingredient of bureaucratic homicide. In Nazi Germany one could make such an argument. By the standards of Germany's own traditions and culture the Nazis were self-destructive men. Hitler's hideous revolution swept the worst elements of German society into power. Albert Speer's memoirs offer a revealing glimpse of how a more or less "normal" bureaucrat (who sounds in many ways much like an efficient American manager) felt among the degenerate, lazy, corrupt, and sadistic Nazi aristocracy. But the men who planned and executed bureaucratic homicide in Vietnam were by the standards of American society the "brightest and the best." That was, to be sure, their own sober self-assessment, but it was widely shared. They were Rhodes Scholars, university professors, business leaders, war heroes—all men who had succeeded brilliantly in their careers. Unlike the Nazi bureaucrats, who always repelled even those upper-class Germans who put up with them as necessary instruments of the times, the American bureaucrats were models of respectability and achievement. They were superior by almost any accepted definition of the society. They performed well on tests. They knew how to make money. They knew how to deal ingratiatingly with people as they leaped over one another in their careers. They were witty and considered good company. They were good citizens contributing their time and energy to numerous charitable causes. They had outwardly stable and respectable personal lives. They represented exactly what the society looked for in its leaders—intelligence, polish, energy, driving ambition, hard work, even a certain idealism. But in their jobs they were dangerously homicidal.

One important force behind bureaucratic homicide is the technological imperative. This is the classic compulsion of modern organizations to push technology to its limits and to exploit it to its fullest. It is, of course, a metaphor to say that technology dictates policy, for people, not machines, make the decisions. Yet the universal impulse in contemporary bureaucracies to seek prestige on the "frontier of technology" and to seek solution of human problems through technological devices is a crucial factor in the exponential rise of the global body count. "Having made the bomb," President Truman told the American people in August 1945, as if restating the obvious, "we used it." A committee of distinguished Americans, incuding the President of Harvard, the President of Massachusetts Institute of Technology, the president of one of the largest insurance companies, a former Supreme Court Justice, and a former Secretary of State recommended unanimously "that the bomb be used against the enemy as soon as it could be done . . . without specific warning and against a target that would clearly show its devastating strength." *

* See R. G. Hewlett and O. E. Anderson, Jr., *The New World* (University Park, Texas, 1962), pp. 358–60 for discussions of Interim Committee.

The President of Harvard made it clear in the committee meetings that the only target meeting such criteria was a population center. The people of Hiroshima and Nagasaki were about as defenseless against a high flying B-29 with an atomic bomb as the Jews in Hitler's Europe were against the gas chambers and ovens. Harry Truman always took personal responsibility for the decision and defended the bomb as "just another weapon." Although there was substantial evidence at the time that the Japanese were considering surrender, the two bombs were dropped "to save lives." Truman's "decision" to drop the bomb was, more accurately, a decision not to stop a bureaucratic process in which more than $2 billion and four years of incredible effort had been invested. The fact that the United States possessed a second bomb, the "Big Boy," which operated on a different, still untested, scientific principle from the "Fat Man" that destroyed Hiroshima, may well account for the totally indefensible Nagasaki attack. Truman never saw anything incongruous about combining his moral defense of Hiroshima and his moral condemnation of hunting in the same book. (One should not shoot at animals that can't shoot back.)

(2)

TECHNOLOGY is not enlisted in the service of bureaucratic homicide until it is harnessed to a political end. That end is usually expansionism in some form—i.e., the drive to extend control over an ever greater portion of the universe. "The thrust of expansionism," as Max Lerner has noted, "has been a continuous impulse in American history. Land hunger, power hunger, newness hunger, have proved wants that feed on themselves." By any historical definition the United States is an empire. From the birth of the Republic in 1776 to the outbreak of World War II the area under the dominion of the United States increased from 400,000 square miles to 3,738,393 square miles, expanding to a continental domain of about 3,026,789 square miles and overseas possessions and territories of 711,604 square miles. In World War II the United States did not legally annex further territory, but it assumed total control of "strategic trust territories" and other bases and thereby increased its global domain by approximately 8,484 square miles.

But rapid and continuous territorial acquisition is only one index of expansionism. The essence of expansionism is the ever-increasing dominion over other people. Political control need not be accomplished by the physical occupation or annexation of territory. In recent decades the techniques of control and domination available to great powers have multiplied and the United States has made more imaginative use of them than its rivals. Because the economy of the noncommunist world is tied in varying degrees to the dollar, the United States is in a position to export pneumonia whenever the American economy catches cold. The United States can exert pressure on single-crop countries through dumping, quotas, and other import practices. A decline of a few cents in the world market price of basic raw materials, over which the United States has great influence, can spell national bankruptcy for a poor country. American corporations are busily buying up corporations in Europe and staking new claims to the resources under the earth, and, now, under the sea as well. Perhaps the best index of America's economic power in the world is the fact that the American people, who represent about 6 per cent of the earth's population, melt, burn, or eat over 50 per cent of the world's consumable resources each year.

The United States government uses a variety of techniques for protecting this expansionist process—the granting and withholding of aid, the penetration of foreign economies by American corporations working closely with government, the export of American tastes and fashions through magazines, movies, TV programs, educational curricula, and, of course, the ubiquitous activities of U.S. intelligence agents. According to former CIA Deputy Director Richard Bissell, in some countries "the CIA representative has served as a close counselor (and in at least one case a drinking companion) of the chief of state." The CIA also resorts periodically to bribery. (The going rate for a chief of state in the 1950's, it appears, was about $3 million. The premier of Singapore publicly announced he was offered that sum, and according to Miles Copeland, a former CIA agent, the Egyptian President, Nasser, turned down a similar "gift." In 1960 the Congo parliament was bought much more cheaply. In the nature of things, details are available only on bribes that are refused.) All such activities are designed to expand influence and control.

But, as George Lichtheim has noted, "an empire is not complete without an imperial creed held by its governing class." From the days of "manifest destiny" to the era of "the American century," the empire of the United States has been well supplied with such a creed. America's imperial creed since World War II has been "world responsibility," no less than one should expect from the number one nation. It has now become time, wrote Henry R. Luce in his widely circulated editorial and pamphlet of 1941, "to accept wholeheartedly our duty and our opportunity as the most powerful and vital nation in the world and in consequence exert upon the world the full impact of our influence, for such purposes as we see fit and by such means as we see fit . . . it now becomes our time to be the powerhouse from which the ideals spread throughout the world." This creed was developed and proclaimed by the leaders of every major American institution. "The United States is the key to the destiny of tomorrow," wrote Hanson Baldwin, military editor of the New York *Times,* in early 1947. "We alone may be able to avert the decline of Western civilization, and a reversion to nihilism and the Dark Ages." As dark as the world crisis was, America's leaders saw it also as an opportunity. In 1946 Leo D. Welch, then Treasurer and later Chairman of Standard Oil of New Jersey, declared:

> American private enterprise is confronted with this choice; it may strike out and save its position all over the world, or sit by and witness its own funeral. That responsibility is positive and vigorous leadership in the affairs of the world—political, social and economic—and it must be fulfilled in the broadest sense of the term. As the largest producer, the largest source of capital, and the biggest contributors to the global mechanism, we must set the pace and assume the responsibility of the majority stockholder in this corporation known as the world. . . . Nor is this for a given term of office. This is a permanent obligation.*

By the mid-sixties the ideology underlying the "hard and bitter peace" of which John F. Kennedy spoke in his neo-Augustan inaugural address had become firmer and ever more audacious. "The interests of the United States are global," wrote Assistant Secretary of State Harlan Cleveland, "and that is good fortune for all the world's people and most of their leaders." America's mission, W. W. Rostow proclaimed, is to create, "no matter how long it may take, a world community in which men and nations can live at peace. No less is required of us." "World responsibility," Under Secretary of State George Ball declared in 1965, "may in today's world, be possible . . . only for nations such as the United States which command resources on a scale adequate to the requirements of leadership in the twentieth century." †
"History and our own achievements have thrust upon us the principal responsibility for the protection of freedom on earth," President Johnson declared at a Lincoln Day dinner in 1965, a trace of sadness mixed with pride in his voice. "For the next ten or twenty years," his predecessor had observed three years earlier, "the burden will be placed completely on our country for the preservation of freedom."

All the elements of a powerful imperial creed are present: a sense of mission, historical necessity, and evangelical fervor. Perhaps, most important, the American imperial creed was fitted with particularly effective rhetorical devices to clothe greed in the language of charity and to obscure the national will to win by calling it the burden of responsibility.

---

* Speech before the National Foreign Trade Convention, November 12, 1964.
† "The Dangers of Nostalgia," Department of State Bulletin, April 12, 1965, pp. 535–36.

The American imperial creed is expressed in anti-imperialist rhetoric. The United States seeks no colonies or territorial annexations. It opposes colonial empires, and indeed helped to preside over the orderly dismantling of the British, French, and Dutch Empires. (It is little noted, however, that along with the imperial responsibilities inherited from these collapsing empires the United States also acquired a considerable amount of the oil, markets, and other benefits that used to flow to London, Paris, and Amsterdam.) George Ball expressed the official altruism of American policy in these words:

> . . . never before in human history has a nation undertaken to play a role of world responsibility except in defense and support of a world empire . . . we find ourselves in a position unique in world history.

The same creed can be found in Max Lerner's popular *America as a Civilization,* which graced suburban coffee tables in the late 1950's:

> There can be no question that America has built one of the big empires of history. But to say this is not to carry along with it all the connotations that "imperialism" conveys as a set of drives towards aggrandizement which colors the nature of the imperium. . . . America did not set out to dominate the world as the Nazis did under Hitler, with a notion that its people were meant to be Herrenvolk while the rest were sub-men. There was no ideological fanaticism behind American expansionism, as in the case of the Communists. The American case is not even like that of the Roman Empire, which was the product of a similar energy system but which rationalized its expansion as Rome's civilizing function in a world of outworn kingships and barbarian hordes.*

This is a good example of the kind of ideological history Americans like to hear: America is exceptional and cannot be judged by the criteria applied to other nations. But of course every expansionist power has felt uniquely justified in helping itself to other people's goods and land or controlling their lives. For Cicero too the fledgling empire of the first century B.C. was a "guardianship," a domain over which the Roman people, whether by force or persuasion, could enforce the law of Rome and secure justice for primitive peoples. The British Empire was the "White Man's Burden," imposed by the stern hand of history. "Empire is congenial enough to the Englishman's temperament," George Unwin wrote during World War I, "but it is repugnant to his political conscience. In order that he may be reconciled to it, it must seem to be imposed upon him by necessity, as a duty. Fate and metaphysical aid must seem to have crowned him." In

---

* (New York: Simon and Schuster, 1957), p. 887.

every century, powerful nations have reluctantly "come of age," playing out their imperial destiny by carrying on a *mission civilisatrice* on the land of some weaker neighbor.

To call the ideology which undergirds the American Empire hypocrisy, however, is to miss the point. The American imperial creed can be understood only by taking the official rationale for expansionism literally. The United States, Secretary of State Dean Rusk noted sadly, is "criticized not for sacrificing our national interests to international interests but for endeavoring to impose the international interest upon other nations." * The imperial creed rests on a theory of law-making. According to the strident globalists, like Johnson, and the muted globalists, like Nixon, the goal of U.S. foreign policy is to bring about a world increasingly subject to the rule of law. But it is the United States which must "organize the peace," to use Secretary of State Rusk's words. The United States imposes the "international interest" by setting the ground rules for economic development and military deployment across the planet. Thus the United States sets rules for Soviet behavior in Cuba, Brazilian behavior in Brazil, Vietnamese behavior in Vietnam. Cold War policy is expressed by a series of directives on such extraterritorial matters as whether Britain may trade with Cuba or the government of British Guiana may have a Marxist dentist to run it. Cicero's definition of the early Roman Empire was remarkably similar. It was the domain over which Rome enjoyed the legal right to enforce the law. Today America's self-appointed writ runs throughout the world, including the Soviet Union and China, over whose territory the U.S. government has asserted the right to fly military aircraft. The United States, uniquely blessed with surpassing riches and an exceptional history, stands above the international system, not within it. Supreme among nations, she stands ready to be the bearer of the Law.

As Hannah Arendt has put it,† the use of *violence* for political ends is an index of the failure of political *power*. The United States has had the misfortune to come to its moment of greatest imperial expansion just as the postimperial era began. In earlier times America's military and economic might would have assured her the role of international "peacekeeper" which the managers of American foreign policy have sought. But the extraordinary cultural and political upheavals of our time have undermined the legitimacy of any single nation playing such a role and have forced the modern imperialist to resort more and more to the sophisticated use of violence. Yet at the very moment the number one nation has perfected the science of killing, it has become an impractical instrument of political domination.

* Harry Magdoff, *The Age of Imperialism* (New York: Monthly Review Press, 1969), p. 41.
† *On Violence* (New York: Harcourt, Brace and World, 1970).

Shortly after the Kennedy Administration decided to increase its military commitment to Vietnam in 1961, I received a visit from an official of the British Defense Ministry who warned that the United States was heading for catastrophe in Southeast Asia. He said that the moment an empire is forced to fight wars to hold positions of influence, it has already lost. Empires in the modern world can be maintained for a while by police but not by armies. If the resistance of the population is so great that an army must be sent to pacify them, the costs of maintaining imperial privilege always exceed the gains. These words from an experienced imperialist have yet to be heeded by the managers of the American Empire. America has been driven by her ideology and by her appetite to expand her dominion where the political basis for it does not exist. The result has been a form of political frustration which leads as if by reflex to bureaucratic homicide.

The awakening of the Third World—two billion men and women— has fundamentally altered the stage on which imperial politics has customarily been played. Primitive societies that fifty years ago could still be bought, sold, or traded in the chancelleries of Europe and had no control over their own destiny are now fiercely nationalistic. More and more they are resisting pacification by traditional imperial methods. Some have begun to resist not only foreign control but also foreign values. Former colonial countries, like others, do not wish to be run by bureaucrats from or in Washington, and a few of them are even demanding the right to be un-American in the solution of their problems. We now live in a world where fewer and fewer people know their place. A world in which traditional values, traditional assumptions, and traditional loyalties are breaking down is a hard world to manage—even for the number one nation. To be a counterrevolutionary power in what is in many ways a revolutionary world, as the United States has been for a generation, is in itself a commitment to the continuing use of violence.

2

The Bureaucratic Revolution

THE UNITED STATES has been engaged in wars of one kind or another since its birth. Our first "Vietnam" was General Arthur MacArthur's successful pacification campaign in the Philippines at the turn of the century. In the early decades of this century Marines landed regularly in Central America to collect debts, to put down revolutionary threats, and to protect friendly governments. But the scale and organization of warlike activities changed dramatically as a result of World War II, and as a consequence attitudes toward the use of violence as the primary instrument of diplomacy changed. It was a very different national security bureaucracy in the autumn of 1915 when Woodrow Wilson summoned the Acting Secretary of War, Henry Breckinridge. "Trembling and white with passion," Breckinridge recalls, the President pointed to a story in the Baltimore *Sun* which claimed that the General Staff was putting together contingency plans for a war with Germany (which did occur eighteen months later). The President directed the Secretary to investigate the charge and if true to "relieve every officer on the General Staff and order him out of Washington." * Today Pentagon files are stuffed with contingency

* Quoted in Samuel Huntington, *Soldier and the State* (New York: Vintage Books, 1964), p. 144.

plans for future wars, not only with our obvious enemies but with some of our closest allies.

The era of "dollar diplomacy," a time of sporadic, reflex interventions in Latin America when the United States also stationed six thousand Marines in China, has been followed in the post–World War II era by a more deliberate strategy of continuous global military involvement. Each year since 1945, somewhere in the world, American forces have been engaged in battle. The primary thrust of American military operations since 1945 has been counterinsurgency warfare, wars against political movements and people rather than against governments. Thus, in part, it is because the enemy is different from America's antagonists in the prewar period that the U.S. national security bureaucracy has come to look different and to operate under new rules. But, primarily, it is because the national security bureaucracy in a nation that has "come of age" and proclaims itself to be the number one nation has a different function.

The bureaucratic revolution that occurred in the United States during World War II has had a profound impact on the way the nation defines the national interest. How a nation organizes itself—whether for peace or war—largely determines how it will pursue its interests. As a result of the mobilization in World War II the United States organized for war. The essentials of those organizational changes remain to this day. This chapter is a brief survey of some of the major changes that have created the bureaucratic reality within which the managers of American foreign policy operate.

(2)

UNDER THE IMPACT OF WAR, the positions of the federal bureaucracy in American society changed radically in two ways. First, government agencies came to control the creation and disposition of a significant share of the national wealth. Second, the balance of power within the federal bureaucracy shifted decisively to those agencies that concerned themselves with foreign and military affairs. In 1939 the federal government had about eight hundred thousand civilian employees, about 10 per cent of whom worked for national security agencies. At the end of the war the figure approached four million, of which more than 75 per cent were in national security activities. The last premobilization defense budget represented about 1.4 per cent of the Gross National Product.* The lowest postwar defense budget, an interlude of about eighteen months between demobilization and remobilization for

---

* *The U.S. at War,* Bureau of the Budget (Washington, D.C.: Government Printing Office, 1946). See chart on p. 434 and text following.

the Cold War, took 4.7 per cent of the Gross National Product. Defense spending alone for fiscal year 1948 (the year of the lowest postwar defense budget) exceeded by more than one billion dollars the entire budget of the federal government for the last prewar year. Once postwar remobilization was under way, defense spending seldom dipped below 8 per cent of the GNP.

The phenomenal increase in the size and importance of the national security bureaucracies was accompanied by major transformations in their character. The State Department and the military agencies came out of the war with views of their functions and roles that differed substantially from those they had held before the war. In large part this metamorphosis was attributable to a generation of new men, schooled in war, who now stood ready to take over the swollen machinery of government.

Only for a few fleeting moments in her history had the United States attached high importance to the diplomacy of negotiation or awarded more than ceremonial status to the men who practiced it. In the earliest days of the Republic, Jefferson, Jay, and Franklin, the political and intellectual leaders of the United States, had shrewdly carved a place for the new nation as an adjunct of the European state system. In the weakness of infancy the United States relied heavily on persuasion and political maneuver to protect herself. But the Monroe Doctrine, which marked the divorce of America from European politics, also marked the shift of American diplomacy from cosmopolitanism to parochialism. In most of the world the American ambassador limited his role to that of a reporter or a scout for commercial opportunities. The State Department in Washington devoted its energies principally to economic, consular, and trade matters. The diplomatic career was a pleasant life for the rich man's son, the dilettante, or the retired financier who did not mind being outside the mainstream of politics and commerce. It hardly taxed one's intellect or initiative, and the token salary Congress was prepared to appropriate for the diplomat reflected the value it placed on his services. In the late nineteenth century the top ambassadorial posts began to go to prominent businessmen. The embassy, like the honorary degree, had become a ritualized reward for commercial success.

From the Monroe Doctrine to the Truman Doctrine, American diplomats spent much of their time helping the army to wrest control of the continent from the Indians and to extending the United States' sphere of influence to Latin America and the island prizes reaped from the Spanish-American War. While he was a passive agent of American interests in the great courts of Europe, the American diplomat was an active and vigorous defender of American business interests among more backward peoples and an engineer of territorial expansion through purchase and war.

However, as active as American diplomats were in these pursuits in the prewar period, these were not men who were equipped to deal with the unprecedented problems and opportunities that faced America across the ruins of World War II. One nation had been restored and strengthened by the war that had ravaged most of the rest. How the United States should relate to a starving, seething planet was a task for which the diffident socialites who had graced the European embassies and the proconsuls who had managed the United States' interests in Latin America were equally ill fitted. Most of the prewar generation of diplomats soon disappeared from the scene. A generation of career ambassadors, such as Norman Davis, as well as the leading administrators of the State Department in the New Deal period, Cordell Hull and Sumner Welles, did not survive the war in office. Despite repeated reorganizations during the war, the State Department's staff continued to reflect the prewar conception of its function. It was far stronger in economic, trade, and consular matters than in the practice of international politics. Even three years after the war the Department had a total of only 336 officers supposedly dealing with political questions out of a total complement of 5,906.

Franklin D. Roosevelt, who loved to play both the soldier and the diplomat, helped finish off the feeble prewar foreign policy bureaucracy with a series of blows. First, he appointed as Secretary of State a decent, old-fashioned moralist who bored him utterly. When he felt compelled to communicate with the State Department at all, he usually did so privately through Sumner Welles, the old schoolmate he had appointed as Under Secretary. Throughout his memoirs Hull complains about being left in the dark on the great issues. At the outset of the war Hull himself accelerated the State Department's decline by renouncing interest in vital political matters on the grounds that they sounded like "technical military" affairs. He refused even to look at the "ABC" papers, the strategic directives drafted by American and British military leaders in the months preceding Pearl Harbor. On November 27, 1941, Hull, according to his memoirs, "washed his hands" of the Japanese negotiations and "turned the problem over to Stimson and Knox—the Army and the Navy."

The State Department's prestige and power in government declined in other ways as well. Many foreign service officers were drafted. It was not considered an essential occupation. Thus while the officer corps of the military services grew astronomically, the ranks of the professional diplomatic service were depleted. At the same time the professionalism of the foreign service was further challenged. New foreign policy bureaucracies responsible to other, more powerful agencies, such as the Departments of Agriculture, Treasury, and Commerce as well as the emergency agencies, came increasingly to overshadow the State Department. At the height of the war forty-four separate government agencies had representatives stationed at the American embassy in London. At the end of the war the Manpower Act of 1946 encouraged the "lateral entry" of military officers into the top foreign service grades, thus diluting the old club atmosphere and bringing in a new breed of diplomat fresh from the war. Veteran diplomats mourned the passing of the good old days when a half dozen men would gather in the Secretary's office and talk over the state of the world.

(3)

THE DECLINE of the State Department created what diplomats themselves like to call a "power vacuum" and the military rushed in to fill it. In the war years the President turned increasingly to his generals and admirals for foreign policy advice, not only because his primary focus was on winning the war but, perhaps most important, because Marshall and his associates inspired confidence, as Hull did not. The Joint Chiefs, not Hull, attended the Big Three Meetings at Cairo, Teheran, and Casablanca. At Yalta, Roosevelt threw aside the voluminous briefing books that the State Department had provided him because he thought they were, in general, too equivocal with respect to the future of the British, French, and Dutch empires and too hostile to the Soviet Union. When the subject came to China, he banished the State Department representatives from the room. The Joint Chiefs of Staff were the most resourceful agency in the government in obtaining information. They received copies of the Roosevelt-Churchill correspondence "on a strictly personal basis" from the top British general in Washington, Sir John Dill. The military aide in the map room at the White House also smuggled out for his colleagues in the Pentagon memoranda prepared by FDR. All of these were, of course, quite unavailable to the State Department.

The power of the military services had grown swiftly once the President turned his major attention from economic recovery to preparation for war. In December 1941, shortly after his first wartime meeting with Churchill, Roosevelt created the Joint Chiefs of Staff. This bureaucratic innovation, which was based on neither Congressional legislation nor an executive order, greatly strengthened the position of the uniformed military within the government and profoundly affected the future course of American diplomacy. The purpose of the decision was twofold: to create a counterpart to the British Chiefs of Staff, who sat with the American officers on combined planning boards; and to discourage interservice rivalry. The result was the creation of the most efficient governmental structure for devising and implementing national security policy. The Joint Chiefs acquired a huge staff and drew also on the Operations Division of the War Department, which for a while was headed by General Dwight Eisenhower. They had direct access to the President and their influence was strengthened by Admiral William Leahy, who had an office in the White House and served as ambassador between the military chiefs and the President. The military leaders saw the President far more frequently during the war than did their civilian superiors. FDR, who had enormous respect for General Marshall—"I feel I could not sleep at night with you out of the country"—rejected the advice of the Joint Chiefs of Staff no more than two or three times.

Perhaps most important, the military supplied to the rest of the government the conceptual framework for thinking about foreign relations. Thus, not only did the war radically shift the balance of power in the federal bureaucracy, catapulting the military from a marginal institution without a constituency to a position of command over the resources of a whole society, but it also redefined the traditional tasks of the military. The traditional semantic barriers between "political" and "military" functions were eroded; in the development and execution of strategy the military was deep in politics. The military historian Walter Millis has summarized the rise of the policymaking role of the military in these words:

> Because the State Department was so effectively sidetracked, because the military establishment has such a dominant institutional position, and because American experience furnished so little in the way of precedents for guidance, the inherited and ingrained American military doctrines about war and the functions of force in national policy became unusually important.*

The major decisions of the war with the greatest obvious political impact were made by the President, the Joint Chiefs of Staff, and Harry Hopkins. The Chiefs prepared for diplomatic conferences, negotiated with the Allies, and in the war theaters the commanders, Eisenhower and MacArthur, were supreme. Each obtained the power to pass on all civilians sent to his theater and to censor their dispatches. "Through these controls of overseas communications," Walter Millis observes, "JCS was in a position to be informed, forewarned, and therefore, forearmed, to a degree no civilian agency could match."

At a time when Stalingrad was still under siege and it would have taken a lively imagination to conjure up a Soviet threat of world domination, United States military planners had already begun planning a huge postwar military machine. As the war ended, the Army demanded a ground force capable of expanding to 4.5 million men within a year. The Navy thought it wanted to keep 600,000 men, 371 major combat ships, 5,000 auxiliaries, and a "little air force" of 8,000 planes. The Air Force also had specific plans. It wanted to be a separate service and to have a 70-group force with 400,000 men.* With these plans the top military officers made it clear that they were through being fire-fighters called in when the diplomats had failed.

Because of their prestige and their experience and the dearth of obvious alternatives, generals and admirals were invited into key foreign policy positions in the Truman Administration. General Marshall was placed in charge of the China negotiations in 1946, returning the following year to become Secretary of State. General MacArthur was made the czar of Japan and staged a brilliant social and economic reconstruction. General Hildring was put in charge of the critical German policy and was succeeded by another general, Henry C. Byroade. A West Point graduate, Byroade later switched to the Foreign Service and became the key U.S. diplomat on Middle East policy in the early fifties, first as Assistant Secretary for the region and later as Ambassador to Egypt. In the first six years of the Cold War the American ambassadors to the Soviet Union were, successively, a Lieutenant General and an Admiral. The professional military were also assigned as ambassadors to such lesser posts as South Africa, the Philippines, Panama, Paraguay, and Costa Rica. They also staffed top positions in the newly burgeoning "intelligence community." The officers in charge of the National Intelligence Authority, later the Central Intelligence Agency, were General Hoyt S. Vandenberg, later Chief of Staff of the Air Force, Admiral Roscoe Hillenkoeter, and later General Walter B. Smith. Admiral Sidney Souers, a businessman who rose in the government in intelligence work, and James Lay, an intelligence officer, were the first Executive Secretaries of the National Security Council, the President's personal interpreters of major matters of foreign and military policy.

(4)

UNDER THE PRESSURE of war new techniques for manipulating the politics of other countries had been developed; those who had put together the bureaucratic structures for operating these techniques fought to preserve their life. In the postwar world, they argued, the United States would need them whatever the political environment

---

* *The Air Force Plans for Peace* (Baltimore: Johns Hopkins Press, 1969), pp. 7 and 8.

would look like. The world-wide deployment of United States forces at the end of the war represented an opportunity for projecting power that a nation aspiring to the "responsibilities of world leadership" would not renounce. Thus the Joint Chiefs of Staff argued successfully for retaining most of the network of bases acquired during the war. The research and development program, the public relations and propaganda networks, the military assistance program, and the subversion and intelligence apparatus, which hardly existed in 1940, continued to be major recipients of government funds after peace returned.

Let us look for a moment at three of these networks. Before the war the United States had naval bases in Guam, Hawaii, and the Philippines, and one or two other minor installations. During the 1930's it had been difficult to persuade Congress to agree to their fortification. In September 1945, as the war ended, U.S. military forces were in control of 434 bases around the world, built or occupied since 1940. Of these, 195 were in the Far East. During the war Secretary of the Navy James V. Forrestal and the military chiefs insisted that the United States retain the Pacific bases it had captured or built. "I am working on the idea," President Roosevelt wrote the Joint Chiefs of Staff in the summer of 1944, "that the United Nations will ask the United States to act as trustee for the Japanese mandated islands." Congressional committees visited the new Pacific acquisitions and, while the war was still on, recorded their demand that the United States keep them. A trusteeship with sufficiently flexible terms to amount to national control was negotiated at the end of the war, and the United States found itself with a permanent system of overseas bases that soon extended to every continent.

Even while some of the wartime bases were being given back, others were being acquired. By 1969 approximately 1,222,000 men were manning 399 major overseas installations and 1,930 minor installations. In many of these bases U.S. presence evolved from wartime occupation and thus preceded the onset of the Cold War. In countries such as Spain and Turkey, which were Axis-sympathizing neutrals in the war, U.S. forces made their first appearance with the American-Soviet confrontation. Bases that had declined in military value because of the increasing reliance on intercontinental nuclear missiles were retained to show the flag or to exert political influence on the home governments. The effect has been that military officers have outnumbered all other representatives of the United States around the world. The personal relationships they have made have had an important impact on the direction of U.S. policy. Since for the most part these relationships have been with their counterparts in other officer corps, it is not wholly surprising that these junior ambassadors from the military services found much confirmation and support for their own way of looking at the world.

In the prewar years, U.S. espionage activities were minimal. "Gentlemen do not read each other's mail," Secretary of War Henry L. Stimson airily observed as he dismissed a proposal for a national intelligence agency during the Hoover Administration. (This was the same prehistoric era, it should be remembered, when a top general in the War Department could veto plans for a new bomber on the grounds that it was "immoral" to design a plane to bomb civilians and the Navy could turn down the application of a chemist on the ground that it already had one.) Before World War II the Chief of Staff had a Military Intelligence Division which was responsible for conducting espionage and counterespionage, but he was so strapped for funds that the best he could do, as the intelligence specialist Roger Hilsman has put it, was to "occasionally sponsor an individual secret agent on a temporary job." But the day of hard times for spies was over. During the war the Office of Strategic Services, the first U.S. intelligence and espionage bureaucracy, recruited more than thirty thousand people for its work. Major General William J. (Wild Bill) Donovan—a Medal of Honor winner in World War I and an inspired bureaucratic empire builder—put together an extraordinary collection of scholars, socialites, businessmen, adventurers, and old friends who turned their hands to a series of brand-new activities for the U.S. government. Some infiltrated the European resistance movements and posed as Communists or Socialists. Others produced and distributed counterfeit currency. Still others parachuted behind enemy lines to assist partisan groups in Yugoslavia. There were many who assumed a variety of disguises to ferret out information in Lisbon, Stockholm, Bern, and even in occupied Europe. Most of the thirty thousand, however, were assigned to the pedestrian but more comfortable task of collecting, editing, and rewriting intelligence data. As the war drew to a close, intelligence analysts of the OSS turned to such topics as "The Character of the Belgian Resistance," "Radicalism in Italy," and "The French Police." Reports on these and other topics flooded the government, forerunners of the postwar intelligence production line that would spew forth red, green, brown, and yellow reports on every conceivable subject. (Years later a similar report enabled President Kennedy to dazzle an Israeli visitor with his intimate knowledge of nursery school developments in Israel.)*

Because of Donovan's energy and connections, to say nothing of the glamorous reputation of his agency, the Director of OSS was able to recruit an all-star cast for his world-wide operation. William Van-

---

* The information on OSS personnel and their activities is from Robert H. Alcorn, *No Bugles for Spies* (New York: David McKay and Co., 1962), p. 80.

derbilt, former Governor of Rhode Island, became his administrative deputy. David Bruce, Andrew Mellon's son-in-law, headed the European Theater activities, and later took charge of all espionage activities. Professor William L. Langer organized and ran the Research and Analysis branch and recruited a brilliant army of historians, economists, and other academics to what came to be known as "the intelligence community." The OSS alumni, including such men as Carl Kaysen, Herbert Marcuse, and Arthur Schlesinger, have held some of the most influential academic positions during the last generation. Within its ranks OSS also included Mellons, Morgans, Armours, and Goddards, and other scions of famous upper-class families, mostly recruited by David Bruce—a fact that gave rise to the quip that OSS stood for Oh So Social. At the same time it was a home for radicals. "I'd put Stalin on the OSS payroll if I thought it would help us defeat Hitler," General Donovan retorted to a critic.

General Donovan's thinking, as peace dawned, offers an insight into the indestructibility of bureaucratic instruments. His assistant, Robert H. Alcorn, has described his views:

> With the vision that had characterized his development of OSS, General Donovan had, before leaving the organization, made provision for the future of espionage in our country's way of life. Through both government and private means he had indicated the need for a long-range, built-in espionage network. He saw the postwar years as periods of confusion and readjustment affording the perfect opportunity to establish such networks. We were everywhere already, he argued, and it was only wisdom and good policy to dig in, quietly and efficiently, for the long pull. Overseas branches of large corporations, the expanding business picture, the rebuilding of war areas, Government programs for economic, social, and health aid to foreign lands, all these were made to order for the infiltration of espionage agents.*

Thus, before the Soviet spy revelations of 1946, before the first clashes of the Cold War, decisions were made to use "for the long pull" the instruments of subversion fashioned in war.

This process by which bureaucracies expand to take advantage of opportunities is particularly important in the area of technology. In both World War II and the Cold War into which it merged new technological discoveries have spawned new bureaucratic empires. Increasingly both threats and opportunities have been defined in terms of available technology. The idea that a country's crops may be a legitimate military target does not really take hold in the national security bureaucracy until there is a crop destruction "capa-

---

* Alcorn, Robert H., *op. cit.,* p. 195.

bility." What begins as a technologist's flight of imagination ends up as a social system, for every modern weapon must come equipped not only with its own means of delivery but with its own bureaucracy skilled in inventing threats to justify its use and lobbying for its further development. Americans have such a weakness for the "sweetness" of technology (How often we use the word for a new car!) that a sophisticated piece of equipment easily sells itself. Stewart Alsop tells the story that President Eisenhower finally agreed to the U-2 flights over the Soviet Union after being shown a photograph of the Augusta golf course at seventy thousand feet. "Every detail of the familiar well-loved golf course was clear to the President, who delightedly picked out a golf ball on the green." If you have a marvelous instrument, how can you afford not to use it?

The tyranny of technique pervades the whole national security bureaucracy. It is very hard for any individual to resist it. David Lilienthal describes in his diaries the arguments used by the Pentagon to gain control of atomic weapons and make them part of its regular arsenal right after the war. He quotes Truman as saying, in contradiction to his own public statements on the subject, that the atomic bomb "isn't a military weapon," but one "used to wipe out women and children and unarmed people."

"But, Mr. President," Secretary of Defense Forrestal argued, following time-tested procedures for presidential flattery, "as an old weaponeer yourself, you know how important it is to get used to handling a new weapon." "Yes," agreed Kenneth Royall, the Secretary of the Army, "we have been spending 98 per cent of all the money for atomic energy for weapons. Now if we aren't going to use them, that doesn't make sense." More than twenty years later officers working for the Joint Chiefs of Staff would write that it made no sense to have all those tactical nuclear weapons in the Pacific if you were never going to use them.

(5)

IN ADDITION to such traditional military instruments for promoting national security policy as bases and spies, the United States government learned from the war new techniques for projecting its power and influence. These, too, remained. One was military assistance. In 1938 the U.S. Army had begun to send military missions to Latin America to replace the French and British officers who had been the traditional mentors of the Latin armies. The purpose was mainly to keep out German influence. In 1942 the Inter-American Defense Board was created. This was a permanent bureaucratic structure through which the United States took charge of weapons supply, ordnance standardization, and training for the armies of the hemisphere. In early 1946 the War Department announced the plans which had been developed during the war for a permanent military assistance program to Latin America. As the proponents of the program have frequently stated in Congressional testimony, its purpose has been to establish close ties with Latin American officer corps so as to insure continued U.S. influence in their countries. The United States has extended its military aid program far beyond the Western Hemisphere. Starting with the exchange of over-age destroyers for bases on British territories in 1940, an arrangement made without Congressional approval and handled by Dean Acheson as his first national security assignment, the United States quickly established itself as "the arsenal of democracy." During the first twenty years of the Cold War, the military assistance bureaucracy spent more than $35 billion.

Other foreign policy agencies, originally organized to perform emergency tasks, were also later incorporated into the permanent national security apparatus. For example, on July 2, 1940, the United States established export licensing as a device for controlling the traffic of strategic goods to Japan. Originally set up under the Office of Export Control, later shifted to the Office of Economic Warfare, the licensing function ended up after the war as a regular function of the Commerce Department and a much-used, though largely ineffective, instrument for fighting the Cold War.

The United States had no permanent information or propaganda agencies before the war. As the Bureau of the Budget's official history, *The United States at War,* puts it, "the customs of diplomacy as well as its lack of legal authority restrained the State Department from participation in commercial, cultural, and educational activities that might embarrass it in the conduct of its normal business." The first effort to develop a bureaucracy for the official use of culture and education as an instrument of foreign policy grew out of a suggestion by Nelson Rockefeller. He believed that there should be "an organization which would not be hampered by the limitations of traditional diplomacy in the promotion of good will among the Latin American Republics." As frequently happens to influential insiders who propose new bureaucracies, Rockefeller was invited to head the new organization. On August 16, 1940, he became head of the Office for Coordination of Commercial and Cultural Relations between the American Republics, with a mandate to make "effective use of governmental and private facilities in such fields as the arts and sciences, education and travel, radio, the press, and cinema" to "further national defense and strengthen the bonds between the nations of the Western Hemisphere." Later the Office of War Information carried on greatly expanded activities of the same character but on a global scale. At the end of the war OWI's foreign information functions were transferred to the State Department, which, on December 31, 1945, created an Office of International Information and Cultural Affairs. This was the beginning of an expanding network of peacetime propaganda and information agencies which culminated in the permanent world-wide operations of the United States Information Agency and the Voice of America.*

(6)

THE MILITARY-INDUSTRIAL complex is another legacy of World War II. The five-year mobilization transformed the relationship of government and the defense industry and created the symbiotic partnership that exists today. Before their wartime association, there were few issues on which the two partners thought alike. Before the war most businessmen looked upon the military as boon-dogglers and practitioners of an obsolete and barbaric art. Some of the most prominent businessmen, such as Andrew Carnegie and Henry Ford, were commercial pacifists who believed that the salvation of mankind lay in trade expansion. One day the whole world would become one great market. The choice for America, as they saw it, was between industrial progress and militarism, and the latter they equated with waste. The professional military were equally contemptuous of businessmen, who, in their view, constituted a money-grubbing leisure class. Businessmen "never consider the propriety of devoting themselves or their sons to the public service unless it be as ambassadors or ministers at foreign courts," General William Carter complained in a 1906 issue of the *North American Review*. Patriotism was one thing and profits were quite another. There were, to be sure, exceptions. The Navy League, a lobby composed of naval officers and shipbuilders devoted to extracting more money from Congress for ships, was an early prototype of the military-industrial complex.

Big business was dragged reluctantly into rearmament in 1940 by the New Deal. The War Resources Board, under Edward Stettinius, president of U.S. Steel, set modest rearmament goals despite the fact that the steel industry was operating at less than 54-per-cent capacity at the time. The New Dealers with the biggest reputations for being antibusiness—Henry Wallace, Harry Hopkins, and Leon Henderson—were constantly pressing for faster and more drastic

---

* Discussions of wartime propaganda activities are in *The United States at War*, pp. 203–233.

rearmament than either the businessmen in charge of procurement or the Army itself. Generals were aghast when Roosevelt set a production goal of fifty thousand planes a year.*

Business feared full-scale mobilization because they were nervous about being saddled with excess productive capacity if the war should turn out to be too small. The model on which they operated was World War I, in which the government manufactured most of its own armaments in federal arsenals. General Motors kept producing automobiles throughout World War I and did a total of $35 million in war work without expanding its plant at all. In World War II, on the other hand, GM had $12 billion in government contracts. From February 1942 to September 1945, the company did not produce a single automobile. At the same time it went into production on 377 totally new items.† Other firms were even more totally transformed by the war. Whole new fields, such as radar, advanced communications, and nuclear energy, were opened. Entire new industries, which had not existed in the prewar period, were now flourishing captive suppliers of the federal government.

The relationship that evolved in the war was a marriage of necessity, but the government brought to it a handsome dowry. Contracts went to the companies that were able to marshal talent and facilities quickly. These were the biggest corporations in the nation. Forty per cent of all research contracts, for example, went to the ten top corporations. The government financed hundreds of new plants and then at the end of the war sold many of them to the industrial giants at nominal cost. The Geneva Steel Plant, which cost $202.4 million to build, was given to U.S. Steel for $47.5 million. The government also paid for research that ended up as private patents. It gave fast tax write-offs, and at the end of the war terminated contracts on terms so favorable to the contractors that the Comptroller-General later found that in one out of every seven cases the contractor received excessive or fraudulent payment.

Big business had faced a crisis in the war. Some, such as Bernard Baruch, proposed that the government nationalize the war effort, draft industry into the war economy, and set industry profits itself. General Brehon Somervell, chief of the military procurement agency, the Services of Supply, with 42 per cent of the annual war budget to spend, called for the total militarization of the economy. The Army would take over the plants. Corporation presidents would

---

* For additional discussion of wartime production, see Bruce Catton, *The Warlords of Washington* (New York: Harcourt, Brace and Co., 1948), and Donald M. Nelson, *Arsenal of Democracy* (New York: Harcourt, Brace and Co., 1946).

† General Motors operations in the two world wars are described by Alfred P. Sloan, *My Years at General Motors* (Garden City, N.Y.: Doubleday and Co., 1964), pp. 375–76 ff.

wear uniforms and be subject to military law. But the mobilization crisis was solved, instead, by giving business a variety of incentives to produce. The free-enterprise system, helped by government funds, caused the Gross National Product to increase more than twofold in five years. A galloping economy—$687 billion in gross national product during the war years—overwhelmed the enemy with America's productive might. But in the process the relationship of government and business was transformed. In 1944 Charles E. Wilson, president of General Electric, speaking to the Army Ordnance Association, proposed a "permanent war economy." What he had in mind was a permanent set of relationships between business and the military which could be the nucleus of any future general mobilization effort and the conduit for the substantial military production he assumed would continue in the postwar world. Every major producer of war materials, he advised, should appoint a senior executive, with a reserve rank of colonel, to act as liaison with the Pentagon. "There must be once and for all," he said, "a continuing program." *

The experience of war made American business ready to accept the military as a permanent, legitimate force in American life with which industry could form profitable coalitions. By the same token, the war restored the public image of big business, which had been badly tarnished in the Depression years of the 1930's. In creating the arsenal of democracy, business demonstrated its capacity for patriotic service. There was no doubt that what was good for General Motors was good for the country when GM was producing tanks to fight Hitler. In addition, the rapprochement of business and the military was eased by the changing character of the military task. As the military became increasingly involved in problems of technology and politics—and particularly in the job of managing billions of dollars' worth of assets in the civilian economy, such as factories, hospitals, housing, and transportation—the historic distinctions between the soldier's heroic ethic and the capitalist creed faded.

(7)

THE ORGANIZATIONAL REVOLUTION, which brought the federal bureaucracy to a new position of command over American society and secured the dominance of the national security institutions within that bureaucracy, took place against a background of profound social changes. These too were accelerated by war. Many of them

* Quoted in Tristram Coffin, *The Armed Society* (Baltimore: Penguin Books, 1964), p. 169.

were closely linked to the bureaucratic revolution itself. They also helped to change the definition of the American national interest.

As the role of the federal bureaucracy expanded, the role of Congress correspondingly diminished. In the 1930's Congress exercised a powerful veto on military spending, refusing to fortify Guam and, only a few months before Pearl Harbor, passing the Selective Service Act by a single vote. In 1938 President Roosevelt had to summon all his political powers to block the Ludlow Resolution for a constitutional amendment forbidding the President to send troops overseas without a national referendum. Less than ten years after its narrow defeat his successor secured broad Congressional support for the President's right to use American military power at his discretion to put down revolutionary movements abroad. This was the Truman Doctrine, later to be amplified in the Eisenhower Doctrine, the Gulf of Tonkin Resolution, and forty-two treaties of assistance stating "commitments" which the President, not Congress, has the right to decide when and how to meet. Congress had abdicated its war powers under the Constitution, and the President was now in a position to carry on vest-pocket wars in such places as Laos (where the CIA has recruited a 100,000 man foreign legion made up of various Southeast Asian tribes), beyond the scrutiny of the people or their elected representatives and in violation of such provisions of U.S. law as the prohibition against using Thai mercenaries in Laos. Military appropriations, which before the war were subjected to the Congressional meat ax, in the postwar years were passed unanimously after friendly hearings in the armed services committees and perfunctory debate on the floor. "I never voted against a defense appropriation," former Congressman and later Secretary of the Interior Stewart Udall testified before the Joint Economic Committee. Such appropriations, he said, were "sacrosanct." The constitutional historian Edward Corwin has noted that each war the United States has fought has increased the power of the executive and speeded the centralization of government.* This is a process which Lewis Mumford finds repeated throughout history. Centralized, bureaucratic government, or what he calls the Megamachine, is both the product and the cause of war.† We can see this process at work in the remarks of a typical Congressman during the Second World War:

> I am taking the word of the General Staff of the War Department, the people who are running this show. If they tell me this is what they need for the successful prosecution of this war and

---

* See Edward S. Corwin, *The "Higher Law" Background of American Constitutional Law* (Ithaca, N.Y.: Great Seal Books, 1955).

† Lewis Mumford, *The Myth of the Machine* (New York: Harcourt, Brace and World, 1970), p. 317.

for ultimate victory, I am for it. Whether it staggers me according to its proportions or not, I am still for it.

The war brought about a change in the role of organized labor in the United States that has had far-reaching implications for national security policy. Labor shared in the great economic gains of the war. Because industry prospered workers' wages rose. Despite wage controls, weekly earnings in manufacturing industries doubled between January 1939 and January 1945. Union membership rose during the same period by more than six million. Most of the new members were in manufacturing and the building trades. As new workers were recruited, they joined the union. The War Labor Board aided the wartime organizing effort by ordering "maintenance of membership" clauses written into union agreements. This meant that every union member or would-be member had to maintain his membership during the life of the contract. Both these developments lent great additional strength to the union movement.

The immediate prewar years had witnessed a series of bloody sit-down strikes in the automobile and steel industry. During the Little Steel strike on Memorial Day 1937 Chicago police had shot and killed ten strikers. But by 1941 the War Labor Board had pressured the Little Steel companies to come to terms with the Union. Ford had been forced to recognize the United Auto Workers. Meatpackers and rubber workers were organized. In a time of extreme labor shortage the unions' bargaining power was evident. It was at this point that labor leaders became labor statesmen, joining the war effort and subordinating their constituents' demands to the nation's needs.

The labor leader who took on the task of healing the deep resentments of the past and bringing labor into cooperation with the national security establishment was Sidney Hillman. On May 28, 1940, Hillman, who was President of the Amalgamated Clothing Workers and an important figure in the CIO, was appointed to the National Defense Advisory Commission along with six others including the President of General Motors. It was the first time a labor leader had been called to the highest councils of government. In his job he persuaded the War and Navy Departments to require observance of federal labor legislation in all defense contracts and succeeded in having the AFL building trades unions recognized on all government construction projects. At the same time he persuaded labor to curb its power to strike. "I find no difficulty in reconciling the objectives of labor and the objectives of national defense," he told the CIO convention in 1940. "They are intertwined, they are inseparable." He successfully resisted a no-strike law urged by a number of the businessmen who had come to Washington, although after Pearl Harbor the major unions gave a voluntary no-strike pledge. During the war the President seized war plants on forty occasions, but the overwhelming majority of disputes were settled without strike, largely because of the cooperative role of labor leaders, who now found themselves called in more and more for conferences on the war effort. After the German invasion of Russia in June 1941 the communist factions in CIO unions stopped strikes and slowdowns in war industries and outpaced the rest in sacrificing union demands to the war effort. Of all the major union figures only John L. Lewis refused to cooperate with the President. In war a strike against a major industry is a strike against government. When the government-industry partnership continued into the postwar period this meant a loss of power for the unions vis-à-vis management because industry could continue to invoke "national security" in discouraging or preventing the use of labor's weapons.

Shortly after Pearl Harbor Walter Reuther of the United Auto Workers had proposed that labor officials serve with management leaders on joint committees to supervise conversion to war industry. Labor wanted more than an "advisory" role, he insisted. But industry leaders whose leanings were antiunion nervously rejected such "socialistic" ideas. As the war continued, labor leaders increased their power by building their unions' treasuries and pension funds and playing a larger political role in the Democratic Party. But their influence in the top management of the war effort declined and they were unable to transform their new respectability into gains for workers commensurate with the new prosperity. In 1942 Sidney Hillman left government. The national security managers, who had been recruited from industry and finance, now ran the war effort alone.

In the area of foreign policy labor leaders became government servants. The American Federation of Labor had long worked to support U.S. foreign policy. In 1918, Samuel Gompers had gone to Europe to proselytize European labor for the Wilsonian foreign policy, although his presence appears to have had the opposite effect. But with World War II the most powerful segments of organized labor, which might have been in a position to pursue an independent or critical foreign policy, were integrated into the foreign policy establishment. In 1944 the AFL set up the Free Trade Union Committee, which was designed to combat the growth of communism as a world force. Jay Lovestone, a former top U.S. Communist who had been purged by Stalin for supporting his ideological rival, Nikolai Bukharin, was made Executive Secretary. Lovestone, by now a militant anticommunist, had already built a career for himself as professional adviser on communism to unions, such as David Dubinsky's International Ladies Garment Workers' Union, which were engaged in fighting their own communist factions.

Thus the war, particularly in its closing months as it shaded almost imperceptibly into the Cold War with the Soviet Union, provided new incentives to organized labor to join the foreign policy consensus. First, labor leaders gained prestige by being consulted on major national issues, and, as Walter Reuther would point out in the heated debates on the Truman Doctrine in the 1947 CIO convention, labor gained legitimacy by joining the team. Second, the "threat" of world communism was an invaluable ideological weapon for union leaders battling local Communists for control of their unions. As the Cold War intensified, the AFL would play a major role in supporting U.S. diplomacy and would offer the American labor movement as a cover for the operations of the Central Intelligence Agency, particularly in Latin America. Labor leaders, such as Lovestone's associate Irving Brown, would transmit U.S. government cash in France and Italy to buy elections and to break strikes in the furtherance of the American national interest. These activities, which reached a height in the years 1947–51, were also natural outgrowths of the war. In the closing months of the war, for example, Brown was serving in Europe as director of the Labor and Manpower Division of the Foreign Economic Administration making contacts with "reliable" local labor leaders and developing a strategy for fighting the European Communists, who, he knew, would emerge from the war with new prestige. The relationship between such labor leaders and the wartime intelligence agencies laid the basis for labor's major foreign policy role in the postwar period and must be seen as an important part of the bureaucratic revolution.*

(8)

A CRUCIAL ASPECT of the bureaucratic revolution was the mobilization of the universities. The Manhattan Project, which produced the first atomic bomb, was the most famous instance of the militarization of science. Thousands of the nation's most competent scientists, working under world-renowned physicists, many of them unaware of what their colleagues in the next laboratory were doing, devoted their talent to weaponry. The "war of the laboratories" was rightly regarded as one of the most crucial fronts in the global fight against

* For a discussion of labor cooperation, see Ronald Radosch, *American Labor and United States Foreign Policy* (New York: Random House, 1969), and Matthew Josephson, *Sidney Hillman: Statesman of American Labor* (Garden City, N.Y.: Doubleday and Co., 1952).

Hitler and the Japanese. Gerard Piel, editor of the *Scientific American,* summarizes what happened to American science during World War II:

> The universities transformed themselves into vast weapons development laboratories. Theoretical physicists became engineers, and engineers forced solutions at the frontiers of knowledge. MIT and Harvard undertook to create the strategy and tactics as well as the instruments of radar and counter-radar; from Johns Hopkins came the proximity fuse that brought the conventional high-explosive artillery shell to its peak of lethality, and Columbia, Chicago, and California joined in the successful engineering and manufacture of the most fateful weapon of all. The universities and the scientists then dealt with the military not as contractors, but as privateers bringing along their own novel weapons.*

When the war ended Massachusetts Institute of Technology was as eager to dismantle its Instrumentation Laboratory and California to give up Los Alamos as the War Department was to convert the Pentagon into the hospital it was originally designed to be. These enormous scientific complexes brought huge federal subsidies to the campuses. For the new breed of academic operator that had been developed in the war it meant a chance to exercise power on the national scene. Building on the wartime scientific network, the Defense Department and the Atomic Energy Commission developed weapons laboratories or pools of scientific consultants at all major universities and a good many minor ones. University administrators welcomed the infusions of federal money which enabled them to build and keep departments of prestigious scientists. Professors, who had had a taste of history-making in the war, were eager to continue serving on White House advisory boards and Pentagon panels.

In July 1945, Vannevar Bush, Director of the Office of Scientific Research and Development, drawing on the experience of the war then drawing to a close, outlined for the President a continuing policy of scientific mobilization:

> There must be more—and more adequate—military research during peacetime. We cannot again rely on our allies to hold off the enemy while we struggle to catch up. Further, it is clear that only the Government can undertake military research; for it must be carried on in secret, much of it has no commercial

---

* Gerard Piel has developed these ideas in *Science in the Cause of Man* (New York: Alfred Knopf, 1962), pp. 103–112.

value, and it is expensive. The obligation of Government to support research on military problems is inescapable. . . .

Military preparedness requires a permanent independent, civilian-controlled organization, having close liaison with the Army and Navy, but with funds directly from Congress and with the clear power to initiate military research which will supplement and strengthen that carried on directly under the control of the Army and Navy. . . .

Publicly and privately supported colleges and universities and the endowed research institutes must furnish both the new scientific knowledge and the trained research workers. These institutions are uniquely qualified by tradition and by their special characteristics to carry on basic research. They are charged with the responsibility of conserving the knowledge accumulated by the past, imparting that knowledge to students, and contributing new knowledge of all kinds. . . .

If the colleges, universities, and research institutes are to meet the rapidly increasing demands of industry and Government for new scientific knowledge, their basic research should be strengthened by use of public funds.*

In the process the great universities became instruments of the state. By the 1960's MIT's attorney would characterize the university as "a scientific arsenal of democracy," the President of the University of California would conclude that "intellect" has "become an instrument of national purpose, a component part of the 'military-industrial complex,' " and the President of Michigan State would call the nation's colleges and universities "bastions of our defense, as essential as . . . supersonic bombers. . . ."

The mobilization of social science had an even more profound effect on the university. During the war government discovered that social scientists could be useful, particularly in the areas of testing, opinion manipulation, and propaganda. Social scientists, organized by anthropologists such as Margaret Mead and Clyde Kluckhohn, flattered that the academic interests they had been pursuing for poor pay and with scant attention should now be deemed relevant to universal political questions, flocked to Washington to become "problem-solvers" for the government. In the process new techniques of analysis such as operations analysis, systems analysis, and game theory were refined.

Government subsidization of social science had profound effects on the state of knowledge in America. Professors who could obtain

* Vannevar Bush, *Science: The Endless Frontier* (Washington, D.C.: National Science Foundation Office of Scientific Research and Development, 1960), pp. 17–20.

support from the Department of Defense grew in prestige and power in the university community while those whose work was "irrelevant" to the great problems of the day got along without secretaries, research assistants, and travel funds. To be "relevant" a social scientist had to look at problems as if he were a bureaucrat looking for an answer. His job was to tell officials how to do what they wanted to do in the most efficient way and then to help them measure what they had done. Criticizing policy goals or challenging the implicit values behind a policy were considered "counterproductive" by the managers of university contract teams and by ambitious professors themselves because the government was not disposed to renew contracts with academics too dense to realize that they were being paid for technical assistance, not wisdom. Thus the government, through the research contract, exerted an extraordinary influence on what was thought and said in the major universities. Built into the contract relationship were profound unspoken assumptions such as: Government is an instrument of problem-solving, not a problem itself; efficiency is more to be prized than freedom; scientific development equals scientific "progress"; the techniques of social control and manipulation of taste developed through motivational research, data processing, and communications research are neutral knowledge.*

On foreign policy issues the government-university relationship helped reinforce the new orthodoxy that was quickly developing. Academics who had been part of the OSS constellation, such as John Gardner and William Langer, helped organize area studies programs in major universities. The Russian Research Center at Harvard is a notable example. These centers, meant to reflect and rationalize official government views of the Soviet Union, concentrated on developing information for implementing official policy rather than on testing its validity. Thus, one of the earliest studies of the Russian Research Center was a survey of Soviet minerals prepared by a CIA employee on leave. The war potential of the U.S.S.R. and the stability of the regime were the principal "academic" questions to be examined.* This use of academic talent was a direct outgrowth of organizational experiments during the war and was crucial in molding the foreign policy consensus.

The war changed America in many other subtle ways. By any definition America's participation in World War II was a huge national success. Therefore, it taught habits of mind and organization that have persisted to the present. Above all, it shaped national attitudes toward war. For 296,000 Americans World War II meant death in battle; for 680,000, wounds from enemy fire. But for most of the remaining 150,000,000 inhabitants of the nation the war

---

* The major project at the Center in its early years was an Air Force financial interrogation of Soviet refugees.

meant dramatic increases in cash, and despite some shortages and rationing, more goods to spend it on. By 1943, after two years of war, spendable income had climbed more than 65 per cent. Individual savings went from $50 billion to $140 billion for the years 1940–44. Retail sales measured in prewar dollars were significantly higher than in the years before 1939. Food consumption increased dramatically, particularly for lower-income groups. By 1943 the average American was eating fourteen pounds of food more than he had eaten in 1939 and in general the quality was better. Wages and farm prices soared. For millions of poor Americans the armed forces offered the first chance for decent medical care, adequate nutrition, and training. For blacks the war brought important gains in civil rights and, for millions in the South, the possibility of migration to the cities of the North. For business the war meant not only handsome subsidies—new facilities worth some $16 billion, built entirely with government funds, remained in private hands at the end of the war—but a technological revolution on which a generation of rapid industrial expansion could be built. Jet engines, computers, packaging, nuclear energy, synthetics, drugs, and electronics had all been given an enormous boost as a result of the war effort. Because the big companies had been given the bulk of the government contracts —fifty-six companies had 80 per cent of the prime contracts—the war accelerated the concentration of capital and the spectacular growth of the national company.* The new stage in American business was symbolized by the disappearance of the corner grocery and the rise of the supermarket chain.

The war helped build national markets for all kinds of commodities because it helped to build a national consciousness and to break down localism in taste and style. The years 1941–45 were a supreme homogenizing experience for the American people. Men who had reached their twenties and thirties without venturing beyond the next town were suddenly scooped up by the selective service system, thrown with fellow soldiers of all types, and scattered to England, France, Italy, to exotic islands in the Pacific, or to parts of the United States they did not know existed. The war stimulated mobility in America, social as well as geographical. The shared experience of World War II served as a national classroom for a whole generation.

Perhaps the most important lesson of the war was what it taught Americans about the political and economic benefits of massive military power. The war was the greatest single American success of the century in which all but a relatively few shared. Beyond the much-needed economic stimulation it provided, the war fulfilled an

* For a discussion of concentration in government contracts, see Catton, *Warlords of Washington. op. cit.*

important psychological need by giving a common purpose to what in 1940 was still a country threatened with serious economic unrest. Nine days after the attack on Pearl Harbor Congressman John W. Flannagan, Jr., sensing that the "war of purification" was an American opportunity, assessed those benefits on the floor of Congress:

> Oh, no doubt there are those who will think I should not say it—I only give expression to my innermost thoughts when I do —but probably we needed a Pearl Harbor—a Golgotha—to arouse us from our self-sufficient complacency, to make us rise above greed and hate, to awaken us to a realization of our spiritual duties and responsibilities, and unite us in defense of the God-given ideals of liberty, freedom, and equality, of peace, justice, decency, and morality, upon which this Republic rests.*

World War II was an ideal war for promoting national unity because the enemy was so much the embodiment of evil that all could support the Allied crusade. Because it seemed to be the least ambiguous war in history, the fight against the criminally insane Nazis and the sneaky bombers of Pearl Harbor made mass destruction and war against enemy populations legitimate. "We must hate with every fiber of our being," Lieutenant-General Lesley J. McNair, director of the training program for U.S. ground forces, declared on a radio broadcast to the troops in November 1942. "We must lust for battle; our object in life must be to kill; we must scheme night and day to kill." A young lieutenant, in charge of ranger training, haranguing his men before an admiring general, screamed, "The dirtier you are the better we like it. A stab in the back is one of the finest principles we know of." The general, impressed by what training had done, exclaimed, "And that lieutenant used to be a clerk on Wall Street!"

Undisguised racial prejudice was used as a weapon of war. In its March 19, 1945, issue, *Time* magazine titled its description of the battle of Iwo Jima "Rodent Exterminators." The "ordinary unreasoning Jap," the writers of *Time* concluded, "is ignorant." "We are drowning and burning the bestial apes all over the Pacific," Admiral William F. ("Bull") Halsey commented on a newsreel, "and it is just as much pleasure to burn them as to drown them." An advertisement in the New York *Times* approved by the War Production Board, pictured a toothy Japanese face with the headline "RAT POISON WANTED." The point of the ad was that there is "only one way to exterminate the slant-eyes . . . with gunpowder."

Dehumanizing the enemy is a psychological precondition for killing him because most human beings have been socialized against

* Remarks in Congress on December 16, 1941. Quoted in Richard Polanberg, ed., *America at War* (Englewood Cliffs, N.J.: Prentice-Hall, 1968), p. 6.

homicide. One can only surmise that childhood memories of the apelike "Jap" made it easier for some of America's postwar soldiers to exterminate "gooks" and "dinks" in the line of duty. But there is no doubt that the experience of war changed many prewar attitudes toward political violence in general. Pacifism and antimilitarism, which had been a strong minor theme in American politics and had served as a check on "big stick" chauvinism, were now thoroughly discredited. "The preachment and practice of pacifists in Britain and American were a cause of the World War," the columnist Walter Lippmann told his newspaper readers. Norman Vincent Peale summed up the dangers of positive thinking about peace in a capsule history of the prewar generation: "Due to popular feeling against war we allowed ourselves to get into such a position that we were totally unprepared, thus giving the Germans an opportunity to make this war." * Members of the Denver Committee on Foreign Relations warned against "being ashamed of power and afraid to use it." The United States must "enforce world peace by force."

The myth of perpetual peace—that peace, not war, is the normal state of human affairs—which had been kept alive on Wilsonian rhetoric all during the rise of fascism, had now been replaced by the myth of permanent war. "You are the soldiers and nurses of the next war," General George S. Patton told a Sunday-school class of eight-year-olds a month after Hitler's collapse. "There will be another war. There always has been." † About 70 per cent of the men in the armed forces, agreeing with him, favored compulsory military training.

"What does it mean to go to war?" Woodrow Wilson asked in 1917. "It means an attempt to reconstruct a peacetime civilization with war standards, and at the end of the war there will be no by-standers with sufficient peace standards left to work with. There will be only war standards." His fears were premature. It would take one more world war.

---

* Quoted in Lawrence S. Wittner, *Rebels Against War* (New York: Columbia University Press, 1969), p. 101.

† *Ibid.*, p. 98.

3

The Education of a Governing Class

O NE OF THE most profound consequences of the bureaucratic revolution was the coming to power of a national security elite remarkable for its cohesiveness, consistency, and, above all, persistence. Nothing like it existed before it in the United States, and outside the area of foreign affairs, its equivalent cannot be found. The founding fathers of the Republic were, and indeed thought of themselves as, a governing class. But there were far deeper ideological cleavages—the most celebrated being between Jefferson and Hamilton—than can be discerned among a whole generation of national security managers. Again, individuals, such as Henry Clay, William Jennings Bryan, and Sam Rayburn, have performed feats of political longevity, but never has a self-defining, self-selecting and self-perpetuating group held power so long in American politics.

Between 1940 and 1967, when I stopped counting, all the first- and second-level posts in a huge national security bureaucracy were held by fewer than four hundred individuals who rotate through a variety of key posts. The temporary civilian managers who come to Washington to run America's wars and preparations for wars, the national security managers, were so like one another in occupation, religion, style, and social status that, apart from a few Washington lawyers, Texans, and mavericks, it was possible to locate the offices of all of them within fifteen city blocks in New York, Boston, and Detroit. Most of their biographies in *Who's Who* read like minor variations on a single theme—wealthy parents, Ivy-League education, leading law firm or bank (or entrepreneur in a war industry), introduction to government in World War II. In Part II, we shall consider what it means that seventy of the ninety-one people who have held the very top jobs—Secretaries of Defense and State, Secretaries of the three services, the Chairman of the Atomic Energy Commission, and the Director of the CIA—have all been businessmen, lawyers for businessmen, and investment bankers. Here we shall seek only to describe the small, durable, and exclusive club that has been in charge of American foreign policy for a generation. What sort of person gets to be a member?

In 1961, John F. Kennedy offered Robert A. Lovett his choice of running the State, Defense, or Treasury Departments. He turned all three down and suggested an old assistant by the name of Dean Rusk. Ten years earlier, both men had held key positions as national security managers in the Truman Administration. Dean Acheson entered the State Department as an Assistant Secretary in 1941. Twenty-seven years later, he supplied crucial advice that persuaded Lyndon Johnson to de-escalate the Vietnam war. Clark Clifford, who drafted a key Cold War planning document in September 1946 as Counsel to the President, was Secretary of Defense twenty-two years later. In the interim, men such as Acheson, Clifford, and John J. McCloy (High Commissioner in Germany in the late 1940's, Kennedy adviser on disarmament, NATO, and the Cuban missile crisis in the 1960's) continuously served as unofficial consultants, certifiers of younger men, and opinion makers in the service of the Administration. In addition, the elder statesmen of the Truman Administration have exerted steady and continuing influence on subsequent Republican and Democratic administrations by serving on presidential commissions and by mixing with their successors at the Council on Foreign Relations, celebrated alike by left and right as the sinister headquarters of the Establishment.*

---

* Membership in the Council on Foreign Relations, it should be noted, is a rite of passage for an aspiring national security manager. It is a convenient list of about 1,500 potentially eligible "responsible" and "informed" individuals with reasonably predictable views, temperaments, and associations. Not every member qualifies, to be sure, for an occasional crank is admitted, and in recent years a few symbolic policy critics have actually been recruited, but failure to be asked to be a member of the Council has been regarded for a generation as a presumption of unsuitability for high office in the national security bureaucracy. The Council takes itself very seriously, and the security procedures invoked for its frequent off-the-record sessions with Chiefs of Naval Operations, Australian Prime Ministers, German Chancellors, French bankers, and presidential assistants are reminiscent of the national security bureaucracy itself. When the Council, which formally takes no position on any issue, decided, or more accurately, a few powerful members of its board decided, to oppose the escalation of the Vietnam War, it prepared a plan for de-escalation which

A few former officials such as Paul Nitze in the 1950's and a number of Kennedy intellectuals in the 1960's took academic cover on leaving office and helped during Republican administrations to convert such Washington institutions as the Johns Hopkins School for Advanced International Studies and the Brookings Institution into occasionally influential governments in exile. Thus, in various ways, the national security managers have preserved the continuity of their influence.

Is continuity of influence a bad thing? One of the criticisms of the American system in the past is the charge of amateurism. It is often said that the American government, unlike the British Empire with its venerable permanent civil service, has been run by part-timers, dollar-a-year men, recipients of political payoffs, and others who reserve their real managerial talents for floating bonds, making cars, arranging mergers, and other activities more remunerative than foreign affairs. Even during the past generation in which so many inevitable faces persisted, the average time any one of them held any single office in the national security bureaucracy was less than two years. Could not one argue that it is fortunate in the midst of turnover and bureaucratic chaos to have men who are willing to take on the burdens and responsibilities of power for a generation and to hand their experience and wisdom on to the naïve generation to come?

These are serious questions which, it seems to me, must be answered in general and specific terms. As a general observation, there appears to be a serious risk in permitting any self-perpetuating establishment, whatever its outlook, to be in charge of defining problems and proposing solutions too long. The world changes faster than anyone can comprehend. Those whose world view was formed a chronological generation ago may, in fact, be overtaken by two or three political generations and five or six technological generations. The road map by which the national security managers locate themselves, plot the route, and identify the landscape is the history of the 1930's as they learned it under fire in World War II, the central political event in their lives that remains to the present day their most profound learning experience. People do not recognize change when it contradicts deeply held beliefs. Sometimes an experience is so central to their own view of themselves that they refuse to admit even the possibility of change.

Thus the national security managers have consistently applied the logic, analysis, and strategy of World War II to the postwar world. The war against "world communism" was a continuation of the

---

was received in the State Department with all the pomp reserved for diplomatic messages of foreign governments.

crusade against Hitler. Any entrenched establishment is vulnerable to future shock and under its impact is likely to make tragic errors. Errors such as exaggerating or misinterpreting a threat tend to be self-serving in the short run, in the sense that they justify and rationalize expansionist policies, but they are ultimately self-defeating. The slowness of social adaptation in the midst of rapid technological change poses one of the most serious threats to civilization. This is a problem inherent in government and indeed in all human organization. The time-consuming process of education and experience people must go through to become capable of making judgments carries them into a strange new world in which the lessons are already obsolete. To a certain extent, conceptual lag is inherent in the human condition, but, as we shall see, it is positively courted in the national security bureaucracy. The predisposition of the national security managers to look at the world of 1948 as if it were the world of 1937 provided the crucial ideological backdrop for postwar American expansionism. The problem was "aggression" and every U.S. military thrust was a "response."

However, the evaluation of the American foreign policy establishment that has governed for more than thirty years must ultimately rest on an assessment of its performance rather than on any organizational theory. The defenders of this establishment, often its members in their memoirs, ask whether anyone else could have done better. I have made no secret in this book thus far of my own belief that on the whole they have not done well. This belief does not stem from any confidence that an alternative establishment would have done better, although in retrospect it appears that some of the foreign policy pariahs of this generation—Henry Wallace, Robert Taft, Harold Stassen, Chester Bowles—might well have made fewer disastrous decisions. The disillusionment with the foreign policy managers of the last generation now growing among the new generation is based on more than the loss of the Vietnam War. It springs from a new awareness that the objective requirements of survival demand a different policy. Americans coming to consciousness in the 1970's are struck by the tragic and absurd contrast between what is plainly needed to reach the twenty-first century in such a way as to want to arrive there and what their highest officials say and do. This contrast has frequently been dramatized by the national security managers themselves. Proclaiming that there is no alternative to peace in a world of atomic weapons, the national security managers waged a generation of "brushfire" war under the cover of a horrendous nuclear arms race. While giving lip service to the deep human aspiration for independence and dignity, they sought security by dominating others. Wringing their hands in public about the human failure represented by every bullet and tank produced, they poured money into the military and strained the civilian economy. They uttered solemn warnings about distorted priorities, pollution, poverty gaps, and the deteriorating quality of human life for billions caught up in the cataclysmic changes of the twentieth century, but they had no response but to perpetuate the very policies they themselves discredited. They talked about taking "risks for peace" and "bold new approaches" to rescue mankind from war, the supreme social sickness, but they sought to conquer war by increasing its risks.

Measured against such fundamental requirements of civilization as the growth of freedom, the alleviation of poverty, the prevention of the killing of the innocent, and the reduction of mass misery, the performance of the national security managers has clearly fallen far short of what anyone with a claim on the future has a right to expect. Judged even by the national security managers' own criteria, the generation in which the United States has spent $1,500 billion on armaments has witnessed a sharp increase in threats to American national security, an erosion of U.S. military and political power, and serious cracks in the U.S. corporate economy itself. The very longevity of the national security managers has helped to compound and finally to enshrine their failures. There was no room in the official orthodoxy even to contemplate the changes in the political organization of the planet that are needed for survival, and no interest in trying to bring them about.

These then are the biased criteria I use to evaluate the performance of the national security managers—no less neutral, it seems to me, than the "sincerity," "effort," and "high purpose" for which they award each other high marks, or the unprovable but dubious claim that without their efforts things would have been much worse. Whether the national security managers' view of reality or their critics makes more sense is a debate to which I have contributed elsewhere, but it is beyond the scope of this book. We are interested here in understanding them. What kind of men were they? Why did they think as they did? What was the moral and intellectual ground on which they built public policy? *

(2)

THE ASCENDENCY of the foreign policy establishment can be dated from June 19, 1940. On that day, Franklin D. Roosevelt, eager to share the responsibilities of war preparation with some prominent

---

* National security bureaucracy personnel is described in Richard J. Barnet, "The National Security Managers and the National Interest," *Politics and Society*, Vol. 1, No. 2 (February 1971), pp. 260–62.

Republicans, took the advice of Felix Frankfurter and Grenville Clark and telephoned Henry L. Stimson to offer him the post of Secretary of War. Stimson's political ancestry went back to Theodore Roosevelt, who had appointed him a United States attorney in 1906. He was strongly devoted to Theodore Roosevelt's ideal of the "strenuous life" and a firm believer in compulsory military service. He had been Secretary of State in the Hoover Administration in 1931 and had vainly tried to resist Japanese aggression in Manchuria. Within six months of FDR's call Stimson had put together an impressive staff of like-minded people who also were imbued with TR's values—struggle, honor, and glory. Robert Patterson, John J. McCloy, Robert A. Lovett, and Harvey H. Bundy, his principal assistants, ran the War Department under Stimson's direction all through World War II. Peculiarly sensitive to the charges then being hurled by Axis propagandists that the democracies were soft, he dedicated the final years of his own long career and the generation-long careers that lay ahead for many of his principal associates to proving that this was not so. Foreign policy, Stimson believed, was the testing of character.

Stimson's recruits and their colleagues in FDR's wartime government became the key architects of American national security policy during the Cold War. Their assistants and protégés in turn became the technicians and managers of that policy. Men of the vintage of Lovett, McCloy, Acheson, Dulles, and Forrestal built the structures —the intellectual concepts, the rhetoric, the alliances, the military networks. Men such as Maxwell Taylor, Dean Rusk, Walt Rostow, and McGeorge Bundy tried to maintain and to extend these structures, and in the end, stretched them to the breaking point.

Another key recruiter of future national security managers was James V. Forrestal, wartime Secretary of the Navy and the first Secretary of Defense. He brought in a number of his old colleagues at Dillon Read & Co., such as William Draper and Paul Nitze. It is common practice for men to staff bureaucracies with trusted associates. What is significant about these particular associates is that they represented a new breed in government. A few of these men, bankers and lawyers for bankers, had held government office before, usually dealing with monetary or financial matters, but most had had no acquaintance with government at all. Thus, 1940 is a turning point. Before that year, a small and ineffective foreign policy bureaucracy was presided over by Foreign Service officers, with a Tennessee politician at the top. Most important decisions were made by Roosevelt himself with the help of New Dealers in the White House. After 1940, the national security managers, working with the military, began to redefine the national interest. It was Stimson's and Forrestal's recruits, plus a few others with similar backgrounds, including Dean Acheson, William Clayton, and Averell Harriman, who, after Roosevelt's sudden death, formed the collective picture of the world adopted by the uninformed and ill-prepared Harry Truman.

While every national security manager came to Washington either with a personal fortune or a final paycheck from a well-paying job, a small number of them started out in genteel poverty. Dean Rusk, the Georgia Presbyterian preacher's son who became President of the Rockefeller Foundation and Kennedy's Secretary of State, was born poor. John J. McCloy's father was an auditor for an insurance company who died when the boy was six. Supported by his mother, who was a nurse, he worked his way through Amherst waiting on tables. John Foster Dulles came from a celebrated, well-connected family that boasted two secretaries of state (the Foster in Dulles' name and the Lansing in his sister Eleanor's), but the Dulles household, with another Presbyterian preacher at its head, lived on an annual budget of $3,600 a year, well above the poverty line at the turn of the century, yet still modest.

When we come to Dean Acheson's family, the scene brightens. Acheson's father, the Episcopal bishop of Connecticut, was able to offer his son a childhood he remembers as a "radiant morn," complete with pony and Groton. Robert Lovett's father was the general counsel of the Union Pacific Railroad, and the family was of adequate social status for the future Secretary of Defense to make Skull and Bones at Yale. (Like McGeorge Bundy. Acheson was a Scroll and Key man, a notch or two below.) It was not an obstacle in the path to wealth and influence at an early age for young Lovett to marry the daughter of the senior partner of the Brown Brothers banking firm. Forrestal's father had a successful construction business. Averell Harriman's father had an empire.

As a group, then, these men started out in life with more than ordinary advantages in connections, status, and wealth. Each of them had the good fortune to know strategic people at strategic times, which is essential to any successful bureaucratic career. But membership in the foreign policy establishment cannot be assured by class position or wealth alone. Money and connections obviously help, but the upper reaches of the national security bureaucracy are, above all, a meritocracy of a very special kind. The one thing these men had in common was not money or class but ambition and skill. Dean Rusk's brother summed up what was a pressure common to all of them. "We were under constant admonition to excel, to go out in the world and do something. We were always striving for excellence." The national security managers, to a man, have been strivers for and achievers of excellence in precisely the terms in which our society has defined this goal. They were prizewinners. In the Kennedy era, there were more former Rhodes Scholars on the seventh floor of the

State Department than in most first-rate university faculties. Vale-
dictorians, recent and not so recent, wearers of Phi Beta Kappa keys,
former *Harvard Law Review* editors, and Supreme Court clerks
abounded. On the whole, the national security managers have been
men who raced through their academic careers with seeming ease
and were remarkably early achievers in their careers. It was more
than the good fortune of having married the boss's daughter that
made Robert Lovett a partner at Brown Brothers, Harriman at the
age of thirty-one. John Foster Dulles was the directing partner of
what was probably the most prestigious law firm on Wall Street,
Sullivan & Cromwell, at the age of thirty-eight. Dean Acheson had
resigned as Under Secretary of the Treasury by the age of forty.
McGeorge Bundy was dean of Harvard at thirty-four and McNamara
was President of Ford at forty-one. These men, more perhaps than
any other group one can think of, were America's winners.

(3)

THE MEN who became the managers of American foreign policy
came to national prominence because they had developed certain
skills in the practice of their professions. These skills determined to
a considerable extent the way they conducted their offices. Some,
like McCloy and Lovett, were originally brought into government
because of specific expertise. Stimson immediately thought of McCloy
to advise him on counterintelligence—German espionage and subversion was a serious problem in 1940—because McCloy had made
a reputation investigating the Black Tom explosion case, a spectacular piece of World War I sabotage. Lovett, an enthusiastic flier
in World War I, was captivated personally, professionally, and fi-
nancially by airplanes. He was an ideal man to take charge of the
Army Air Forces.

Most national security managers, however, have been appointed
under the theory that successful lawyers and bankers can do anything. This is a theory—limited, to be sure, to lawyers—that I remember hearing forcefully and frequently expounded at Harvard
Law School. A number of the principal architects of American foreign policy—the men of the Truman Administration who initiated in
each major national security area policies that persisted for a generation—were corporation lawyers in large firms. The hold of lawyers
on American foreign policy has been the subject of fashionable and
insistent criticism by such practitioners of political realism as George
Kennan. The problem, as they see it, is that the plethora of lawyers in

the State Department has introduced the evils of "legalism" into American foreign policy.

My own view is almost exactly the contrary. Far from importing too many legal prohibitions or setting unrealistic legal standards, lawyers who become national security managers are too ready to defer to their client, the state, and to ignore the law or to make it up. A lawyer is paid to be partisan. John Foster Dulles, perhaps the most lawyerly of the national security managers, was a superb bargainer for the bankers and large bondholders who were his clients. He was a man who, according to one of his biographers, had in his law profession "an inspired ability to calculate risks and gamble on them." The practice of high-powered business law is a continuing battle of wits. It does not matter who the client is or what he wants. The challenge is to get it for him if at all possible. The successful "can-do" lawyer never counsels his client to moderate his appetite unless there is absolutely no choice. When Dulles' colleagues at Sullivan & Cromwell were asked to reminisce about him for Richard Goold-Adams' biography, the phrase that leaped to mind was "Well, don't go down unless you have to"—i.e., don't give an unnecessary inch or dollar. Goold-Adams notes that this habit of mind carried over into his diplomacy, where countries "were all instinctively rivals and opponents of his own client, America." *

Acheson's gifts—lucidity, pungent language, and an instinct for the telling argument—were used to the same effect. Lawyers with a weakness for seeing the merits of the other side end up being employed by neither. "Negotiation from strength," Acheson's favorite concept, looks like elementary common sense in diplomacy as in business. However, the never-ending race to build "situations of strength" in a contest between two great powers produces intransigence and prolonged stalemate. Unlike ordinary people, who at some point must sell things, make contracts, or carry out some other business transaction, great nations often do not have to make any deal at all. They can wait.

As ubiquitous as lawyers are in the world of national security, bankers have played an equally important role. National security memoranda frequently read like investment prospectuses. It is not uncommon for them to speak of countries as "assets" which must not be lost. When President Truman urged the appropriation of $400 million for aid to Greece and Turkey under the "Truman Doctrine," he explained that it was a small investment to protect the big investment made in World War II.†

---

* Richard S. M. Goold-Adams, *John Foster Dulles* (New York: Appleton-Century-Crofts, 1962), p. 9.

† The Truman Doctrine, an address to a Joint Session of Congress on March 12, 1947, in *Public Papers of the Presidents*, 1947.

It has been stated by political scientists that the key role of bankers in the world of national security is in part responsible for the conservative cast of American foreign policy. It is not surprising that bankers are conservative, for that is literally what their job entails. They are conservators of property. But at the same time, they are professional risk takers. They are paid for taking chances. Their skill is in risk selection and risk minimization. For this reason, the banker has a passion for certainty. He feels compelled to control and to manage the environment in which he is dealing because uncertainty is often a greater risk than a dependable disaster against which he can hedge. If you don't know what other people are going to do, it is much harder to minimize risks. Thus, the banker's preferred world is one where everyone knows and plays out his assigned role, where words mean the same to everyone, and where there are few surprises. That was not the world in which the national security managers were called to manage risks for the nation.

The international bankers and their lawyers who became national security managers are for the most part widely traveled, but their foreign contacts are narrow. For John Foster Dulles, the French banker Jean Monnet was France, and McCloy's hand-picked German Chancellor, Konrad Adenauer, was Germany. The contacts that men such as McCloy and Acheson had with their Continental counterparts, especially Monnet, during the 1920's and 1930's had a profound impact on the policies they pursued in the 1940's and 1950's. These contacts helped to build the group consciousness of an international governing class. In the early postwar period, when the governments of Western Europe were under the control of strong Catholic, anticommunist governments in which men such as Monnet were strong influences, the national security managers felt more at home in the chanceries and clubs of Europe than in most places in their own country. This was indeed a moment, much celebrated at the time, when there appeared to be the dawning of a real internationalism, but it was an internationalism held together by class ties, old business associations, and a common fear of communism. In the end, it was overwhelmed by the resurgence of nationalism, European and American.

Though the national security managers of the Truman Administration were able to mix easily and congenially with the political and business elite of Western Europe, in a sense they were émigrés in America. The world in which they moved—the Metropolitan Club, the Council on Foreign Relations, the intimate dinners with ambassadors, newspaper publishers, financiers—bore little more resemblance to the America in which most citizens were struggling to make their lives than the court of Louis XVI bore to prerevolutionary France. To say that the national security managers were out of touch with the country is an understatement. There was a substantial part of the country—beyond Lincoln, Scarsdale, and Winnetka, of whose existence they were quite unaware. Their contact with poor people or blacks was limited to the doorman at the Metropolitan Club. The closest they came to seeing hunger in America was when a dinner partner was treated to bad service at a declining French restaurant. They saw themselves as a benevolent aristocracy without obligation to spend time with or on lesser people. True to the Calvinist upbringing so many of them shared, they considered themselves an elect whose virtue had been divinely certified by their elevation to the ruling elite. The elegance, the arrogant style, and the careful cultivation of the uncommon touch, personified by Dean Acheson but shared by others to a lesser degree, set them apart from the American people, who were supposedly their clients. But the real client was the state, and most managers, when they came to weigh the risks and make high policy, left the hopes, fears, failures, and suffering of the nonelect out of the balance. The notion that the pursuit of foreign policy could have subtle, lasting effects on what was discovered in the late 1960's as "the quality of life" in America, was utterly foreign to them.

The right-wing pseudopopulist attacks on Acheson were pure demogoguery, but they struck a responsive chord because the Secretary did appear "un-American." It was absurd to charge that he was not *for* the country, as the McCarthyites did, but it was less clear in what sense he was *of* it. "I watch his smart-aleck manner and his British clothes, and that New Dealism," Nebraska Senator Hugh Butler fumed after one of Acheson's virtuoso performances at the Senate, "and I want to shout, 'Get out. Get out. You stand for everything that has been wrong with the country for years.' " *It was ironical that Acheson, the architect of a tough policy of anticommunism, should have been painted in the McCarthy era as a pink subversive, for his career had a consistently conservative bent to it—enough alienation from the New Deal by 1936 to attend the famous Mayflower Hotel dinner of the Liberty League to hear Al Smith denounce FDR as Lenin in disguise, enough invulnerability to conventional liberalism to be able at the end of his career to be a vigorous propagandist for Rhodesia.† John Foster Dulles and the Republican bankers recruited in the war and promoted by President Truman made no secret of their political conservatism. It was not supposed to be important because everybody knew that foreign policy was above

* Quoted in Fred J. Cook, *The Nightmare Decade: The Life and Times of Senator Joe McCarthy* (New York: Random House, 1971), p. 69.

† Illustrations of Dean Acheson's position on Rhodesia are in Acheson, *On the Rhodesian Question* (Washington, D.C.: Rhodesian Information Service, 1970).

politics. It was a matter of managerial skill, and that was precisely what the bankers and their lawyers had demonstrated.

With a handful of exceptions the national security managers have never held or run for elective office. It is noteworthy that among the few exceptions—Harold Stassen, Chester Bowles—are to be found the few mavericks and dissenters from the national security consensus. John Foster Dulles was appointed by Dewey to fill an unexpired term and ran unsuccessfully for election in his own right in 1949 against Herbert Lehman. His conduct of the campaign gives a clue to an important side of his character. He charged Lehman with being soft on communism because as UNRRA administrator he had been shocked by starvation in the Ukraine and had made public statements about helping Russia to get back on her feet. The incident suggests where compassion fit in the Dulles hierarchy of values. Goold-Adams develops the point in his sketch of Dulles' life.

> . . . he was never in touch with people who knew hunger, poverty, or personal failure. Believing in addition that everyone must make the most of themselves in life and that those who do not have something wrong with them, he never seriously tried to understand the people whose misfortune it is to get left on the bottom rungs of the ladder. Nor did he ever read fiction about them.

Once, shortly after taking over at the State Department, Dulles asked a friend why his speeches never elicited any enthusiasm among the poorer countries. "When the friend frankly explained," Goold-Adams relates, "that his words were cold and lacking in any genuine appreciation of the outlook and problems of these countries because he had never understood any kind of underdog, Dulles accepted the point and asked, 'Is it too late to learn?' " The friend replied that it was.*

Dulles' peers in the national security elite, who regarded him as atypical, actually resembled him in basic attitudes more than they liked to admit. The national security managers as a class have not had the training or incentive to develop understanding, compassion, or empathy for people in different circumstances from their own. This is a handicap in the conduct of foreign relations because there are about three billion such people on the planet.

This insulation from the real world, as well as their special brand of Calvinism, a topic to which we shall turn below, go far to explain the giant misunderstanding of the past generation: the nature and dynamics of revolution. As a group, the national security managers have been so removed emotionally from the human desperation that

* Goold-Adams, *op. cit.,* pp. 6 and 7.

afflicts a majority of the world that they cannot understand why people will join a revolution. Revolutionaries must be agents, dupes, or romantics. As Wolin and Schaar have put it, "The bureaucratic search for 'understanding' does not begin in wonder, but in the reduction of the world to the ordinary and manageable." Revolution, by definition, threatens stability and introduces uncertainty. It is therefore a threat that must be suppressed. It is this lack of understanding or feeling and the accompanying fear of the unknown which feeds the power fantasies of the managers and helps them to rationalize the use of terror, starvation, and intrigue to bring societies threatened by revolution back to "normal."

I once had the opportunity of comparing the capacity of the North Vietnamese and American leadership for understanding and empathy. Within a few days, I talked to Pham Van Dong, the Premier of North Vietnam, in Hanoi, and to Henry Kissinger, President Nixon's national security adviser, in the White House. I was struck by how well the Vietnamese politician understood Nixon's character and situation as well as the pressures that operated on him. The Premier had the ability to put himself in Nixon's place. Kissinger, on the other hand, while evidencing respect and even a little admiration for his adversary's skill, seemed to have no genuine understanding of what motivated him. In Hanoi, Nixon was a human being, not liked, but seriously considered. In the White House, Pham Van Dong was a chessboard figure. Those with power easily convince themselves that they do not need to understand their adversaries. Those without power know they cannot afford not to understand.

There is a process of natural selection through which leaders emerge with a certain social character that meets the requirements of the institutions through which they rise. It is possible to be an eccentric if you are fortunate enough to invent a cheap automobile like Henry Ford or to corner a good part of the steel market like Andrew Carnegie. Artists, entrepreneurs, robber barons, and big-time racketeers can afford to have extravagant dreams, to be exuberant philanthropists, wild gamblers, or insatiable lovers. The managerial class, even at its top echelons, are of necessity sober men who present a picture to the world of moderation, self-control, and probity. To use the word they so often apply to each other, they are "upright" men. (The characterization most frequently on the lips of some of their children, a number of whom have broken with their fathers over the Vietnam War, is "uptight.")

Robert McNamara was the classic example of the cool administrator who would never allow emotions to interfere with the smooth-functioning circuitry of his brain. The word newspaper reporters habitually applied to the managers of the Kennedy era was "steely." McNamara had a steel-trap mind, McGeorge Bundy had steely nerves, etcetera. Yet these were deeply emotional men given to strong feelings of anger, sorrow, love, and hate. Dean Acheson writes that lawyers make fine diplomats because "they have learned to remain detached from the emotional involvement of their clients," but it was often painfully obvious when he was Secretary of State how much will power he had to summon merely to suffer fools as gladly as he did. McNamara sometimes betrayed his feelings late in his career when he would weep in public at ceremonies honoring a war hero. Anyone who saw his TV interview the morning after his close friend Robert Kennedy was shot must have realized that the detachment for which he became famous was studied, not natural. He was capable of quite human reactions. He could function as the famous McNamara machine only after the object of his attention, notably the two to three million victims created in Vietnam during his Pentagon service, were quantified and dehumanized. How this process works in the national security bureaucracy we will consider later.

To be a successful manager or senior counselor of a large organization in America, it is supremely important to be agreeable, and, if possible, to have charm. The ability to put a visitor at ease, to run a meeting with grace, and to break the tension with engaging small talk is an art that most of the managers have developed on their way to the top floor of the law office or bank. Wit is a specialty. Acheson was a master of the snappy comeback, sometimes leavened with a touch of self-deprecation, as in the story he liked to tell of the taxi driver who picked him up at the height of the McCarthy attacks. "Aren't you the Secretary of State?" the driver asked. "Yes," replied Acheson with an imperious twinkle. "Do I have to get out?" He was also given to outrageous puns: "I learned it at my mother's knee and other low joints." Wit, as Freud has pointed out, is the humor of detachment. Some managers, such as McGeorge Bundy, liked to use imitation La Rochfoucauld *bon mots* to lessen the emotional impact of acts that may have caused moral qualms. Thus, when Kennedy's press secretary Pierre Salinger prepared a brilliantly obfuscatory communiqué after the assassination of Diem, Bundy wrote the following congratulatory marginal note: "Pierre, Champion! Excellent Prose. No Surprise. 'A communique should say nothing in such a way as to fool the press without deceiving them.' " *

The two qualities these men prize in themselves and in others are loyalty and duty. Loyalty is the supreme bureaucratic virtue. In the foreign policy establishment, it is far more forgivable to do something incompetent or dangerous inside than to talk about it on the outside. Thus, the few internal critics of the Vietnam War rushed to the defense of their colleagues after the publication of the Pentagon papers, lamenting the disclosures, certifying motives, and refusing to

* New York *Times,* August 27, 1970.

discuss the substantive issues raised. What you say to an outsider must be circumspect and reflect no discredit on any member of the club. What you say to an insider is another matter. In a TV interview, George Ball was unperturbed when he acknowledged that inside the government he was writing opinions on the Vietnam War diametrically opposite from his public speeches at the time.

Loyalty is so highly prized because a bureaucracy cannot run without it. For this reason, it is crucial to the advancement of personal careers. But only certain kinds of loyalty are prized. John Foster Dulles demanded what he called "positive loyalty" from all employees of the State Department, but he felt none himself toward subordinates who were unjustly attacked by McCarthy. His loyalty to the President, as he no doubt rationalized it, took precedence over any obligation to be fair. Similarly, McGeorge Bundy in both word and deed makes it clear that his loyalty to the presidency outranked loyalty to friends. Thus he agreed to be Lyndon Johnson's instrument to inform Robert Kennedy, with whom he had a close personal relationship, that he was unwanted as Vice-President in the Johnson Administration.

The national security managers have been organization men *par excellence,* but they do not fit the model celebrated in the fiction and pop sociology of the 1950's. They are hardly plodders and they are quite prepared to take risks. They are looking for much more than security in their old age. In their early careers, particularly, they do unconventional things outside of the established career patterns. Bundy, Lovett, McNamara, organization men all, were risk takers at crucial stages in their early careers. But above all else, they are loyal to superiors because the bureaucratic ethic demands it. They know that their only capital is their marketability. To get power, they must prove acceptable to men who already have it.

Dean Acheson is a classic case. He was fiercely loyal to President Truman, endearing himself to "the Boss" forever by being the only high official to meet the presidential train at Union Station after the 1946 elections had swept the Republicans into power in the Congress and reduced Truman's prestige to the vanishing point. Truman, who, more perhaps than any other recent President except Harding, had built his career on personal associations, responded to a show of loyalty more than to any other quality. His own career had been built on little else. He had neither professional skill nor a successful business background nor money. He made his career in the Missouri National Guard and "Battery D" in World War I. He came to the attention of the Pendergast machine because Mike Pendergast was impressed at finding a captain "whose men didn't want to shoot him." These same men were honored guests at his inaugural in 1949. Truman was accused of "cronyism" but it was a code of honor to take care of your friends, and friends, by definition, were people you could trust. The same strong sense of loyalty that caused the President to threaten to kick music critics who failed to be charmed by his daughter's singing also prompted him to brave public criticism to attend Boss Pendergast's funeral. Dean Acheson displayed some of the same sort of loyalty at great cost in his famous declaration that he would not turn his back on Alger Hiss, who had been his friend and colleague. It was not merely, as he recounts in his memoirs, a dictate of Christian charity remembered from that golden childhood in Middletown. A gentleman does not turn on associates in an organization unless it is absolutely necessary.

Acheson tells a story in his memoirs which shows the pride he took in loyalty as a virtue. Roosevelt had him appointed Under Secretary of the Treasury in 1933. He did not like FDR personally. The President's baronial informality struck Acheson as "patronizing and humiliating." When the future Secretary of State rather quickly found himself in disagreement with the monetary policies of the Roosevelt Administration, he was summarily fired. He voiced no public criticism and never received the customary "Dear Dean" letter from the White House. Years later, Acheson recalls, he heard that FDR had rejected an angry letter of resignation from one of his successors with the words, "Return it to him and tell him to ask Dean Acheson how a gentleman resigns." Acheson writes that he treasures the story; for servants of power there is no higher accolade.

It is ironical that so many of the early generation of national security managers were accused of disloyalty to the nation by McCarthy and his followers because of their very loyalty to subordinates. (McCarthyite attacks against Acheson, and later against his son-in-law William P. Bundy, for being "soft on communism" because he had contributed money to Hiss's defense, had the effect of making their anticommunism stronger and more strident.) Even so formidable an establishment figure as John J. McCloy was attacked by McCarthy for having written a directive during World War II specifying that any employee of the War Department could hold communist views provided that they did not override his loyalty to the United States. Men like McCloy and Acheson had civil-libertarian inclinations when it came to the rights of employees, although Acheson went along with a State Department loyalty program principally designed to steal Republican thunder. McCloy was a fair-minded man; yet he supervised the relocation of Japanese-American citizens early in World War II. There is a poignant example of the split between private and public morality from the last days of John Foster Dulles. Moralist though he was, Dulles was a great dissembler, for bluff is the essence of the bargainer's art. In the practice of brinksmanship, he was forever hurling Jovian threats that would, he was sure, never have to be carried out. "Never forget, Bill," he told his old assistant William Macomber as he lay dying in Walter Reed Hospital, "that if the United States is willing to go to war over Berlin—there won't be any war over Berlin." Yet he was so afraid he had misled Adenauer when he told the Chancellor at their last meeting that his impending operation was for a hernia and not for a recurrence of cancer, that minutes after coming out of the anaesthetic, upon hearing the dreadful truth, he insisted upon sending a message to Bonn.*

(4)

THE NATIONAL SECURITY MANAGERS who have played the leading roles in developing American foreign policy are deeply moral men. This may strike the reader as a peculiar statement, for these were indeed the men who proposed the gratuitous destruction of China in the event of a war with Russia, who planned, executed, and congratulated themselves for the fire bombing of Hamburg, Tokyo, and Dresden, the atomic slaughter of Hiroshima and Nagasaki, the sabotage teams parachuted into Communist China, and a variety of other "dirty tricks," secret and unsecret, in the pursuit of what they called the national interest. The prolonged torture of Vietnam alone—by "free fire" zones, napalm, and crop destruction, by hunting and hounding the people with murderous antipersonnel weapons, by herding them into stinking refugee camps and driving them into bloated cities, and by assassinating tens of thousands of civilians—would earn these men the right to be considered among the great killers and pillagers of history. Yet most of them were moral men, driven by a strong sense of right and wrong.

The acknowledged crimes perpetrated in the course of the Vietnam war have raised again the old question about morality and foreign policy. Many of the national security managers were profoundly influenced by the dichotomy popularized by Reinhold Niebuhr in his influential book *Moral Man and Immoral Society*. Niebuhr insisted that nations and other social groups could not follow the dictates of individual morality. Arthur Schlesinger, Jr., a disciple of Niebuhr, chronicler of the Kennedy era in which he also participated as a presidential adviser, once summarized Niebuhr's argument.

Niebuhr insisted on the distinction between the moral behavior of individuals and of social groups. The obligation of the individual was to obey the law of love and sacrifice; "from the viewpoint of the author of an action, unselfishness must remain the

---

* Goold-Adams, *op. cit.*, p. 162.

criterion of the highest morality." But nations cannot be sacrificial. Governments are not individuals. They are trustees for individuals. Niebuhr quotes Hugh Cecil's argument that unselfishness "is inappropriate to the action of a state. No one has a right to be unselfish with other people's interests." *

There is scarcely a subject about which more self-serving confusion has been generated than the relationship of morals and statecraft. For much of our history, men such as Woodrow Wilson treated foreign policy, in Schlesinger's words, as a branch of ethics. It is not that the policies they pursued were particularly notable for their ethical or moral quality, but that the articulated purpose of policy was the pursuit of moral values, notably freedom. John Foster Dulles was probably the most unabashed moralist ever to sit in the cavernous office of the Secretary of State, but his value system was widely shared by other top managers. The "realist tradition," for which Niebuhr was so important in providing the philosophical underpinnings, grew up in reaction to the horrors and mistakes of the periodic moral crusades unleashed by self-righteous statesmen in the preceding era. The realists noted that the product of all the crusades of history was a mountain of corpses and little else. Intelligent self-interest, not moral uplift, is what foreign policy is about, they argued. They would quote Churchill with approval: "The Sermon on the Mount is the last word in Christian ethics. . . . Still it is not on those terms that Ministers assume their responsibilities of guiding states." Those who run nations cannot be unselfish, generous, or even honest in the jungle world of international relations because such impulses are not reciprocated. To recognize external limits on discretion is to compromise the interests of the American people and of future generations for whom the statesman is supposed to act as trustee.

Thus, men who were on the whole scrupulous in their private lives came to believe that when they stepped into their public role, everything was permitted. Impressed by the philosophical tension between moralism and pragmatism in public policy, they confused the two in the making of it. What was expedient also became right. It was not that they did not believe in limits to the exercise of power, for by inclination these were moderate men, but they did not believe in limits which were not of their own making. Neither God, law, world opinion, right reason, or any other outside standard was recognized as a limit on their own discretion, for that discretion, they convinced themselves, would be exercised in the pursuit of the highest moral values.

Thus the debate about whether foreign policy should be based on morals or expediency seems wholly unreal. Every human being brings

* "The Necessary Amorality of Foreign Affairs," *Harper's Magazine,* August 1971, p. 72.

his own set of values and moral principles to the making of policy. Sometimes career interests and moral principles of an individual clash, but usually it is not hard to reconcile them. A recurring theme of this book is that career and bureaucratic interests have a great deal to do with shaping moral outlooks, but they are nonetheless genuine for that. The question is not *whether* moral principles should guide the formation of policy but rather *which* ones? Whose moral principles? Barry Goldwater's? His belief in the duty to eliminate communism in Cuba was so great that he wrote President Kennedy after the Bay of Pigs invasion urging him to invade the island even though it would mean nuclear war:

> I have come to the conclusion that even though Russia will probably invade Berlin or Iran or some other place, our main force, Strategic Air Command, could complete the necessary Cuban operations very quickly and be available for tasks elsewhere. . . . [In 1961, SAC was capable of carrying out nuclear strikes only, a fact of which Goldwater, an Air Force reserve major general, was aware.] I would not hesitate to make the decision to invade Cuba to rid this hemisphere of the threat of extending Communism.*

Should Walt Rostow's values be the guide? Martin Luther King's?

Foreign policy is not and cannot be amoral because it is made by men who make instant choices on the basis of one set of values or another. The important issue is what kind of moral values are encouraged or discouraged within our national security structures. However, important as it is, in my view, to have foreign policy managed by men with a very different set of values from those that have prevailed in the last generation—more humanism, more reverence for life, more tolerance of diversity—it is crucial to maintain a healthy skepticism toward everybody's morality. As I would not choose bankers and ambitious college professors to decide when duty and honor require invading other countries and killing their people, so I would not grant such discretion to saints. That is why the "rule of law," so celebrated in rhetoric and so consistently violated in practice, is such a clear, practical necessity. It is exactly because moral standards are so difficult to apply wisely to foreign policy issues that it becomes necessary for survival to submit to objective, even arbitrary standards. There are some things that should not be done, whatever the circumstances or however plausible the provocation. The rules of war and the limitations on national sovereignty in the United Nations Charter were developed out of the shared experience of nations that a world where everything is permitted is not worth living in.

* New York *Times,* August 27, 1970.

The very flexibility and multiplicity of options which the national security managers constantly seek are responsible for some of their most monumental errors. The broader the canvas, the wider the discretion, the more remote the objects of one's plans, and the freer one is of outside restraint, the greater the risks of error. Advancing the national interest is no guide at all, since it means whatever a policymaker wants it to mean.

The terrible problem for policy planners in mid-century America was that they did not and could not know what their long-term interests really were. To be sure, they used the code word "national interest" to sanctify policies they perceived to be in their own class interests, i.e., the ever-increasing capitalist system from which they, their friends and employers had amassed great wealth. But within a generation it had become clear that they lacked a sufficiently coherent understanding of the world and a sufficiently flexible strategy to realize their parochial definition of the "national interest." The world was moving too fast. They explained and rationalized their choices by constantly using the analogies of Hitler and Munich. But the political forces in motion did not in fact resemble those of the familiar world in which they had received their political education. Ho Chi Minh was not Hitler. Mao was not Stalin. Castro was not Mossedegh. De Gaulle was not Napoleon. Thus it was that some of the greatest short-term manipulative triumphs turned out to be longer-term disasters. The American complicity in the assassination of Diem was a technical masterpiece. Everything worked beautifully—Kennedy's precautions for keeping most of the U.S. government in the dark, Henry Cabot Lodge's suave deception of the Premier a few hours before he was dragged out of his office and killed, Pierre Salinger's "champion" communiqué, which compounded the deception. But from the standpoint of U.S. interests narrowly conceived, the decision to get rid of Diem was a disaster. It opened the political floodgates of Saigon and narrowly led to an NLF victory in 1964. But who should have known whether it was in "the American national interest" to "sink or swim with Diem," as some advisers were insisting, or to try to replace him with a more pliable puppet. This is the kind of question no government can answer with respect to another in a world that is no longer simple. American policymakers have assumed that anything that increases the capacity of the United States to control political and economic developments around the world and to penetrate foreign markets contributes to the power of the United States and ultimately to the welfare of her people. But, as we shall see, the evidence is mounting that the costs of empire, not only financial but political and psychological, have weakened the United States. Indeed, the loss of American hegemony appears to be directly related to the strategies adopted to maintain it.

(5)

WHAT WAS the internal moral code that the national security managers applied? What did they value? What were they striving for? As a rule, they stood their personal moral codes on their heads when they assumed their public roles. They believed in the honor of gentlemen, and, in dealing with one another, it pained them to lie. But they took pride in public deception. A man who would stoop to help a fallen bird to its nest would exhibit the most callous indifference to the pain, torture, and death it was his business to cause to the people of Indochina. Harry Truman typifies this moral ambivalence better perhaps than anyone else of his generation. Warm, friendly, capable of inspiring the strongest loyalties, he exhibited many of the best qualities of Americans. He loved life. He had courage. He was generous with his time and with his praise. Yet he stoutly insisted to the end of his career that he never lost a moment's sleep over his decisions, which ultimately were his alone, to incinerate and poison the people of Hiroshima and Nagasaki with two atomic bombs.

The war planners, responsible for so much of the suffering of Indochina, never betrayed a trace of remorse. Perhaps one can understand the pride that would keep them from issuing public *mea culpas*. But it is hard to understand how some of them, upon hearing of the revelations of the Pentagon papers, would address one another at Cambridge cocktail parties with a breezy, "Hi, war criminal." Yet these were the men who set the standards of uprightness and sanity for the society.

In Chapter 5, we will describe some of the absolution systems operating within the national security structures that, in effect, help the national security managers invert their private morality. Here we shall explore their personal moral code. We have noted that many of the national security managers have been Presbyterians—Dulles, Rusk, McCloy, and McNamara, among many others. John Foster Dulles, of course, was the one who took Calvinism most seriously and who assumed the most active public role as a churchman. As a boy, he learned long Bible passages and was reputed to have memorized the entire gospel of St. John. Bishop Acheson was, of course, not a Presbyterian, but his practical theology was not so different. Dean Acheson recalls his father as a man of "olympian detachment."

[My father] was a baffling man, widely read in theology and Christian doctrine, yet rarely speaking of either, privately or in his sermons, which so far as I can remember dealt more with ethics and conduct. But no conviction could have been deeper than his in a code of conduct, based upon perceptions of what was decent and civilized for man inextricably caught up in social relationships. If his goal was the salvation of his soul, it was a salvation by works, performed with charity and humor as well as zeal. Through this mixture of belief ran a strong strain of stoicism. Much in life could not be affected or mitigated, and hence, must be borne. Borne without complaint, because complaints were a bore and nuisance to others and undermined the serenity essential to endurance.*

The peculiar American brand of Calvinism combines a number of beliefs that have helped shape the attitudes of a governing class toward power. At the heart of their moral universe was a belief in the profound corruption of the human soul. Human existence is nasty, brutish, and short, and also exceedingly dangerous. Unless man is controlled or dominated he will control and dominate others. This belief underlies the whole theory of the balance of power. Eugene V. Rostow, Under Secretary of State in the Johnson Administration, summarized the national security manager's view of man a few months after leaving office: "universal taste for violence" and "an instinct for destruction for its own sake, normally but not always kept in check by the texture of his social system." †

How then shall man's depravity be kept in check? James V. Forrestal told the Bond Club in 1943, long before Russia had been identified within the government as an enemy, that the "cornerstone in any plan which undertakes to rid us of the curse of war must be the armed might of the United States." ‡ Twenty-five years later, Eugene Rostow, arguing that at "no time in history has effortless peace been the normal state of affairs," called the "rational control of force" man's noblest secular achievement. The ultimate threat to civilization is disorder and the instrument for combating it is law backed by some superior military power.

But who are the lawgivers and the law enforcers? Here we come to the second great principle of American political Calvinism. "The Utopians have always imagined that the world is naturally harmonious," Rostow writes, "and that the freedom of every man to do as he pleases would lead naturally to a peaceful order. . . . On the real front, however, we quickly learn the lesson of *High Noon*—that without organized power to maintain the law, freedom is impossible."

* *Morning and Noon* (Boston: Houghton Mifflin, 1965), p. 18.

† *Law, Power, and the Pursuit of Peace* (New York: Harper and Row, 1968), Introduction, p. xviii.

‡ Quoted in Arnold Rogow, *James Forrestal* (New York: Macmillan, 1963), p. 125.

Who shall be sheriff? The Calvinist answer is: The best among us. And who are they? None other than those whose virtue has been certified by worldly success. It is altogether fitting that the most powerful nation run the world, for what other nation has comparable achievements to boast of as outward symbols of inward grace? It is equally fitting that the achievers run the nation. Those who rise to the top in a fiercely competitive society are by definition "excellent." They are the elect; their success is tangible evidence of God's favor.

The cult of excellence reached its zenith with Kennedy. Observing him as he was about to launch his campaign for the presidency in 1960, Theodore H. White noted, "In the personal Kennedy lexicon, no phrase is more damning than 'He's a very common man' or 'That's a very ordinary type.'" The arrogance so characteristic of the Kennedy advisers, a quality that made it so easy for them to dismiss unwelcome advice by dismissing those who proffered it, was the pride of the men who believed that they were the chosen.

McGeorge Bundy, who made a brilliant reputation in the White House with crisp memos, cutting comments, and facile summations at the end of complicated discussions, once advanced the thesis that man's "real motivating force" was not the profit motive but "the simple, natural, almost unexaminable human desire to do something really well." This indeed, without exception, fitted the national security managers, early achievers as we have seen, firm believers in the American achievement ethic. David McClelland has called America "the achieving society" and has advanced the thesis, much as McGeorge Bundy put it in the remarks just quoted, that the sense of achieving is what gives meaning to life. The drives to make things, to bend the physical environment to man's will, to develop the techniques for controlling economic growth, and social development— these are the source of the incredible energy that propels America. McClelland argues that the American educational and social environment challenges, develops, reinforces, and rewards the achieving personality. Everything we know about the childhood of the national security managers bears out this theory. Each of them was under relentless pressure to be a winner and each succeeded. McGeorge Bundy, for example, reacting to the competitive atmosphere of his family, spent one boyhood summer looking up an obscure word a day in the dictionary trying to stump his father at the dinner table. It is not surprising that such a cool, driven personality should have appealed to a President who had survived the fierce competitive training of the Kennedy family.

In the language of the national security manager, achievement is called duty. The Boy Scout virtues—"duty," "service," "responsibility"—recur again and again in private conversation as well as in official prose. McGeorge Bundy, to take one example, is forever using these words. His first book, the Stimson memoirs, was called *On Active Service;* his second, the edited speeches of Dean Acheson, was entitled *The Pattern of Responsibility.* His recent articles on the presidency and foreign affairs are filled with references to duty and service. A child of the Establishment—Dexter School, Groton, Skull and Bones, a wartime career smoothed by such family friends as Archibald MacLeish and Vice Admiral Alan G. Kirk—Bundy was in the Theodore Roosevelt tradition. To use Bernard Shaw's term, he believed that life is a moral gymnasium. Assigned to the Admiral's Paris headquarters, after the Normandy invasion, he demanded to be transferred to combat duty with the infantry even if it meant a loss of rank. Like his contemporary, John F. Kennedy, who turned his undergraduate thesis into an interventionist tract, *Why England Slept,* Bundy, too, at an early age, felt a deep personal responsibility to fight evil. On graduating from Yale in 1940, he contributed a chapter to a book called *Zero Hour,* in which he set out his own interventionist creed. "Let me put my whole proposition in one sentence. I believe in the dignity of the individual, in government by law, in respect for the truth and in a good God; those beliefs are worth my life." * Twenty years later in the White House, the name of the Evil One had changed, but underneath the snappy comeback, sophisticated analysis, and icy manners, the Boy Scout code still operated. A succession of new Hitlers had arisen to challenge the brave and the best.

The celebration of duty is an effective way to disguise the lust for power from oneself as much as from the outside world. As a group, the national security managers have probably wielded as much power as any group of mortals in history. They relish power—using it, dissecting it, discussing its uses. Yet, by the Calvinist code, it is obscene to revel in power. A politician who aspires to a back seat in Congress can ask for power, but the men who manage the mightiest armies in history are responding only to duty. Their offices are burdens, their life sacrificial. Margaret Mead has noted that the Puritan tradition of denying pleasure runs so deep in America that it has pervaded our language. With the hedonistic explosion of the postwar era, traces of Puritanism are becoming harder to find. But in the formative years of the national security managers, America was still a place where a pleasant-tasting drink that melted your teeth was sold as "tonic" and mothers sighed "It's such a nice day. We *ought* to have a picnic," as they dutifully pushed their children into the sun. A Calvinist establishment is particularly adept at denying the pleasures of power for a still Puritan people. Thus, just as the nation's expansionist drives were rationalized as "responsibility," so the managers' personal will to rule became "service."

* William MacKaye, "Bundy at the White House," *Saturday Evening Post,* March 10, 1962, p. 84.

Yet it would be a profound mistake, I believe, to question the sincerity of the service ethic. Indeed, this is one reason why the standards of "sincerity" are so useless in trying to understand the motivations of the national security managers. Neither critics who insist upon discovering venal motives for murderous policies nor the participants' often honest defense that their motives were "pure" are much help. The world has been brought close to ruin by a variety of sincere men, who have honestly believed that their personal interests and the interests of humanity happily coincided. The issue is not *whether* the national security managers believed that what was expedient was right—the evidence is strong that they did—but *why* they believed it.

The answer, I believe, requires us to return to the Calvinist concept of the elect. If, as McGeorge Bundy suggests, the "simple, natural, almost unexaminable human desire to do something really well" is man's basic drive and the real source of meaning in life, then power and technique indeed become gods. Power worship is based on a denial of the importance of content. One "something" to do really well is as good as another. As Lionel Rubinoff put it in *The Pornography of Power,* "the act which serves the goals of power, regardless of its content, is invested with a moral character of its own by the mere fact that it does so. The evil which serves politics ceases to be evil and becomes good, and the *autonomy of morality* is thereby replaced by the *morality of power*." * The fascination with technique and the definition of achievement as the perfection of technique go far in explaining why the rules of individual morality are suspended when men act for the state.

If the impulse to achievement is the source of ultimate meaning, and power—which the managers themselves define as the capacity to bend the world to their will—is crucial to achievement, then the elect have a moral duty to hoard their power. Bureaucratic homicide becomes a disagreeable duty with no purpose other than to maintain power. But for the national security managers, there is no higher moral purpose because power gives meaning to life.

Power thus becomes the criterion for evaluating other countries—not just military power but techniques of all kinds. For example, the leaders of the U.S. army of occupation in Germany immediately warmed to the Germans because of their efficiency. They understood machines. Unlike the Italians and the French, they made bathrooms and telephones that worked. By the same token, much of American racism is rooted in the achievement ethic as well. Blacks are inferior because they are shiftless. Latin Americans do not keep appointments. Asians would rather dream than work. The official theory of development is to identify the local elect who can be rescued from

* (Chicago: Quadrangle Books, 1968), p. 46.

3. *The Education of a Governing Class*   **73**

their sloth through the application of proper motivational techniques. Thus, David McClelland writes in "Achievement Drive and Economic Growth":

> How can foreign aid be most efficiently used to help poor countries develop rapidly? Not by simply handing money over to their politicians and budget makers but by using it in ways that will select, encourage, and develop those of their business executives who have a vigorous entrepreneurial spirit or a strong drive for achievement.*

The managers of the Vietnam War in their internal discussions have consistently demonstrated far more respect for the North Vietnamese enemy than for the South Vietnamese allies. This is hardly surprising, for Ho Chi Minh, Pham Van Dong, and General Giap share both the achievement ethic and a mastery of technique, whereas the third-rate generals in Saigon are an embarrassment to American leaders who value excellence above all things.

Dean Acheson's preferences in countries offer a good illustration of how decisive considerations of power are in the formation of official prejudices. He was brought up as an Anglophile. His father, the son of a professional British soldier, migrated to Canada and served in the Queen's Own Rifles before settling in Connecticut. On the Queen's birthday, the Union Jack fluttered from the rectory flagpole and they toasted the Queen at dinner. British in manner, as his Midwest critics never tired of pointing out, Acheson was noticeably pro-British in his years in the State Department. But when the impact of the loss of empire was finally felt and British influence waned as troubles at home mounted, Acheson traveled to Britain to make a famous speech berating the English for their loss of power. He was unabashed about defending South Africa and Rhodesia, clearly his favorite African countries, despite the fact that most of the people who live there are mistreated, humiliated, and exploited because of their race. The white governments in Southern Africa know how to keep order and to manage growing economies. The managers of the State Department rationalize their support of Brazil in much the same terms. The government may torture people by attaching electrodes to their genitals, but they do seem to know how to control inflation.

For the national security manager, the most basic enemy is not communism. Even John Foster Dulles could manage a friendly word for Tito. Nor is it, despite official speeches to that effect, violence. The national security managers notice violence selectively. The

* *The Roots of Consciousness* (Princeton, N.J.: Van Nostrand, 1964), pp. 16–17.

French managed to slaughter thousands of Vietnamese and Algerians
in the vain attempt to hold on to their empire during the early postwar years without eliciting an official reaction from Washington, too
busy commiserating with the "captive peoples" of Eastern Europe.
Vietcong violence or Cuban violence is a sure sign of moral depravity.
Brazilian violence or Greek violence is, at worst, "regrettable."

At what can only be described as a religious level, the real enemies
are chaos and disorder, which threaten to undermine one's power.
Despite his devotion to the rhetoric of "freedom," the national
security manager puts his trust in hierarchy. Because the world is
dangerous, because man's nature is essentially evil, structures must
be maintained within which people will know and keep their place.
The most threatening political development of the postwar world is
revolution, because the essence of revolution is a redefinition of
place. For the number one nation any disturbance of existing power
relations (even in the enemy's domain) holds certain risks. The managers' fear of uncertainty is so great that a stable authoritarian government is infinitely preferable to an experimental government, whatever its ideology. A world where clear lines are drawn and old positions firmly held can be preserved and perhaps, over the long run,
even improved a little. On the other hand, as the national security
manager sees it, war breeds in an environment of chaos and turmoil,
and unless it is tightly controlled by a reliable elect, change is exceedingly dangerous. The Kennedy managers' enthusiasm for counterinsurgency grew out of their belief that they had finally hit upon
a technique to control and to moderate political change in the world.
Perhaps the world was not really out of control but would respond
to the right combination of political, economic, and military techniques.

Of all those who have been top advisers, Walt Whitman Rostow—
"in the bombing business," as he puts it, in World War II as an OSS
major; economist; theorist; Rhodes Scholar—has put together the
most coherent philosophical statement about the use of American
power. (Rostow was Johnson's Special Assistant for National Security
during the last three years of his Administration.) His colleagues
would twit him for his manic optimism—Vietnam, he promised,
"might be the last great confrontation of the postwar era"—for his
peculiar blend of liberalism and militarism—"Chester Bowles with
machine guns" they called him in the Kennedy White House—and for
a fundamentalist anticommunism no less burning then Dulles'—in
his writings, Communists are "scavengers," communism "a disease."
But he was a caricature, not an eccentric. He would not have lasted
so many years as a top presidential assistant had his views not been
an eloquent exaggeration of official policy.

Rostow had the optimism and the naïveté and the nerve to visualize the denouement of the American Century. It was to be the technocrat's peace. Vietnam was Armageddon. The communist scavenger would slink back into the night, defeated, and the American elect would proceed to organize the peace through technology. The poor would be helped to achieve the "take-off" to a "high mass consumption" economy within a system of stability and order. Rostow sees "a new day in which organized violence finally ends." It will come through the spread of American technology and technique throughout the world, for according to the impervious Rostovian faith, "aggressive impulses diminish in technologically mature societies." Rostow brings to its logical completion the moral system developed by a generation of national security managers. The world will be rescued through American power and technique. Those who know how to use power and are not afraid to use it will save themselves and all humanity.*

* See Walt Rostow, "The Great Transition: Tasks of the First and Second Post-War Generations," a speech delivered at the University of Leeds, in England, and published by the Leeds University Press, 1967.

4

The National Security Managers
and the President

I N THIS CHAPTER we shall look at the principal role of the national security managers—advising the President. These men exercise their power chiefly by filtering the information that reaches the President and by interpreting the outside world for him. They structure his choices. The advisers who actually work in the White House, the McGeorge Bundys and the Henry Kissingers, see the President at the beginning of the day and at the end. They are his immediate link with a vast bureaucratic machine for collecting intelligence and evaluating it, for thinking up options and possibilities, for "staffing out" risks, and for defining the "threats" posed by the outside world. The heads of the military establishment—the Secretary of Defense, his principal advisers, and the Joint Chiefs of Staff—tell the President the limits and possibilities of using military power to promote what they define as "national security." The Secretary of State shares responsibility for discovering "vital interests" across the world, sanctioning and legitimizing the use of force to protect them, and advising the President on the reaction of other governments to American moves. Bureaucratic responsibility for discovering, interpreting, and managing global "interests" and "threats" produces a distinctive world view, which General Maxwell Taylor, one of John F. Kennedy's most influential advisers, once elegantly summarized:

The United States can no longer be a one-eyed Cyclops. Its power of attention must partake of the many-eyed vigilance of Argus—constantly watching in all directions in anticipation of the emergence of forces inimical to our national purposes.*

The relationship between the President and the national security managers is truly symbiotic. They are engaged in a complex and continuous process of mutual persuasion. The President, as we shall see, is as concerned with how to move the bureaucracy as the advisers are concerned with how to convince the President. In the Vietnam War Lyndon Johnson and Richard Nixon pressed their advisers to formulate plans that would avoid the defeat they could not accept. The advisers in turn pressed the President to take the risks and to sanction the homicidal power necessary to achieve victory.

Political scientists like to talk about the "decision-making process." In one sense everyone in the national security bureaucracy is a "decision-maker." This includes the B-52 pilot who decides where to unload his excess bombs after destroying his assigned target, for in a literal sense he has the power of God over hundreds, possibly thousands of people on the ground beneath. The State Department desk officer who sends a routine cable to an embassy in a minor country on a "back burner" issue is making policy for the United States. But on the great issues, the President is the one who decides. It is for him alone to say "yes" or "no" or, as is often the case, "wait!" President Truman used to keep a sign on his desk: "The buck stops here." On the great issues of the Vietnam War the President made the final decisions. But the thrust of the bureaucratic machine, particularly the activity of his closest advisers, narrowly circumscribed his choices.

Because he is so dependent upon his principal assistants, the President in effect makes policy when he selects them. Indeed he probably exerts his greatest influence over future policy when he recruits his leading advisers. It is in the nature of his job that most of his decisions be affirmations, or at most modifications, of proposals from below. "I am the responsible officer of the government," John F. Kennedy told reporters the day after the Bay of Pigs fiasco, but within a few weeks he had fired Allen Dulles, the head of the CIA and the leading advocate and technician of the ill-fated invasion.† President Johnson used to defend himself and his policy on Vietnam by pointing out that all his advisers were "unanimous" in approving his course. Eisenhower insisted that the Joint Chiefs of Staff bring him unanimous recommendations. No President, of course, will tolerate public dis-

---

* Maxwell Taylor, *Responsibility and Response* (New York: Harper and Row, 1967), p. 6.

† Arthur Schlesinger, Jr., *A Thousand Days* (Boston: Houghton Mifflin, 1965), pp. 290 ff.

agreement among his advisers. Even private disagreement on the premises and goals of policy is exceedingly threatening and for this reason advisers feel pressure "to get their ducks in order" before they face the President. So when policy bubbles up from the bureaucracy, to use Dean Acheson's phrase, there is a consistency to it.

There is also a certain predictability. The President can get a good idea in advance of the kind of advice he is likely to get. For one thing, the pool of eligible national security managers is extremely narrow. When President Kennedy was putting together his Cabinet, Robert A. Lovett, according to Arthur Schlesinger, "exerted a quiet influence on his tastes." * The former Secretary of Defense, senior partner of Brown Brothers, Harriman, and key Truman adviser in the early crucial days of the Cold War, was the man who suggested both Dean Rusk and Robert McNamara for the two top national security posts. To become a national security manager you must know the President personally, as McGeorge Bundy did, or you must be endorsed by another national security manager. "I'd like to have some new faces here, but all I get is the same old names," Kennedy complained to his biographer. But having asked Robert Lovett he could hardly have expected the list to include Norman Thomas or Martin Luther King. A prospective appointee who has been certified as "responsible" by the man Schlesinger calls "the chief agent" of "the New York Establishment" is not likely to depart significantly from the national security wisdom of the past.

The pool of eligibles is further narrowed by the security procedures. Unconventional associations, heretical views, or "derogatory information," which need be no more than an unfriendly remark by a reasonably credible "informant," are enough to eliminate potential national security managers from the list. Then appointments must also be checked against various Congressional lists, such as that compiled by the House Un-American Activities Committee. (In the early Kennedy Administration a Congressional committee had obtained "information" that Paul Nitze, investment banker, Truman adviser, and Cold War hard-liner, was "soft" on the United Nations and disarmament, and he weathered some hostile questioning after he was appointed Assistant Secretary of Defense and later Secretary of the Navy. A less certifiably "responsible," experienced, and conventionally valuable man would have been dropped from the list.) Thus the range of advice a President will get is circumscribed from the start by the selection process.

Presidents do encourage a certain range of opinion among their top advisers and they often make decisions by giving responsibility to one rather than to another. Thus at an early crucial stage in the de-

* Schlesinger, *op. cit.,* pp. 129–31.

liberations on Vietnam, President Kennedy sent General Maxwell Taylor to Saigon for a first-hand analysis and recommendation for action. Sending Taylor (along with Walt Rostow, whose views on the subject were almost as fixed) was a virtual guarantee of getting back a recommendation for war. Had he entrusted the mission to John Kenneth Galbraith instead of asking him to "stop off in Saigon and forward his views," he would have received entirely different advice.

The Taylor mission and the President's reaction to it offer a good illustration of the workings of the national security bureaucracy. The decision on November 16, 1961, to send additional military advisers and equipment in violation of the limits agreed to at the Geneva Conference was a crucial point in the escalation of the war. It was Kennedy's first major decision on Vietnam and it set other forces in motion. One result of the Taylor-Rostow mission was the establishment of MACV, a major theater headquarters in Saigon. Once this headquarters was staffed it became a powerful advocate for increased military involvement. An organization whose mission was preserving Vietnam by military means was now a major factor in bureaucratic politics.

John F. Kennedy knew General Taylor's views on Vietnam because during the 1960 campaign the General had lectured the candidate on the need for a "flexible response" against all forms of "communist aggression." Moreover, the General had resigned from the U.S. Army during the Eisenhower Administration because Ike was unwilling to give the Army money to fight just such "brushfire wars." Kennedy came to the White House convinced that the great battle of his Administration would be the fate of the Third World and that that fate would be decided by the ordeal of guerrilla warfare. Shortly after his inauguration he appointed Taylor a special White House Assistant and put him in charge of "Special Group Counterinsurgency." Supported by the ideological notions of Walt Rostow, who was coming to believe that the whole future of mankind hung on the outcome of jungle wars, and the energetic commitment of his brother Robert, Kennedy devoted much early attention in his Administration to the rehabilitation of the Special Forces. The new President vigorously backed those bureaucracies committed to unconventional warfare and personally restored the Green Beret, which, as the symbol of the new elite fighting force, had inspired the derision and jealousy of the regular army. He was briefed on the euphoric literature on counterguerrilla warfare then beginning to emerge from the CIA-sponsored research in leading universities, and turned his personal attention to improving the technology of guerrilla warfare. At his carved oak desk he pored over the design of a new sneaker for America's jungle warriors.

In a bureaucracy contingency plans play a crucial role because they set the terms of the bureaucratic debate. If a plan is in existence, its bureaucratic advocates have an advantage over those who oppose it but have no plan of their own. "Well, what would you do?" is as effective a ploy in political debate inside the national security bureaucracy as it is anywhere else. It is most unlikely that President Nixon would have ordered the sudden invasion of Cambodia had the Joint Chiefs of Staff not already had well-worked-out contingency plans. In a crisis, real or exaggerated, the President reaches for a plan. The second effect of contingency plans is to spread illusions of success. The military do not write "scenarios" that predict their own defeat. If they have "staffed out" a military operation and have indicated which units should move where, they have, in effect, certified victory.

Thus the planning at the beginning of the Kennedy Administration helped set the climate for future decisions. When Taylor, the chief planner, was sent to report on whether to implement his own plans, his recommendations were predictable: send in more advisers and a "military task force" of about eight thousand men. The risks of backing into a big war, he assured the President grandly, were "not impressive." Vietnam was not an unpleasant place to operate, much better than Korea. North Vietnam, he was glad to report, was "extremely vulnerable to conventional bombing." Taylor's final paragraph in his report to the President was a brilliant piece of bureaucratic argumentation:

> It is my judgment and that of my colleagues that the United States must decide how it will cope with Khrushchev's "wars of liberation" which are really para-wars of guerrilla aggression. This is a new and dangerous Communist technique which bypasses our traditional political and military responses. While the final answer lies beyond the scope of this report, it is clear to me that the time may come in our relations to Southeast Asia when we must declare our intention to attack the source of guerrilla aggression in North Vietnam and impose on the Hanoi Government a price for participating in the current war which is commensurate with the damage being inflicted on its neighbors to the south.*

Taylor here demonstrates a flair for presidential advocacy. No one advises the President without being an advocate for something. (There are, to be sure, always a certain number of sycophants, valets, raconteurs, even an occasional friend, who amuse the President, but if they are ever asked for "advice" they know that it is reassurance that

* Neil Sheehan, Hendrick Smith et al., *The Pentagon Papers* (New York: Bantam, 1971); see the Taylor Report of 1961, pp. 141–48.

is wanted and they provide it.) Advisers represent bureaucratic constituencies such as the Department of Defense, or if they have none, like White House advisers, they are in the business of selling their own reputations, which means generally that they must keep defending last week's advice.

The Taylor memorandum reveals an understanding of the peculiar way the President, the only nationally elected official, the only man with the authority to push the button for nuclear war, looks at the world. As a good professional adviser, he frames issues for the President in such a way as to put maximum psychological pressure on him to make the "right" decision—i.e., the adviser's choice. As is often the case, this is done in a deceptively neutral framework which creates the illusion that "all options have been presented" merely because they may have been stated.

In his report Taylor puts the Vietnam conflict into the larger context of a world struggle with communism. The still-small conflict in a tiny faraway country was not the issue. The conflict, as Taylor described it, assumed the proportions of a historic battle that could decide the political organization of the earth. It was the great test of America's power. To engage the President's attention, much less his commitment, it is necessary to exaggerate the importance of an issue and to paint all alternatives to the recommended course of action in hopeless black. No sane President will start a war over Berlin, Laos, Vietnam, or more obscure places. But "Berlin," "Vietnam," even "Quemoy and Matsu," once invested with the symbolic importance developed and rationalized in a hundred state papers, become causes worth dying for and killing for. The sacrifice of American lives is a crucial step in the ritual of commitment. Thus John T. McNaughton and others stressed in working papers the importance of "spilling American blood" not only to whip up the public to support a war that could touch their emotions in no other way, but also to make clear to the enemy that the President now had no alternative to massive intervention. Just as the "symbolic" deaths of American soldiers in a war in Europe would, according to U.S. war plans, serve as a "tripwire" for a retaliatory attack on the U.S.S.R., leaving the President no option but to drop hydrogen bombs on Soviet cities, so sending Americans to face death in Indochina was designed to convince Ho Chi Minh that the United States also "meant business" in Southeast Asia.

The deliberate inflation and distortion of issues in the advocacy process leads to what might be called the bureaucratic model of reality. It is a collective view of the world put together through the process of bureaucratic struggle, the final purpose of which is to induce the President to do something or to make him feel comfortable about something the bureaucracy has already done. (We will explore in

Chapter 5 the elements of this synthetic world view and how it arises out of the bureaucratic process.)

To persuade the President to take risks it is often necessary for an adviser to paint conflict between nations as a personal joust between leaders. Thus, Taylor tells Kennedy that it is "Khrushchev's new and dangerous technique" that is at stake in Vietnam. The ambitious adviser comes quickly to see that the national interest viewed from the President's desk is indistinguishable from the President's ego. Like monarchs in Shakespearean plays who call each other "England" or "France," Presidents quickly come to see themselves as personifications of the nation. For this reason there are dangers in world leaders' getting to know each other better. "If Khrushchev wants to rub my nose in the dirt," Kennedy told a visiting newspaper editor after their Vienna meeting, "it's all over." The "it" was world civilization, for the President was talking about nuclear war. "What worried him," Arthur Schlesinger reports, "was that Khrushchev might interpret his reluctance to wage war as a symptom of an American loss of nerve. Some day, he said, the time might come when he would have to run the supreme risk to convince Khrushchev that conciliation did not mean humiliation." *

The bureaucratic advocate, aware that powerful leaders come to have an egocentric view of the universe, finds them peculiarly susceptible to paranoid analysis. Thus, other nations seldom have reasons of their own for their foreign policy moves. They exist as sparring partners for the United States. A foreign service officer specializing in Chinese matters recalls his astonishment at listening to John Foster Dulles ascribe an obscure and inconsequential Chinese troop movement to Eisenhower's heart attack which had occurred a few days before. President Kennedy was constantly being told that foreign policy moves by other nations were personal tests of him. The State Department convinced him that the Vienna meeting with Khrushchev in June 1961 was a confrontation designed to intimidate a young, inexperienced President. Dean Acheson lectured him after Vienna to the effect that Khrushchev's policy in Europe "had nothing to do with Berlin, Germany, or Europe" (just as "Vietnam is not really the issue" in Vietnam). Khrushchev's aim, as Acheson saw it, "was not to rectify a local situation but to test the general American will to resist." Acheson used an Aesopian way of talking about Kennedy's will. Kennedy understood that his short-term political reputation and his longer-term historical reputation depended upon whether he could "stand up to Khrushchev." "I can't take a 1954 defeat today," he told Walt Rostow in the spring of 1961, a few weeks after the Cuban disaster.† His two successors

* Quoted in Schlesinger, *op. cit.*, p. 391.
† *Ibid.*, p. 339.

held to the same refrain, using almost literally the same words, *"I will not be defeated in Vietnam."* In Johnson's case his two closest personal nonofficial advisers, Clark Clifford and Abe Fortas, kept feeding his personalized conception of the national interest, the latter reminding him almost nightly, "You do not want to be the first President to lose a war."

(2)

PRESIDENTIAL ADVISERS are in the business of simplifying the world for their employer. Nuances, doubts, complications are eliminated in the effort to come up with a tough, lean analysis and a practical plan of action. When McGeorge Bundy reflected on his role while still in office, he pictured the presidential adviser as a "prism through which the President saw public problems." In the great game of making policy each adviser had his own "spin," but advisers have "got to do things his way." Loyalty to the President is the adviser's most important asset.

As we have seen, the shrewd adviser tailors his advice to the President's prejudices as best he knows them. This is, of course, an example of the universal practice of telling superiors what they want to hear or "protecting" them from bad news and from discouraging predictions. Choleric kings of old used to have messengers who were indiscreet enough to bring the wrong answer executed on the spot. Presidential displeasure in Johnson's time used to take the form of tongue lashings. So frightened were LBJ's advisers that, according to the White House Vietnam adviser, Chester Cooper, they did not dare to counsel delay of bombing raids on North Vietnam when diplomats were at a delicate and crucial stage in the attempt to arrange negotiations because Johnson was in a bad mood. A glimpse of what regularly lay in store for advisers who stumbled was given in an interview by President Johnson to a visiting history professor. Dean Rusk, the President's most loyal counselor, had inadvertently leaked some information. In "an unmodulated voice," the professor reports, the President went on about the "disloyalty" and "unpatriotic sentiments" in the State Department. "It's gotten so that you can't have intercourse with your wife without it being spread around by traitors." * Any subordinate willing to put up with such a man will try very hard to please him.

Advisers must have sensitive antennae to what is salable advice and what is not. National security managers, in defending their rec-

---

* Quoted in Henry F. Graff, *The Tuesday Cabinet* (Englewood Cliffs, N.J.: Prentice-Hall, 1970), p. 148.

ommendations or their failure to speak up, talk about preserving their "credit points" with the President. You cannot propose too many ideas that are unfamiliar or incompatible with presidential beliefs. McGeorge Bundy used to tell his staff that an adviser has only so many swings at the ball. (In the Pentagon the vernacular is to have a "chop" at the "action," but it is the same game.) Opportunities for influencing policy are limited. Opportunities misused destroy "credibility" and "effectiveness."

The President, for his part, is deeply conscious of his dependence upon the bureaucracy—not only the senior advisers he has personally selected but also the thousands farther down the line. After all, they were discovering "vital interests" in some distant country long before he may have even heard of it and they will remain long after he has gone home to write his memoirs and build his library. Every President has complained about the difficulty of moving the bureaucracies below him. Sometimes they see themselves fighting the government they are supposed to be leading. In an interview with Jean Daniel shortly before his death, John F. Kennedy hinted that he was ready to change American policy on Cuba, but he didn't know whether "the government" was.

Presidents are keenly aware that they will never know more than a fraction of what subordinate agents do every day in the name of their administrations. Indeed, even the most autocratic rulers face the same problem. Nicholas I, who ruled Russia with a terror not equaled until Stalin's day, used to complain that it was not the Czar of all the Russias but ten thousand clerks who really ruled that vast domain. In his memoirs, Albert Speer notes that Hitler, who could have anyone within the Third Reich shot within hours, was unable at times to get the bureaucracy to carry out his orders.

As he was about to leave office Harry Truman remarked of his successor, General Eisenhower, "He'll say 'do this' and 'do that,' and nothing will happen. Poor Ike—it won't be a bit like the army." * Presidents have resorted to great secrecy to avoid having their policies sabotaged by what they believed to be hostile bureaucracies. With the outbreak of war, communication between President Roosevelt and the State Department broke down almost entirely. "Don't tell anybody in the State Department about this," the President told Robert Murphy, then a junior foreign service officer about to leave on a presidential mission to North Africa. "That place is a sieve." † To insure against State Department interference in his foreign policy, Roosevelt carried on his most important correspondence in Navy

---

* Richard E. Neustadt, *Presidential Power* (New York: Signet Books, 1964), p. 22.

† See Robert Murphy, *Diplomat Among Warriors* (Garden City, N.Y.: Doubleday and Co., 1964).

Department codes. When President Kennedy decided to introduce a wholly new rhetoric on U.S.–Soviet relations in his American University speech in June 1963, the text was prepared by his intimate advisers in the White House, and the State Department bureaucracy learned about the new direction in foreign policy along with the public.

The way "to get America moving again," Kennedy believed, was to circumvent the conventional bureaucracies and to take charge of America's most crucial foreign policy involvements through new, streamlined bureaucracies over which the President could hope to exercise some direct control. The State Department, he said, was a "bowl of jelly."

Presidential effort to control bureaucracies by circumventing them through the use of personal assistants and elite units has been a trend of American government for many years. Roosevelt's use of Harry Hopkins as "troubleshooter" is a prime example. In the Kennedy-Johnson era, however, the process became institutionalized. President Kennedy's "detailed support" of the Special Forces against what Schlesinger calls the "organization generals" of the Joint Chiefs of Staff and President Johnson's dispatch of his assistant Robert Komer to be in charge of the pacification program are typical of presidential attempts to create loyal channels and dependable instruments of policy outside the regular bureaucracy. The effect of course is to build up the personal power of the President and to eliminate some of the organizational checks and balances within the executive department.

The planning of the Vietnam War makes an excellent case study of the mutual dependence and tension that characterize the relationship of the President and his principal advisers, not only because it is typical in many ways of the bureaucratic process, but also because it was a conspicuous failure. At least one hundred bureaucratic accomplices in the tragedy have rushed into print with their own exculpatory versions of the story. One of them, John Roche, grandly declassified a secret memorandum written by Assistant Secretary of State Roger Hilsman in the pages of the New York *Times Magazine* the better to impeach the historical testimony of his bureaucratic rival, along with his character.* Anyone interested in understanding the phenomenon of bureaucratic homicide can only welcome such public display. In politics, as in medicine, often the only way to gain insight into the way an organism works is to wait for the pathologist's report.

Advisers are bound by the fundamental beliefs and prejudices the President brings with him to the White House. They assume

* John Roche, "The Jigsaw Puzzle of History," New York *Times Magazine,* January 24, 1971.

that his goals are about as Henry Adams described them a hundred years ago in his novel *Democracy:*

> He came to Washington determined to be the Father of his country; to gain a proud immortality—and re-election.

Therefore, in recommending policy, advisers must be sensitive to the President's psychological and political history. In the case of the Vietnam War, for example, both Kennedy and Johnson were publicly committed to the preservation of South Vietnam as a non-communist state and an American sphere of influence long before they sat in the President's chair. As early as June 1956, Senator John F. Kennedy had given a speech defining America's vital interests in Southeast Asia:

> Vietnam represents the cornerstone of the Free World in South-east Asia, the keystone to the arch, the finger in the dike. Burma, Thailand, India, Japan, the Philippines and, obviously, Laos and Cambodia are among those whose security would be threatened if the red tide of Communism overflowed into Viet-nam. . . . Moreover, the independence of Free Vietnam is crucial to the free world in fields other than the military. Her economy is essential to the economy of all of Southeast Asia; and her political liberty is an inspiration to those seeking to obtain or maintain their liberty in all parts of Asia—and indeed the world. The fundamental tenets of this nation's foreign policy, in short, depend in considerable measure upon a strong and free Vietnamese nation.*

Lyndon Johnson came to the White House even more of a committed partisan. Less fascinated with the technology of counter-insurgency or the rhetoric of "wars of national liberation" than his predecessor, he was more committed than Kennedy, personally and psychologically, to preserving the American role in Vietnam. In May 1961 Kennedy had sent him to Southeast Asia on a fact-finding mission. He came back talking about Diem as "the Winston Churchill of Southeast Asia." Ringing in his ears were the warnings of the leaders of Thailand and the Philippines that their pro-American regimes would be imperiled if the United States were humiliated in Vietnam. Johnson privately recommended to Kennedy the dispatch of combat troops:

> Our mission arrested the decline of confidence in the United States. It did not—in my judgment—restore any confidence already lost . . .

* Chester Cooper, *The Lost Crusade* (New York: Dodd, Mead and Co., 1970), p. 168.

I cannot stress too strongly the extreme importance of following up this mission with other measures, other actions, and other efforts. . . .*

Thus Johnson was already on record within the Administration as a hard-liner on Vietnam. Two days after taking office he had a conversation with Kennedy's ambassador to Vietnam, Henry Cabot Lodge, who told him that hard decisions were in the offing. Johnson replied, "I am not going to lose Vietnam. I am not going to be the President who saw Southeast Asia go the way China went."

For the generation of national security managers who lived through the early postwar era the great political trap was "appeasement." Alger Hiss, the old China hands, the Poland losers, the Czechoslovakia losers, and other "venders of compromise" in the State Department, as Senator John F. Kennedy would later call them, had become symbols of wrecked careers and warnings to the wise many months before Senator Joseph McCarthy went on the rampage. John Foster Dulles' security officer, a friend of McCarthy, had a sign on his desk: "An ounce of loyalty is worth a pound of brains." The point was not lost on the men who came to Washington in the 1960's to advise the President.

Lyndon Johnson did not know much about the outside world, and nothing whatever about Southeast Asia. But he knew a lot about politics in the United States and he had powerful hunches about what motivated men everywhere else. "I grew up with Mexicans," he told some reporters shortly after he moved into the White House. "They'll come right into your yard and take it over if you let them. And the next day they'll be on your porch, barefoot and weighing one hundred and thirty pounds and they'll take that, too. But if you say to 'em right at the start, 'Hold on, just wait a minute,' they'll know they're dealing with somebody who'll stand up. And after that you can get along fine." † There is a whole world view in the story. It is the same world view Johnson expressed before the troops in Vietnam when he told them to "nail the coonskin to the wall" because we are "outnumbered fifteen to one" and the poor of the world, if not put decisively in their place, will "sweep over the United States and take what we have." A President, particularly one with a powerful personality, who feels strongly and expresses himself strongly about such elemental fears, creates a climate for his subordinates. He is sure to have his prejudices packaged for him in the form of neatly rationalized options.

---

* Lyndon Johnson, "Mission to S.E. Asia, India, and Pakistan," May 23, 1961, in Sheehan et al., *The Pentagon Papers.*
† Johnson's tale is repeated in Tom Wicker, *JFK and LBJ* (Baltimore: Penguin Books, 1970), p. 196.

A President who is strongly committed to a foreign policy objective that can only be achieved through force presents a problem for his advisers because no matter how zealous the President may be, he also exhibits the caution that comes with having ultimate responsibility. This ambivalence at the highest level of government—a mixture of dread of being branded a "loser" and terror at the prospect of being the man who started World War III—goes far to explain the pattern of escalation in Vietnam. As Daniel Ellsberg and Leslie Gelb, who were both second-level advisers during the process, have noted, the President invariably accepted less military escalation than his advisers proposed. Maxwell Taylor presented to President Kennedy his recommendations for an initial task force of eight thousand men. "I do not believe that our program to save South Vietnam will succeed without it," General Taylor flatly asserted. In so recommending he was backing up the Joint Chiefs of Staff. As Kennedy's assistant, Theodore Sorenson, has revealed, the Joint Chiefs had called for the sending of ground troops to Vietnam and Laos within four months of Kennedy's inauguration. Even Taylor pointed out that sending the task force would not necessarily avert defeat. It would show Diem and the Communists that the United States "meant business" and would shore up America's sagging "credibility" in Asia, but if Hanoi and "Peiping" were to intervene, the United States would have to be prepared to commit six divisions, or about 205,000 men.

Kennedy, in Sorenson's words, "in effect voted 'no'—and only his vote counted." He increased the established advisers and set up a major headquarters in Vietnam. He did not send in the troops, but he set forces in motion he knew would compel him to make further decisions. He told Schlesinger in November 1961:

> They want a force of American troops. . . . They say it's necessary to restore confidence and maintain morale. But it will be just like Berlin. The troops will march in; the bands will play; the crowds will cheer; and in four days everyone will have forgotten. Then we will be told we have to send in more troops. It's like taking a drink. The effect wears off, and you have to take another.*

Like his successor, John Kennedy wanted to do only the minimum necessary to avoid immediate defeat. He wished to postpone the politically unpalatable decision, just eight years after the Korean armistice, of ordering American boys into another land war in Asia.

In 1961, according to Arthur Schlesinger, Kennedy had made a "conscious decision" to turn the Vietnam problem over to the Secre-

* Quoted in Schlesinger, *op. cit.,* p. 547.

tary of Defense. The Secretary of State did not object, writes Roger Hilsman, who at the time was the Assistant Secretary of State in charge of Asia, because Rusk always regarded Vietnam "as essentially a military problem." President Kennedy had approved a program of covert actions against North Vietnam which had been recommended by a Vietnam Task Force established in the early weeks of the Administration. These actions included the dispatch of agents into North Vietnam to set up "networks of resistance, covert bases and teams for sabotage and light harassment." Other proposals were for increased overflights of North Vietnam and for U.S.-supported South Vietnamese guerrilla operations in Laos, especially against communist aerial resupply missions in the vicinity of Tchepone. During this period the State Department was particularly strong in pushing for military operations in Laos, and some of these President Kennedy rejected. On March 9, 1962, U.S. officials announced that American pilots were accompanying Vietnamese pilots on combat missions as part of a "combat training" program. By the fall of 1963 the Joint Chiefs of Staff had approved a plan developed by Admiral Ulysses Grant Sharp, the Commander of the Pacific Fleet, which called for amphibious raids using Vietnamese Rangers and Airborne and Marine units against targets in North Vietnam.

The fourteen months between the assassination of John F. Kennedy and the inauguration of Lyndon B. Johnson as President in his own right was a period when the national security managers had the greatest flexibility in developing and promoting policy. This was the era of "McNamara's war" during which the crucial planning on the escalation of the Vietnam war took place. In the previous period Vietnam was still a "back burner" issue and bureaucrats "in the field," such as the CIA station chief, John Richardson, had great latitude to set American policy. A few months later the President himself would be the Vietnam desk officer, squadron commander, sometimes even patrol leader, personally approving bombing targets and waiting up through the early hours of the morning until the planes had returned from their missions. But in his first year of office Johnson was engaged with other matters, passing the Kennedy legislative program, developing one of his own, emerging from the shadow of Camelot, and getting himself re-elected. A few days after he took office, he called for renewed planning for possible increased activity against North Vietnam. Within two weeks MACV, the military headquarters in Saigon, had obliged with OPLAN 34A which offered "a spectrum of capabilities" against North Vietnam including air attacks, all designed to "convince the DRV leadership" that they should stop supporting insurgent activities in South Vietnam and Laos. Thus by posing essentially military questions to national security bureaucrats the President effectively guaranteed that the

Vietnam drama would be a war story. Since the events in Southeast Asia were moving too fast to be ignored and the President was otherwise occupied, this meant that the handful of men who had already become "old Vietnam hands" had the "action." Within broad limits they were free to frame the issues and to pose the alternatives.

(3)

ALL THROUGH 1964 the tempo of contingency planning quickened. The idea men at the Pentagon worked overtime. Various proposals for demonstrating American displeasure—bombing, defoliating, conducting reconnaissance, infiltrating agents, even using the supersonic boom of B-52's to break windows in Hanoi—were forwarded up the bureaucratic ladder. McNamara insisted on managing the planning process himself, sharing his war primarily with his trusted lieutenant, Assistant Secretary John T. McNaughton. The planning process consisted of evaluating the risks and effectiveness of various combinations of military and paramilitary measures put forward by specialists in the military services and in the "intelligence community." Chester Cooper, an old CIA hand on Vietnam, has written, somewhat unfairly, that "serious thinking with respect to the choices available was desultory." (It was indeed highly imaginative: a dozen James Bond scripts could be written from a month's output of Joint Chiefs of Staff recommendations.) In noting the militarized nature of the planning process Cooper observes:

> By and large the non-defense elements of the government were neither psychologically nor organizationally able to come to grips with an insurgency that was quickly getting out of hand. None of the courses at the Foreign Service Institute, and none of the experiences of AID specialists and Foreign Service officers elsewhere, seemed relevant to what was going on in Vietnam.*

Why was it that while the Pentagon bureaucracy churned out dozens of recommendations for making the life of the Vietnamese more miserable in imaginative new ways, no staff work of any consequence was devoted to the kind of peace settlement the United States wanted or had reason to expect, or how to get it? Why was the fear of negotiation so great that proposals for settlement from U Thant, the Soviet Union, and de Gaulle as well as peace feelers from Hanoi, were turned aside? "We do not believe in conferences to ratify terror, so our policy is unchanged," the President an-

---

* Cooper, *op. cit.,* pp. 253 and 255.

nounced. Meanwhile, Assistant Secretary of State William Bundy was exploring a Laos conference as a possible diplomatic "gambit" which could be used as a "plausible way of holding off Vietnam negotiations." * The national security managers understood that U.S. minimum objectives in Indochina could not be achieved by negotiation because the Saigon government had so little political power. The NLF's political advantage could only be overcome, they reasoned, by massive military power.

The same preoccupation with military solutions and the virtual exclusion of serious consideration of nonmilitary solutions has been noted in connection with other national security crises. According to Adam Yarmolinsky, at the time a second-level but strategically placed national security manager, the Executive Committee of the National Security Council, during the Cuban missile crisis (October 14–28, 1962), "spent at least 90 per cent of its time studying alternative uses of troops, bombers, and warships." Although "the possibility of seeking withdrawal of the missiles by straightforward diplomatic negotiation received some attention within the State Department, it seems hardly to have been considered by the President." Nor was any significant attention given to the use of economic leverage on the Soviet Union in preference to the confrontation and eventual ultimatum. Yarmolinsky finds it "curious" that nonmilitary agencies should have had so few options to put before the President.†

There are profound reasons why it is not particularly "curious" that the U.S. government specializes in violence in its approach to national security. The basic characteristics of our institutional structures, the rewards and incentives that operate on men when they become national security managers, and the elaborate private language and ideology that has been developed to absolve men from personal responsibility for bureaucratic homicide all reinforce each other. The actors in the Vietnam tragedy by and large did what they were trained to do, were paid to do, and, under happier circumstances, would have been praised for doing. In short, they were following the rules for governing an empire.

(4)

THE OFFICE of the Presidency itself has a profound effect on the way foreign affairs are conducted. The nature of the Presidency is no longer a political issue dividing the major parties. Every presidential

---

* See Sheehan et al., *The Pentagon Papers,* Chapter 6.

† Adam Yarmolinsky, "American Foreign Policy and the Decision to Intervene," *Journal of International Affairs,* No. 2, 1968, pp. 231–35.

candidate promises to be a "strong" chief executive. Eleven months before he took office, Senator John F. Kennedy told the National Press Club:

Whatever the political affiliation of our next President, whatever his views may be on all the issues and problems that rush in upon us, he must above all be the chief executive in every sense of the word. He must be prepared to exercise the fullest powers of his office—all that are specified and some that are not . . . the President is alone, at the top.*

Although most candidates campaign on such views, each President has ended his administration impressed with the limitations of his office. "The President," John Kennedy wrote in the year of his death, "is rightly described as a man of extraordinary powers. Yet it is also true that he must wield those powers under extraordinary limitations —and it is these limitations which so often give the problem of choice its complexity and even poignancy." † It is these limitations which also determine presidential priorities and encourage him to act where his space to act is greatest.

The principal goal of a President in office, more even than re-election or historical vindication, is to govern. In domestic affairs he barely governs. He presides. John Kennedy died having failed to enact any major piece of domestic legislation. During the years in which he was making life-and-death decisions affecting the fate of the Northern Hemisphere he could not persuade Congress to enact a minimum-wage bill or a federal education act. When he tried in 1962 to use the power of command of his office to halt inflation and publicly denounced steel-company executives for raising their prices, he spent the rest of his term apologizing for his bitterly criticized "strong arm methods." Harry Truman remarked, "I sit here all day trying to persuade people to do things they ought to have sense enough to do without persuading them. . . . That's all the powers of the President amount to." ‡ Where the President resorts to command to solve problems at home, he usually ends up looking foolish. Truman was ordered by the Supreme Court to give back the steel mills he seized during the Korean War. His earlier attempt to draft striking railroad workers into the army was blocked by Congress. Because of a remarkable constellation of circumstances— his predecessor's assassination, mounting civil disturbance and a sense of crisis, and his own special skills and associations—Lyndon Johnson was able to enact much of John Kennedy's legislative pro-

* Speech before the National Press Club, January 14, 1960.

† Theodore Sorensen, *Decision-Making in the White House* (New York: Columbia University Press, 1963), p. xii.

‡ Neustadt, *op. cit.*, p. 22.

gram, but by the time the war escalated he too had run out of steam. As a wartime President he lacked the power or leadership authority to curb crippling inflation. As Richard Neustadt has observed in his book *Presidential Power,* command "is not a method suitable for everyday employment" in domestic affairs. In controversial issues of social reconstruction the President's power is hobbled.

It is only when the President acts in' his capacity as commander-in-chief that he can command and count on a high probability that he will get obedience and even results. Only in foreign and military affairs, insulated as they are from the political restraints of domestic conflict, can the President exercise the full scope of his enormous powers.

This does not mean that foreign problems are ultimately any more tractable than domestic problems, but it does mean that a President can have the illusion of success when he acts as commander-in-chief. A President who lacks the power to raise the price of postage stamps is peculiarly susceptible to the illusion that he can manage the world. In national security affairs, particularly in the twilight world of half-secret brushfire wars, the President is in command of his own reputation in a way that he never can be in domestic affairs. If he claims to be winning the "war on inflation" it is possible to determine the accuracy of his claim at the local supermarket. But who can successfully challenge his claim to be winning the hearts and minds of Southeast Asia by improving the "kill ratio"? Only when a foreign war meets with obvious disaster does the President lose his firm (and exclusive) grip on the flag.

The bureaucratic structure of the national security establishment over which the President presides is built on the principles of hierarchy and command. The art of governing by persuasion, which is essential in domestic affairs, is a rare political skill. It is far easier to govern by command, and the only area where this is possible is beyond the shore. Whether there is to be "action" or not in domestic affairs depends in large measure on the feelings, interests, fears, and hopes of unpredictable human beings. Military operations, on the other hand, deal with "hard" data. Where is the enemy? How many are there? How many men do we move from here to there in order to destroy them? When the President decides to order the movement of troops, he can be reasonably sure, in contrast to many areas of domestic policy, that his commands will be carried out with dispatch and even a touch of virtuosity. Moreover, the possibilities for the experimental use of power beyond the frontiers of American society are tempting, while legal and political restraints still operate within our borders. Thus Kennedy could consider solving the "Cuban problem" by involving the island or the Congo problem by bribing the entire parliament. However much he may be tempted, a President cannot solve his tax problems or inflation problems by using similar methods.

In Vietnam the President was presented with a seemingly limitless panoply of "options," all of which made use of homicidal technology organized under commandable bureaucratic structures. Although, as we have seen, the long-range intelligence prognoses on the war were guarded or pessimistic, the President was offered a variety of tools to try. He could do something. He did not have to "sit in my rocking chair," to use Lyndon Johnson's words, and admit that he, the President of the United States, was as powerless to influence the dangerous outside world as he was to change America.

5

The Operational Code of the
National Security Managers

LIKE REALLY important rules anywhere—in families, corporations, country clubs, and street gangs—the operational code of the national security managers is not written down. The rules are in the air and the successful bureaucrat learns them quickly. To avoid becoming a bureaucratic casualty a national security manager must accept the conditions for exercising power. For someone entering office in the 1960's this meant embracing a well-worked-out bureaucratic model of reality, resting on a set of assumptions about human nature in general, the behavior of enemies in particular, the appointed mission of America, and the very purpose of international politics. These assumptions have been widely shared by other great empires. They were articulated most clearly, and debated somewhat, in the early formative years of the Truman Administration when the main contours of postwar American foreign policy were laid out. By the time of the escalation of the Vietnam War they were no longer debatable. Indeed, they had become so much a part of the consciousness of the militarized civilians who ran the national security bureaucracy that it was seldom necessary even to articulate them.

The basic premise of the national security manager is that international politics is a game. As an Egyptian politician once put it, in the game of nations "there are no winners, only losers. The objective of each player is not so much to win as to avoid loss." * Problems do not get solved. They are managed. Success is achieved if disaster is averted or even postponed until the next administration. When his term of office came to an end in the ignominious stalemate of Vietnam, Rusk looked back on his eight years with satisfaction, he said, because nuclear weapons had not been used.

The "name of the game" (a favorite expression in the national security world) is to avoid losing "influence" and if possible to gain more. It is much less clear what you do with the influence once you get it. Power has a primarily psychological meaning. The national security bureaucrat does not seek to change the physical environment of the world so much as to inspire what he regards as a healthy fear in his opposite numbers in other nations. The modest but important triumphs of the Public Health Service in eradicating disease or of the Agriculture Department in boosting productivity abroad barely count as field goals. The touchdowns are the triumphs of will. When the enemy backs down, in Cuba, Berlin, or wherever, then you know that you have not lost power. In short, power, as it is conceived in the national security bureaucracy and in the chanceries of all nations big enough to be contestants, is the capacity to dominate by using the technology of intimidation. It is a game in an exact sense because it is without higher purpose beyond winning (or, more accurately, avoiding loss). Once the capacity to dominate is established, the winners may, as in the case of defeated Germany and Japan, pay the losers substantial amounts of money for the privilege of winning. Indeed, they have to do it to keep the playing field in repair. Playing the game, even when you win, is an uneconomic, indeed very expensive, activity. (The United States has expended about one ton of copper per man per year in Vietnam to preserve a "credibility" which may or may not help it in the future to get strategic raw materials such as copper at favorable prices. It would surely have been cheaper to buy copper at five times the current market price). But that hardly matters, for the game cannot be justified in rational terms.

All great nations play the game. There are only two principal rules. The first is that no rival nation or combination of rivals can be allowed to become powerful enough to threaten your own power—not merely your physical safety but your capacity to impose your will on such others as you choose. That is the time-honored principle of balance of power. The second rule is that all the world is the playing field. There are no spectators. Every nation, no matter

* Egyptian Vice-President Zaharia Mohieddin in a lecture at the Egyptian War College, quoted in Miles Copeland, *The Game of Nations* (New York: Simon and Schuster, 1969), p. 18.

how small, insular, or neutralist in outlook, is a potential member of somebody's team. If it has not yet been chosen, or more accurately, dominated, then there is a "power vacuum" which you must exploit before the other team does. Taken together, the two rules guarantee an unending competition for high stakes on a vast and absorbing scale.

To keep the game going you must be prepared to be flexible about your enemies, being prepared to change them when the game so requires. Institutions which have a vested interest in preserving their own bureaucratic empires are threatened by historical change. The most fundamental law of any organization is bureaucratic inertia. Institutions like to continue doing what they have been doing, always on a grander scale, if possible. When old enemies disappear, mellow, or turn into allies, as frequently happens in international relations, new enemies must be found and new threats must be discovered. The failure to replenish the supply of enemies is the supreme threat facing any national security bureaucracy. But the U.S. national security establishment has been remarkably adept at keeping up with history. NATO and the rearmament of Germany, which originally was promoted in Congress and sold to the public as an essential barrier to a Soviet sweep to the English Channel, has for years been primarily justified inside the national security bureaucracy as a necessary device for containing West Germany by keeping her closely integrated into a Western system. As relations with China begin to ease, and the United States prepares to adjust to the departure of Chiang Kai-shek from the scene and the final collapse of the dream of restoring the *ancien régime* on the mainland, a new rationale has developed for retaining American bases on Taiwan and deploying an armada in the far Pacific. It is the threat of renewed Japanese militarism.

For the national security manager the game is what makes the job exciting. "I couldn't stand this job if I didn't love it," Assistant Secretary of Defense John T. McNaughton, who had been working fourteen hours a day weeks on end, exclaimed to his assistant at the height of the pre-escalation planning on the Vietnam War.* A man is attracted to a job as national security manager because he is intrigued by power, more than money and more than fame. Dean Rusk, Robert McNamara, and McGeorge Bundy did not expect to enrich themselves serving the state. Indeed, Robert McNamara, whose desire for financial success had been satisfied by his becoming a millionaire, is reputed to have lost a considerable sum when he was obliged to sell his stocks to gain his office, like Charles Wilson and other Secretaries of Defense before him. McGeorge Bundy, whose mother was of the Boston Lowells, did not need money either. He

---

* I am indebted to Daniel Ellsberg for this information about John McNaughton.

could and subsequently did make much more than his starting salary of twenty-one thousand dollars as a White House Special Assistant. Dean Rusk, who on one occasion at least let it slip to the gossip columns that he had exhausted his savings and did need money, hardly expected that his job would make his fortune, and it didn't. He told a visiting professor a few weeks before leaving office that he was "broke and unemployed."

What makes the game worth unending hours of dreary meetings and sleepless nights? One national security manager to whom I put the question answered immediately, "The sense of playing for high stakes." Once the national security managers have been exhilarated by the proximity to Promethean power, it is hard to go back to corporate bonds, advising clients on mergers, making raincoats, lecturing students, or anything else in the comfortable world from which they come. In the Kennedy era they called themselves "crisis managers" and liked to think of themselves as judicious specialists in violence. Their "finest hour," as many of them have written, was the Cuban missile crisis, where, for perhaps the first time in human history, the fate of world civilization hung in the balance. Like Henry V on the eve of the battle of Agincourt, the modern militarized civilian believes that he will be remembered and measured by the great contests in which he participates. It is here that he can put his stamp on the future. His tests are, of course, not tests of bravery but of toughness. The challenges come as portentous decisions in an atmosphere electric with risk.

In a sense international politics has always been treated by diplomats as something of a game. (Winners get to be called statesmen.) But the game used to be played primarily with the tools of "old-fashioned diplomacy"—what Harold Nicolson called "the art of negotiation." The words of the prewar diplomat Jules Cambon—". . . the best instrument at the disposal of a government wishing to persuade another government is the word of an honest man" *— have a hollow ring in the era of the Green Beret, assassination teams, U-2's, defoliation programs, black propaganda, Bay of Pigs invasions, bribed parliaments, and the "slow squeeze" around Hanoi. The rules of the game have changed for the United States because the point of the game has changed. Negotiation is a good instrument only if your objectives are limited and concrete, only if you are willing to "win some and lose some." But for a nation exhilarated by the game of nations the whole field of international relations is a confrontation.

Thus, one State Department official greeted the preliminary skirmish over a site for the "contacts" that were supposed to lead to

* Quoted from Harold Nicolson, *The Evolution of Diplomacy* (New York: Collier, 1962), in John Campbell, *The Fudge Factory* (New York: Basic Books, 1971), p. 22.

"discussions" for ending the Vietnam War as if it were Armageddon. When the Vietnamese agreed to meet in Paris instead of Warsaw, the official exclaimed proudly to a New York *Times* reporter: "There we were right off the bat—eyeball to eyeball on a question of prestige as well as procedure. And they're the ones who blinked. Now we're one up." When the Soviet Union canceled the tour of the Broadway company of "Hello, Dolly" in Moscow, presumably in furtherance of its aid commitments to Hanoi, Lyndon Johnson, "mad as hell," summoned Dean Acheson to think up an appropriate response to so ignominious a defeat. When the former Secretary of State, to his credit, told the President to forget about it, Johnson angrily dispatched the troupe for a retaliatory run in Saigon.

(2)

THERE IS a second foundation stone in the bureaucratic model of reality which no one who likes to be driven to the office in an official limousine or have his desk banked with flags or thrill to a hurried summons to the White House Situation Room is disposed to cast aside. It is the official theory of human motivation. All killing in the national interest is carried out in strict accordance with certain scientific principles concerning human behavior. It is those principles that persuade Presbyterian elders, Episcopal wardens, liberal professors, and practitioners of game-theory rationalism that bureaucratic homicide is neither wanton nor purposeless.

The official theory of human motivation is a hopelessly oversimplified derivative of the rat psychology many of the national security managers learned in college. If you want to motivate a rat give him a pellet or shock him with a bolt of electricity. In international politics it is dangerous to be overgenerous with positive inducements. That is "appeasement," which, as the history of the prewar period showed, merely whets rats' appetites. Unlike the well-stocked laboratory, a modern militarized nation such as the United States has a shortage of positive inducements, for politicians feel they cannot make very many political concessions without losing the game. But the panoply of weapons to burn, blast, poison, or vaporize the rat is limitless. Such "negative reinforcement" will make him less dangerous and will be a good example to all other rats.

The rat view of human nature has been at the heart of American Cold War policy. In September 1946, Presidential Counsel Clark M. Clifford prepared a memorandum on U.S.–Soviet relations which laid out the analysis and policy recommendations that have dominated the last generation. In his letter to the President, Clifford reported, "I have consulted the Secretary of State, the Secretary of

War, the Attorney General, the Secretary of the Navy, Fleet Admiral Leahy, Ambassador Pauley, the Director of Central Intelligence. . . . There is remarkable agreement among the officials with whom I have talked. . . ." The crucial paragraph of the long memorandum embodies the classic rat-psychology view of politics:

> The language of military power is the only language which disciples of power politics understand. [Clifford here means them, not us.] The United States must use that language in order that Soviet leaders will realize that our government is determined to uphold the interest of its citizens and the rights of small nations. Compromise and concessions are considered, by the Soviets, to be evidence of weakness and they are encouraged by our "retreats" to make new and greater demands.*

Since compromise is "retreat" the only way of making the Soviet Union behave is to threaten it with superior military power. "Therefore," Clifford continued, "in order to maintain our strength at a level which will be effective in restraining the Soviet Union, the United States must be prepared to wage atomic and biological warfare. . . . The United States, with a military potential composed primarily of highly effective technical weapons, should entertain no proposal for disarmament or limitation of armament as long as the possibility of Soviet aggression exists."

This view of human nature in general and of enemies in particular effectively rules out nonmilitary approaches to international conflict. The cold warriors themselves have, oddly enough, tended to berate themselves for their softness rather than for their belligerency. During the last thirty years there have been innumerable boards, task forces, groups, and special "exercises" designed to fight the Cold War harder, specifically to make our threats more credible. Yet consider so redoubtable a warrior diplomat as Charles Bohlen, who, having been attacked by Senator Joseph McCarthy for being a typical upper-class pink, spent a distinguished career trying to prove that he had not sold out the country to Stalin by translating for FDR at Yalta. Despite the fact that the United States has spent all but a fraction of its foreign policy dollar on building the mightiest arsenal in history (there is more firepower on a single aircraft carrier than was available to all the armies of history up to 1945) and is the only country on earth with its troops on every continent, Bohlen is concerned that Americans "believe rather excessively in the virtue of good will between nations." †

---

* Appendix to Arthur Krock, *Memoirs* (London: Cassell and Co., Ltd., 1968), pp. 228–29.

† Charles E. Bohlen, *Transformation of American Foreign Policy* (New York: W. W. Norton & Co., 1969), p. 97.

So pervasive is the stimulus-response view of human motivation in the upper reaches of the national security bureaucracy that it can withstand a great deal of hard empirical evidence about how human beings actually react to coercion. In the Clark Clifford memorandum the policy of threatening the Soviet Union with atomic and biological warfare is recommended as part of "a diligent effort to improve . . . relations" with the Soviet Union. George Kennan, whose influential analyses of Soviet conduct in 1946 are reflected in the memorandum Clifford prepared for the President, scaled the bureaucatic heights (before being toppled by Secretary of State Dulles, who thought he was soft) and acquired a lasting reputation for his theories of Soviet motivation. In a long memorandum prepared while he was chargé d'affaires in Moscow, which was promoted like a best seller in the national security bureaucracy by Secretary of the Navy Forrestal, Kennan argues that the Soviet leaders have a paranoid view of the outside world. The Communists believe that the nations of the West, in the interests of preserving capitalism, will "encircle" the Soviet Union and eventually attack it. The prescribed therapy, Kennan suggests, is to fulfill their paranoid fantasies. If the Soviet leaders are subjected to enough "pressure," they will "mellow." Or, as Clifford puts it in his version, "they will change their minds and work out with us a fair and equitable settlement when they realize that we are too strong to be beaten and too determined to be frightened."

Only a few doubters such as Walter Lippmann and Henry Wallace professed to be confused about how "containing" an immense, powerful, though temporarily weakened continental empire with threats of mass destruction—American strategy was nuclear from the start —would make her supposedly paranoid leaders mellow. The history of a generation suggests that what sometimes works on rats in a laboratory has unfortunate consequences in real life. The Soviet reaction to the "negative reinforcement" of American military pressure has been to build up its military forces to equal those of the United States, to use military power to keep its grip on Eastern Europe, the issue over which the confrontation started, and to adopt a much more adventurous policy in the Caribbean and Mediterranean.

(3)

WHEN THE national security managers in 1964 began planning the escalation of the Vietnam War the strategic discussions were permeated by these mechanistic theories of human motivation, for the rat-view of man provides the rationale for the very existence of the national security establishment. Indeed, the goals pursued by the United States government in Indochina have been almost exclusively psychological. Neither territory nor economic advantage has been the principal object of the commitment. Under the "domino theory" the target of military operations in Southeast Asia was important not for its intrinsic strategic or economic value but for its symbolic impact on other countries.* The entire purpose of the enormous and costly effort has been to create a specific state of mind in three different audiences. The war became a disaster because the national security managers misjudged each audience.

The first audience was the South Vietnamese government. As early as May 1961, the Joint Chiefs of Staff had recommended that "U.S. forces should be deployed immediately to South Vietnam" and had said the primary purpose was to "indicate the firmness of our intent." Throughout the Kennedy years the reason given in recommendations for increasing the number of U.S. advisers and military aid in South Vietnam was to show that the United States "means business." As General Taylor put it in his report to Kennedy, we need a "U.S. military presence capable of raising national morale and showing to Southeast Asia the seriousness of U.S. intent." In October 1963 Ambassador Henry Cabot Lodge, reflecting the views of the Vietnamese generals who had taken over after the assassination of Ngo Dinh Diem, urged John Kennedy to apply "various pressures" on North Vietnam and suggested that regular bombing of North Vietnam be commenced. Although the President's Special Assistant for National Security, McGeorge Bundy, also favored bombing at this time, the decision was postponed for almost a year.†

Instead, the President appointed a working group under Assistant Secretary of State William Bundy, McGeorge's brother, to propose a "thirty-day scenario" of actions to lift morale in Saigon and strike fear in Hanoi. The national security action memorandum setting up the group (NSAM 288) specified the U.S. objective in Vietnam as an "independent noncommunist South Vietnam." Years later, in bureaucratic fights with civilians who were losing stomach for the war, the Joint Chiefs of Staff would cite this document, much as lawyers wave a Supreme Court decision under the noses of inferior court judges. Meeting in May 1964, the group conceived an elaborate series of "graduated" measures, a careful orchestration of covert actions, diplomatic warnings, and public statements. A Canadian

---

* Once the commitment is made, however, military services, banks, oil companies, and insurance agencies quickly enlist in the continuing struggle against world communism and air-conditioned office buildings, drilling rigs, bowling alleys, used-car lots, and supermarkets follow the flag.

† Much of the material in this and the following paragraphs comes from Neil Sheehan et al., *The Pentagon Papers* (New York: Bantam, 1971).

diplomat would be dispatched to warn Hanoi. "Diplomatic preparations" for bombing the North (a euphemism for a propaganda campaign to convince the world that they deserved to be bombed) would be undertaken. A draft Joint Congressional Resolution, much like the text of the Tonkin Gulf Resolution actually submitted three months later, was prepared. The scenario culminated in air strikes against North Vietnam. The planners were attempting to concoct the right mixture of carrots and sticks, but, as one State Department participant at these meetings put it, "it was all stick."

The Executive Committee of the National Security Council (Rusk, McNamara, Bundy, JCS Chairman Wheeler) decided to postpone the opening of this drama until all less dangerous alternatives had been exhausted. In July President Johnson directed all appropriate government agencies to "seek to identify actions which can be taken to improve the situation in Vietnam: action which would produce maximum effect with minimum escalation." Meanwhile the planning of stepped-up covert actions against North Vietnam went on. "General Khan," Ambassador Taylor reported, needs "to be reassured that the U.S. continues to mean business." Assistant Secretary of Defense, John T. McNaughton, McNamara's leading thinker on the war, mused about "the extent to which we should add elements [in the scenario] . . . that would tend deliberately to provoke a DRV reaction, and consequent retaliation by us." The purpose of such actions, he noted, would be to assist morale in South Vietnam and show the Communists we still "mean business." When the decision was finally made in February 1965 to initiate Operation Rolling Thunder, the daily bombardment of North Vietnam, the primary bureaucratic reason stated in the planning documents was to buoy up the rapidly failing morale of the South Vietnamese government. It worked for a while. "The happiest day of my life," Marshall Ky exclaimed when he heard that American bombs were falling on North Vietnam, where he had been born. "It's like taking a drink," President Kennedy had said of the policy of charging up weak governments by a display of military power. But the United States was now firmly committed to this particular form of intoxication in the "battle for men's minds" in Southeast Asia.

By the summer of 1964 the national security managers were concentrating more on Hanoi as the audience. Shortly before President Kennedy's death one of his most trusted assistants had gone to Vietnam and concluded that there was no evidence that any weapons captured in the South had been infiltrated from the North since 1954. (After 1965 and the U.S. intervention the massive supplying from the North would begin.) He corroborated the view of the CIA and the State Department intelligence experts at the "working level" that the insurgency in the South grew out of local Southern issues, was led by Southerners, although supported by the North, and that the insurgency could not be crushed by pressuring the North. Indeed, the "Sigma" war games, the report of the interagency study group chaired by Robert Johnson of the State Department Policy Planning Council that began meeting in February 1964, and studies of bombing effectiveness by McNamara's then prestigious systems analysts in the Defense Department all led to the conclusion that bombing could not win the war. The "will" that had to be "broken," to use a favorite JCS term, was of the Vietnamese in the South who preferred to fight rather than live under the Saigon government. There was no cheap way to do that by breaking Hanoi's "will."

Nevertheless, the bureaucratic model had completely displaced reality and the hard and stubborn facts, which so many intelligence analysts were paid so much to collect, were ignored. Any view that tended to buttress the rat-psychology premises of the national security managers, who in their frustration were straining to lash out at Hanoi, was welcomed. Thus, when Bernard Fall, an expert on Indochina who had been critical of the French military effort, suggested after a visit to Hanoi that Ho Chi Minh might feel different about the war in the South if some of his new industrial plants were made a target, his ill-considered speculation created something of a stir in the Pentagon. (In the succeeding three years when he became one of the most informed and accurate critics of the U.S. war strategy, he was ignored, and as an alien was subjected to a certain amount of harassment.)

Since there was little that could be done to arrest the deteriorating political and military situation in the South, the national security managers began to bank all their hopes on "squeezing" Hanoi. The planning alternatives soon divided into the Joint Chiefs of Staff "option," a recommendation for "a sharp, sudden blow" based on the blitz bombardment of ninety-four strategic targets in North Vietnam, and the civilian alternative, the "slow squeeze." The "moderates" prevailed and the "slow squeeze"—i.e., inflicting measured amounts of "pain" in greater increments by bombing increasingly sensitive targets, was adopted. The Pentagon planners used the language of the professional torturer and they shared the torturer's classic problem. How do you keep the victim alive long enough to surrender? "Too much" coercion is as bad as "too little," General Maxwell Taylor warned, for "at some point we will need a relatively cooperative leadership in Hanoi."

As the war in the South appeared more and more hopeless in the second half of 1964, with dramatic rises in desertions from the South Vietnamese army, loss of control by the Saigon government of vast areas of the country, and mounting Vietcong terrorist and military operations almost everywhere, the national security managers began to develop what could best be described as the faucet theory of how to end the war. It was impossible to stop the torrent in the South except by turning off the faucet in the North. Once again the theory violated the best intelligence about the nature of the Vietcong, their relationships with Hanoi, and the political dynamics of revolutionary movements. According to one analysis in October 1964, "the basic elements of Communist strength in South Vietnam remain indigenous South Vietnam grievances, war weariness, defection and political disarray, VC terror, arms capture, disciplined organization, highly developed intelligence systems and the ability to recruit locally. . . ." * The faucet theory had only one thing to recommend it. It seemed to fit American technology. It was the only plausible strategy that could work at acceptable cost.

Under the theory Ho Chi Minh would eventually feel enough "pain" once the "screw" was "twisted" tight enough (the words were used in planning documents prepared by William P. Bundy) or enough "economic strangulation" (Maxwell Taylor) that he would broadcast an order on the radio for the Vietcong to give up and turn in their arms at the local police station. The guerrillas naïve enough to comply would be caught and the rest would "fade away" in the hills, much as the Greek guerrillas—Walt Rostow, Johnson's resident historian, would remind skeptics—faded in 1949 when U.S. guns had brought an abrupt end to the Greek civil war. This fantasy became the official goal of the escalation planning despite the fact that the intelligence community, with the not surprising exception of Air Force Intelligence, was most skeptical. Moreover, a number of high officials of the Administration, Deputy Secretary of Defense Paul Nitze for one, had participated in the post–World War II Strategic Bombing Survey which assembled in a remarkably thorough manner data from Nazi Germany which demonstrated why strategic bombing will not compel surrender. (As it later developed, the bombing solved serious domestic political problems for Ho Chi Minh, uniting the country against the foreign invader, and, once Roman Catholic churches were bombed in large numbers, effectively ending Catholic dissidence.)

As the planning process continued into the fall of 1964 the national security managers began to talk one another into greater optimism. In late November Walt Rostow prepared some "observations as we come to the crunch in South East Asia." At this stage of history," he asserted, "we are the greatest power in the world— if we behave like it." Thus, he added, "our assets are sufficient to see this thing through if we enter the exercise [*sic!*] with adequate

---

* Quoted in Ralph L. Stavins, Marcus Raskin, and Richard J. Barnet, *Washington Plans an Aggressive War* (New York: Random House, 1971), p. 136.

determination to succeed." * New and drastic action, General Taylor cabled from Saigon, is "needed to overcome the war weariness and hopelessness of South Vietnam." The Joint Chiefs of Staff, reacting strongly against the "slow squeeze," warned against being "swayed unduly" by such civilian concerns as "world opinion." It is not useful, one JCS officer asserted, to claim that America's proposed war plans are "defensible." It is enough to affirm that they need no defense. (One should not assume, however, that there is a substantial disagreement between civilians and military in the national security bureaucracy on the matter of "world opinion." The typical view of the foreign policy managers was once expressed by John J. McCloy, veteran crisis consultant, when he recommended to President Kennedy that he resume nuclear testing: "World opinion? I don't believe in world opinion. The only thing that matters is power." †)

Of course "world opinion" in one sense was absolutely crucial to the decision to escalate. John T. McNaughton estimated that about 70 per cent of the reason to begin bombing North Vietnam and to step up the ground war in the South had to do with prestige. "Our judgment, skill, capability, prestige, and national honor are at stake," the JCS had written, and the civilian planners could hardly disagree, for the President and Secretary of State had already said so publicly many times. For us, Rusk had told newsmen, Vietnam is like Berlin, an issue over which the United States had always insisted it was ready to go to nuclear war, if necessary. In the rat-psychology model of international politics all responses of world opinion are based on either fear or greed. As long as the United States is able to do what it says it will do, whether it is wise or foolish, legal or illegal, moral or immoral, the leaders of all other countries will continue to have a healthy respect for American greatness.

Other nations can also be influenced by direct concessions such as military aid. (Thailand was able to work up considerable enthusiasm for the Vietnam War once the United States began to underwrite the Thai army.) But no points are won by acting generously, graciously, or even legally. The national security managers were essentially accurate in their analysis of "world opinion." The international bully enjoys an enviable reputation as long as he is successfully plying his trade. The silence of world statesmen over the American atrocities in Vietnam has been shattering. The very definition of a statesman is to know when to keep one's mouth shut, and an essential skill of a leader is to know how to keep in check the small unruly minority who actually care about bureaucratic homicide in some distant part of the world. (General de Gaulle

---

* Sheehan et al., *The Pentagon Papers.*

† Quoted in Arthur Schlesinger, Jr., *A Thousand Days* (Boston: Houghton Mifflin, 1965), p. 481.

by these definitions sometimes slipped as a statesman, but he took his responsibilities as a leader seriously and regularly banned anti-war demonstrations he thought might get out of hand.)

The importance of "world opinion" as an index of America's power to intimidate was reflected even in the "fallback positions" prepared during the escalation planning of 1964. "Fallback positions" outline the concessions to be "surfaced" at some crucial stage of a future negotiation, and as such they are vulnerable to the charge of being called surrender documents. This is one reason why bureaucrats do not like to write them. They are always highly classified—"closely held" in the self-important vernacular of the national security world—not only to protect any future bargaining with the enemy but also to keep them beyond the reach of the hard-liners in the next office. In September 1964 Assistant Secretary of Defense John T. McNaughton asked his assistant Daniel Ellsberg to look into what losing in Vietnam would mean. "You realize," Ellsberg recalls him saying, "to work on this subject is to sign your own death warrant." McNaughton did his own typing on this high-risk assignment. When George Ball in July 1965 recommended cutting losses in Vietnam, these papers were hand carried to a few key individuals. When the question of real negotiation is raised, only a very few have "a need to know."

At about the same time, William P. Bundy was also writing more acceptable "fallback position" papers, although these too ran into heavy "flak" from the Joint Chiefs of Staff. These analyses stressed that the United States must make a "good try" before extricating itself from Indochina. Like a "good doctor" who does everything humanly possible to save his patient, these papers argued, it is better for the American reputation to make heroic efforts to "meet our commitments" and fail than not to make the try. Other potential "dominoes," such as Thailand, will feel more secure as a result of the try, even if it is abortive, because they will assume that the United States will take similar risks in their behalf, perhaps even with greater success. This was perhaps the greatest miscalculation into which the national security managers were led by their rat-psychology notions. Nothing has so shaken the reputation of the United States as the number one nation than its spectacular and costly failure to impose its will on North Vietnam. A demonstration that the United States could not defeat that small country after sending in millions of Americans and spending hundreds of billions of dollars in the longest war in her history did nothing to enhance the national reputation.

Thus, to the extent that "world opinion" was considered at all, it was used more as an argument for escalation than restraint. The opinion of the American people received only slightly more attention. True, once the decisions were taken major bureaucratic efforts were made to persuade both the world and the American public that the war was just, inevitable, and winnable. In 1965 Johnson dispatched every senior diplomat he could corral on a whirlwind "peace blitz" to convince world leaders how much he wanted to negotiate an end to the war. At the same time State Department officers were engaging in debates on college campuses, distributing false accounts of the war in White Papers, and showing films such as *Why Vietnam?* (Pictures of Vietcong terrorist attacks and GI's bringing candy to Vietnamese children; no U.S. use of herbicides, napalm, and antipersonnel cluster bombs.) In the planning papers prepared in late 1964 it was occasionally mentioned that some Americans might object to a wider war in Asia and would have to be talked out of their "isolationist" objections. McNamara, for one, wondered whether the American people would support a "slow squeeze" that did not bring quick results. If the war dragged on, and it was never assumed that victory would come quickly, Americans would have to be "educated" to the reality that the number one nation might have to fight a long time to preserve its credibility. Once the decision was made in July 1965 to send in a large expeditionary force, the President's advisers unanimously recommended calling up the reserves as John F. Kennedy had done in the Berlin crisis. It was not only a necessary source of manpower, they argued, but it was also a way of waking up the country and enlisting the people for "the long haul." Lyndon Johnson's well-developed political instincts guided him to the opposite conclusion.

However, almost no thought was given to the actual impact of the war on the American economy and the American society. While they predicted the military course of the war with remarkable accuracy, and to some extent the public reaction, both the national security managers and the consummate domestic politician in the White House totally miscalculated the impact of the war on the United States. The war planners operated on the assumption that they had limitless resources. Although the "war on poverty in America" had been declared with considerable fanfare, no one saw in 1964 that a reformer's crusade extending from Harlem to Danang meant a two-front war that was beyond even the number one nation. On September 10, 1964, for example, the National Security Council issued an action memorandum to those engaged in planning economic programs and covert political action in South Vietnam:

> The President emphasizes again that no activity of this kind should be delayed in any way by any feeling that our resources for these purposes are restricted. We can find the money. . . .

It was not until 1966 that the Johnson Administration began to understand the disastrous economic consequences of the war. Twenty years of mindless Keynesianism, an economic faith in which a dollar spent on guns is considered of equal value to a dollar spent on butter or anything else, had left the national security managers quite unprepared for the galloping inflation that the $25-billion-a-year war soon brought.

(4)

ONE OF THE first lessons a national security manager learns after a day in the bureaucratic climate of the Pentagon, State Department, White House, or CIA is that toughness is the most highly prized virtue. Some of the national security managers of the Kennedy-Johnson era, looking back on their experience, talk about the "hairy chest syndrome." The man who is ready to recommend using violence against foreigners, even where he is overruled, does not damage his reputation for prudence, soundness, or imagination, but the man who recommends putting an issue to the U.N., seeking negotiations, or, horror of horrors, "doing nothing" quickly becomes known as "soft." To be "soft"—i.e., unbelligerent, compassionate, willing to settle for less—or simply to be repelled by mass homicide, is to be "irresponsible." It means walking out of the club.

Bureaucratic *machismo* is cultivated in hundreds of little ways. There is the style of talking to a subordinate—the driving command masked by superficial informality—or to a superior—fact-loaded, quantitative, gutsy. The Kennedy operators, particularly, cultivated a machine-gun delivery. The man who could talk fast and loud often proved he was "on top of the job." Speed reading too became a kind of badge of prowess. To be an operator is to be active in "putting out fires," a free-wheeling generalist who is "in on the action" wherever it might be. The ambitious and successful bureaucrat reaches for the great issues. He specializes in the crisp, uncomplicated, usually mechanistic analysis of a problem because in a militarized bureaucracy that is the easiest view to sell. Those who specialize in the "long view" soon get a deadly reputation for writing "interesting think-pieces" which by definition have "no status." (A paper acquires "status" in the bureaucracy by being passed around from department to department for appropriate officials to initial. The less the paper disturbs the prevailing bureaucratic climate, the faster the signatures are collected and the sooner the author of the paper is on his way to making history.)

Arthur Schlesinger, Jr., describes the "rhetorical advantage" which the advocates of the Bay of Pigs adventure had over those who privately doubted the wisdom of the operation:

They could strike virile poses and talk of tangible things—
fire power, air strikes, landing craft, and so on. To oppose the
plan, one had to invoke intangibles—the moral position of the
United States, the reputation of the President, the response of
the United Nations, "world public opinion," and other such
odious concepts. These matters were as much the institutional
concern of the State Department as military hardware was of
Defense. . . . I could not help feeling that the desire to prove
to the CIA and the Joint Chiefs that they were not softheaded
idealists but were really tough guys, too, influenced State's representatives at the Cabinet table.*

The most important way bureaucratic *machismo* manifests itself
is in attitudes toward violence. Those who are in the business of
defining the national interest are fascinated by lethal technology
because, in the national security bureaucracy, weaponry is revolutionary and politics is relatively static. For years the only real movement in the national security bureaucracy was provided by the
momentum of the arms race. On the political issues positions were
frozen. Officials could handle the recurring NATO "crises" by
dredging up papers prepared ten years earlier. But the weapons
revolutions that occurred every five years presented a new, dangerous, and exciting reality that had to be dealt with. To be a specialist in the new violence was to be on the frontier.

To demonstrate toughness a national security manager must accept the use of violence as routine. Proposals for the use of violence
are inserted into the normal rush of bureaucratic business. Thus
messages on the commencement of the bombing campaign in North
Vietnam also included such routine matters as the procurement of
PX supplies. Crises in which violence is to be used are treated in
the national security bureaucracy as normal extensions of everyday
life. When President Kennedy informed the country in 1961 that
the Berlin crisis might result in imminent nuclear war, he took the
occasion to lament the Post Office deficit. Even the language of
the bureaucracy—the diminutive "nucs" for instruments that kill
and mutilate millions of human beings, "surgical strike" for chasing
and mowing down peasants from the air by spraying them with
eight thousand bullets a minute—takes the mystery, awe, and the
pain out of violence. The socialization process is designed to accus-
tom bankers, lawyers, and military technocrats with no more than
normal homicidal inclinations to the idea of killing in the national
interest, much as at lower levels recruits are trained to grunt and
shout "Kill!" as they thrust their bayonets into sawdust bags.

The man who agonizes about taking human life is regarded by

* Schlesinger, *op. cit.,* p. 225.

his colleagues at the very least as "woolly" and probably something of an idealistic "slob." Thus the critics of the Vietnam escalation never raised the issue that "taking out" great areas of Vietnam, a euphemism for killing large numbers of Vietnamese, was wrong. Their arguments were invariably pragmatic—bombing doesn't work, don't get bogged down in a land war in Asia—or they relied on the torturer's idiom—keep the victim alive for later. When we asked one of the most strategically placed doves in the State Department why the moral issue was never raised, he replied that such a discussion "would be as if from another world." Perhaps he was aware of the brief encounter J. Robert Oppenheimer, the ambivalent father of the atomic bomb, had with President Truman. After the scientist had blurted out, "There's blood on my hands," Truman took aside Secretary of State Acheson, who had accompanied him, and said, "Don't ever bring that man in here again."

The best evidence that the "tough"—i.e., specialists in violence—prevail in the bureaucracy is provided by looking at what "making it" means in the national security world. Those who recommend more killing than the President is willing to sanction do not seriously jeopardize their position. The generals who urged President Johnson to obliterate eleven Chinese targets or to mine Haiphong Harbor (along with any Soviet ships that happened to be there) neither lost their jobs nor were reprimanded when the President rejected their advice. Members of the Joint Chiefs of Staff during the Cuban missile crisis recommended solving the problem by bombing the Soviet missile sites, advice which the President rejected because he thought it risked a nuclear war and a minimum of 150 million fatalities. Once the crisis was over the chiefs resumed business as usual. A general such as William Westmoreland, who was allowed to play out his own "scenario" in Vietnam to the point of disaster, was rewarded with an appointment as Army Chief of Staff. We are not suggesting that bad advice, or even good advice that is rejected, should necessarily result in dismissal. The point is that only certain kinds of bad advice or rejected advice are likely to have that result. This fact of life is not lost on careerist bureaucrats. Certain kinds of advice are safe to give, even if rejected, and certain kinds involve immense personal risks. That reality sustains a bureaucratic atmosphere that supports permanent military involvement.

The outstanding bureaucratic casualties of the Cold War have all been men who took modest risks to promote conciliation rather than confrontation. Secretary of State James Byrnes was, although orthodox in his view of the U.S.S.R., accused by Congressional critics of being an "appeaser" because he was ready to explore exchange of scientific information with the Russians at the Moscow conference, in December 1945. In 1952 Truman published a letter he claimed to have written to Byrnes at the time (which Byrnes denied receiving): "I'm tired of babying the Soviets." * Whether the letter was written in 1946 or 1952, its release, coming at the same time as McCarthy's gathering storm, taught a clear bureaucratic lesson. So also, as we have noted, did the loyalty investigations of the "old China hands," John Carter Vincent, John Paton Davies, and others. Even their cautious defenders, such as George Kennan, sought to rehabilitate them by testifying before a Congressional committee that they used quotation marks around the word "imperialism" whenever they discussed Chinese ideology. Anyone who attempts to write dispassionately or understandingly about "the other side" runs certain risks. I, myself, recall writing an eighty-page analysis of Chinese attitudes on disarmament for Jacob Beam, a senior diplomat who later became Ambassador to the Soviet Union. His only comment on the whole effort was a scrawl across the cover: "Use 'Chicom' and 'Peiping' throughout." †

In the 1950's the "appeasers," such as George Kennan and Harold Stassen, disappeared as swiftly as the proponents of negotiation of the 1960's, such as Chester Bowles. These men were not exactly radical. Stassen was peremptorily relieved by Secretary of State Dulles for vigorously seeking a limited arms agreement with the Soviet Union. Kennan, the father of "containment," had by the early 1950's come to believe that negotiation was preferable to continued confrontation in Europe. He was invited to expound those views at the Institute for Advanced Study so that the State Department could get on with the business of building NATO. In 1962 Chester Bowles proposed a plan for the neutralization of Southeast Asia which ten years later would look like a blueprint for a U.S. victory. For this and other initiatives seeking to downgrade the use of force in pursuing the national interest, he acquired a reputaiton for "woolliness" and soon found that he had exchanged the office of Under Secretary of State for an honorific title and a White House car. John Kenneth Galbraith recalls being continually challenged by colleagues in the national security bureaucracy to admit that he was a man who didn't like to use force.

Bureaucratic *machismo* greatly hobbled the effectiveness of the critics of the Vietnam War. Vice-President Humphrey, for example,

* Harry Truman, *Memoirs, Vol. 2: Years of Trial and Hope* (New York: New American Library, 1965).

† State Department magic words to make Mao's regime disappear. "Chicom" is an Orwellian word for a Chinese communist which by definition is a non-Chinese. "Peiping" is a recondite way of saying that Mao's seat of government is not the real capital—a kind of "in" joke between the half-dozen Chinese specialists in the State Department and seven hundred million Chinese. (The Nixon Administration began its new China policy by showing a willingness to call the Chinese capital by its right name.)

argued against the crucial escalation of the Vietnam war in February 1965 on the ground that the attempt to gain a military solution in Vietnam would take years. "His views," according to Townsend Hoopes, a Pentagon official at the time, "were received at the White House with particular coldness, and he was banished from the inner councils for some months thereafter, until he decided to 'get back on the team.' " * Unable to say that the war was wrong, if indeed he believed it, he was reduced to challenging the military judgments of the Joint Chiefs of Staff.

The most publicized critic was George Ball, the Under Secretary of State. He argued vigorously against a major troop commitment in Vietnam and continued to oppose further escalations. Indeed, he became known as the "devil's advocate"—the only top adviser to register continuing dissent. According to his close associates it was his strong personal conviction that the Vietnam commitment would lead to disaster. Neither he nor anyone else challenged the legitimacy or purpose of the effort, but he did strenuously question its practicality. America stood to lose more in terms of world power than it would gain by the effort since it would divert resources and attention from the area he considered most vital to protect and develop— Western Europe. The "devil's advocate" role was taken on as a protective cover in a bureaucracy committed to the view that the war could and should be won. Even the second-highest official in the State Department did not dare to say that he actually believed his own heretical views. As Chester Cooper, a second-level bureaucrat who has had a long involvement with Vietnam, has put it, being a self-styled "devil's advocate" is "a good way of saying I think you are all wet without resigning from the club."

As a domesticated critic Ball was virtually without influence. He had little credibility to start with, despite his office, because Asia was not his area of responsibility. He was regarded as an amateur, despite the fact that he had once as a lawyer represented the French during the Indochina war. Second, he compromised his opposition by giving his assent to Operation Rolling Thunder, the decision for continuous bombardment of North Vietnam made in February 1965. Having endorsed the war in principle, he was in a weak position to argue strategy with the Pentagon.† Third, he exaggerated the risks of widening the war. On the advice of China experts in the State De-

---

* Townsend Hoopes, *The Limits of Intervention* (New York: David McKay and Co., 1969), p. 31.

† Because of the prevailing bureaucratic climate the cautious critic often tries to wrap his heretical pacific views in protective compromise. "I'm really for bombing A so I have standing to argue against bombing B." A frequent result is that his tactic is used against him. "See, even those who are against bombing B—an absurd position that can be safely dismissed—support our efforts to bomb A."

partment he warned of the risks of Chinese intervention as in Korea. When they did not intervene, he lost credibility.*

The only critic of the policy of escalation who dared to tell the President exactly what he believed was Dean Acheson, and that only because of extraordinary circumstances. The Tet offensive of February 1968 was the event that finally convinced Johnson he faced a long war. The claims of the military that they could "hurt" North Vietnam enough to make them call off the insurgency had proved utterly groundless. During 1967 there was a continuing debate in the government on the level of troops needed for the war. The Joint Chiefs of Staff argued that the level should be increased to seven hundred thousand and that it would take at least two years to win. If the troop level remained below five hundred thousand it would take three years. But by this time the top civilian advisers in the Pentagon, including Secretary McNamara and Assistant Secretaries McNaughton and Enthoven, were arguing that to accept the recommendations for more troops would amount to giving the JCS a "blank check." Against this background of growing internal debate in the Pentagon and the Tet offensive Johnson consulted Dean Acheson, who had a deserved reputation as the principle architect of American Cold War policy. Acheson, according to Hoope's "inside account," told Johnson, "With all due respect, Mr. President, the Joint Chiefs don't know what they are talking about." When the President said that he was shocked by the statement, Acheson pressed the point, saying that the war could not be won without the application of totally unlimited resources "and maybe five years." †

The luncheon meeting led to a full-scale independent review and eventually to a decision by the President not to escalate the war. He announced the new policy on March 31, 1968, along with his decision not to seek re-election. While the commitment of the new Secretary of Defense Clark Clifford to de-escalation was crucial, the Acheson intervention appears to have been important in providing the space within which the dissenters in the bureaucracy could operate.

The luncheon encounter with Acheson is revealing in many ways. It took a senior statesman of established reputation for toughness and with no further career ambitions in government to talk honestly to the President. It is not that Acheson challenged the conception of the war, its legal or its moral legitimacy. He repeatedly stated that he had no doubts on those matters. He was merely presenting facts which were common knowledge among members of the national security "club" but which had not penetrated the White House be-

* *Ibid.*
† *Ibid.*, pp. 204 ff.

cause no one in the bureaucracy felt strong or brave enough to confront the President with them.

(5)

WHEN HE was surrounded by angry Harvard students milling around his car, Secretary of Defense McNamara, standing on the hood, suddenly weary of plastic explanations of the Vietnam War, screamed, "I was tougher than you are then [in World War II] and I'm tougher than you now." He would not even see that the students doubted his humanity, not his *machismo*. Why is toughness, defined as being comfortable with violence, so admired a character trait and so essential to reputation in the national security bureaucracy?

One can attempt to answer the question on many levels. Wilhelm Reich developed a whole theory connecting political sadism with the sexual inadequacies of the fascist overlords. Enough is known about Mussolini's office sex life to suggest that there may be something to the theory. But, based on the superficial knowledge we have about the private life of the national security managers, this particular theory does not seem to offer much insight into the problem of bureaucratic homicide in America. As a general rule national security managers stay married longer, and apparently more happily, than the average American.

Nor can one say, as with Hitler, that early personal frustrations provided the dynamic for the national security managers' predilection for violence. As a rule, the men who have made it to the top of the national security bureaucracy have had a smoother ride on the American escalator of success than the rest of their countrymen. As we have seen, they have been early achievers. Robert McNamara, Dean Rusk, and McGeorge Bundy all moved from the opportunities offered them by the Second World War into senior clerkships in the most powerful institutions of the society in their thirties.

True, these were obviously men with well-developed power drives. One national security manager, who held a high position in the Defense Department, told a visiting psychoanalyst, without a trace of embarrassment, that the recurring dream of his boyhood was to be king of the world. McGeorge Bundy, borrowing from Dean Acheson, liked to talk about the United States as the "locomotive at the head of mankind pulling the 'caboose' of humanity along behind" (with himself, presumably, at the throttle). They spared themselves little in the climb to the top. Working evenings and weekends was itself a badge of success. But men with enormous power needs abound in American society. Board rooms, gentlemen's clubs, flag officers' dining rooms, the Senate, and university laboratories are filled with them. Indeed, Americans have so come to expect the power-hungry look in their leaders that when a figure with a less developed craving, such as Adlai Stevenson or Eugene McCarthy, comes along, he is regarded as something of an American Hamlet.

However, men of power in America are not usually violent in everyday life. Indeed, one essential element of the *gravitas* characteristic of the successful manager is a capacity for exquisite self-control. In talking with equals the national security manager goes out of his way not to ruffle feelings and he has an absolute horror of making a scene (this abhorrence of personal confrontation across a table as opposed to nation-to-nation confrontation across a distant battlefield explains a good deal of the behavior of the secret dove). The predilection for violence which characterizes the national security bureaucrat results from the conjunction of a power-hungry social character and an inherently frustrating bureaucratic role. Of the two factors the latter seems far more important.

The obvious but fundamental fact is that for the number one nation using or threatening to use violence to get its way is easier than all other methods of dealing with the outside world. There is a huge superfluity of force. If a foreign policy problem can be converted into a military operation, the responsible officer can count on getting action. The problem may not be solved. It may eventually be complicated, as in Vietnam, but the wheels of government will move. Managers are concerned with process, not results, because in the game view of international politics there is no end. It is tempting for Americans to make fun of the State Department as a "bowl of jelly," a "bunch of cooky pushers," or a "foreign affairs fudge factory," because foreign service officers are often cautious, conservative, and absurdly unconnected with the world they are supposed to be watching. But, more important, diplomacy is by nature slow and frustrating business. "I don't feel I have an action group at my command as they do in other departments," Secretary of State William Rogers confessed to reporters a few months after taking office. Americans demand action and results. In the age of well-developed lethal technology it takes much less time to kill a man than to change his mind or change your own. To solve a political problem nonviolently requires extraordinary patience, understanding, and objectivity. The national security manager is lacking in all three by the very nature of the job.

The top managers of an institution that defines its mission as being the "locomotive of humanity," "the guardian at the gates," staying "number one," or exercising "world responsibility" are clearly very busy men. They hop from crisis to crisis, spending most of their time in meetings or reading reports of subordinates. In rapid succession the national security manager figuratively roams the globe, "putting out fires," as he likes to call it, with a telegram here, a strong statement there. Frenetic activity becomes a substitute for reflection and analysis. Not only has he no time to think, but he would be suspicious if someone tried to present him with the opportunity. He wants to be where "the action" is. Slightly contemptuous of the specialist who gets bogged down in facts, the global operators, buoyed by their own considerable self-confidence and a religious faith in technology, believed that managerial talent and a little determination was a substitute for understanding. Many of them had risen by doing little more than improvising, taking manageable risks, and exuding confidence. Was it not reasonable to assume that these same qualities which had brought them success in their personal careers would also bring success to the nation?

The national security manager operates under another handicap which has a direct bearing upon the predilection for violence in the bureaucracy—ignorance. James C. Thomson, Jr., who was an officer in the National Security Council during the Vietnam escalation, notes that the men who made the basic decisions about Vietnam had only the most superficial knowledge of the area.* One reason Vietnam was so quickly elevated as a symbol in the world of national security is that people at the top knew virtually nothing about the reality. Walt Rostow liked to write learned memos about the "Southeast Asians," lumping people of a hundred cultures divided by ancient animosities into a single convenient target much as the statesmen of the Eisenhower era converted the rest of the world outside North America and Western Europe into a manageable unity by calling it the "gray areas." Top national security managers are forced by the circumstances of their job to be generalists. To serve the President and retain his confidence, which is the only source of their power, they must be prepared to commit themselves to any crisis wherever it appears. They must also try to relate the chaotic rush of events into some coherent pattern which the President can understand. This means that facts must be fitted into available theories, for there is neither the time nor the energy to change theories in which bureaucracies have huge investments. Obscure events must be immediately located in a familiar ideological landscape. It is for this reason that State Department planners were talking about the "Sino-Soviet bloc" four years after the split in the communist world had exploded into public view. The global manager cannot afford to compromise his ideology with uncongenial facts, for his power rests on his reputation for being able to manipulate events in accordance with a theory.

There was, of course, no particular reason why investment bank-

* "Why Are We in Vietnam?" *Atlantic Monthly,* April 1968, pp. 47–53.

ers, generals, Texas politicians, or foreign service officers should know anything about Vietnamese politics. Often they knew little about the political forces in their own immediate communities. In addition, once they occupied their offices, they became willing victims of a social process that compounded their ignorance. In a bureaucracy there is a clear correlation between rank and credibility. Generals, ambassadors, and Cabinet ministers can safely pronounce inanities that would end the careers of junior officers. Secretary of State Rusk once disposed of a complicated disarmament issue by observing that "we must project our power." All present nodded and the meeting ended in a corporate delusion that a rational decision had been made.

Most of the information the national security manager receives in the course of an official day tends to reinforce his prejudices and insulate him from unwelcome facts and opinions. He also becomes adept at filtering out anything that contradicts official wisdom. The learning experience of the national security manager begins with the morning newspaper. Newspaper reports such as those which suggested the United States was not winning the Vietnam War are viewed not as truth, for the personal implications of accepting them as true are too serious, but as public relations problems to be dealt with in some other way. Perhaps another briefing should be scheduled. Then begins what is probably the longest working day put in by any American since the abolition of the sweatshop. For McNamara the job began around 7:00 A.M. and he left the Pentagon around 8:00 P.M., usually to go to a dinner or reception where he would continue to discuss the same problems he talked about all day, essentially with the same people. This means that the national security manager will hear his views reinforced and have his illusions fed during his "off duty" hours. He never gets away from the exhilarating but crushing problems of the "shop." True, there may be a fast game of squash in the Pentagon gym or for McGeorge Bundy an afternoon tennis game with another national security official. Once a year McNamara would climb a mountain. But there was little release for the mounting fatigue.

The top bureaucrat is surrounded day after day by essentially the same people. It is an almost exclusively male society. (Of the more than four hundred people who have been national security managers between 1940 and 1967, only one was a woman.) Nor is there much time for wives, children, or friends who are not professional associates. The women at parties are either professional hostesses or shy wives of other officials who make small talk about life in official Washington or feel compelled to interview their dinner partner on the news of the day. At the crucial stage of the dinner the women are whisked away to a separate parlor and over brandy and cigars the national security managers continue their business.

Anthony Downs, in his study *Inside Bureaucracy,* has observed that at the top of all bureaucracies official and nonofficial life merges. (Hitler's unbearably banal evenings to which he summoned the chief Nazis to listen to recorded performances of *Die Fledermaus* and Stalin's nightly movie parties which no Politburo member dared to miss are examples.) William H. Whyte, Jr., in his study *The Executive Life,* notes that there is "between work and other aspects of one's life a unity he can never fully explain. . . . How can you overwork, executives ask, if your work is your life?" The difference between the old job at the bank or the law firm and the new job in the Pentagon or the White House is the excitement that comes with being a minor historical figure, and the pressure.*

For the Kennedy-Johnson professors, particularly, who in Cambridge had moved at a brisk but comfortable pace, the demands of the national security world dictated a new life style. Fatigue became a badge of importance. Officials could measure their significance by the demands their office made on their time. The favorite word of the self-important bureaucrat to describe his immediate plans on laying down the burden of office is "decompress." There is a cost, however, in measuring prestige by effort rather than output. It is worth noting that the first Secretary of Defense jumped out of a window, the second convinced Dean Acheson, who was, to be sure, somewhat too ready to believe it, that he was "mentally ill," and a third, Robert McNamara, was by the time he was relieved of his office given to weeping in public.

The pace in the national security world leads bureaucrats into the trap of collecting isolated facts and figures. Robert McNamara was, of course, the leading specimen of *homo mathematicus*—i.e., men who behave and believe other men behave primarily in response to "hard data," usually numbers (infiltration rates, "kill ratios," bomb tonnage). Like the classic private eye on television, they are always looking for "the facts," but usually the wrong ones. They miss reality, for they never get close enough or related enough to another society to do more than count things in it. If you relate to a country as a military target you do not need to know anything about it except such details as are easily supplied by reconnaissance satellites, spy ships, secret agents, etcetera. You need never know who the victims of your attack were. Your task is merely to assess the results of what you have done and this is done by counting bodies, destroyed factories, enemy soldiers. Things that stay still long enough to be counted are either inanimate or dead. Living human beings, complex

* For further reading on bureaucrats' lives, see Anthony Downs, *Inside Bureaucracy* (Boston: Little, Brown and Co., 1967), and William H. Whyte, Jr., *The Executive Life* (Garden City, N.Y.: Doubleday and Co., 1956).

and changing political relationships, intangibles like national pride elude the best analysis. All foreigners who do not know a society are at an enormous disadvantage, but *homo mathematicus* is intellectually crippled in special ways. When Desmond Fitzgerald, top CIA specialist in covert intelligence operations, briefed McNamara and told him that he had a "feeling" for the events in Vietnam that contradicted the optimistic "hard data" which lower echelons were feeding Washington, the Secretary of Defense glared icily at him and never invited him to give another briefing.*

Most of the proposals for reforming the State Department miss the point. The smartest, best-informed men, operating in the most streamlined bureaucracy, cannot perform the task which the national security managers assigned themselves. They cannot run the world. They cannot even try without destroying pieces of it.

Many of the national security managers prided themselves on taking a systems analysis approach to foreign relations—collect the facts, calculate the costs and the benefits, outline the possible options, and select the best course. The problem was that they did not know enough that was relevant about the rest of the world to understand what system they were operating in. They saw no need to understand foreign societies they thought they knew how to manage. (Nor, for that matter, did they feel any compulsion to consider the impact of national security policy on the American people.) Chester Cooper gives an illuminating, if biased, picture of the meeting of East and West at a crucial point in the Vietnam War:

> Much more worrisome than the meetings with government officials were those with the dissident Buddhists and students. Bundy came out reeling from a two-hour session with a leading member of the Buddhist hierarchy. His razor-sharp mind just couldn't cut through the ooze of generalities. Two cultures and two educational backgrounds did not directly conflict but rather slid past one another.†

(It would be interesting to get the Buddhists' impression of Bundy's "razor-sharp mind.")

(6)

PERHAPS the most important quality in a man seeking nonviolent, political solutions rather than violent solutions to national security problems is objectivity, and this is the quality that is least in evi-

* David Halberstam, "Programming of Robert McNamara," *Harper's Magazine,* May 1971, pp. 37–40.

† Chester Cooper, *The Lost Crusade* (New York: Dodd, Mead and Co., 1970), p. 257.

dence. The man who tries to see the point of view of the adversary or explain his perspective has to defend himself against the charge that he is defending the adversary. For someone to have suggested in April 1961 that the Cuban people were not likely to revolt against Castro because he was a popular leader, far more popular than the émigrés the U.S. was supporting, was to sound pro-Castro. To suggest that the Soviet Union's moves in Eastern Europe after the war were a reflection of deep-seated security fears rather than the first step toward world conquest was to be a Soviet apologist.

In the game of international politics practitioners must be fiercely partisan. The United States is the client, and the task of the manager is to increase her power and influence in the world, whatever the cost. *Raison d'état,* the historic principle asserted by sovereign nations that they are above all law, is a daily operating rule in the national security bureaucracy. In the jungle world of international politics the duty of the national security manager is to pursue every seeming advantage he can get away with, regardless of law. Thus the issue of war crimes in Vietnam only became a matter of concern in the national security bureaucracy after the public disclosures of My Lai. Indiscriminate bombing, free-fire zones, torture of prisoners, wholesale crop destruction, and other acts that violate the letter and spirit of solemn treaties signed by the United States and should shock any civilized conscience were common knowledge throughout the national security bureaucracy. The 1949 Geneva Conventions signed by the United States with respect to the treatment of civilian populations and the treatment of prisoners are not regarded as objective standards for regulating American conduct but as diplomatic weapons to be used against the enemy or as minor embarrassments in the path of policy which a skilled legal adviser can deftly remove.

In the national security world there are neither neutral principles nor reciprocal obligations. The fact that the United States would be outraged if Chinese, Cuban, Soviet, or Cambodian aircraft flew over Washington is not viewed as having a bearing on the right of the United States to carry on such activities over other peoples' territories at will. Dean Acheson summarized the prevailing code. In discussing the Cuban missile crisis he said that since the "power, prestige, and position" of the United States had been challenged, "law simply does not deal with such questions of ultimate power." Where any state itself concludes that its survival (including prestige) is at stake, it can ignore the law. "No law can destroy the state creating the law. The survival of states is not a matter of law." *

* See the Proceedings of the American Society of International Law, 1963, pp. 14–15, and discussed in Richard J. Barnet and Marcus Raskin, *After 20 Years* (New York: Random House, 1965), p. 229 n.

Objectivity has never been a notable characteristic of political power-seekers. "The man of politics," Boccalini of Loreto wrote in the late seventeenth century, "gets firmly into his head the principle that everything else must give way before the absolute necessity of asserting and maintaining oneself in the State; he sets his foot on the neck of every other value in heaven and earth. The desire to govern is a daemon which even holy water will not drive out." The way to "maintain oneself in the State" is to promote the State. The politician who works for the aggrandizement of the State, for its glory and expansion, is a hero (until he fails); the man who counsels moderation and restraint is a nuisance. No politician has felt called to preside over the liquidation of an empire (although some have ended up reluctantly doing so). For rulers and their clerks personal satisfaction has always been the reflected glory of state power. In the age of the organization man this is especially true.

Like the manager of a soap company who paces himself by the bars of soap the corporation sells, the national security manager also measures his worth by how well his organization is doing. As John Kenneth Galbraith has pointed out,* people in government, unlike poets, opera singers, and brain surgeons, are sustained by organizations. The defeated politician, retiring ambassador or general, or, one might add, the former Cabinet officer, who fails to get a bank, foundation, or university to manage, "faces total obscurity." They were "sustained by an organization," Galbraith observes, and "on losing its support they pass permanently into the shadows." This being so, national security managers have a personal investment in the health and aggrandizement of their own bureaucratic organizations. They equate the national interest and their organization's interest as a matter of course. They will fight to maintain an obsolete air base, build redundant weapons systems, proliferate arms around the world by certifying that the nation's "vital interests" are at stake when it is merely their own budgets. Thus they demonstrate the same objectivity as advocates for their own bureaucratic components as advocates for the nation display in dealing with the rights of other nations.

Generals and admirals invariably believe that what is good for the Air Force or the Navy is good for America. A few days after becoming Secretary of the Navy, Paul Nitze discovered a "power vacuum" in the Indian Ocean and a new "requirement" for the fleet. At a Congressional hearing on the B-36, a proposed new bomber for the Air Force, Admiral Arthur Radford denounced nuclear deterrence as "morally reprehensible." It was not until the Navy invented the Polaris submarine-launched nuclear missile that the Admiral decided that the peace of the world depended upon the

---

* *The New Industrial State* (Boston: Houghton Mifflin, 1967).

hydrogen bomb. Each service embellishes "the threat" to serve its bureaucratic interests. The Office of Naval Intelligence is especially good at finding extra Soviet ships which Air Force intelligence always manages to miss. There are tens of thousands of mysterious objects in the Soviet Union which the Army is convinced are tanks but which any Air Force intelligence officer knows are really airplanes.

Each military service has also worked out a view of the world that justifies its own self-proclaimed mission. For the Army, the job is to preserve a "balance of power" and to keep order around the world through counterinsurgency campaigns and limited wars. It should be no surprise that the Air Force view of the world is much more alarmist. "The Soviet leadership is irrevocably committed to the achievement of the ultimate Communist objective, which is annihilation of the capitalist system and establishment of Communist dictatorship over all nations of the world," * wrote former SAC Commander General Thomas Power. According to General Nathan Twining, former Chief of Staff of the Air Force, "the leaders of an organized conspiracy have sworn to destroy America." It is essential to have an enemy worthy of your own weapons and your own war plans. A strategy based on the nuclear annihilation of the Soviet Union is far easier to accept if that country is the embodiment of evil. To rationalize a nuclear arsenal of eleven thousand megaton bombs, it is vital to assume that the leaders in the Kremlin are too depraved to be deterred by less. The anticommunist reflex is the Air Force's biggest political asset.

So fierce is organizational loyalty that it leads to open bureaucratic warfare. In the Pentagon the Joint Chiefs of Staff protect their domain as if it were a duchy separate from the rest of the Department of Defense. Indeed, their corridor has a special guard and no official, however exalted, can casually enter their premises. In the McNamara era the office of Systems Analysis became the *bête noire* of the JCS because the "whiz kids," as disgruntled generals called them, questioned inflated intelligence estimates of the size of Soviet forces and challenged the efficacy of certain weapons systems which the military were promoting. So strained were relationships that formal "treaties" were drawn up reflecting compromise agreements on intelligence estimates of the number of Soviet aircraft.

In a bureaucracy knowledge is power and secrecy is an effective weapon. The Secretary of Defense is frequently unable to obtain technical studies prepared by the Joint Chiefs of Staff on weapons systems and force levels. Whenever the JCS believe that such studies could be used against them in bureaucratic conflict they assert their prerogative and withhold them. It is a measure of their power that

---

* For this and similar statements, see General Thomas S. Power, *Design for Survival* (New York: Coward McCann, 1965).

they are almost always successful in keeping such crucial information from their civilian superiors.

Bargaining and struggle are normal modes of carrying on business in the national security bureaucracy. Each bureaucratic unit represents and promotes its own conception of the national interest, in which higher budgets and more power for itself are invariably a key factor. In the 1950's the Air Force and the Army struggled over control of the missile program. The counterinsurgency obsession of the early sixties was in large part a campaign by the U.S. Army to get "a piece of the action" back from the CIA and the Air Force, which reigned supreme all through the Eisenhower era. In the State Department U.S. policy toward the new states of Africa, frequently contradictory, evolved out of a bureaucratic conflict between the Bureau of European Affairs, representing the interests of the former colonial powers now U.S. partners in NATO, and the Bureau of African Affairs, representing what they believed to be the growing U.S. strategic interests in Africa.

The most bizarre bureaucratic conflicts have involved the CIA. As Smith Simpson, former Foreign Service Officer, has written, "State is kept in the dark about many CIA operations abroad and especially about those which run counter to the Department's policies." Although he omits the most dramatic confrontation, in which the State Department and the CIA supported opposing armies in Laos in 1960, his own account of the running battle between the covert and overt arms of U.S. diplomacy is worth quoting:

> Living with CIA has thus become more and more difficult. The Agency supported Indonesian rebels against Sukarno while State was trying to work with Sukarno. It supplied and emboldened the anticommunist Chinese guerrillas in Burma over the protests of the Burmese Government and the repeated protestations of the State Department in Washington and our ambassador in Burma that we were doing no such thing. In Viet Nam, too, CIA and State have worked at cross-purposes.
>
> But the Agency has not confined its activities to unstable countries. It has meddled elsewhere, to the consternation of the State Department and friendly governments. In the mid-1950's, its agents intruded awkwardly in Costa Rica, the most stable and democratic country in Latin America. While the Agency was trying to oust Jose Figueres, the moderate socialist who became the Costa Rican President in a fair election in 1953, the State Department was working with him and our ambassador was urging President Eisenhower to invite him to the United States to enhance his prestige. So it went the world around.*

* Smith Simpson, *Anatomy of the State Department* (Boston: Houghton Mifflin, 1967), p. 103.

(7)

IN THE ATTEMPT to understand why. the "brightest and the best" in American society, all "honorable gentlemen," as the severest critics among their own number always concede, defined the national interest as requiring the prosecution of an aggressive war, as brutal as any in history, two principal theories are adduced—the "mistake" theory and the "conspiracy" theory. Under the "mistake" theory, which we have already discussed, the national security managers did not mean to do what they did. They were misled by history and their own misguided good intentions. Such a theory cannot stand up to either legal or moral scrutiny. The national security managers understood the homicidal nature of the policies they recommended although they were clearly "mistaken" as to their consequences, as indeed is every ruler who embarks on a war and fails to achieve victory. As we have seen, it was to achieve certain specific results and to protect specific values that the United States committed and recommitted itself to a war in Vietnam. To have avoided the war would have meant a major revision of the operational code of the national security managers.

But there are problems with the "conspiracy" model as well. Two questions arise: Did the national security managers have a conscious plan, an imperial design? Did they believe that they were transgressing legal or moral standards?

Anyone willing to read the historical record will find it hard to deny that American policymakers for a generation have had a rather clear design for expanding American power. Americans acquired their global empire in the same mythical fit of absent-mindedness in which Great Britain gathered hers. The maintenance of strategic territory occupied in World War II, the containment of the two great potential power rivals, Russia and China, the filling of "power vacuums" left by the collapse of French and British imperial power, the expansion of American influence into all open areas of the "developing world," and the maintenance of a world capitalist economic system dominated by the United States have been, as we shall show more specifically in Part II, conscious policies. To accomplish any of them the United States has been prepared to use various forms of violence against other nations and people. The great documents of the Cold War that have come to public light—the Clark Clifford memorandum, NSC-68, NASM288—to the extent that official government documents prove anything, bear out the existence of a reasonably coherent grand design. True, American officials often stumbled and faltered in carrying out the design. Sometimes their actions were self-defeating. But faulty execution does not negate the existence of a plan.

Yet the "conspiracy" concept does not fit the facts, because conspiracy, for the layman if not for the lawyer, implies some consciousness of guilt. Conspirators, according to popular understanding of the term, are men who plot to commit acts they know to be wrong. Here is the crux of the problem. The men who were ready in the Cuban missile crisis to risk civilization for prestige, for what Dean Acheson calls "the shadow of power," and to destroy Indochina to save America's reputation for toughness, to lie and kill on a grand scale, all believed that they were doing right, that, indeed, they were acting under duty. It is impossible to understand how dangerous the structures of the national security bureaucracy are without also understanding the systems of absolution that operate within those structures. It is these systems of absolution that serve to stand ordinary principles of private morality on their head and to transform reasonably law-abiding professors and bankers into killers.

When President Eisenhower was caught telling a lie, by denying the existence of the U-2 flights over the Soviet Union after Gary Powers had been inconveniently shot down over Sverdlovsk, many Americans were shocked. Taught to believe that Presidents may chop down their fathers' cherry trees, but never lie about it, they began to worry about a "credibility gap." By the time Lyndon Johnson had left the White House the gap had assumed cavernous proportions. But lies have always been standard equipment in promoting the national interest. A jocular but accepted nineteenth-century definition of a diplomat was an "honorable gentleman sent to lie abroad for his country." In the age of covert operations the opportunities for deception have grown greatly. No one expects nations at war to tell the truth about their war plans, motivations, conditions of settlement, or the atrocities they are committing. National security managers who manage truth in these areas feel little compunction about it, for they are performing a clear and traditional duty in behalf of the state.

However, the unconscious lie—something one should know to be false but has come to believe is true—is even more common. This psychological mechanism offers protection against unpleasant and disturbing truth. It can be found everywhere. No doubt there are cigarette manufacturers who believe that smoking prolongs life. But the unconscious lie is rampant in the national security bureaucracy. Any organization that devotes so much of its resources to propaganda is bound to fall victim to a certain amount itself. Many of the statements on Vietnam, for example, were analogous to the kind of advertising claims which Jules Henry has dubbed "pecuniary pseudotruth." This is a false statement made for the purpose of selling something, which is uttered as if it is true but is not intended to be believed. One of the clearest analyses of pseudo-truth in the national security establishment came in the form of testimony by Air Force Secretary Harold Brown. Defending his budget request for a new bomber before a Congressional committee by claiming the Soviets were probably building one of their own, he observed: "The Air Force view is at least as much a view that 'they ought to have one' as it is 'they will have one.' " The repeated public claims in the Vietnam War that victory was around the corner were of this character. The claims were contradicted by all available intelligence and were sufficiently at odds with public reporting that no reasonably informed citizen could swallow them. They were meant to be taken literally no more than the claim that Seven Crown whisky "holds within its icy depths a world of summertime." They were part of what national security managers like to call "atmospherics," official expressions of confidence designed to pep up the public. The remarkable thing, however, is that the national security managers came to believe them. In 1965 Robert McNamara, one of his aides recalls, had waved aside the suggestion that a full-time man be put on Vietnam in the International Security Affairs office of the Pentagon on the ground that "it will all be over soon."

Confusion between what is true and what people would like to be true is an occupational hazard in any institution that spends a great deal of time projecting an image. It is a narcotic that protects people not only from public confrontations, but from their own consciences. When the truth about the Vietnam War began to come out in 1967 and 1968 and the national security managers were forced to defend their policy at dinner parties, the strains associated with the job began to outweigh the thrills. One high-level White House assistant told us he would become physically sick at such dinner party confrontations. Forced to face the truth, other national security managers began to show such signs of strain as snapping at subordinates and succumbing to fits of depression. Albert Speer gives an interesting picture in his memoirs of what happens to political operators when the bubble of illusion bursts and they come to see themselves as conspirators.

However, the official lie in its myriad forms is only one of the systems of absolution operating in the national security bureaucracy. Another, clearly related, is the "need not to know" phenomenon. In approving a stepped up defoliation program in Vietnam in late 1965, Secretary of State Rusk observed to his staff assistant in charge of counterinsurgency that Vietnam was really an "empty jungle." The only people "who would get hurt by defoliation" would be Vietcong. The statement, absurd on its face, was clutched at by the Secretary to resolve inner moral doubts and to legitimize the ordering of a crime.

Just as there is a "need to know" requirement which restricts classified information to the fewest possible hands, there is a "need not to know" which makes it possible for conscientious men to authorize bureaucratic homicide. I came upon another example of the "need not to know" after I returned from a visit to North Vietnam and reported to a senior American statesman, by that time an opponent of the war, that the U.S. Air Force had systematically bombed churches and pagodas in the province I had toured. His immediate response was that these buildings had been used to hide trucks and were therefore legitimate targets. The reality which I saw was that the churches were for the most part in the middle of fields and could not have been used for military purposes. The bombings took place not because of specific orders to hit churches but because of a standing order to hit everything. In a primitive economy there is a shortage of good targets, and a pilot under orders not to come back with left-over bombs finds the biggest structure in the village irresistible. There is no easier way to deal with such typical examples of bureaucratic homicide than "not to know."

There is also the need "not to understand." The crucial factor that upset all the calculations of the optimists in the national security bureaucracy was the willingness of the enemy to accept a staggering loss of life. From 1965 to 1968 the Pentagon reported the destruction of the whole Vietcong force more than once. Even allowing for official U.S. exaggeration, the actual number of enemy deaths was enormous. But the implications of the fact that the Vietnamese were ready to die on a vast scale rather than give up were clouded in official ignorance. No one at the top knew or considered it important that the Vietnamese had been fighting foreign invaders for almost two thousand years. No one understood the depth of their nationalist feeling. The official explanation inside the Pentagon was that Vietnamese value life cheaply and are accustomed to dying in droves. The implication of this racist analysis, with its connotations of human waves, yellow hordes, and kamikazes, is that they are exceedingly dangerous people and deserve to be killed in even greater numbers.

Another absolution system goes by the name of pragmatism. A policy involving the use of force is initiated without any idea of the consequences. In his study of "coercive diplomacy," Alexander L. George calls this the "try-and-see" approach. At the height of the Cuban missile crisis, for example, according to Robert Kennedy's account, the United States was prepared to drop depth charges on Soviet submarines operating on the high seas near the area on which the United States had established a quarantine and may have actually done so. The President, aware of the implications of beginning a shooting war with the Soviet Navy, asked, "Isn't there some way we can avoid having our first exchange with a Russian submarine—almost anything but that?" McNamara replied, "No, there's too much danger to our ships. There is no alternative." * Because of the felt need to "show determination," the incalculable risks of firing on the Soviet flag on the high seas received no attention. The herbicide program in Vietnam, to take another example, was begun on a vast scale without any consideration of the consequences, either in permanent ecological or genetic damage or risk to human life.

Pragmatism of the "try-and-see" variety is a comfortable stance for a bureaucracy with a superfluity of power at its command. The enormous margin of military superiority which the United States has enjoyed since the end of the Second World War encourages experimentation. Covert operations are particularly attractive to the pragmatists because they can be disowned if they fail (except in the rare case in which a live pilot from a spy plane falls into enemy hands, as in the U-2 incident). Thus the United States has parachuted men into China, and has flown its planes regularly over Chinese territory, but it has also engaged in overtly provocative maneuvers such as the harassment of the Soviet fleet in the Mediterranean, all because the risks were seen as manageable. The "try-and-see" syndrome provides the principal dynamic of escalation. In Vietnam no one had a plausible "scenario" for bringing victory. Each service, however, had plausible recommendations for limited operations which could prevent immediate defeat and which seemed to have limited risks. The President had the illusion that he was "keeping the options open," to use the favorite phrase of the Kennedy days, but it was no more than illusion. Once he had committed some military forces, he was under extreme pressure to commit more, not only to protect the men already there, but, more important, to redeem their failing efforts. Psychologically, it is always easier to escalate in stages with distinct pauses separating the critical decisions.

(8)

THE STRUCTURE of bureaucratic language is itself an absolution system. For the national security managers the flavor and connotation of the words they use on the job reinforce the legitimacy of what they are doing and obscure the reality of bureaucratic homicide. We have already noted the use of such obvious examples of verbal camouflage as "surgical strike." "Taking out" a "base" implies that the operation is therapeutic. No pictures of flaming chil-

---

* The Kennedy-McNamara exchange appears in Robert F. Kennedy, *Thirteen Days* (New York: W. W. Norton, 1969), p. 48.

dren, torn limbs, or shattered bodies pinned under rubble come to mind. "Attack objectives" are easier to think about than the mutilated, weeping, and dazed human beings who will be the actual target of the bombs. "Pacification" trips off the tongue far more easily in a Pentagon briefing and looks better on the page of a neat memorandum than phrases that would actually describe the death and suffering to which the antiseptic term refers. Emotional distance from the homicidal consequences of his planning is essential to the mental health of the planner and bureaucratic language is rich in the terminology of obfuscation.

But there are more subtle uses of language as well. The routine use of such words as "power vacuum" disguises a major policy premise and forecloses debate on what is actually a highly debatable proposition. The idea concealed by the term "power vacuum" is that a weak country must inevitably be dominated by a stronger one, that the power of one or the other of the Great Powers will "flow into" the country. The implication of those who use the term in the American bureaucracy, of course, is that it had better be U.S. power that flows in. Thus the idea of the impossibility of neutralism, national independence for weak countries, or avoiding the spread of American power is built into the working vocabulary of the national security manager.

Once substantial numbers of U.S. "advisers" began to accompany South Vietnamese units into battle in 1964 and the Vietcong began to attack U.S. installations as at Pleiku, Pentagon planners used the language of reprisal so as to make their plans for carrying the war to North Vietnam appear defensive, not only to the outside world,* but, at the emotional level, to themselves. The same psychological pattern is even clearer at lower levels of the bureaucratic ladder. In the air war in Vietnam, as Frank Harvey has pointed out, pilots of the Tactical Air Command "cruise around over the Delta like a vigilante posse, holding the power of life and death over the Vietnamese villagers living beneath." So convinced are the pilots of their right to spray Vietnam with bullets at will that they are genuinely outraged when "the little mothers" begin "shooting back." As Robert Crichton notes, Americans accustomed to a thousand-to-one superiority in firepower over the enemy have come to feel that it is their inherent right to kill people without retaliation.† Bureaucratic language of

* Actually, the national security managers were ambivalent about justifying American operations to the outside world as reprisals for attacks on U.S. personnel, as that position appeared to undercut the commitment to the government of South Vietnam, which was the reason the U.S. advisers were there in the first place. But the feelings of revenge which the "reprisal" rhetoric fed helped the national security managers feel that their war plans were both justified and necessary.

† Robert Crichton, "Our Air War," *New York Review of Books,* January 4, 1968, is quoted in Philip Slater, *The Pursuit of Loneliness* (Boston: Beacon Press, 1970), p. 37.

reprisal sustains this incredible assumption at the same time as it obscures its real meaning.

Perhaps the most striking characteristic of bureaucratic language is the recurrence of the imagery of manipulation. "The timing and crescendo" of operations "should be under our control." "We should rev up Mr. ——— to explore negotiations." "The United States Government might do better to carry forward the war on a purely unilateral basis." "How should we permit negotiations to develop?" Such random quotations from official documents recalled by former national security managers whom we have interviewed all have one quality in common. They reinforce the myth of control—i.e., that the national security manager, with all the technological power at his command, can play upon the world like a giant console. Indeed, James C. Thomson, Jr., recalls an Assistant Secretary of State in late 1964 proposed bombing and strafing patterns with these words: "It seems to me that our orchestration should be mainly violins, but with periodic touches of brass."

The most compelling absolution systems are the myths which exalt the significance of the targets of American military operations. These myths come in two principal varieties: the myth of monolithic conspiracy and the myth of the inexorable blueprint. The second had more of a vogue in the early days of the Cold War. The first, to which we have already alluded, played a crucial role in the Vietnam escalation.

One of the principal problems in justifying the magnitude of the American commitment to keep South Vietnam from having an indigenous communist government is that it is a very small country, very far away, with no record of having harmed any American interest. If it is to be the object of ten years of ferocious attention by the world's most powerful nation, it must be invested with sufficient importance. The myth of monolithic conspiracy was an ideal device for finding an enemy in Vietnam worthy of the U.S. effort. Who that enemy was changed from time to time. In 1961, when the Vietcong insurgency was still at a relatively low level, a State Department White Paper conceded that the enemy were the "Vietnamese Communists" but they were using "the same methods," including "Mao Tse Tung's theories," which were used "in Malaya, in Greece, in the Philippines, in Cuba, and in Laos." By 1965, before North Vietnamese regulars had crossed the seventeenth parallel and before Chinese and Soviet weapons had been found in any quantities in the South and just before the United States itself sent an army to South Vietnam and began bombing North Vietnam around the clock, the State Department had changed the enemy. "In Viet-Nam a Communist government (North Vietnam) has set out deliberately to conquer a sovereign people in a neighboring state." By 1967, after the United States had committed more than half a million men in

South Vietnam and had dropped more bombs on Indochina than were dropped in five years of World War II, the enemy was escalated again. When asked at a press conference why he thought "our security is at stake in Vietnam," Secretary of State Rusk replied unhesitatingly:

> Within the next decade or two, there will be a billion Chinese on the mainland, armed with nuclear weapons, with no certainty about what their attitude toward the rest of Asia will be.

> Now the free nations of Asia will make up at least a billion people. They don't want China to overrun them on the basis of a doctrine of the world revolution.

The same confusion as to the real enemy was manifested in internal debates inside the bureaucracy because there never was a credible theory for making the war the principal project of the United States. Unless one believed in a literal sense in the "dominoes" theory, it was perfectly obvious that the costs of fighting the war far outweighed the gains. But, as in any human activity, acts bring with them their own explanations. The more aggressive the act, the more elaborate the explanation. Thus, for Rusk, Vietnam was a "test case" of "wars of liberation" supported by Moscow as well as Peking. International communism had a design to control all Asia, Africa and Latin America, "thus encircling and strangling the Atlantic world." If we do not defeat "them" in Vietnam, President Johnson warned, we will have to fight "them" in San Francisco. At last the cause in Vietnam had been made worthy of the destruction and the suffering being visited upon it.

The other myth, the myth of the inexorable blueprint, is clearly related. The basic idea is that the Communists are so autistic that nothing the "free world" does, save credible military threats, influences their conduct. Inside the government intelligence reports are sifted daily which contradict so inherently absurd a proposition. The communist system is changing. The Soviet Union is changing. Soviet leaders clearly react to moves in the outside world, and not only to threats. Indeed their principal concession, the test-ban treaty, for example, has come in response to conciliatory initiatives by the United States. The national security managers know all these things. For years they have been familiar ideas in their daily work. Yet in making crucial decisions they cling to the myth of the blueprint. Put most simply, "the underlying crisis of our time," according to Secretary Rusk, "arises from this fundamental conflict: between those who would impose their blueprint on mankind and those who believe in self-determination." The myth had been preserved almost intact since 1950, when Dean Acheson, speaking on the "Communist Menace," observed that the conflict with the Soviet Union transcended ordinary international disputes and declared that "there can be no greater disagreement than when someone wants to eliminate your existence altogether." The Soviet plan to "bury" America along with the capitalist system was inexorable. Indeed, as early as 1946 Harry Truman, dispatching an aircraft carrier, four cruisers, a destroyer flotilla, and the battleship *Missouri* to the Eastern Mediterranean to counter Soviet pressure on Turkey for a share in the control of the Straits, told Acheson that "we might as well find out whether the Russians were bent on world conquest now as in five or ten years." *

The myth of the blueprint gives credibility to the idea of "defensive expansionism and preventive war." If communist design to rule the world is implacable, it makes sense to fight them now in a small war when they are relatively weak than to wait for Armageddon. With the Nazi takeover of the Rhineland, Austria, and Czechoslovakia etched in their minds, the national security managers determined to treat any communist advance anywhere as a harbinger of that final confrontation and as a justification for a final solution. A speech of Senator Lyndon B. Johnson in 1952 (when the Soviet Union had yet to develop a way of delivering the atomic bomb on the United States) typifies widely held American attitudes on preventive nuclear war:

> We should announce, I believe, that any act of aggression, anywhere, by any Communist forces, will be regarded as an act of aggression by the Soviet Union. . . . If anywhere in the world —by any means, open or concealed—Communism trespasses upon the soil of the free world, we should unleash all the power at our command upon the vitals of the Soviet Union. That is the policy we should build toward.†

A Soviet government which can be dealt with only through ever increasing military power rather than diplomacy is the perfect adversary for an American government whose primary activity is war preparation. It is the indispensable partner. That Communists everywhere are guided by a fixed hostile ideology rather than limited and possibly flexible interests is a convenient, indeed an essential, analysis for the number one nation still bent on expanding its power. It has absolved the national security managers of responsibility for waging a generation of war.

* Quoted in Walter Millis, ed., *The Forrestal Diaries* (New York: Viking Press, 1951), p. 192.

† Michael Parenti, *The Anti-Communist Impulse* (New York: Random House, 1969), p. 152. In the following quote from the same book, the racist overtones of Lyndon Johnson's rhetoric are clearly evident: "No matter what else we have of offensive or defensive weapons, without superior air power, America is a bound and throttled giant, impotent and easy prey to any yellow dwarf with a pocket knife."

II

THE POLITICAL
ECONOMY OF
EXPANSIONISM

6

The American Business Creed
and the National Interest

I n part i we described the men who are in the business of defining the national interest and the bureaucratic climate in which they operate. It is the thesis of this book that the decisions they make can be understood only by relating them to the struggles of bureaucratic politics. Bureaucracies respond to their own inner logic and to their own laws. Bureaucracies lose touch with the original purposes for which they are founded, and bureaucratic momentum often carries men far beyond the point to which they originally intend to go. But bureaucracies do not exist in the air. They are an expression of the social, political, and economic organization of a society. We are concerned in this part with relating the national security institutions to their economic roots.

Just as the huge complex system that has been established to manage U.S. national security policy does not resemble Max Weber's idealized picture of an orderly, obedient, rational, and responsive instrument of government,* so Marx's famous phrase "executive committee of the ruling class" also fails to take adequate account of the

---

* Max Weber, *Theory of Social and Economic Organization*, trans. Talcott Parsons (Glencoe: Free Press, 1947).

concentration of independent power within the national security bureaucracy. To a degree undreamed by Marx, the national security bureaucracy exercises power on its own.

However, bureaucracies are established to carry out functions, and it is these tasks which determine its basic character. Thus, while the national security managers, as we have seen, have virtually complete discretion to decide which "threats" and "vital interests" should engage America's attention at any given moment and to select the appropriate "responses" and "options," they exercise that discretion within a political and economic context. The national security bureaucracy was established not only to provide physical security for American territory but also to protect certain key American values sometimes characterized as the American way of life. Within the hierarchy of traditional American values the most basic have to do with the relationship of property, freedom, and order. In their study of American business ideology, Seymour Harris, Carl Kaysen, James Tobin, and Francis X. Sutton call this constellation of fundamental beliefs "the American business creed." * In Part II we shall be looking at the role of economic institutions in the setting and carrying out of American foreign policy. In simple terms: What is the role of business in setting U.S. foreign policy? The question that dominates this part is whether the evolving American economic system—late-twentieth-century capitalism—is responsible for America's expansionist foreign policy and wars, and to what extent. How much can American foreign policy change without major changes in our basic economic assumptions and institutions? The discussion begins in this chapter with an analysis of the business creed.

For much of the last generation America's economic stake in the global status quo has been treated by most political scientists and foreign policy analysts as a state secret. Like most state secrets, the economic roots of American expansionism are better known abroad than at home. During twenty years of Cold War, courses and seminars on national security abounded in the leading American universities, but rarely, if ever, could a student deduce that national security had anything to do with so mundane a matter as money. A few yards away in the business school or economics department colleagues would subject international trade, balance of payments, and raw materials policy to elegant analysis without corrupting it with politics. The pursuit of compartmentalized truth in the academy reflected and buttressed the public ideology. The purposes of domestic policy are largely economic, but foreign policy is essentially a spiritual activity. Entities called nations compete with one another at great economic cost without obvious economic benefit in the pursuit of noneconomic values.

* *The American Business Creed* (Cambridge: Harvard University Press, 1956).

Most foreigners who observe the United States from abroad do not believe it.

American businessmen themselves have on the whole been more candid and less naïve than professors in articulating some of the economic drives behind national security policy. Many of the nation's leading industrialists and bankers are convinced that the projection of American power and influence abroad is rooted in economic necessity, in the needs of an expanding economy for new markets and new resources unavailable at home. Whether it is true that domestic prosperity requires continuing foreign economic and military expansion is an issue to which we shall return in Chapter 8. But, whether it is true or not, American leaders at critical moments in the development of foreign policy have believed it.

Businessmen make two major points in arguing that the expansionist interests of corporations, primarily large corporations, are identical with the national interest. The first concerns the importance of foreign trade. Overseas expansionism is so crucial to the domestic economy, as William Clayton, the world's richest cotton merchant, temporarily serving as Assistant Secretary of State, told the National Foreign Trade Convention in 1943, that the only alternative to a continuing effort to open up new markets is "to turn our country into an armed camp, police the seven seas, tighten our belts, and live by the ration books for the next century or so." Dean Acheson, who had just come from a large corporate law practice to the State Department, told a Congressional committee the same year that "we cannot expect domestic prosperity without a constantly expanded trade with other nations. . . . To keep prosperity, levels of employment, production and income . . . we shall have to find increasing markets for our production and increasing investment outlets for our capital." Of course, he agreed, you could "fix it so that everything produced here would be consumed here," but "that would completely change our Constitution, our relations to property, human liberty, our very conception of law." To be sure, this was a hard sell of free trade to a still protectionist-leaning Congress, but the words accurately expressed the strong sentiments of the new liberal business community.*

The second national security argument advanced by business spokesmen for encouraging corporate expansion overseas is that the great strength of America is her productive capacity and that the maintenance of that strength demands ever-increasing control of critical resources by American corporations. It was oil that "licked

---

* William Clayton's statement is from *Foreign Commerce Weekly,* November 20, 1943, p. 11. Quoted in David Horowitz, ed., *Corporations and the Cold War* (New York: Monthly Review Press, 1969), p. 149. The Acheson statement is from the same book, in an article by William A. Williams entitled "The Large Corporation in American Foreign Policy," p. 96.

the Nazis and the Japs," Eugene Holman, President of Jersey Standard, asserted in 1946, emphasizing that the petroleum empire over
which he presided, though privately owned, was a national weapon.
Businessmen have invested millions of public relations dollars and
thousands of hours of speechmaking in arguing what Bernard Baruch
once called the "essential oneness of economic, political, and strategic
interests."

(2)

THE MOST DYNAMIC expansionist period in American history, whether
judged by the spread of economic control or that of military deployment, has been the post–World War II era. The same years have also
witnessed the triumph of the American business creed. The two developments are related, for, as we shall see more fully below, each element of that creed supports a crucial tenet of American foreign
policy. By the same token, American national security policy has
played an important role in promoting broad acceptance of the business creed among the American people.

It is curious that the ideology of the free-enterprise system should
have taken such strong hold in the United States at the very moment
that the nation was for all practical purposes abandoning the system
in favor of a highly managed, subsidized economy. Though one out
of every eleven workers in the United States now works directly for a
unit of local, state, or the federal government and the government now
dispenses, according to the Joint Economic Committee, about $40
billion a year in direct subsidies, mostly to corporations, Americans
have preserved an image of themselves as a nation of independent
private entrepreneurs.* Even in the age of the organization man and a
90-per-cent failure rate for new small businesses, Americans are sustained by the faith that for those without special disabilities of race or
color there is reasonably equal access to the escalator of success.
Despite recent attacks on traditional capitalist values among upper-
middle-class college students (celebrated in such books as *The Green-
ing of America*), Richard Hofstadter's judgment that Americans
"have accepted the economic virtues of capitalist culture as necessary
qualities of man" is still valid. Fifty years after Calvin Coolidge re-
stated the obvious, the business of America is still business.

* The figure for government employment is derived from *U.S. Statistical
Abstract*, 1969, from tables on pp. 211, 395, and 429, and is based on 1968
data. Presumably the ratio in 1971 is greater.

Forty billion dollars is based on a study of subsidization prepared by the
staff of the Joint Economic Committee, entitled *The Economics of Federal
Subsidy Programs*, which appeared in January 1972.

The bureaucratic revolution had an important role to play in resurrecting the ideology of the free enterprise system. At the depths of the Depression, William E. Leuchtenburg wrote, "the businessman had lost his magic and was as discredited as a Hopi rainmaker in a prolonged drought." On the eve of World War II, 17.2 per cent of the work force was still unemployed. But the war wiped out unemployment almost overnight and brought instant prosperity. The engine for this miracle was business. The very men denounced a few years earlier as "economic royalists" now succeeded in refurbishing their public image by taking charge of the "arsenal of democracy" and working a "production miracle" which kept American losses and American suffering to a minimum. By 1946 businessmen ranked second only to religious leaders in public-opinion polls as "the group that was doing the most for the country."

The war also helped to dissipate much of the traditional American suspicion of bigness in business, as expressed in earlier times in the trust-busting rhetoric of Theodore Roosevelt and in the judicial opinions of Louis Brandeis. "The American people like, admire, and respect bigness," the President of Jersey Standard was happy to report in 1948. "Most of America's young men and women would rather work for big companies." * This was fortunate, for the choice was rapidly narrowing. One of the great consequences of the bureaucratic revolution was the impetus it gave to the rapid concentration of economic power. As we have already noted, the large corporations received an overwhelming share of the war production contracts that provided the steam for economic recovery. As a result, by 1947, 139 corporations owned 45 per cent of all industrial assets.

Business, which was rescued by the war, was thus helped to new heights of prosperity and to unprecedented concentration of wealth and power by the permanent national security crisis of the postwar era. As the historian William H. McNeil has noted, businessmen in the war "came to know their way around in the maze of Washington officialdom and realized that modern government was not merely a policeman but a very good customer and a soft-hearted banker as well." Even the most rugged individualists were willing to make an exception to their general distaste for "government interference" when that interference took the form of fast tax write-offs, tax rebates, free licenses, patents, interest-free loans, and straight subsidies. Each of the postwar administrations, including the Democratic administrations, were, despite their populist rhetoric, pro-business in their basic policies. The Truman Administration projected an image at election time of being against "mossbacks" and for the "little fel-

---

* Quoted in Thomas G. Paterson, "The Economic Cold War," an unpublished Ph.D. thesis completed in 1968 at the University of California at Berkeley.

low," but its policies, as Adams and Gray have shown in their study *Monopoly in America,* promoted big business. "You have a partner in the White House," *Nation's Business* reassured its readers. The same point could have been made about John F. Kennedy twelve years later. Despite Kennedy's preference for people who had money to those who were in the business of making it and the annoyance his style caused in business circles, the owners and managers of large corporations had very little reason to object to his tax, fiscal, or anti-trust policies. A government in permanent mobilization, however conservative or liberal its leadership, cannot turn on its industrial giants, even if it should want to. Thus, the Lockheed Corporation, unable to survive after massive infusions of federal funds for successive generations of superfluous missiles, is now kept alive by large gifts from the Treasury because the company is deemed a "national asset."

(3)

UNTIL THE explosive sixties, when racial tension, the collapse of urban services, consumer revolts, and, above all, the Vietnam War began to disturb the corporate vision of permanent, orderly boom, the business creed was accepted by everybody. (A surprising number of the radicals hounded out of government and universities in the McCarthy era became instant millionaires by starting electronics firms or riding the bull market on Wall Street.) The inevitability of prosperity was a theme well addressed in advertising budgets. "Step by step, rung by rung," the Bell Telephone System proclaimed proudly in a full-page ad in the March 1948 *Harper's,* new leaders "will mount the ladder to the top. . . . There will be more good jobs in the telephone business in 1958 and 1998 than now. It just can't help being this way. . . ." We have recounted how the permanent national security crisis helped to make the business creed a truly popular religion in the postwar era and solved major political problems for the large corporations in the process. Now we shall look at the substance of that creed and see to what extent it is reflected in the making of foreign policy.

It should be said at the outset that the American business creed is far more a cluster of attitudes than a well-worked-out theology, a fact which business spokesmen often note with regret. Introducing the McKinsey lectures at the Columbia Graduate School of Business in 1956, Ralph Cordiner, Chairman of General Electric, lamented the fact that "somehow we have not been able to do it well—to describe this new people's capitalism. . . ." * It should also be noted

* Robert Heilbroner, *The Limits of American Capitalism* (New York: Harper and Row, 1965), p. 31.

that there are profound ideological differences within the business world—between reactionary entrepreneurs such as H. L. Hunt and J. Howard Pew who finance ultrarightist causes and demand that communist nations be "driven" from the United Nations and the more moderate managers associated with the Committee on Economic Development who run most of the major corporations. But there are certain first principles which American capitalists of all political persuasions accept in varying degrees, and it is these principles that have an important impact on the setting of American foreign policy. The first tenet is that political freedom is indissolubly linked with free enterprise. (The modern definition of free enterprise makes room for government subsidies for successful industries and even for forms of nationalization for failing ones, such as the Penn Central.) At the fiftieth anniversary of the National Association of Manufacturers, their former president declared that "competitive enterprise, civil and religious freedom, and political freedom are inseparably bound up together." If in any country one of these freedoms is undermined, "all liberty they now so smugly enjoy will soon be devoured in the maw of dictatorship." * Almost a generation later Nelson Rockefeller embellished the same point in his report to President Nixon on Latin America:

> There is no system in all of history better than our own flexible structure of political democracy, individual initiative, and responsible citizenship. . . . It makes the individual of central importance; its subordinates the role of government as a servant of the people. . . .†

The free enterprise system protects individual liberty because it reduces the legitimate sphere of government. By protecting private space for private enrichment, the system keeps tyrannical government in check. As long as the market rather than the commissar determines what shall be produced and where men shall work and how much they shall be paid, the political liberties embodied in the Bill of Rights will be safe, and the "consumer freedoms"—the right to choose your own brand of toothpaste—will be preserved. The free enterprise system is also essential for political democracy, according to the creed, because dynamic capitalism has the best chance of producing the high standard of living in which successful democracy can flourish. (In Chapter 7 we shall be examining some of these suppositions as they relate to poor countries.)

According to the business creed, man can be motivated to help society only by being encouraged to help himself. Experiments which seek to inculcate community loyalty and collective responsibility on

---

* Kaysen et al., *op. cit.*, p. 31.

† Nelson A. Rockefeller, *The Rockefeller Report on the Americas* (Chicago: Quadrangle Books, 1969), p. 39.

some basis other than the profit motive are dismissed as hopelessly "romantic" by such sophisticated exponents of the business creed as W. W. Rostow. The true believer has a view of human nature which dovetails almost perfectly with the rat-psychology views of the national security manager. There are only two ways to get a man to produce, just as, it will be recalled, there are only two ways to make rival nations behave. One is to reward him according to his achievement and the other is to coerce him into producing. A society that does not reward achievement will end up with some form of Stalinism.

The second tenet of the business creed is that freedom is indivisible. It is often tempting to be cynical about such rhetoric, especially since the "free world," including as it does the Thieu regime in Saigon, the dictatorship in Taipei, and the brutal military juntas in Greece and Brazil, is obviously an honorary association in which freedom is not a requirement of membership. But just as the imperial creed of the national security manager cannot be understood without taking the "rule of law" seriously enough to seek its exact meaning, so we also need to look more closely at the "indivisibility" of freedom. It too has a precise meaning. It is the economic counterpart of the "dominoes theory." Nations cannot maintain free enterprise economies except within a system of capitalist states. When nations abandon the capitalist system, particularly when they withdraw from the "free world," such revolutionary acts of defiance are contagious. The further divisibility of freedom is likely to follow. The United States, despite its enormous power, will not be able to maintain its domestic freedom if it is politically and economically isolated from the rest of the world. In Nelson Rockefeller's words, such isolation would be a "barrier" to growth, and growth is a precondition of freedom. "The destruction of free enterprise abroad, like the destruction of democracy abroad, is a threat to free enterprise and democracy at home." These words of liberal Republican Charles P. Taft could be taken as the slogan of a generation. If Communists, state traders, and nationalists bent on hoarding their resources or driving hard bargains are permitted to restrict American economic opportunity, Americans will be pushed for their very survival toward a controlled economy and the garrison state.

Perhaps the tenet of the creed most crucial to foreign policy is the celebration of growth.* A business enterprise cannot survive by standing still. Indeed, expansion rather than quality of product or pure profitability is the most important criterion of business success. The pressure to expand in American industry is so great that companies that increase their sales or earnings at no faster rate than they did during the previous year find that their stock has tumbled. "Without

---

* See Walt W. Rostow, *Politics and the Stages of Economic Growth* (Cambridge: Cambridge University Press, 1971).

large-scale economic enterprises," Ralph Cordiner preaches, "a nation is today a second-rate power." Or in Roger Blough's words: Larger and larger groups "are necessary to perform America's larger production tasks."

The modern corporate manager takes it as axiomatic that his object is to extend the control held by his organization in every possible way—a greater share of the market, greater access to suppliers and advanced technology, a greater diversification of product. As Galbraith and others have argued, the quest for more profit is only one of many drives and not always the most important. The goal is the creation of a stable environment in which all obstacles to limitless growth will be removed. When businessmen come to play the game of nations they take it as a matter of course that expansion is the object of the game. Creating a controlled global political environment for the number one nation is merely an extension of the principles of prudent corporate management. The uncertain and unknown are threats. Domination and control need no justification.

Growth is celebrated in another sense too. In the business creed the measure of success in American society is the standard of living. "Ours may not be a perfect system," Paul Hoffman, automobile manufacturer and foreign policy adviser told the National Board of Fire Underwriters in 1950, "but under it 7 per cent of the people of the world do produce nearly 50 per cent of the world's manufactured goods. . . ." The genius of the system, as Benson Ford of the Ford Motor Company told the Los Angeles Chamber of Commerce in a typical speech of the late 1940's, is that everyone keeps getting more:

> In the year 1900, there was one automobile for every 9,500 people in this country. Today there is one automobile for every 4½ to 5 people in the United States.
>
> In the year 1925, 2,700 families had radios. Today 37,000 families—or 95 percent of families of spending units in this country—had an income of over $2000. Last year 64 percent had incomes over $2000 a year.
>
> . . . Progress is always an unfinished business in America.*

Now, twenty years later, when it has become fashionable to be concerned about the polluting side effects of limitless accumulation, and many young Americans are resisting being drawn into the race to consume, the exponents of the business creed continue to preach growth. To those few economists who are beginning to advocate a "zero growth" economy—stabilization of production and consumption of scarce resources—the business answer is that that is a "romantic" and "Luddite" solution. The inner dynamics of technology,

* Kaysen et al., *op. cit.,* p. 20.

the population growth, and the increasingly "sophisticated" appetites of a society with a lot of spending money make such a solution impossible. The issue, according to the business creed, is not whether to expand but how.

(4)

AS WILLIAM APPLEMAN WILLIAMS and his students have shown, foreign expansion, the Open Door, control of foreign resources, and the drive for new markets have been primary concerns of American businessmen, labor leaders, and farmers throughout the last century.* The IBM slogan "World Peace through World Trade" or, as Harry Truman put it, "peace, freedom, and world trade—are inseparable" is an important continuing theme of American history. In the postwar era, however, because of the high productivity of the American economy and the pre-eminent position of the United States in the world economy, corporations have been under special pressures to expand by acquiring foreign assets, foreign raw materials, and foreign markets.

James O'Connor has shown how economic prosperity in the United States since World War II has increasingly depended on overseas expansion:

> Between 1950 and 1964, United States commodity exports, including the sales of overseas facilities of United States corporations, rose nearly 270 per cent, while commodity sales at home increased only 125 per cent. Expectedly, earnings on foreign investments make up a rising portion of after-tax corporate profits —ten per cent in 1950, and 22 per cent in 1964. In the strategic capital goods sector of the United States economy, military and foreign purchases account for a surprisingly large share of total output—between 20 and 50 per cent in twenty-one of twenty-five industries, and over 80 per cent in two industries.†

In 1946 direct foreign investments totalled $7.2 billion, slightly less than in 1929. In the next four years the total foreign investment increased by more than 50 per cent. Within ten years the total tripled. Today the total value of U.S. corporate assets overseas is in excess of $70 billion.

Raymond Vernon has shown that the most powerful corporate units

---

* For an extended discussion of these concerns, see William A. Williams, *The Tragedy of American Diplomacy* (New York: World Publishing Co., 1962) and *The Roots of the Modern American Empire* (New York: Random House, 1969).

† James O'Connor, "The Meaning of Economic Imperialism," in K. T. Fann and Donald Hodges, eds., *Readings in U.S. Imperialism* (Boston: Porter Sargent, 1971), p. 48.

now depend increasingly upon their overseas operations.* As *American Banker* noted in 1970, banks are now under intense competitive pressure to expand their international operations. The Mellon National Bank began to operate in Latin America because "huge banks from New York, California, and Chicago were taking advantage of their international expertise to obtain larger shares of the domestic business of Mellon's traditional customers."

A report of McKinsey and Company, a firm of business consultants, published for corporate executives in 1962, summarized the spectacular growth of U.S. foreign investment in the 1950's and what it meant for those companies who participated in it. By 1960 one out of seven of the one hundred largest U.S. companies obtained more than 40 per cent of its total profit from foreign activities. Eighty of the largest corporations reported foreign profits 30 per cent higher than domestic profits. "The feeling grows," *U.S. News & World Report* noted in a 1964 survey, that the U.S. market, while huge, is relatively "saturated." An official of the Colgate-Palmolive Company, which had indeed been saved from serious difficulties at home by its foreign profits, burbled at the thought of the "millions of people each year who reach the stage in their cultural, social, and economic development where they buy soap, toothpaste, and other things we sell." Most of the corporate executives interviewed by *U.S. News* attributed the high rate of profit for overseas operations to low wages and light competition.

Because limitless economic expansion abroad is essential for the maintenance of liberty and prosperity at home, government, according to the business creed, has a duty to promote a favorable business climate throughout the world. Other countries, particularly poor countries with a shortage of capital, have a "responsibility" to develop a "climate" that will attract private investment; the United States government has the responsibility to persuade them to meet this responsibility.

"The promotion of such a favorable 'climate' for international investment and foreign operations is a legitimate function of government," W. R. Herod, President of the International General Electric Company, told the National Foreign Trade Convention in 1949, "through such grants as may be made on the one hand and through withholding on the other. . . ." † Speaking before the Miami Beach

* In his study *Sovereignty at Bay: The Multinational Spread of U.S. Enterprises* (New York: Basic Books, 1971), Vernon finds that after-tax earnings of 187 multinational corporations for 1964 were 7.2 per cent of sales. The comparable figure for the top U.S. corporations without extensive foreign operations was 5.9 per cent. For U.S. manufacturing enterprises not on *Fortune*'s list of the 500 leading corporations the figure was 3.1 per cent.

† Paterson, *op cit.* A collection of similar statements by business leaders can be found in Oliver Cox, *Capitalism as a System* (New York: Monthly Review Press, 1970).

chapter of the Committee of One Hundred four years later, the Executive Vice-President of the Ford Motor Company, Ernest R. Breech, defined what he meant by a bad "climate":

> There is . . . a spirit of indifference and even outright hostility in some countries towards American investments and the efforts of our people to see that those investments are managed properly. We have already seen a growing tendency in some nations to nationalize private property, foreign owned as well as locally owned. The give us your money and know-how, but keep your hands off attitude is one of the most serious bars to further American investment abroad.

According to the business creed, it is the job of the United States government to use the full panoply of instruments at its command to maintain a congenial climate in foreign countries for American economic expansion. In the 1960's businessmen were enthusiastic supporters of interventionist techniques developed by the Kennedy and Johnson Administrations. Military aid would build up a stable professional military, the only class in many countries capable of marshaling entrepreneurial skills and energy and of applying technology to public problems. Counterinsurgency teams, Green Berets, and police advisers would crush or contain revolutionary forces and thus provide "stability" necessary for properly managed growth. Economic aid would be used to build up a middle class that would welcome partnership with American industry. Loans and grants would also go to construct "infrastructure"—roads, airfields, harbors, schools, and other institutions necessary to support large-scale corporate activities in primitive economies. Educational reform and more explicit U.S. government propaganda and "information" activities would be used to awaken local interest in the good things of life, specifically American wants and American products. For national security bureaucrats, managing a local economy, experimenting with its educational program or agriculture, or playing *éminence grise* in its local politics was a source of excitement and satisfaction and the building of official American influence was an end in itself. But to businessmen who followed their activities closely these men were promoting more than their own bureaucracies. They were missionaries for the American way. In recent years, businessmen have begun to have second thoughts about the utility of both heavy-handed military intervention and the emphasis on using aid to bring about "stabilizing" political and social reforms, a policy that had a brief vogue in the Kennedy era. Now they are pushing for U.S. government financing of "infrastructure," i.e., the construction of highways, ports, and other facilities which U.S. companies need for manufacturing, marketing, and exploitation of raw materials.

Like the operational code of the national security managers, the business creed has its built-in absolution systems. The managers of major corporations are aware that the American corporation in many parts of the world has the image of marauder and exploiter. Some will acknowledge that in the past outrageously favorable concessions have been negotiated, mines have been raped, and cheap native labor exploited, but that day, they insist, is over. Just as the "professional" manager in the United States has "a responsibility to society as a whole," as *Fortune* puts it, so the enlightened corporate venturer abroad must justify the high profits he earns abroad in social and even moral terms. (By definition corporations do not take the risks or go to the inconvenience of establishing operations abroad unless they do expect higher profits or some other economic advantage, such as patents, or access to raw materials, that would not be available in the domestic economy.) In setting criteria and in evaluating their own performance, corporate managers and their advisers demonstrate some of the same capacity for endless self-deception that we saw in the national security bureaucracy.

How the absolution system of the corporate managers works is most obvious in relation to poor countries. True, the galloping acquisition process in Western Europe, much of it facilitated in the beginning by U.S. government financing, foreign aid, and favorable tax laws, was often publicly explained as "spreading technology," "stimulating local economies," and "building the Atlantic Community" rather than crushing competition, cornering markets, tariff hopping, or other traditional business objectives. But such negotiations among corporations in advanced industrial countries did not raise the issues of exploitation that are obvious when huge American corporations invest in small poor countries. Why they are obvious has been explained by Herbert Salzman, Assistant Administrator for Private Resources for the Agency for International Development:

Alongside this picture of rapidly-growing, diversified, international giant companies who have access to the world market, we must now place the picture of emergent, sometimes newly-independent, national states. If we rank together gross national product of nation states and gross annual sales of the large corporations, 13 of the largest are private companies. Of the 100 largest, half are private companies, and two-thirds of the private companies are American.

Nigeria is 39th after General Motors, Ford, Jersey Standard, Royal Dutch Shell, General Electric, Chrysler, Unilever, Mobil Oil—
Algeria is 61st after Western Electric and Bethlehem Steel—

Morocco is 64th after International Harvester and Westinghouse—
Ghana is 78th after National Dairy and Union Carbide—and
there are no other African countries in the first 100.*

(5)

IT IS THEREFORE essential to the business creed to show how a business bargain between two such unequal partners could possibly benefit the weaker party, particularly when American corporations, unlike
the government, do not even claim to have philanthropic functions
overseas. This miracle is accomplished by proclaiming an identity of
interests on two levels. The first is the comfortable assumption that
there is no conflict between the expansion of American power and
American consumption and the interests of the global poor. The second flows from the first: there is no conflict between the interest of a
particular corporation seeking economic opportunities abroad and
the national interest. Indeed, for all practical purposes, they are the
same.

In order for poor countries to become rich ones, the exponent of
the business creed argues, they must cultivate two important social
characteristics: efficiency and stability. Efficiency is making the most
of scarce resources. This can be done only through educating an
entrepreneurial class in efficient techniques and in the interim relying
on foreign technical advice. The economy can grow efficiently only
if a country develops a strong technocratic infrastructure to service
it. This means supporting a rising entrepreneurial class where it exists,
or relying on the army where it does not. Since private enterprise is
the system that best stimulates entrepreneurship, socialism and government planning of the economy should, wherever possible, be discouraged. Reforms should be administered from the top to prevent
revolutionary violence from bubbling up from the bottom.

Thus efficiency can lead to a stable nonrevolutionary social structure, which is a precondition for economic progress and political
democracy. Stability, the corporate managers properly point out, is
not stagnation. It is orderly, controlled growth. The exponents of the
business creed mark their own performance in the poor countries by
comparing "growth rates" or monitoring the Gross National Product.
GNP is like an economic body count. It measures with about the
same accuracy things that are lying around to be measured and thus
leaves out of account most of reality. Thus Brazil, now in the hands

* From a speech quoted in "International Dependency in the 1970's," by
the African Research Group, February 1970, p. 60.

of torturers, has shown a modest economic growth in the last few years and an impressive ability to control inflation, but these statistics, celebrated though they are by foreign investors and national security managers alike, fail to inform the unsuspecting that over half the country is so poor as to be outside the money economy.

Because corporations do good in the process of doing well, corporate managers argue that they are essential instruments of American foreign policy. They tell the American story, replenish the reservoir of good will, and constitute a "presence" which keeps potentially unfriendly countries on the American side. An oil company "study," *Foreign Oil and the Free World,* celebrates the "foreign service oilmen who as unsung ambassadors of goodwill serve their country and the Free World as they serve their companies." In Latin America it has been traditional for copper and oil companies to proclaim themselves as the embodiment of the national interest, much as General Motors President Charles E. Wilson once proclaimed that what was good for America was good for General Motors, and vice versa. Like old-fashioned nineteenth-century imperialists, some U.S. investors, particularly in Latin America, still expect to be rescued by the State Department or the Marines. Why the power of the state should necessarily be committed to save rugged individualists who gamble for high stakes in foreign countries and lose (often after expatriating two generations of extraordinary profits) is not self-evident as a matter of logic. Yet until recent years when the rise of nationalism began to complicate the task of protecting the foreign investment of American corporations with traditional strong-arm methods, the intervention of the State Department, in response to the righteous wrath of wounded corporations, was politically ordained. Because the corporation promoted the myth that it represented the flag, it could commit public resources to protect private wealth.

(6)

To WHAT EXTENT is the American business creed actually translated into foreign policy? In his study *Imperialism,* Joseph Schumpeter argues that there is but one way to understand the phenomenon of expansionism in a society. It is to undertake the "scrutiny of domestic class interests, the question of who stood to gain." We have reviewed what business has had to gain from the continuing national security crisis and from the promotion of expansionist economic policies and have explored the ideology by which a business-oriented foreign policy can be justified. Now we need to ask how responsive has the national security bureaucracy been to the requirements of business.

The foreign policy most obviously designed to serve the interests of American business is development policy. The Marshall Plan, which began the postwar aid program and under which 95 per cent of all aid was extended in early postwar years, had two complementary aims. The political objective was to strengthen the stability of noncommunist centrist, pro-American regimes in Western Europe, then under strong domestic communist challenge. The economic objective was to restore Europe as quickly as possible as the prime market for American goods.* "The loss of European markets would cause serious and painful readjustments in our own country," State Department Counselor Benjamin V. Cohen argued in support of the Marshall Plan. The Council of Economic Advisers, taking note of the fact that roughly one-third of all U.S. exports went to the West European market, warned:

> Without new foreign aid, Europe is threatened with starvation and disease; lack of raw materials and equipment impede further recoveries in agricultural and industrial production. Moreover, Europe would be forced into an entirely different character of production and a reorientation of trade. European resources would have to be organized in such a manner that all but the most essential imports from the Western Hemisphere were dispensed with. This would have a detrimental influence on a number of our important industries which have been accustomed to considerable exports to Europe.

Without a substantial new foreign aid program, the Council concluded, U.S. exports would drop by almost one-third.

The managers of leading American corporations enthusiastically supported the aid program from the start. The Committee for the Marshall Plan, organized by the State Department, included Philip Reed of General Electric, Alfred Sloan of General Motors, Charles Merrill of Merrill Lynch, Allen Dulles of Sullivan Cromwell, Thomas Lamont of J. P. Morgan, and Winthrop Aldrich of the Chase Bank. "What would happen to our farmers, our cotton growers, our manufacturers or to our productive capacity," the Committee asked, if the government did not step in to serve the European markets?

The Marshall Plan was presented to Congress and to the pub-

---

* The Marshall Plan is a good illustration of both compatibility and conflict in economic and political policy formation. According to Raymond Vernon, "during the Marshall Plan years the United States made strenuous official and private efforts to reinvigorate European industry." Although such policy was primarily dictated by the desire to strengthen the European economy to withstand communist subversion and to build a trading partner, the growth of European industry was of course a potential threat to U.S. exporters. But the risk was not seriously considered in the State Department when the Marshall Plan was being developed.

lic as a measure to strengthen the American economy in general, but it was also a pork barrel at which many special economic interests were invited to feed. Professor Thomas Paterson has listed some of the special interests served by the Marshall Plan:

> Flour millers secured a provision that twenty-five percent of the total wheat or wheat products sent to Europe under the ERP had to be in the form of flour, milled, of course, in the United States. American products declared in surplus by the Secretary of Agriculture were to be procured by the participating countries only in the United States. The freight forwarders obtained a statement in the act that insured them that private channels of trade would be used, and the oil interests secured a provision that petroleum products be purchased as much as possible from sources outside the United States. Shipping interests, backed by the Congress of Industrial Organization Maritime Committee, obtained a provision that later rankled Europeans. Fifty percent of ECA goods (gross tonnage) were to be shipped in American bottoms.*

When the focus of the aid program shifted in the late 1950's to the poor countries of Asia, Africa, and Latin America, its crucial U.S.-business-serving purpose became even clearer. By coordinating its aid program, commodity policy, tariff schedules, and international trade policy, the U.S. government has been able to use its power to secure extraordinary economic advantages for American corporations. The P.L. 480 program, subtitled "an act to increase the consumption of United States agricultural commodities in foreign countries, to improve the foreign relations of the United States, and for other purposes," has enabled the government to market U.S. farm surpluses and ease the balance of payments problems at the same time. (Money generated abroad is used to pay embassy and other official costs, thus saving the outlay of dollars.) It has been used, as the 1970 annual report makes clear, for "expansion of dollar sales" which owe much "to aggressive world-wide development efforts initiated under P.L. 480." During the period from 1955 to 1959, as Michael Hudson has calculated, government export programs financed 29 per cent of the total U.S. farm exports.† (About 42 per cent of U.S. aid in recent years has been directly related to the financing of exports.) The secondary benefits to U.S. corporations of the aid policy are enormous. The introduction of high-technology agriculture in poor countries causes such countries to be dependent upon U.S. companies for

---

* Paterson, *op. cit.*

† Michael Hudson and Denis Goulet, *The Myth of Aid* (New York: IDOL North America, 1971), prepared by the Center for Study and Development of Social Change, p. 86.

machines, parts, and technical assistance. We have already mentioned the importance of government-financed infrastructure—chiefly roads and communications—in facilitating further U.S. private investment.

At the same time United States policy is designed to protect American firms from foreign competition, including the competition of the poor countries themselves. Indeed, as the development economist Harry Johnson has written, U.S. policies such as "price supports, restriction of market access, subsidized export of agricultural surplus, and heavy taxation of imports . . . are directly harmful in various ways to the competing exports of less developed countries." * At the 1964 United Nations Conference on Trade and Development, the United States voted "no" to virtually every proposal of poor countries to improve their relative economic position vis-à-vis the rich nations. Various provisions of American law and economic policy discourage the accumulation of local capital in poor countries. The U.S. market is barred to many products of poor countries because of high tariffs and quotas. But the United States opposes similar efforts by poor countries to use protectionist measures to build up their own "infant industries" and to save foreign exchange. The United States has been largely unsympathetic to commodity agreements or compensatory financing such as the prefinancing of buffer stocks. Instead, it has stockpiled raw materials and used its economic power to control world markets to the disadvantage of raw-material-producing countries.

United States officials make no secret of the fact that aid is a way of increasing the power of the American state and the wealth of American business by writing a single check. Since the days of the Truman Doctrine and the Marshall Plan, which Secretary of Defense Forrestal defended as "hard and selfish" policies, the national security managers have been enlisting the support of their colleagues in business by appealing to their self-interest. So important has foreign aid been to the "internationalist" outlook of the postwar corporate executive that Senator Robert A. Taft lost considerable support in the business community in his 1952 bid for the Presidency because he refused to pledge himself to continue the aid program at the then current levels.

In an effort to fend off the attacks of unsophisticated conservatives who, confused by the philanthropic rhetoric associated with the aid program, denounce it as a "giveaway," government officials took pains to point out to the business community that aid is really protection for foreign business operations. Assistant Secretary of Commerce Andrew F. Brimmer reminded a group of businessmen in

* Harry G. Johnson, *Economic Policies Toward Less Developed Countries* (Washington, D.C.: Brookings Institution, 1967), p. 28.

1965 that "if these aid programs were discontinued, private investments might be a waste, because it would not be safe enough for
you to make them." President Kennedy liked to point out to U.S.
businessmen how "an early exposure to American goods, skills, and
American ways of doing things" can play an important role in "forming the tastes and desires of newly emerging countries" so that "even
when our aid ends, the desire and need for products continue. . . ." *

American law restricts the aid program in a number of ways that
have no purpose other than to provide immediate benefit to American
corporations, for they increase costs to the poor countries without
offering them any commensurate advantages. Except in exceptional
circumstances, it has been a requirement of American law that
American aid shipments be carried in American bottoms, purchases
be made in the United States, and American branch-banking be
used for financing.† This has meant, as former AID Director William
Gaud explained it, that in 1968, for example, 93 per cent of AID
funds were spent directly in the United States, benefiting about four
thousand firms in all fifty states. Such subsidies from AID funds
play an important part in certain key industries. In 1961, for example, 39 per cent of ocean freight shipped abroad under the U.S.
flag came from AID shipments.‡ But because of such provisions, as
the White House–sponsored Peterson Report points out, U.S. aid
costs recipients on the average about 15 per cent more than world
market prices.

(7)

THESE, THEN, are a few of the ways in which the power of the government is used to promote foreign investment and exports for the
benefit of American industry. The same power is also used to protect American assets abroad once they are acquired. This protection
is accomplished in many ways. Under the Hickenlooper Amendment
the President is forbidden to send foreign aid to any country that
nationalizes U.S. property without paying what the companies and
the State Department consider adequate compensation. (In 1962
this provision was invoked against Honduras, which had passed a
land-reform program involving expropriation of United Fruit properties, and against Ceylon when the Ceylonese nationalized sixty-three
gas stations belonging to Esso Standard and Caltex Ceylon.)

* Both the Brimmer and the Kennedy remarks appear in Harry Magdoff,
The Age of Imperialism (New York: Monthly Review Press, 1969), pp. 133
and 135.
† "U.S. Foreign Assistance in the 1970's: A New Approach" (The Peter-
son Report, Washington, D.C., March 4, 1970), especially pp. 31 ff.
‡ Hudson and Goulet, *op. cit.,* p. 93.

The State Department has other weapons short of cutting off all aid. It can regulate the flow of benefits in accordance with the recipient country's attitude toward American investment. Governments that pursued nationalist economic policies considered inconsistent with a good investment climate, such as the Goulart government in Brazil or the Bosch government in the Dominican Republic, found their aid reduced to a trickle. When they were overthrown and replaced by less independent governments that made a policy of attracting U.S. private investment, the flow of AID funds increased dramatically. By the same token, the orderly transfer of power in Chile from the pro-American Eduardo Frei to the Marxist Salvador Allende was accompanied by a steep decline in U.S. aid in anticipation that the new government would expropriate the U.S. copper mines (which it did).

The use of American military power to protect threatened American investments abroad was standard practice in the days of "dollar diplomacy." In 1869 the President of the Dominican Republic signed an annexation treaty aboard a U.S. gunboat selling his whole country for $150,000 in cash and guns.* In the first three decades of this century Central America was almost a second home for the U.S. Marine Corps, so frequent were their debt collection and police duties there. In the postwar era the use of military power has been much more subtle. Military assistance funds are largely subsidies for an officer class and are justified as such before Congressional committees. In most poor countries the officer class supports traditional oligarchies that are not disposed to make trouble for American investors. Increasingly, however, the officer corps in underdeveloped countries sees itself as a modernizing force and is seizing power. During the 1960's the new military were favorite recipients of U.S. aid because they were firm believers in the business creed and welcomed American capital and technology. It is true that in recent years a new generation of military officer, in Peru for example, is proclaiming nationalist policies, including some expropriation. But in most of the world military dictatorships—Greece, Brazil, Indonesia—find American private investment and military assistance crucial to their rule. (I was once asked at a dinner party by the Indonesian military attaché shortly after Sukarno was overthrown whether I would like to invest in an electronics firm in Jakarta in which he was interested. Since there could not have been a more unlikely prospect, I assume that he put the same proposition to anyone he encountered.)

The granting of military aid is often a more effective instrument of control than the withholding of economic aid. Typically, because

* Richard J. Barnet, *Intervention and Revolution* (New York: David McKay and Co., 1969), p. 153.

of their failure to solve the basic economic problems—lack of capital, inflation, mass misery—the leaders of poor countries can maintain their own power only by military rule. "Counterinsurgency support" has been an effective instrument for persuading such governments not to try to solve their economic problems by wringing more money out of American firms, for they know that without American military aid they are vulnerable to the revolutionary forces in their society. Thus, a beleaguered government such as that of Guatemala, which has been under attack by local guerrillas for years, will take a benign attitude toward American corporations as long as the United States is willing to lend it money for police cars, bullet-proof vests, and similar items, which make up a major share of the aid program.

The one throwback in the postwar years to the era of gunboat diplomacy in Latin America was the CIA operation in Guatemala in 1954.* It all began in March 1953, when Jacobo Arbenz, the leftist President of Guatemala, expropriated 234,000 uncultivated acres belonging to the United Fruit Company. The State Department, at the time headed by John Foster Dulles, intervened to suggest that the compensation demanded by the company, $15,854,849, was precisely the amount required under international law. When Arbenz refused, the CIA trained an army of exiles and mercenaries, sent them to Guatemala, and bombed the capital city. The President went into exile and was replaced with someone who lost no time in giving United Fruit back the land. David Tobis summarizes some of the favorable development for U.S. investors that has occurred since the Dulles brothers converged on the little banana republic:

> There are no transfer restrictions of any kind on foreign owned assets, dividends and interest. There is no fixed amount of profit which must be reinvested in industry. The industrial laws of 1952, which gave preferential treatment to domestic capital over foreign capital, were repealed in 1959. Today new foreign industries are exempt for ten years from payment of duties on imports of construction materials, factory machinery and equipment, raw materials, and automotive vehicles for industrial use. These industries receive exemption from payment of taxes for the following five years.†

Other services rendered to U.S. investors with tax dollars include loans and guarantees. If an investor is willing to finance an industrial operation in a "less developed country" which will promise not to

---

* For a more detailed description of the CIA operations in Guatemala, see Barnet, *Intervention and Revolution*, Chapter 10.

† "Foreign Aid: The Case of Guatemala," in K. T. Fann and Donald Hodges, eds., *Readings in U.S. Imperialism* (Boston: Porter Sargent, 1971), p. 250.

produce goods in competition with U.S.-produced exports or will actually increase the flow of such exports, he can get a loan from the Agency for International Development. AID will also, according to its brochure *Foreign Aid through Private Initiative,* "finance up to fifty percent of the cost of pre-investment surveys undertaken by United States investors." The United States also provides investment guarantees for United States corporations abroad, which, according to the same brochure, amount to more than $2 billion. These investment guarantees have a significance beyond their insurance function. The United States as insurer takes over the corporation's claim for the expropriated properties once it has paid the corporation for its loss. This means that the host government faces the most powerful plaintiff in the world.

The Nixon Administration established the Overseas Private Investment Corporation to handle insurance for American corporations who venture abroad. These insurance programs have limited use. Most corporations prefer to be their own insurers because they judge the risks to be minimal. On the other hand, large-scale expropriations such as the nationalization of the Chilean copper mines quickly exceed the assets appropriated for compensation. But the programs are an important symbol of the crucial significance of overseas business expansion in American foreign policy. It is noteworthy that no similar insurance programs exist to persuade business to accept the risks of moving to or remaining in the ghetto which the center of virtually every large city in America has become.

The most common sort of protection afforded American investors abroad is diplomatic negotiation. The relationship between the United States and a foreign government can be completely colored by the attempt of the State Department to protect specific American corporate interests. Thus the swift deterioration in United States relations with Cuba was a direct outgrowth of the expropriation of American sugar interests. The unsuccessful attempt by the State Department to save American corporate assets in Eastern Europe was hardly responsible for the Cold War, but the zealous advocacy by American diplomats of the interests of TWA, Standard Oil, American Telephone and Telegraph, IBM, and Anaconda in Eastern Europe did nothing to improve relations with the Soviet Union. It also, as it turned out, did nothing for the companies either. In the attempt to save U.S. corporate interests, the U.S. government exerted strong pressures of various kinds on the Soviet Union and the governments of Eastern Europe, but the efforts largely failed. The total U.S. investment in Eastern Europe amounted to about $500 million.

The American ambassador to Czechoslovakia, Lawrence Steinhardt, promised a Standard Oil executive that Russia would get no loan until ESSO properties were returned. When Hungary refused to grant TWA air rights in Budapest in 1947 the U.S. retaliated by barring Hungarian planes from the U.S. zone in Germany. These efforts added fuel to the growing conflict with the Soviet Union, but they did not accomplish their objective. Nor did the attempt to obtain a payment of $25 million for ESSO properties in Hungary succeed. The Hungarians originally offered to pay twice the original investment but in response to State Department pressure ended up paying nothing. (The British government, incidentally, which generally took a softer line, achieved much better results for its investors.)*

(8)

IT IS HARDLY surprising that the national interest should conveniently coincide with the interests of the large corporations in the area of foreign economic policy. It has been a fundamental tenet of the business creed that the economy as a whole grows if business expands, that such expansion depends critically upon the exploitation of opportunities overseas, and that, therefore, all Americans benefit if the path to overseas expansion for the corporate giants is smoothed by the state. Thus who else should be the principal beneficiaries of trade, investment, tariff, and monetary policies?

But what about the great issues of war and peace? Standing firm in Berlin. Rearming Germany. Intervention in the Greek Civil War. High levels of defense spending. Vietnam. To what extent are these also a reflection of the business creed? Is there an economic dimension to national security decisions and what is it?

It should be said at the outset that none of these decisions is exclusively determined by economic factors. As we saw in Part I major decisions are the products of bureaucratic coalitions. It is impossible to ascribe them to any single cause and the attempt is often ludicrous. Thus many people in the effort to make sense out of the seemingly irrational persistence of the United States in Vietnam fastened on oil or minerals as *the* answer. When it was discovered that oil companies were investing heavily in exploration in South Vietnam some of the outrage was mingled with relief at finding a hard-headed explanation for the adventure. But there is no evidence that the expectation of finding oil lured the Americans to South Vietnam in the first place and not much to suggest that it is oil that is keeping them there. President Eisenhower once explained the American commitment to Vietnam by stressing the importance of minerals, but his testimony is of questionable historical weight

* Paterson, *op. cit.*

because he seemed to have only the haziest idea of what was there. This is not to say that U.S. officials have not been heavily influenced by the present and potential value of raw materials in Southeast Asia, Latin America, and parts of Africa where the U.S. has intervened militarily, for, as we shall see, the national security managers frequently justify such penetration to each other in precisely these terms. The "dominoes theory" reflects a profound fear of economic loss. But the desire to control global political and economic development in the world transcends economics. Leaders as well as citizens often try to make the irrational rational by emphasizing dollars-and-cents reasons when the real decisions may be made for such costly uneconomic reasons as glory, honor, fear, or the sheer fun of winning.

Indeed, the distinction between economic and noneconomic reasons for going to war has become blurred in the nuclear age. In former times academic quibbles about "strategic" versus "economic" motivations made a certain amount of sense. In the past a nation could pursue physical safety by acquiring strategic territory. In some cases the acquisition would also add to the material wealth of the empire but in others the costs of maintaining strategic outposts far outweighed any indirect commercial advantages that might be associated with it. In the nuclear age territorial expansion does not promote national security because no matter where the United States deploys its forces around the world, it is still powerless to prevent another major nuclear power from incinerating forty to sixty per cent of the U.S. population. Whether Vietnam is united or divided, communist or noncommunist, whether Guatemala, Iran, Indonesia, Greece, or the Congo have governments which encourage their people to drink Coca-Cola or to burn USIA libraries has nothing to do with the physical safety of the United States. In the prenuclear age the nation that commanded strategic geographical positions had an added measure of safety, but the revolution in warfare has made relics of those prized bits of terrain that generals traditionally covet. (They still covet them, to be sure, for famous military bases build military morale. By the same token, the Navy insists upon keeping a five-ocean navy afloat and a string of bases to service them because of a self-serving, but totally implausible, belief that the next war will be like the last one.) As the control of real estate has declined in importance as a means of promoting physical security, economic factors have achieved greater significance. The United States won World War II primarily through the mobilization of technological and industrial power. The increasing economic interdependence of the globe and the increasing dependence of military machines on high technology and scarce mineral resources mean that national security is more than ever dependent upon the state of the economy. Such economic considerations were instrumental in reversing previous politico-military decisions in the case of U.S. policy on German industry immediately after World War II. In 1944 Henry Morgenthau had proposed a plan for "converting Germany into a country primarily agricultural and pastoral in character." Although the plan was opposed from the start by businessmen on loan serving as national security managers, it was accepted in broad outline by political leaders and by the military themselves as fitting retribution for a monstrous enemy. When the Joint Chiefs of Staff were put in charge of the political and economic administration of Germany, their orders reflected Morgenthau's thinking. The American Supreme Commander in Germany was directed to proceed with denazification, disarmament, and decartelization. The Potsdam agreements between the Western Allies and the Soviet Union provided for the elimination of Germany's war potential, decentralization of the economy, and a drastic reduction of heavy industry.

However, General Lucius Clay, the U.S. Commander, soon dragged his feet in implementing these policies. The business community in the United States was strongly opposed to the dismantling of German industry. Alfred P. Sloan, the Chairman of the Board of General Motors, which had had considerable business in Germany before the war, wrote that this country was the "spark plug or motivating center of the whole European economy" and that de-industrialization would seriously hurt the U.S. economy. Clay believed that those pushing for decartelization were well-intentioned "extremists" and he and Eisenhower interpreted the decartelization and dismantling orders accordingly. By late 1946 political arguments stemming from the Cold War could be added to the economic arguments for building up Germany instead of tearing her down, and a few months later John Foster Dulles (who represented a number of German interests) declared in the Senate that the U.S. "should not [feel] bound in any way to the commitments of Potsdam and the so-called level-of-industry agreements that were reached in Berlin." *

The Truman Doctrine, which set the pattern for future interventions in civil wars and revolutions, was primarily a show of political power designed to contain the spread of Russian influence in the Mediterranean and to demonstrate that despite the consolidation of Stalin's empire in Eastern Europe, communism was not the wave of the future in the rest of the continent. But in developing bureaucratic support for the unprecedented open-ended commitment by the United States, in President Truman's words, "to support free peoples who are resisting attempted subjugation by armed minorities or by outside pressures," economic considerations played an important

* Patterson, *op. cit.*

role. Secretary of Defense Forrestal outlined in a letter to Paul C. Smith of the San Francisco *Chronicle* why he believed the intervention to be vital to the American economy. Seventy-three per cent of America's imports, he said, consisted of vital raw materials and over half of these essential products came from areas under the control of the British Empire. "These raw materials have to come over the sea and a good many have to go through the Mediterranean. That is *one* reason why the Mediterranean must remain a free highway." On the telephone the next day with Paul Shields the Secretary developed this line of thinking further:

FORRESTAL: What we are talking is raw materials and we haven't got them.

SHIELDS: Of course you're talking real stuff when you talk that.

FORRESTAL: . . . not only for war but for peace we haven't got the basic stuff.

SHIELDS: It is a question of the survival of our economy through procuring materials in those countries. . . .

FORRESTAL: That is the only thing that makes any impression on me at all.

Another Truman Administration official who stressed economic arguments for the intervention in Greece was Clark Clifford, the Counsel to the President. One week before the President delivered his message, Clifford drafted the following paragraph for inclusion in the speech:

If by default, we permit free enterprise to disappear in the other nations of the world, the very existence of our own economy and our own democracy will be gravely threatened. . . . This is an area of great natural resources which must be accessible to all nations and must not be under the exclusive control or domination of any single nation. The weakening of Turkey, or the further weakening of Greece, would invite such control.

Acheson took exception to it because it exaggerated, he thought, the economic arguments. The United States was on stronger ground, he sensed, if it talked about freedom rather than free enterprise. "Using General Marshall's great prestige," Acheson recalls in his memoirs, "I got Clark to withdraw his additions and recommend the message as the General had approved it." *

Also cut from the final draft was an explicit reference to the oil deposits of the Middle East, but these were by no means ignored by the men who planned the Truman Doctrine. By 1947 Standard Oil

* Dean Acheson, *Present at the Creation: My Years in the State Department* (New York: W. W. Norton, 1969), p. 221.

and Texas owned a joint concession covering two-thirds of Saudi Arabia and Bahrein Island. Standard Oil and Socony owned a 24-per-cent interest in a concession which covered all of Iraq and was valued, according to the *State Department Bulletin,* at 6 billion barrels. Gulf's concession in Kuwait was estimated at 4.5 billion barrels. The strategic importance of these oil deposits as well as mineral deposits in Greece itself, chiefly bauxite, had not escaped the attention of the business community. *Business Week, Nation's Business,* and the *Wall Street Journal* all carried articles while the Truman Doctrine was being debated within the government, stressing the economic importance of the Middle East and the strategic importance of the Mediterranean in assuring continued American access to the region. The Chief Consulting Engineer of Mines, Inc., which had important holdings in Greece, testified on the Truman Doctrine before the House Foreign Affairs Committee that Greece was a "fortress" controlling the eastern Mediterranean.

(9)

THE MOST IMPORTANT national security policy relates to the level of defense spending; for the size and shape of the budget of the Department of Defense has a profound effect on virtually every issue touching on the foreign relations of the United States. The existence of military capabilities, we have noted, shapes future policies. If military power is available, it tends to be used, if only as a threat. We have seen how military bureaucracies seek to expand as a result of inner dynamism and are largely independent of the external "threat" which is their *raison d'être.* Their vigilance in discovering new threats when old ones wear out is well known. But are there business reasons in addition to these familiar dynamics which account for the extraordinary arms race which until recent years the United States was largely running with itself? (Since the ouster of Khrushchev the Soviet Union for the first time in the postwar era has been engaged in a serious effort to catch up to the United States in nuclear arms.)

Writing in 1913, Rosa Luxemburg argued that nations were driven to militarism—i.e., permanent mobilization and the maintenance of large standing armies—primarily because the military soaked up the surplus generated by capitalist economies which for political reasons could be absorbed in a capitalist society in no other way. Big military budgets are irresistible for capitalist states, she argued, because they cannot maintain prosperity without massive public spending, and military spending, unlike government subsidies for housing, health, and education, does not compete with powerful private interests.* What relevance, if any, does this theory have to the postwar American experience?

The idea that the defense budget could solve instead of complicate America's economic problems grew slowly after World War II. The major corporations, it will be recalled, greeted the Roosevelt Administration's call for mobilization with suspicion at first. They feared that they would be saddled with excess production and did not dream of the extraordinary advantages that huge military procurement contracts could bring them. Even after the war had provided such an obvious stimulus to the economy most industrial managers could not conceive of the military budget playing a remotely analogous role in the peacetime economy. A few, such as General Electric's Charles E. Wilson, talked of building a permanent mobilization capability, "a permanent war economy," to use his famous phrase, but, given the long-standing American tradition against maintaining a big standing army, no one anticipated that military spending would absorb 10 per cent of the Gross National Product year after year for most of the next generation. As the war drew to a close economists worried about what the National Planning Association called the "enormous backlog of idle and underemployed capital," † but the solutions advocated were expanded foreign trade and foreign aid. No one dared to suggest using the military budget as a tool of fiscal management if, indeed, anyone had thought of it.

As soon as the war ended Harry Truman proceeded to cut the defense budget from a peak annual wartime rate of $90.9 billion in the first quarter of 1945 to the all-time postwar low of $10.3 billion in the second quarter of 1947. The steep rise in the military budget after the Korean War provoked sharp debate inside the Administration. "Hard money" advocates in the Truman Cabinet expressed concern that continued high levels of defense spending would produce inflation and would cut into domestic programs. It is true that the Korean rearmament did arrest a business downturn that began in 1948 after the economic stimulus of pent-up consumer demand had begun to wear off somewhat. But there is no evidence that the Truman Cabinet consciously sought to use military spending in this way. Indeed, Korea had been preceded by an economy drive sponsored by a budget-cutting Secretary of Defense.‡ This drive, which had resulted in troops being withdrawn from Korea,

---

* For Rosa Luxemburg's arguments, see her *Accumulation of Capital* (New York: Monthly Review Press, 1964).

† David W. Eakins, "Business Planners and America's Post-War Expansion," in Horowitz, *op. cit.*, p. 156.

‡ Samuel Huntington, *The Common Defense* (New York: Columbia University Press, 1961).

was approved by Acheson and most of the national security managers.

Truman used the Korean War to bring about the permanent world-wide expansion of the military establishment that the national security managers had been urging for more than two years. In the pre-Korea days the military services bitterly fought one another for larger shares of what they thought was an unexpandable pie. It was the civilian national security managers, as Samuel Huntington's studies have shown, who, in the planning document NSC-68, had introduced the idea of the infinitely expandable defense budget. The Truman Administration raised taxes and imposed controls in an effort to balance the budget, for they were worried about the long-term effect of high military spending.

The Eisenhower Administration came in convinced that the competition with the Soviet Union would last a generation and that Soviet strategy in part was to spend the United States into bankruptcy. Therefore, the businessmen who made up the Eisenhower Cabinet reasoned, the defense budget must be kept within limits to preserve the economy. The "new look," with its increased reliance on smaller forces and nuclear weapons, was primarily an attempt, in the words of Secretary of Defense Wilson, to get "more bang for the buck." The Administration also felt the pressure to make modest increases in domestic programs, such as farm support, roads, and urban redevelopment, which were at the same dollar amount in 1955 as they were in 1949, despite six years of population growth and inflation. The Eisenhower Administration under Secretary of the Treasury George Humphrey was committed to balanced budgets and maximum savings in military spending.

Military Keynesianism, the idea that high levels of military spending do not damage the economy but indeed can stimulate it, began to take root among economics professors and liberal politicians during the Eisenhower years. The 20-per-cent reduction in national security expenditures after the Korean War was, according to many economists, a principal cause of the 1953–54 recession. The $2 billion cut in the budget in 1957 contributed to the recession of that year. Outside the Administration a Keynesian consensus was forming. The National Planning Association was arguing that the defense budget could be increased by $22 billion without imposing controls and the Committee on Economic Development announced that defense spending could safely rise to 15 per cent of the Gross National Product. By the end of the Eisenhower Administration some of the nation's leading businessmen, serving as members of the Gaither and Rockefeller panels on national security, called for immediate steep rises in defense expenditures, including $40 billion for blast shelters to keep the whole population safe from atomic attack. The

AFL-CIO was quite candid in calling for increases in defense spending as a way to stimulate the economy and to save jobs. The change in mood was best symbolized by the passing of the old penny-pinching, budget-cutting entrepreneurs such as George Humphrey and the ascendency of the McNamara generation. Men such as George Humphrey treated the money they managed as though it were their own—and, indeed, in the Mark Hanna Company from which he came, it was; but the McNamaras believed that their patriotic duty was to be generous spenders of other people's money.

The Kennedy Administration was committed to military Keynesianism from the start. The Kennedy advisers believed that national security spending had, in Murray Weidenbaum's words, a "catalytic role" in getting the country moving again. It was, in the words of Frank Pace, President of General Dynamics, the leading defense contractor, an economic "stimulus." A dollar spent on the military was as good as any other way to increase the flow of money into the country, to stimulate demand, and no other spending in the public sector was so politically acceptable. Keynes had said that "public works" was the way to fight recession. As Luxemburg had pointed out in 1913, a military public works program which competes with no one and is certified as necessary for the public safety is acceptable to a competitive capitalist society at almost any level, but government housing, government medicine, or any other federal programs that compete with private enterprise, whether it be real estate interests or doctors, are a threat to a capitalist economy.

The Kennedy Administration increased the military budget by $4 billion in a single year. Within the next five years space research and military technical development expenditures climbed about $5 billion. Since then the economy has been addicted to military spending. The government purchases about 10 per cent of the entire output of the steel mills, a crucial subsidy to a stagnant industry unable to meet foreign competition. Thirty-six per cent of the entire output of the durable goods of industry is purchased by the government for military and military-related purposes. Almost 10 per cent of the country's labor force is employed directly or indirectly by the Department of Defense, including substantially over half of the country's engineers and technologists. (The Department of Labor estimates that the escalation of the Vietnam War from mid-1965 to mid-1967 created more than one million jobs, or about one quarter of the increases in job openings during that period.*) Key areas of the country are dependent upon the military economy. Most defense contracts have been concentrated in nine areas: New London-

---

* Richard P. Oliver, "The Employment Effect of Defense Expenditures," *Monthly Labor Review*, September 1967, pp. 9 and 16.

Groton-Norwich, Connecticut; Binghamton, New York; Baltimore, Maryland; Charleston, S.C.; Dallas-Fort Worth, Texas; San Diego, San Jose, and San Francisco-Oakland, California; and Seattle-Tacoma, Washington.* Any substantial cuts in defense spending would seriously disrupt these communities.

The Marxist economist Victor Perlo once calculated that disarmament would help many large corporate units that do not live off the defense budget and would hurt about an equal number.† The interests of big business are not monolithic as far as the level of military spending is concerned. But despite the benefits that would undoubtedly accrue to important segments of the economy if the defense budget were cut, such groups lack both the organized power and the concrete plans to accomplish such a shift in priorities without endangering the economy as a whole. Although a series of government reports and statements assert that reconversion involves no serious problem for the economy, the disastrous local effects of minor military cutbacks in Boston and parts of California show that such reports are more wish than analysis. The stock market, which is not a particularly reliable index of anything, now tends to rise at announcements of military cutbacks and improved prospects of peace whereas in the 1950's it thrived on war scares and new weapons systems, but this means only that investors now sense that the bloated military budget constitutes an economic and political problem. It does not suggest that they or anyone else know what to do about it. Although the image of the Pentagon has become a casualty of the Vietnam War, and it no longer occurs to the White House, as it did in McNamara's day, to sell politically controversial poverty and education programs by having the Department of Defense manage them, the Pentagon retains its key role in the society. Each year it allocates more than $40 billion in the economy and represents a greater concentration of economic decision-making power than any other unit. Despite the increasing awareness of many leading businessmen of the long-term disastrous impact of having more than half the federal budget go year after year to an economically nonproductive military public works program, no consensus has developed in support of an alternative economic policy that would perform the function in the economy now performed by the Department of Defense.

While most corporations that do not directly benefit significantly from the military budget quietly acquiesce in the use of the military

* National Planning Association and the U.S. Arms Control and Disarmament Agency, *Community Information Systems* (Washington, D.C.: Government Printing Office, 1967).

† Victor Perlo, *Militarism and Industry* (New York: International Publishers Co., 1963), p. 124.

budget for economic management, some of the most powerful firms benefit from the defense economy to such an extent that they could not survive without it. A military contractor who derives most of his income from the Pentagon is no longer in the free enterprise economy. Typically, the government picks up a major part of the costs of his plant and capital equipment. He is likely to have the equivalent of substantial interest-free loans in the form of "progress payments." He will have economic "fallout" from military contracts worth millions, such as patents and technical assistance. (Thus Boeing was able to produce the 707 jetliner as a direct outgrowth of its defense-financed development of the KC-135 tanker.) Most important, a long-term government contract permits long-range planning. The contractor can count on continuing support for at least five years from the initial research stage to production in a major contract and can be sure that the government will buy whatever he makes at prices which are subject to continuous upward renegotiation. (This practice results in the "cost overruns" revealed by the Joint Economic Committee, which mean that many weapons systems end up costing many times the original amount Congress was told they would cost.) For these and other reasons, profits on military contracts are on the average substantially higher than those on nonsubsidized production in the free market economy. In short, the military contractor has an enormous competitive advantage. It should be noted that the group of industries which derive such benefits and which depend for their survival on their continuing relationship with the Department of Defense are among the biggest, most powerful, and most technologically advanced units of economic power in the country.

(10)

WE HAVE TRACED the ways in which some of the major national security decisions are made for the benefit of business. It should not surprise us that national security policy in a country that runs on the business creed should be managed by an elite largely recruited from the world of business. (If we looked at the Soviet Union we would find that the foreign policy decisions tended to reinforce the position of the ruling elite in that country, the leadership of the Communist Party.) We have seen that there is a business creed, that it is reflected in foreign policy decisions, but that these decisions are also presumed to serve something called the national interest. We must now ask whether the interests of the corporation and the public interest are in fact the same in the area of national security policy.

We will look at the impact on the country at large of two of the major policies we have been discussing. The first is the policy of economic expansionism—i.e., the collection of programs, diplomatic initiatives, and economic decisions designed to promote expanding foreign investment by United States companies. The second is the policy of military expansionism—i.e., high levels of military spending, continuous military and paramilitary interventions, and permanent war.

In the era of rapid domestic industrial expansion that took place in the United States from the Civil War to the New Deal, it was fair to say that what was good for General Motors was good for America, and vice versa. It was not so good, to be sure, for workers laboring under sweatshop conditions. The cruel social consequences that accompanied the Industrial Revolution everywhere—overcrowding, child labor, the exploitation of men as machines—are part of the history of Western man. But economic growth spearheaded by the expansion of industrial giants did raise general levels of prosperity. The "trickle down" theory which is the essence of the business creed worked, at least to the extent of keeping much of the country in a reasonable state of anticipation that better times lay ahead. In earlier periods it appears that initiatives taken by the government to stimulate foreign trade and investment did have the desired effect by creating more jobs for Americans and putting more money in their pockets with which to buy American goods.

The foreign economic expansion since World War II, however, has followed a different pattern from the prewar expansion, and as a result has had certain consequences which have not been favorable for most Americans or for long-term American prosperity. It has been official policy to promote in various ways the takeover by U.S. firms of foreign corporations, particularly in Western Europe. U.S.-controlled firms in Europe now represent the third most powerful economic unit in the world.* The Common Market, which the United States pushed as a political dream to bring about the unification of Western Europe and as an economic scheme to increase U.S. exports, has encouraged U.S. firms to buy up their European competitors. Safe behind the tariff walls, the U.S.-owned European firm sells to the European and world market, and competes with its parent for a greater share of the American market. The result is a loss of jobs for Americans, as the major labor unions are beginning to point out.

The American firm operating abroad is committed to maximizing profits and other economic advantages. When it shifts operations abroad it feels no more responsibility for maintaining American jobs than it does when it moves from a high-wage Northern city to the South. American corporations with government assistance are making

* See J. J. Servan-Schreiber, *The American Challenge* (New York: Atheneum, 1968).

profits by employing foreigners at lower wages than they would have to pay to American workers. Official policies of economic expansion encourage U.S. corporations to pursue a global "runaway shop" strategy. There is no equivalent government policy for encouraging investment in the vast underdeveloped sectors of the American economy.

The Europeans are particularly annoyed about this development because they have been forced, because of the political strength of the United States, to cooperate in the takeover of their own leading industries. The big outflow of capital to acquire European corporate assets that began in the late 1950's was crucial to the U.S. gold crisis. The U.S. balance of payments deficit was soon running at the rate of $4 billion a year. Just before President Nixon imposed the emergency measures of his new economic policy the annual balance of payments deficit was running at the rate of $22 billion a year. The United States began the postwar era in the strongest economic position of any country in history with a gold surplus in Fort Knox of $24 billion and a world agreement under which other currencies were tied to the dollar and the dollar was tied to gold (most of which the United States owned). By the mid-1960's only about $10 billion was left in Fort Knox. Europeans held some $45 billion of dollar claims (called Eurodollars) primarily useful for buying high-priced American goods they did not want. Appealing to their common interest in preserving the Western alliance and the free world, the United States for many years prevailed upon European governments and central bankers not to demand the transfer of gold which they had a legal right to demand. Thus, Europeans gave up productive assets for claims on the American economy which, because of U.S. inflation, looked less and less attractive.

American corporations could now show dramatic increases in net worth and in profits because of the consolidation of their European and American assets. But the impact on the American economy as a whole was uneven. While the 1.6 per cent of the population (mostly institutions) which owns 80 per cent of corporate securities (according to the 1962 study by Robert Lampman *) earned a staggering return on the European investments, there was a falloff in employment and a further loss of potential jobs when U.S. firms chose to expand their investments in Europe rather than in the United States. Equally important, there was a falloff in exports as the European subsidiaries of U.S. firms took over an increasing share of what had formerly been a U.S. export market. In 1970, the United States had an unfavorable balance of *trade*—for the first time in this century.

The vigorous promotion of expansion abroad had backfired. While

---

* National Bureau of Economic Research Occasional Paper # 71, p. 31.

individual corporations were in some cases saved by their foreign acquisitions—Chrysler in the early 1960's for example—a cycle had started which led to the abandonment of some of the most sacred tenets of the business creed. The emergency gold-flow remedies and import surcharge to which the Nixon Administration had felt driven as a result of the expansionist foreign investment policies of the preceding twenty years meant an end to the supremacy of the dollar and free trade, both long considered vital advantages for the number one nation. According to the business creed, the world's most powerful nation stood to benefit if the market were allowed to operate free of government intervention to the greatest possible extent. But the sheer overpowering economic might of the United States had frightened other nations, particularly Japan, into taking extreme protectionist and isolationist measures. American retaliation threatened to open up a foreign trade war. The specter of cut-throat competition for markets which Lenin insisted was inevitable under capitalism now appeared to be a growing risk.

The policy of encouraging gold flow for military operations abroad has finally forced the United States to abandon the Bretton Woods agreements under which the dollar enjoyed a uniquely favorable position. Floating the dollar (a form of devaluation which undermines the competitive advantage of other currencies) had a depressing effect around the world, and the world market may well shrink in coming years. There is no reason to believe that the United States can maintain its level of prosperity as an island in an economically depressed world any better in the 1970's than it did in the 1930's.

America's economic empire, as the economist John Hobson pointed out with respect to the British Empire seventy years ago, benefits a relatively few investors and managers at the expense of the general population.* If the promotion of jobs and general prosperity were the primary goal, it could be accomplished far more easily and directly by redistributing income and stimulating purchase power in the United States rather than subsidizing wealthy Americans to invest abroad. As the U.S. economy continues to deteriorate we are likely to see the biggest corporate units putting more and more of their assets abroad, all the while invoking the national interest. It may be instructive to recall that before Rome fell those with money had already transferred it to Byzantium.

Americans are now being forced to face some of the questions the British had to face at the height of their empire. The issue is not whether empire pays, as an abstract proposition, but who must pay for it and who derives the benefits. Most of the balance of payments

* J. A. Hobson, *Imperialism: A Study* (London: Allen and Unwin, rev. ed., 1902).

deficit is directly attributable to military and military-related government spending abroad—particularly, since 1965, in connection with the war in Indochina.

Terence McCarthy, noting that by 1968 the war had already resulted in $54 billion in direct military costs, summed up the additional costs of war:

> raised the annual rate of Vietnam War expenditures to $29 billion in calendar 1968;
>
> reduced the purchasing power of the consumer's dollar by almost 9 per cent;
>
> distorted the economy by adding only 1.6 million production workers to manufacturing payrolls compared with 2.3 million to government payrolls;
>
> caused a loss in housing construction of at least 750,000 dwelling units;
>
> raised interest rates to the highest levels in a century;
>
> deepened the poverty of the poor by increasing food prices 10 per cent;
>
> raised the interest bearing federal debt by $23 billion;
>
> produced a $20 billion federal deficit in fiscal 1968 even assuming a tax increase;
>
> rendered impossible required expenditures on renovation of America's decaying cities;
>
> increased the adverse balance of payments insupportably;
>
> cost the nation the gold cover of its dollar;
>
> forced the establishing of a two-tier price for gold throughout the world;
>
> generated the greatest threat of inflation since the Civil War . . .*

The continued high levels of military spending are also directly related to the two principal American economic problems, inflation and insufficient productivity. Inflation, as the economist Samuel Greenhouse explains it, "is caused by investment, which, while enriching the money stream . . . fails to expand the *marketable* goods stream to a comparable extent." † The products procured by the Department of Defense are largely nonproductive and nonmarketable. Guns, tanks, and aircraft cannot produce wealth. Factories that produce them cannot produce marketable goods at the same rate or with the same efficiency as factories not involved in the military

---

* Terence McCarthy, "What the Vietnam War Has Cost," *New University Thought,* Vol. 6, No. 4 (Summer 1968).

† "Our Overheated Economy: A Heretical View of Inflation," *The Washington Monthly,* April 1970, p. 7.

economy. Government subsidies to oligopolistic industries, lax accounting procedures, and lack of incentive to keep costs down drive prices up throughout the economy. The inflationary impact of the Vietnam War has discouraged investment in industrial expansion and modernization. The resulting high interest rates have seriously affected many industries, most notably the construction industry. The most cruel effect has been the decline in real wages of American workers that has occurred each year since the war escalated in 1965. Inflation also eats up savings, pensions, and welfare payments of those on the bottom of society. The economic costs of militarism fall most heavily on the poor, just as the human costs fall most heavily on the young.

But the costs of spending over one and one half trillion dollars on armaments in a generation have been felt by the whole population. The benefits of the massive military budget have gone for the most part to the owners and managers of contracting corporations, high-salaried engineers and scientists, better-than-average-paid bureaucrats, military officers, and those who service them. If one were to imagine the defense budget as a pie, there would be little left after the above groups took their slices. There are few jobs for unskilled workers. While the military budget is crucial to the maintenance of employment levels given the lack of politically acceptable public-works alternatives, it offers no solution to the problem of poverty in the United States. It tends to encourage concentration of economic power, the breakdown of competition, and the continued channeling of money to those who have it rather than to those who don't.

The deterioration in the "quality of life" and the resulting psychological distress are costs of empire which must be balanced against the excitement some derive from being a manager (or a citizen) of the number one nation and the money others make from acting out the business creed. It surely deserves to be considered in determining the national interest. What Seymour Melman has called "our depleted society" * is a direct consequence of our putting our major

---

* Here is part of his inventory of human depletion:
1. By 1968, there were 6 million grossly substandard dwellings, mainly in the cities.
2. Ten million Americans suffered from hunger in 1968–69.
3. The United States ranked eighteenth at last report (1966) among nations in infant mortality rate (23.7 infant deaths per 1,000 live births). In Sweden (1966) the rate was 12.6.
4. In 1967, 40.7 per cent of the young men examined were disqualified for military service (28.5 per cent for medical reasons).
5. In 1950, there were 109 physicians in the United States per 100,000 population. By 1966 there were 98.
6. About 30 million Americans are an economically underdeveloped sector of the society.
The human cost of military priority is paralleled by the industrial-techno-

resources into an economy of death.* The huge investment in the military is the official excuse for the fact that the number one nation lags behind the democracies of Western Europe in providing basic social services to the population. It is the explanation "economy-minded" administrators give for the high infant mortality rate, the destitute condition of old people, the hunger in the rural South, the lack of medical care and housing for poor and middle-income people, low teachers' salaries, and the fact that there is no money to clean up the nation's rivers or its air. A less obvious cost of maintaining the military machine to man the empire is the deterioration of American industry. Our factories can no longer compete in the technologies of peace because the nation's investment has been so heavy in the technologies of war. Money, talent, and energy have gone year after year to support the military while other industrial countries have overtaken the United States in the technology of machine tools, mass transport, and steel production.

The United States steel industry, which is a major supplier of the Department of Defense, cannot compete in civilian markets in part because for years the managements of the great steel companies have felt no compulsion to innovate. Why should they? As Charles B. Baker, administrative vice-president of the United States Steel Corporation, reported to the National Foreign Trade Convention, the government is a steady and none too demanding customer.

> . . . it is largely due to the operation of our foreign aid program that the steel industry has managed to escape the full effects of the forces at work in the world market place. We estimate that AID procurement in the United States of steel mill products currently accounts for some 30 per cent of the value of our steel exports, and for an even higher per cent of the tonnage shipped—perhaps as much as 40 per cent.†

The two major technological advances in the industry of the last generation, the L-D process oxygen furnace and the pelletizing

---

logical depletion caused by the concentration of technical manpower and capital on military technology and in military industry. For example:

1. By 1968, United States industry operated the world's oldest stock of metal-working machinery; 64 per cent was 10 years old and over.
2. No United States railroad has anything in motion that compares with the Japanese and French fast trains.
3. The United States merchant fleet ranks 23rd in age of vessels. In 1966, world average-age of vessels was 17 years, United States 21, Japan 9.
4. While the United States uses the largest number of research scientists and engineers in the world, key United States industries, such as steel and machine tools, are in trouble in domestic markets: in 1967, for the first time, the United States imported more machine tools than it exported.

* Seymour Melman, *Our Depleted Society* (New York: Holt, Rinehart and Winston, 1965).

† Quoted in Magdoff, *op. cit.,* p. 149.

process, have yet to be adopted widely in U.S. plants, despite the fact that they are used routinely in Japan and other countries. The weak competitive position of U.S. industries is of course reflected in wage, employment, and productivity rates which are lower than they would be if proper investment and modernizing practices had been followed. Until now those who bear the cost of this failure are not the managers and stockholders of the large corporations, who can keep profits high by acquiring productive assets abroad at favorable prices, but the workers and customers who must stay in the United States and work for wages that are too low and pay prices that are too high. The lack of public investment in schools, clinics, and mass transport of course primarily affects those without the money for private schools, family physicians, and second cars.

The permanent mobilization of American society has served to obscure such issues, for the problems of fair distribution and conflicting class interests within American society, which were the absorbing issues of the 1930's, have been muted in a patriotic consensus. The crucial question in the Cold War years has concerned production rather than distribution. Productivity has become a national weapon to prevent the Soviet Union from "overtaking" the United States as their May Day slogans threatened.

Class conflict is a subject that always makes the rich uncomfortable and they are understandably delighted when the poor are also willing to pretend that it does not exist. The successful effort to make all challenges to the anticommunist business creed look treasonous deserves some of the credit for the strange disappearance of the issues of fair distribution and concentration of corporate power during most of the postwar period. It was not easy during this period to admit the existence of class conflict without running the risk of being labeled a "crypto" or "creeping" subversive. Business groups devoted considerable resources to blunderbuss attacks on leftists and radicals who raised such issues. Big business, the principal target of the Depression era, became a prime mover in forging a patriotic consensus in which the legitimacy of its own rapidly expanding power was never questioned. The effect has been to eliminate serious economic and social criticism of the basic institutions of American life for two decades and to make the business creed the official standard for defining the national interest.

7

The Government-Business Partnership
in Foreign Affairs

I F THE sustaining myth of American capitalism is the identity of interest between the corporations and the public, the sustaining myth of foreign policy is the identity of interest between government and business. Business statesmen and radical critics alike are fond of repeating Bernard Baruch's dictum about the "essential oneness" of the state's strategic interest and the corporations' financial interests. In this chapter, we shall look more closely at the government-business partnership in foreign affairs.

There is a long tradition that business and government should and do work hand in hand in advancing the national interest. The symbiotic relationship known as "dollar diplomacy" was a happy marriage in which state interests and private interests reinforced one another. Corporations would establish a "presence" in a foreign land which would enhance the influence of the government, and, in some cases, would provide the classic pretext for military intervention by the state. At the same time the government would use its power to open up investment and market opportunities, to collect bills, and to regulate competition. The analysis of how the State Department's view of the national interest and the corporate investor's view of the national interest dovetail has never been stated better than by F. M. Huntington Wilson, Taft's Under Secretary of State, in an article written shortly after his retirement. He listed the criteria for investments which served both interests:

—strengthening American influence in spheres where it ought to predominate over any other foreign influence on account of reasons of fundamental policy, like the Monroe Doctrine, or of military strategy or of neighborhood. Such a sphere is "Latin America." . . . In this category falls also, for example, the discharge of our historic obligation to Liberia (for benefits of commerce and emigration of Negroes) . . .
—the maintenance of a traditional position favorable to our trade where trade may go by political favor, as in the Chinese Empire,
—the strengthening of our friendship with other great powers, (such as the English-speaking peoples),
—with countries where it is wise to preempt a share in a dawning development, like Turkey,
—with countries whose markets are especially valuable,
—foreign investments or enterprises which establish permanent and valuable markets or trade while at the same time subserving political strength where the policy of this country demands that it be strong if we are to have security and tranquillity . . .
—investments or enterprises which have these same purely material advantages while carrying with them some political advantages as well, as, for example, in safeguarding our Chinese trade;
—those investments or enterprises which serve in giving us a commercial standing in some valuable market where development may be preempted by others if a footing not be early obtained (like Turkey);
—in cementing friendship with our natural allies, as Canada and the English-speaking peoples generally;
—in bringing profit and employment to the American people in general.*

If retired diplomats were as candid today, they would write something much in the same vein. Obviously the government in a business society has a duty to advance the interests of American business, abroad as well as at home, and to promote overseas commercial expansion as a means of enhancing the power and prosperity of the American nation. But that being said, many questions arise. What kind of power and influence do corporations have in the making of foreign policy? In the government-business partnership who is the

* Charles A. Beard, *The Idea of the National Interest* (Chicago: Quadrangle Books, 1966), pp. 108–109.

senior partner? In Part I we tried to paint a picture of what goes on in the national security bureaucracy. Some would say that we have merely described the clerks at work and that the real decisions are being made in the board rooms at Jersey Standard or the Chase Manhattan Bank. In the classic Marxist analysis, although the Secretary of State may have an office that looks like Mussolini's and receive a nineteen-gun salute as he travels throughout the empire, he is the servant of corporate power, not its master. We have already indicated how the business creed suffuses the ideology of the national security managers. Nor is there anything in their class background and education that enables them easily to distinguish the interests of business from the national interest.

However, this does not tell us where the power to commit the United States to an invasion, a new weapons system, or a new foreign economic policy really lies. Are the national security managers, who need not check and do not check with anyone before they conclude secret alliances, move fleets, authorize new weapons systems, or invade each of the countries of Indochina, really an executive committee of a corporate ruling class? What and whom do they represent? Where and how do they get their orders?

These questions are complicated by a certain unavoidable lack of precision in the meaning of power. It is hard to be precise about the locus of power in a system as complex as the national security partnership. Power is an elusive notion meaning different things in different contexts. For one thing, it is not the same as influence. To say that David Rockefeller can always be heard on American foreign policy toward Latin America or South Africa is not quite the same thing as saying that he sets that policy. To say that John Foster Dulles was once a lawyer for United Fruit Company does not mean that he was taking orders from the company when he authorized the CIA rescue operation of United Fruit properties in Guatemala. It is surely worth noting, but it does not dispose of the case. It does not rule out the possibility that the decisive grounds for the decision had to do with generalized notions about the Cold War and not the United Fruit Company balance sheet. Most major foreign policy decisions, of course, do not demonstrate such a close connection with particular private corporate interests as this one.

For our purposes we will define power as the ability to command men and resources. The essence of power is to be able to make things happen. To the extent that one must consult others before making things happen, one's power is diluted. The problem is further complicated by the important distinction between power as the world perceives it and as the holder of power perceives it. One of the most important characteristics of modern bureaucracy, particularly the national security bureaucracy, is that the increasing concentration of military and economic power has been accompanied by a pervasive feeling of powerlessness on the part of those who command these bureaucracies. In Part I we talked about the feelings of helplessness that afflict men of power, even dictators, as they try to use instruments of government. Lyndon Johnson once said something to the effect that the only real power he had was to drop the Bomb and he couldn't use it.

<h1 style="text-align:center">(2)</h1>

THE CASE for concluding that corporations play the crucial role in the making of foreign policy rests primarily on the network, visible and invisible, that links Wall Street, Detroit, Pittsburgh, and Washington. National security managers are recruited from and return to the leading corporate enterprises in the nation. That part of the case is indisputable.

If we look at the men who have held the very top positions, the Secretaries and Under Secretaries of State and Defense, the Secretaries of the three services, the Chairman of the Atomic Energy Commission, and the Director of the CIA, we find that out of ninety-one individuals who held these offices during the period between 1940 and 1967, seventy of them were from the ranks of big business or high finance, including eight out of ten Secretaries of Defense, seven out of eight Secretaries of the Air Force, every Secretary of the Navy, eight out of nine Secretaries of the Army, every Deputy Secretary of Defense, three out of five Directors of the CIA, and three out of five Chairmen of the Atomic Energy Commission.

According to the historian Gabriel Kolko, who investigated the 234 top foreign policy decision-makers, "men who came from big business, investment and law held 59.6 per cent of the posts." * The Brookings Institution volume, *Men Who Govern,* a comprehensive study of the top federal bureaucracy from 1933 to 1965, reveals that before coming to work in the Pentagon, 86 per cent of the Secretaries of the Army, Navy, and Air Force were either businessmen or lawyers (usually with a business practice). The Truman Administration recruited its principal national security managers from investment houses and leading banks.† The Eisenhower Ad-

---

* Gabriel Kolko, *The Roots of American Foreign Policy* (Boston: Beacon Press, 1969), pp. 19 ff.

† Because 1945–50 was such a critical period in setting the direction of U.S. foreign policy, the Truman appointees are particularly important. In his unpublished study "The Economic Cold War," Professor Thomas Paterson lists some of the businessmen who held key jobs as national security managers during these formative years. "In the 1945–50 period prominent businessmen

ministration, while not inhospitable to bankers, went in more for leading industrialists. The Kennedy Administration appointed a few well-
connected academics but most of the foreign policy posts on the
New Frontier were filled by reaching back for the bankers, oil
entrepreneurs and managers of high technology industry of the
Truman era. In the Kennedy Administration 20 per cent of all civilian
executives in defense-related agencies came from defense contractors.
The Johnson Administration kept most of the Kennedy appointees or
replaced them with men of similar backgrounds. The Nixon national
security managers are mainly from the financial and corporate world
although they tend to represent more varied and somewhat smaller
interests than the New York financial giants that have served as
suppliers of good Democrats.

The influence of businessmen on policymaking extends beyond the
circle of businessmen in government. "Citizens Committees," "Blue
Ribbon Panels," and "Advisory Task Forces" also play an important
role in making policy. One of the earliest postwar advisory groups
was the President's Air Policy Commission Report issued on New
Year's Day, 1948. Entitled "Survival in the Air Age," it was written
primarily by Thomas K. Finletter, whose prewar career had been a

---

held commanding jobs. W. Averell Harriman, noted investment banker, served
as Secretary of Commerce from 1946 to 1948, when he became the American
Representative for the Economic Cooperation Administration in Europe.
Robert A. Lovett, partner in Brown Brothers, Harriman and Company, assumed the office of Under Secretary of State in 1947. One of Lovett's colleagues in the State Department was William Clayton, of Clayton-Anderson
Company, largest cotton exporter in the United States, who served as the busy
Under Secretary for Economic Affairs. James V. Forrestal, former President
of Dillon Read and Company, investment bankers, was Secretary of Navy and
later Secretary of Defense under Truman. William M. Martin, President of
the New York Stock Exchange, left that job to join and later to head the Ex-
port-Import Bank in 1945. Edward R. Stettinius, Jr., former United States
Steel executive, was Secretary of State for the early critical months of 1945.
Richard C. Patterson, formerly of RKO Corporation, was Ambassador to
Yugoslavia, 1944–47. William Benton, member of the Committee for Economic Development and chairman of Encyclopaedia Britannica, was Assistant
Secretary of State from August 1945 to September 1947. In 1946 Truman
named prominent Southern industrialist, Oliver Max Gardner, Ambassador
to Great Britain. Robert P. Patterson, a corporation lawyer in the Wall Street
firm of Patterson, Belknap, and Webb, served as Secretary of War in 1946.
Kuhn, Loeb, and Company banker Lewis L. Strauss served on the Atomic
Energy Commission under Truman. The Chairman of the Army and Navy
Munitions Board for 1947–48 was the President of Eastman Kodak, Thomas
J. Hargrave. In 1948, among the members of the National Security Resources
Board were Frank Crockard of Tennessee Coal, Iron, and Railroad, Joseph
F. Borda, Jr., of Bethlehem Steel, Gayle W. Arnold of the Baltimore and Ohio
Railroad, and Reginald E. Gillmor of Sperry Gyroscope. . . .

"Others would include Paul Nitze, James Bruce, Laurence Steinhardt, Charles
Sawyer, William H. Draper, Charles E. Saltzman, James E. Webb, Lewis W.
Douglas, A. L. M. Wiggins, Richard R. Deupree, Dean Acheson, Stanton
Griffis, Willard Thorp, David K. E. Bruce, John Foster Dulles."

corporate legal practice with the Coudert Brothers firm, and John McCone, who had made his fortune in shipping and iron companies. The report declared that if the United States were to have even "relative security" it must at all times be "ready for war." Noting that "about 80% of our total federal budgets have been spent for war or preparation for war since 1915," the Report proposed that military production be used to subsidize airplane manufacturers. Whether we like it or not, the health of the aircraft industry, for the next few years at least, is dependent largely upon financial support from Government in the form of orders for military aircraft."

The Air Policy Commission played a role repeated many times since. It is an example of a group of businessmen being called together at the initiative of the national security bureaucracy to articulate and to publicize novel and controversial ideas already held by a few influential members of the bureaucratic elite. The Gaither Committee Report in 1957, the work of managers and advisers to the new, mushrooming high-technology industries, confirmed the thinking initiated by influential military officers such as James Gavin and Maxwell Taylor: There was too much reliance on "massive retaliation." Conventional weapons and mobile armies should be built up. There should be a vigorous civil defense program. On November 7, 1957, the leaders of the financial community, including Robert Lovett and John J. McCloy, were invited to meet with the National Security Council to discuss the report. They made it clear that the leading financial interests of the country would support a big rise in defense spending. Although Eisenhower held firm against dramatic rises in military spending for the rest of his term, the Gaither Report recommendations became the basis for the Kennedy defense policy, and indeed several key members of the Committee took over key national security posts in that Administration, including William C. Foster, who became head of the Disarmament Agency, and Jerome Wiesner, who became the President's Science Adviser.

Businessmen are traditionally called upon to review and sometimes to promote major policy programs. Thus, from time to time the foreign aid and military assistance programs have been subjected to the independent, outside scrutiny of commissions headed by the senior partner of Dillon Read, the Chairman of Continental Can, the President of Inland Steel, and the President of the Bank of America. A similar commission, it will be recalled, was used to promote the Marshall Plan in 1948. Thus, outside businessmen are used by the national security managers to help sell potentially unpopular programs to the country because the prestige of business leaders with the public is high.

There are less formal opportunities for businessmen to influence the national security managers. Because the top national security bureaucrats themselves come from the business world, their colleagues and associates have continuous easy access. No other group has anything remotely like the continuous opportunities for informal lobbying that the old friends, business associates, and law partners of the national security managers have. From time to time they all get together on formal occasions at the Council on Foreign Relations or the Business Advisory Council meetings at Hot Springs. (In May 1960 Vice-President Nixon gave a secret preview of U.S. policy on the U-2 at a Hot Springs meeting a few days before President Eisenhower stated the policy at the Paris summit meeting.)

Shortly after the Tet offensive of February 1968, President Johnson sought the advice of the New York financial community on what to do about the war. Men such as George Ball, Douglas Dillon, John J. McCloy, and Arthur Dean were called together as members of a Senior Advisory Group on Vietnam. As Vance put it, they discussed the "social and political effects in the United States" of what was happening in Vietnam and, in particular, "the impact on the U.S. economy." The war had already begun to have seriously unfavorable economic consequences, and the Advisory Group, though made up of some of the leading Cold War statesmen, was for getting rid of it in some way or at least cutting it down. Townsend Hoopes writes that the President "was visibly shocked by the magnitude of the defection." * Five days later President Johnson announced a new policy along with his renunciation of another term. These former national security managers, now symbolizing the might of Wall Street, had something approaching a veto power over the escalation which the military was then pushing. But they prevailed only because they reinforced the views of the men inside the bureaucracy like Clark Clifford, the Secretary of Defense.

(3)

THOSE WHO BELIEVE that business runs U.S. foreign policy also point to the absence of countervailing influence. There has been a business consensus in support of the main lines of American national security policy since World War II and no significant opposition from any other group with power in the society—labor, farmers, small businessmen, communications media, intellectuals. One need only look at the composition of advisory boards throughout the government to see that the managers of the leading industries and banks are the leading outside influence on policymaking.

---

* Townsend Hoopes, *The Limits of Intervention* (New York: David McKay and Co., 1969), p. 217.

But this falls considerably short of proving that the national security bureaucracy takes its orders from big business. Seymour Melman has advanced almost exactly the opposite thesis, with respect to defense expenditures. The Department of Defense, he suggests, is a state-management organization with increasingly centralized control over its suppliers, the leading corporations in the United States. It is the Pentagon that has control of how the annual $40 odd billion procurement budget shall be spent, which firms to reward and which to punish, which to promote and which to permit to sink. Robert Heilbroner also summarizes the basis of the Pentagon's power.

> At the heart of the Pentagon system lies a crucial structure of centralized management through which the economic activities of the industrial empire are shaped according to the wishes of the Pentagon officialdom. To run the military business of the United States takes some 15 million purchasing decisions per year, and a vastly larger number of administrative decisions. Responsibility for this gigantic activity rests with a DOD bureaucracy of 15,000 individuals empowered to arrange terms of contract at various levels of importance, in addition to another 25,000 who administer, oversee, check and carry out the contractual arrangements.
>
> These arrangements give the DOD virtual life-and-death powers over its industrial suppliers, permitting the prepayment of hundreds of millions of dollars, on the one hand, or the dire penalty of contract cancellation, on the other.*

While this picture of government-industry relationships minimizes somewhat the power of industry, it is more accurate than the simplistic view that the State Department gets its orders from defense contractors and foreign investors. Both have a profound influence on U.S. foreign policy but the process by which their power is exercised is often subtle and their role varies according to issue and area of the world. How much influence they have over the decisions of the national security bureaucracy depends upon two major factors. The first is the nature of the decision. If it is a piece of crisis management—i.e., whether to blockade or bomb Cuba—business managers who are not on loan to the government at the moment or who are not brought in specifically to work on it will not be consulted. They may be informed as a courtesy due the powerful, but they will not have an active role in making the decisions. During most of the postwar generation, to be sure, the support of big business for interventionist policies could be taken for granted, provided they succeeded.

* Review of *Pentagon Capitalism*, by Seymour Melman, in *New York Review of Books*, July 23, 1970.

On the other hand, the role of corporate managers in shaping long-term policies, such as those affecting investment, availability, and use of resources, which are ultimately more important, is much greater. On these, businessmen make their weight felt in two ways. The first is through continuous lobbying of the executive and Congress, most of it private and informal. The second is through the conduct of their businesses. By making ordinary business decisions affecting foreign countries, corporate managers set the direction of American foreign policy. How great their power to shape that policy is depends upon whether there are other U.S. interests at work in the particular area. In Central America, which is an economic colony of the United States, and to a lesser extent, South America, the dominant U.S. corporations operating there have virtual free rein since the only other U.S. interests there are representatives of the national security bureaucracy—military attachés, AID advisers, and CIA agents. While they occasionally perceive U.S. interests in a different light from the corporations, they know that their principal role there is to serve them. (Even in Latin America, it should be noted, the influence of particular corporations may to some extent cancel each other out. For example, at the very moment the copper companies were pressing the State Department to retaliate against Chile for nationalizing its mines, Boeing was desperately trying to sell jet aircraft to the Allende government.) In Southeast Asia and the Middle East, the noncorporate interests are much more developed. In these areas, the interests of the Sixth Fleet and the American Jewish Committee have, on occasion, taken precedence over the interests of the oil companies. Nonetheless, even in such situations, corporations exert an enormous influence on policy merely by having made commitments in the area which then set the frame of reference within which the State Department must operate.

The postwar period has witnessed the spectacular growth of both industry and government. But the growth of government has been greater. While the machinery of the state is still at the service of industry in many ways, and indeed, under our theory of government the essential function of the state is to smooth the path to economic growth for the corporations, nevertheless the power of any individual private industry or group of industries to set the direction of policy has declined. No industrialist today has the power that a J. P. Morgan or a John D. Rockefeller had in the pre-Depression era, and because there are many issues which divide the industrial giants, it is hard for them to act as a bloc. (On crucial questions of foreign policy there are deep conflicts of interest with the business community.) Heilbroner argues that "business has experienced a considerable diminution in its ability to influence the immediate course of events, comparing the pre-Depression era with our own." One of the reasons for this is its past success. Having taken advantage of circumstances of the war to persuade government to subsidize them through the defense budget and other means, the big corporations have ended up in the government's power, for the bureaucratic hand which gives can also withhold or even take. Increasingly corporations must look to government for survival. While the federal government is very responsive to the interests of big business in general, it is quite free to turn down the demands of any corporation or group of corporations, particularly in the area of foreign policy. As in Germany and Japan in the 1930's, a militarized state built with the cooperation of business, in expectation of benefiting from it, ends up with ever-increasing power over the economy and ever-increasing pressure to use it. In an economy in which major industries like Penn Central, Lockheed, and Chrysler are failing and in which government has the discretion whether to save them and what means to use to do it, state capitalism has already arrived. As the German industrialists discovered to their chagrin in the 1930's, managers of the state who may once have been their office boys end up giving the orders. It is they, now that they command the power of government, not their former bosses, who can move people and resources in the execution of foreign policy. The corporations continue to exercise the dominant *influence* in the society, but the *power* keeps passing to the state.

The managerial class which has taken over the major corporations exhibits much less initiative in foreign policy matters than the entrepreneurs of a generation or two generations ago. In 1945, for example, Nelson Rockefeller was serving in the State Department. A man with a strong personal interest in Latin America, he lobbied for the inclusion of Article 51 in the United Nations Charter and was instrumental in having it accepted. The purpose was to retain a role for a regional security organization for the Western Hemisphere, which, of course would be dominated by the United States. (At the time, Secretary of State Cordell Hull was strongly for giving the new world organization exclusive jurisdiction even if it meant a weakening of U.S. influence in the area.) The Rockefeller holdings in Latin America, including Creole Oil, International Basic Economy Corporation, supermarkets, ranches, hotels, banks, and factories, were huge at the time and are now staggering.* Article 51 was intended to be used, and has been used, to legitimize U.S. military interventions in Latin America. Here is a clear case of a powerful family using a temporary position with the state to adopt policies designed to protect their private financial holdings.

But the world has become more complicated and the managers of the great corporations do not think like the old entrepreneurs. On the great issues of national security they do not exert much day-to-

* See James Desmond, *Nelson Rockefeller: A Political Biography* (New York: Macmillan, 1964).

day influence. The presidents and chairmen of the board of the top one hundred corporations do not exhibit great excitement about foreign policy issues which do not have an obvious and fairly immediate economic impact. They will scream about nationalization and push hard for military contracts, but they do not have the imperial imagination of the old entrepreneurs. They will go along with the Administration except where such policies have an obvious adverse impact, as in the investment restrictions imposed in the Johnson Administration. They expect the government to protect business interests in general and to keep opening the world to greater economic opportunity. But how that is to be done is left to their friends who become national security managers. Their expansionist drives are concentrated on their corporations and they do not have the energy or the experience to concern themselves with the details of managing the empire. Indeed, the impact of government national security policies on the future of the corporation is in many cases so uncertain that the corporate managers do not even know what they should be for. It is much easier to concentrate on matters in which their interests are clear, such as the tariff and the income tax. (The triumph of the managerial class is attested by the reduction of the top bracket of the income tax on salaries.) It is true, as the Patman committee hearings suggest, that, true to Lenin's prediction, finance capital now plays an ever more crucial role in the U.S. economy. The trust departments of the large Eastern commercial banks and institutional investors, such as mutual funds, pension plans, insurance companies, and investment and brokerage houses, now hold controlling interests in major corporations. There is indeed great concentration of ownership, but this great concentration of ownership is managed by temporary employees, who, while highly paid to protect it and to make it grow, do not seem to know how to manipulate this great wealth to influence the great decisions of war and peace. Nor do they seem to be particularly interested in doing so. Indeed, the most advanced and powerful segment of U.S. industry is increasingly pessimistic about what the government can now do for them to push back economic frontiers abroad. As we shall see in the next chapter, the managers of the multinational corporations believe that in many circumstances they can do better on their own and that an activist U.S. foreign policy may do them more harm than good.

(4)

THESE QUESTIONS would be of only academic interest if in fact the "essential oneness" of the strategic interests of the state and the economic interests of corporations coincided as neatly as business ideologists and Marxist critics assume. But there are conflicts of interest between a state bureaucracy interested in accumulating uneconomic intangibles such as influence and power and corporations interested in short-term economic gain and the expansion of corporate power. That the state may have economic ends in mind in its quest for power may obscure these conflicts, but it does not mean that they do not exist. Nor should it be automatically assumed that the man from Dillon Read or General Motors who becomes a national security manager thinks about things in the same way he did in his Wall Street or Detroit office. Jobs come equipped with their own ideologies. Perspectives attach to functions and roles. The man who comes from business to the Pentagon or the State Department obviously brings his history with him, but when he becomes a manager for the empire he is not the same man he was when he was merely a manager for a bank. When he was president of the Ford Motor Company, Robert McNamara was able to heal the wound which the fabulous lemon, the Edsel, had gashed in the company by simply declaring that the company had lost enough on that particular experiment. Although he eventually came to have the same view of the Vietnam War, neither he nor anyone else was able to make economic rationality prevail despite monumental losses of resources, inflation, balance of payments crises, and a social crisis which threatened to drive the President from office.

The perspective of the national security manager and the corporate manager (even when they are the same man at different stages of his career) are different because the state employee must think in much broader, more long-range, and more general terms than the corporate employee. One obvious example is in the area of economic warfare. During the Cold War the United States established a long "strategic list" containing numerous items which it was forbidden to sell to the Soviet Union on the theory that withholding them would weaken Soviet power. But while businesses interested in selling to the Soviet Union may have found such a political objective laudable, they were not prepared to sacrifice short-term profits for either ideology or politics. Thus many businessmen developed ingenious methods for circumventing U.S. law. They would turn copper, a proscribed commodity, into wire and wire into copper and ship them in and out of third countries. The object of all this economic alchemy was to have the strategic metal end up in communist hands without the company executives' going to jail. Shipments of chrome ore would be shipped to Norway or Sweden and "switched" with apolitical Scandinavian ore which would then be shipped to Russia. The managers of the state attempted without success to enforce patriotism upon the corporate managers. Each was reacting to different perceptions of interest.

Perhaps because American foreign policy has always reflected the business creed and a high proportion of those who set foreign policy come from the world of business, the government has frequently pressed harder than businessmen themselves for opening up the world to American business. In this respect the pattern of American expansionism has been different from the British experience a century ago. In his study *The End of Empire*, John Strachey concludes that private economic interests were primarily responsible for the new wave of imperial expansion in which Britain was caught up after 1870:

> The power of the state was called in on behalf of adventurous British entrepreneurs like Rhodes investing their capital in overseas enterprises. In Egypt, on the other hand, the power of the state was used to protect bondholders, i.e. persons who had lent their money at a fixed rate of interest to a foreign government. What is common to both cases is that it was found that if the investment of British capital overseas was to be adequately promoted and protected, large slices of the world must be, in fact or in form annexed.*

But in the United States it was the State Department and not the major corporations that provided the original impetus for foreign investment in many areas of the world. For a variety of political and long-range economic reasons the national security managers took the lead in creating the Common Market, which has been the principal magnet for U.S. foreign investment in the postwar period and has led to the "American takeover" of European corporations. This was a case of government planners seeing ultimate opportunity better than corporations themselves did and of pushing them to be more adventurous than they themselves were prepared to be. This same phenomenon is especially obvious with respect to the Third World. According to Lenin's analysis of imperialism, capitalists will race each other to invest in backward countries where wages are low and governments are for sale. But except for Latin America, which businessmen have traditionally considered an appendage of the U.S. economy, U.S. corporate executives have not usually made that analysis. In part because labor has become a less important component of many commodities and because of unique advantages accruing to the businessmen of the number one nation in the developed industrial nations, American investors have preferred less sticky and less risky climates within which to operate. The recent U.S. economic expansion in poor countries is the story of an expansionist government pushing timid investors into overseas commitments.

There are good reasons for this. The typical corporation is reluctant

---

* John Strachey, *The End of Empire* (London: Victor Gollancz, Ltd., 1959), p. 96.

to make investments in countries where it is difficult to operate, the risks of nationalization are present, and short-run profits are uncertain. If investment opportunities exist in the more familiar, predictably profitable, industrialized economies, why not leave the exotic opportunities to others? The government, which sees its role as protector of American business in general rather than of any particular corporation, is much more concerned about competition for the Third World from other industrialized nations. This clash of perspective goes back a long way in our history. Paul S. Reinsch, who was Wilson's Minister to Peking, was constantly trying to promote U.S. corporate investment in China. But, he writes in his memoirs, American bankers were "notoriously the most timid beings known to experience when it came to the matter of foreign investments." * Meeting with the executives of the National City Bank, Chase, J. P. Morgan Guarantee Trust, and Standard Oil, the Minister pointed out that the Europeans and the Japanese "were organized to represent a broad national interest in Chinese business" and that they would soon be "scooping off the cream" if American banks didn't get right in. The same conflict has continued into the post–World War II era. The State Department, thinking two decades ahead, is anxious to Americanize the markets and raw materials sources in Asia, Africa, and Latin America before they fall into other hands. Corporations think more of this year's profit and loss statement, possibly of next year's. It is significant that the multinational corporations, which in some ways look like governments and share some of their perspectives, are much more given to long-range thinking about preempting foreign markets than domestic corporations have typically been.

The general pattern of the postwar period has been that U.S. industry has followed the flag. The United States first establishes a military "presence" and the investments follow. During the war the United States exploited its forward military position in the Middle East to move in on what had been an exclusive strategic resource area of the British Empire. As Admiral William Leahy explained it, the United States built an air base in Saudi Arabia "so that we, particularly our Navy, would have access to some of King Ibn Saud's oil." †

When the United States sent its first military advisers to Greece and Turkey in implementation of the Truman Doctrine there was virtually no U.S. investment there. Almost immediately companies such as Westinghouse, General Electric, and engineering firms received contracts for reconstruction of roads and air facilities. The

* Quoted in Beard, *op. cit.*, pp. 181 ff.
† Gabriel Kolko, *The Politics of War* (New York: Random House, 1968), p. 306.

United States gave Greece almost $4 billion. The U.S. Ambassador, especially John Peurifoy who held the post immediately after the civil war, openly supported certain politicians and built close relations with the Greek officer corps. The Greek Central Information Agency, financed and outfitted by the U.S., became in effect an arm of the CIA. Each ministry had its American advisers, many with veto power over domestic programs that appeared to run counter to U.S. interests. Thus it was not surprising that by 1954 Clarence B. Randall, Chairman of President Eisenhower's Commission on Foreign Economic Policy, was able to report that Greece and Turkey (along with the U.S. base known as Panama) "have led the way in modernizing their corporate laws and creating the right sort of atmosphere for our investment." *

The massive military intervention in Vietnam has also opened up commercial opportunities for American business. Construction firms such as President Johnson's political mentors Brown & Root, shipping and transport companies, oil companies, banks, even MGM, have profited directly from operations in Vietnam even while the American economy as a whole and business in general suffered from its consequences. *Business Week* describes the bureaucratic process by which U.S. banking giants such as Bank of America and Chase Manhattan Bank come to establish branches in such unlikely places as war-torn Saigon.†

> If it weren't for the massive U.S. presence there, probably neither bank would be in Vietnam. The banks came into the Vietnam picture last year as a result of the big U.S. buildup that began in 1965. The U.S. government wanted a place to keep funds—for the Embassy, the Agency for International Development, and the military. And it saw no reason to help French or other foreign banks in the country.

(5)

IN THE short run the interests of the state and the interests of the major corporations converged to increase state power and corporate power at the same time. The business creed seemed to be working perfectly. The foreign activities of corporations would enhance the prestige and influence of the U.S. government, for their crucial financial positions in local economies would give the State Depart-

* Quoted in Thomas G. Paterson, "The Economic Cold War," Ph.D. thesis (University of California, Berkeley, 1968).

† For further discussion see Harry Magdoff, *The Age of Imperialism* (New York: Monthly Review Press, 1969), p. 68.

ment a lever in exerting political influence. At the same time the elaborate imperial apparatus by which the number one nation keeps other nations in varying degrees of dependency would create a beneficial climate around the world for corporate profits. Until the 1960's it all worked.

Since the mid-1960's serious conflicts between the self-defined economic interests of the state and the interests of corporations have developed. To put it in its simplest terms, the costs of maintaining the imperial system began to outweigh the benefits as far as the major corporations were concerned, particularly since these costs were in large measure shifted to the corporations themselves. The state's primary economic goal in this period has been to stem the balance of payments crisis without giving up the uniquely favored position of the United States under the monetary arrangements set up after the war. The United States has attempted to use its predominant economic power to buy political influence and to maintain dependent relationships around the world through military and economic instruments which may be of considerable benefit to those companies able to exploit them but which turn out to represent a net economic loss to the country, including some of its most powerful corporations.

Michael Hudson has analyzed the increasing role of state capital as opposed to private capital in the postwar era. He points out that in the developed world the United States has sought to make U.S. corporations renounce their economic interests—free trade, unrestricted investment—to serve the interests of state capitalism. In the Third World it is U.S. government financing—AID, Eximbank —and U.S. government dominated financing—World Bank, International Monetary Fund—that determines the investment patterns.

In the age of revolution and nationalization, the classic imperialist investor in the mold of Cecil Rhodes is in relatively short supply. The U.S. government established the elaborate international system under which it maintains its position as number one nation—the mightiest armada in history, an international monetary system based on the dollar, a variety of lending institutions (national and nominally international), effectively subject to U.S. government direction, a system of selectively free trade, all for the purpose of enhancing political and economic power at the same time. But the effect of U.S. foreign policy has been to purchase political power, which includes the capability of waging economic warfare, at serious economic cost.

The modern government in the era of unbalanced budgets and unlimited taxing power does not run on conventional economic criteria. Despite McNamara's celebration of the principle of cost-effectiveness in the Pentagon, that is in reality the last principle on which government operates. Governments are willing to spend limitless sums to maintain control and to buy order even when the very social and political environment they are seeking to create is unlikely to yield any economic benefit remotely commensurate with the cost of creating it.

(6)

IN THE following chapter we will discuss why the clash between the economic interests of private capital and the politico-economic interests of state capital is intensifying and what significance this has for the future direction of American foreign policy. But despite these strains the government-business partnership remains very much in effect and its impact on many foreign countries continues to be decisive.

In much of the world the foreign relations of the United States are defined by the daily interaction of government and business. As we have noted, the relationship varies from region to region depending upon the power of the corporations involved, the strategic investment of the U.S. government in the area, and the exact nature of the state in particular. On one extreme are U.S. coroprations in Europe that have been hurt by economic policies of the Johnson and Nixon Administrations. On the other are the old-fashioned plantation and extractive industries operating in Central America. The latter are usually able to get the power of the state to work for them in all sorts of ways. The following episode described by the political scientist James Petras is typical of what goes on in those parts of the world U.S. businessmen still treat as American colonies:

The Boston Panama Company owned 500,000 acres of land (an area one-half the size of Rhode Island) and only utilized 5,000. The Panamanian government, applying a tax law on uncultivated land, eventually asked for a 2 million dollar payment. The Boston Panama Company refused to pay the sum and conferred with U.S. government officials on ways to avoid complying with the enforcement of the law. Communications from the U.S. corporation were sent to the Department of Commerce's International Bureau and to Senator Long informing them of the corporation's economic interests, the relationship between the policy outcome in their case and the rest of the investment community in Latin America and between U.S. development policy for Latin America and private investors. Senator Long and Behrman of Commerce sent letters to the State Department. Political pressure was exerted on the Panamanian government through the device of threatening to cut off loans (the Hickenlooper amendment to the Foreign Aid Bill of 1962). In a matter of weeks the Panamanian government acceded to the demands of the corporation. In the process, it was revealed that the President of Panama, Mr. Chiari, was on the board of directors of a processing plant operated by the Boston Panama Company.*

In most cases, however, the U.S. government role is much less obvious but nonetheless vital. We have already mentioned how military aid, economic assistance, loans, technical advice, counter-insurgency and police programs, and agricultural assistance are used to purchase continuing government influence in poor countries and how that influence is used to build and maintain an investment climate favorable to American corporations. It is a fundamental tenet of the business creed, it will be recalled, that the same foreign investment that benefits the American corporation also benefits the host country.

However, the most important single fact about the relationship of American corporations and poor countries is that each has a set of primary interests which do not coincide and in many respects are adverse. It is important to distinguish between leaders and masses in discussing interests. The leaders of poor countries in most of the world are primarily interested in staying in power and, depending upon how progressive they are, developing their countries. In most of the world they buy the American theory that development depends upon the accumulation of capital through private investment. Thus, in much of the world foreign investment is welcomed because there is no other source of capital. According to the business creed, this enthusiasm for foreign investment is the basis for a happy partnership between the American firm and the government of the developing country. In some cases it is. Private investment can be of enormous benefit to leaders at the same time that it damages the national economy. Leaders benefit from the presence of American corporations in many ways. For some the presence of American money in their country means "consulting fees," numbered bank accounts in Switzerland, and the anticipation of a happy Riviera retirement. An executive of General Foods once wrote a "how to do it" book for doing business abroad which discusses the theory and practice of bribery:

> The attitude towards what we would term "bribery" is often quite different abroad from what we have come to expect in the

* Marvin Surkin and Alan Wolfe, eds., *An End to Political Science* (New York: Basic Books, 1970), p. 195.

United States. . . . There are situations in which it is necessary to make some concessions to the customs and methods that are generally accepted in a foreign country. If this should appear to be the case, it is best to have some dependable local representative handle the situation on your behalf.

The Internal Revenue Service has permitted companies to deduct bribes paid to foreign officials as an "ordinary and necessary business expense." *

There are other benefits of foreign investment that are spread somewhat beyond the presidential palace, the police station, and the customs house. American firms do create jobs. As the National Planning Association concludes on the basis of thirteen case studies, foreign firms operating in poor countries "in many cases created entire social infrastructures of schools, housing, health facilities, and transportation in order to conduct their business." According to Harry Magdoff's calculations, some 40 per cent of U.S. private investment is in what the State Department calls less-developed countries. There is no doubt that U.S. capital is flowing into the poor countries.

But there is also no doubt that more capital is flowing out. From 1950 to 1965 the U.S. direct investment in less-developed countries was $9 billion. Earnings on this investment repatriated to the United States, according to Magdoff, amounted to $25.6 billion. In 1965–66 there was new investment, Leo Model tells us in *Foreign Affairs,* amounting to $507 million and in the same period profits, fees, and royalties remitted to the U.S. in the amount of $2.658 billion.†

However, even these devastating figures do not give an adequate picture of the fundamental conflicts of interest between U.S. corporations operating abroad and the interests of the people of the poor countries. Contrary to popular understanding, corporations do not usually bring money with them when they set up shop in poor countries. They raise it on the local economy. Professor Raymond Vernon points out that in 1964, for example, U.S. firms increased their equity interest in enterprises in Asia, Africa, and Latin America by $3.3 billion but brought only $565 million from the U.S. Where

---

* See Robert Engler, *The Politics of Oil* (Chicago: University of Chicago Press, 1967), p. 457.

† "The Politics of Private Foreign Investment," *Foreign Affairs,* 1968, p. 643. U.S. corporations argue that such figures are misleading because the poor countries, in the absence of foreign-owned factories, would have lost even more foreign exchange through importing goods from abroad. See, for example, Raymond Vernon, *Sovereignty at Bay* (New York: Basic Books, 1971), pp. 172–73. But the critics' point, of course, is that foreign investment is not the answer, and that alternative concepts of development exist.

does the money come from? Frederic G. Donner, the Chairman of the Board of General Motors gives the answer:

> Let me summarize our overseas record during the past fifteen years in terms of some objective measures of business accomplishment. At the end of 1950, the value of General Motors net working capital and fixed assets overseas was about $180 million. . . . By the close of 1965, this investment had increased to about $1.1 billion, or approximately six times the amount in 1950. This expansion was accomplished almost entirely from financial resources generated through General Motors operations overseas and through local earnings. As a result . . . our overseas subsidiaries remitted about two-thirds of their earnings to the United States.*

The result is that domestic investment is discouraged and the development of independent (and potentially competitive) local industry is prevented. A government such as the Castelo Branco regime in Brazil, which overthrew the independent-leaning Goulart government (and was recognized with such indecent haste by the Johnson Administration as to raise suspicions in Latin America that Lincoln Gordon, the American Ambassador, was involved in the coup), had a clear policy of favoring foreign capital over local industry. With strong credit U.S. firms have had the option of obtaining financing at optimum rates locally, thus pre-empting scarce local capital or, when it is advantageous, obtaining financing outside Brazil at lower rates. Local firms, on the other hand, have often been restricted to local sources, for which the interest runs as high as 48 per cent.†

Another argument made in favor of foreign investment is that it insures a flow of technology that will benefit poor countries. The argument overlooks the fact that foreign-owned enterprises are in reality enclaves within poor economies. They are far more extensions of the U.S. economy than integral parts of local economies. It is in the interest of U.S. corporations to keep advanced technology out of the hands of potential competitors. Their policy, therefore, is to center research and development operations in the United States and to limit their operations in poor countries to assembly, packaging, and other operations which require only semiskilled or unskilled workers. Thus, as Michael Kidron points out, in India nine-tenths of all registered patents are taken out by or in behalf of foreign corporations. Except in rare cases, there is little incentive to train

* Quoted in André Gunder Frank, "The Underdevelopment Policy of the UN in Latin America," *NACLA Newsletter,* December 1969, p. 2.

† In recent years underdeveloped countries, including Brazil, have toughened their policies on foreign investment and foreign technology.

local researchers or technologists. And to the extent that foreign-owned capital-intensive high-technology industry is introduced into a primitive economy it of course means a loss of jobs. The corporations' decisions about the import of technology, like their decisions about the import of capital, are based entirely on the world-wide interests of their firm, not on the needs of the local economy, about which the corporate managers typically know little and care less. Blind faith in the business creed makes it possible to assume that what is good for Kennecott is also good for Chile, and vice versa.

U.S. corporations do create jobs but the interests of the corporation are once again often adverse to those of the population. True, the U.S. corporation in many parts of the world is interested in locating those parts of its operations which require unskilled or semiskilled labor which can be obtained at low rates. Thus, U.S. corporations do employ many people in Hong Kong, who at twenty cents an hour assemble radios that have been made in the United States or Western Europe. On the other hand, the trend of U.S. investment in Latin America is toward capital-intensive (i.e., labor dispensing) investment. There has been a dramatic rise in foreign investment in Brazil since 1949, when 7.86 per cent of the active population of Brazil was employed in industry. Fifteen years later, despite a much-celebrated rise in the GNP, only 8.26 per cent of the active population is so employed.* Corporations are under economic pressure to cut costs by abolishing jobs.

The classic cases of corporate exploitation have involved extractive industries. National resources are removed from the country. The host country has little control over price or the use of the resources. Profits are repatriated to the foreign corporation. Though in recent years companies have perceived it to be in their interest to improve working conditions and services for their employees, it is clear that they are responsive to the needs of the corporation, not the development needs of the country. The result is a form of development which impedes the integration of independent societies by increasing class differences.

As Professor Franklin R. Root of the Wharton School found in a study of the foreign operations of the five hundred largest U.S. industrial firms:

> None of the executives interviewed mentioned policies aimed at maximizing contributions to national income and public revenues, improving the balance of payments, stimulating general economic growth and employment, or introducing innovations that would benefit the host economy as a whole.

* See Eduardo Galeano, "Denationalization of Brazilian Industry," *Monthly Review*, December 1969, p. 25.

It is hardly surprising that corporate executives think first of the profit-and-loss statement and not the human misery of the countries where they operate. They are not paid to be philanthropists or social engineers. But the human cost to the poor of the world in pretending that corporations are philanthropic is considerable.

In recent years, as we have seen, the trend in private investment has been toward manufacturing, assembling, and processing industries. Here, too, there are serious conflicts of interest. Branch plants located in poor countries are designed to hop tariff walls and increase exports. In a survey of key international companies, the National Industrial Conference Board concluded that "marketing strategy was clearly the dominant element in investment decisions" relating to the location of branch plants. By dominating the local market a U.S. corporation can crowd out existing or potential locally owned competition, over which it has many advantages. At the same time it encourages poor countries with severe shortages of foreign exchange to import more. Branch plants have strong incentives to import from the parent company and thus discriminate against local suppliers. They also have little interest in producing for export where such exports compete with other branches of the U.S. corporation.*

Perhaps the most negative aspect of private investment for poor countries is its impact on taste and culture. The drive of the developed countries, particularly the United States, to increase the flow of consumer products to what is really the undeveloping world through branch plants and subsidized trade creates demands and diffuses tastes that are new to traditional societies. The notion that consumption is the key to happiness is a basic cultural value of developed societies. Consumerism is creating social and psychological problems in the United States, but its effects in poor countries are disastrous. Aggressive advertising and marketing in the undeveloping countries have created demands that cannot be satisfied. The "revolution of rising expectations" is a cruel hoax, for the products poor people are taught to want and hope for are usually beyond their reach and in most cases are exactly what they do not need. In a country without public transportation the marketing of a few cars is destructive. The need is basic transportation for all, not speed or comfort for a few. Tobacco, Coca-Cola, and other destructive or nutritionally useless products are being effectively marketed to poor people in the undeveloping world who subsist on less than fifteen

---

* For further information, see "The International Corporation and the Nation State" (New York: Business International, 1968, mimeograph); Claude McMillan, *International Enterprises in a Developing Economy: A Study of United States Business in Brazil* (East Lansing, Mich.: Bureau of Business and Economic Research, 1964); and Gilbert Clee, "Guidelines for Global Business," *Columbia Journal of World Business,* Winter 1966.

hundred calories a day. Thus U.S. corporations with strong incentives to build global homogenized markets set the consumption patterns and spending priorities for millions of people to whom they have no responsibility and with whom they have no relationship except as suppliers of cheap labor and consumers.

The corporate dream of a world-wide market is best symbolized, perhaps, by the Ritz Cracker Company's consideration of a global TV commercial transmitted by communications satellite which will tell the Ritz Cracker story to three billion potential munchers. Indeed, much of the shaping of tastes which American corporations engage in around the world is done through television. In recent years 80 per cent of the programs shown on TV stations in Latin America have been such standard items of the nightly U.S. TV diet of the 1960's as "Bonanza," "I Love Lucy," "Route 66." Even a series that does not make it in the fiercely competitive U.S. market may be dressed up with Spanish or French subtitles and shipped off to help a country develop. U.S. companies have been pushing to control the TV and communications industry in such parts of the world. The American Broadcasting Company, for example, organized Worldvision to penetrate the foreign market. By early 1968 this collection of commercial TV facilities had sixty-four stations in twenty-seven countries, mostly in Latin America. In 1966 the company estimated that it could reach "60 per cent of all world TV homes where sponsorship is permitted." As Jon Frappier has pointed out in his study, "U.S. Media Empire/Latin America," ABC offers financial support, technical and administrative services, personnel training programs, a program buying service, and in addition acts as the stations' sales representative.* Member stations must accept programs and advertising selected by ABC for prime-time viewing. As *Television* magazine pointed out in October 1966, "ABC can sell Batman to an advertiser and then place Batman along with designated commercials in any Worldvision country where the advertiser wants it to appear." Thus, U.S. companies are able to market canned dreams which in turn create new wants and new markets.

(7)

THE GOVERNMENT-BUSINESS partnership takes on a special character when we come to the major oil companies.† The five U.S. "majors"

---

* *NACLA Newsletter,* Vol. II, No. 9 (January 1969).

† For further reading on topics touched on in this chapter, see Raymond A. Bauer et al., *American Business and Public Policy* (New York: Atherton Press, 1968). See also Engler, *op. cit.*

control 70 per cent of the oil in the noncommunist world. Oil accounts for more than one-third of all direct U.S. investment abroad, 40 per cent of all U.S. investment in the Third World, and more than 60 per cent of all earnings realized from U.S. operations in underdeveloped countries. In 1967, to take a typical year, the combined sales of Jersey Standard, Gulf, Standard of California, Mobil, and Texaco was $32 billion. Warren M. Cannon, in his survey *The Expansion of American Corporations Abroad,* found that during the 1950's oil company profits in the Middle East were as high as 62.6 per cent.

The extraordinary place of the oil companies in the world economy and the controlling influence they have in many producing countries could not have been accomplished without a close and continuing partnership with the U.S. government. The "public" operations of the State Department and the "private" operations of the oil companies blend in what the petroleum analyst Michael Tanzer, himself a former employee of an oil company abroad, calls a "symbiosis." It is a symbiosis based on mutual dependency. Just as the active diplomatic and, where necessary, military intervention of the U.S. government has been considered by the oil companies to be a necessary adjunct of their business operations, so the continuing productivity of the companies is considered by the government to be a national security asset. In the Middle East, Robert Engler reports, "American foreign service officials are transported in Aramco's sizeable air fleet, and the 13,000 native workers are warned by the Saudi Arabian Government that a strike against Aramco would be a strike against their own government." During World War II, oilmen argued for strong U.S. intervention in Saudi Arabia to help them in their fight for oil concessions against British-owned companies. The British had contacts with their own government which were so intimate, a U.S. State Department official testified, "that it is difficult to discuss where the oil companies end and where the Government begins." The U.S. quickly countered and overwhelmed the British imperial partnership. James Terry Duce of Aramco gave the justification for building Ibn Saud an air field and an aid program, much of which ended up in his personal treasury:

> . . . when you begin to find oil in billions of barrels and it looks as though those billions will grow, it becomes not so much a matter of your interest, it becomes a matter of public interest and the national interest. . . .

The British government's involvement and the American stake in the Middle East oil, Secretary of the Interior Harold Ickes declared, meant that if the United States were to acquire "foreign petroleum reserves for the benefit of the United States . . . American partici-

pation must be of a sovereign character compatible with the strength
of the competitive forces encountered in any such undertaking." The
primary task of the American government, Augustus C. Long, chairman of Texaco, told the New York Chamber of Commerce in June
1957, is to create a "political and financial climate both here and
abroad . . . conducive to overseas investment." This message, as
Robert Engler has written, "is echoed on the mimeograph machines
and at the luncheon clubs by executives of all the international oil
companies." Under the slogan "equal access to oil development,"
the world's most powerful corporations, drawing on the strength of
the world's most powerful nation, have extended their control over
the earth's oil resources, and are laying claim to the oil beneath the
sea. The United States government has eagerly embraced the same
slogan, due in no small measure to the large number of oil company
executives and advisers who have held important positions in the
State, Defense, Commerce, and Interior Departments in which decisions affecting petroleum have been made. Men such as Robert B.
Anderson, Herbert Hoover, Edwin Pauley, Ralph K. Davies, George
McGhee, and John McCone are a few of the men from the world of
oil who have held key posts in the National Security State.* They
and their colleagues are living reminders of the seriousness with which
the industry received the words of Standard Oil Treasurer Leo D.
Welch in November 1946.

> As our country has begun to evolve its over-all postwar
> foreign policy, private enterprise must begin to evolve its
> foreign and domestic policy, starting with the most important
> contribution it can make—"men in government."

Starting in the post–World War I era, the State Department insisted
that, having "contributed to the common victory, this Government
. . . has a right, therefore, to insist that American nationals shall
not be excluded from a reasonable share in developing the resources
. . ." of the Middle East. To protect American oil interests in
Mexico, Philander C. Knox, Taft's Secretary of State, explained it,

---

* For a State Department official with knowledge and contacts in some
areas of interest to oil companies there are good career prospects on retirement
from public service. Harold B. Minor, for example, a former ambassador to
Lebanon, became assistant to Aramco's vice-president for government relations. William A. Eddy, the first U.S. resident minister to Saudi Arabia, also
joined Aramco's public relations staff. Henry F. Holland, the Assistant Secretary of State for Inter-American Affairs at the time of the Guatemalan coup
of 1954 subsequently represented oil interests in Latin America. Jersey
Standard's specialist in government relations, Melvin Conant, is an alumnus of
the CIA. Kenneth Young had been chief of the Southeast Asia desk at the
State Department before going to work for Standard Oil. Later he became
an ambassador to Thailand, which presumably did not adversely affect Esso
in its successful bid for oil concessions in the Gulf of Siam.

the United States sent its naval vessels to patrol the Gulf Coast, hoping thereby to keep the Mexicans "in a salutary equilibrium, between a dangerous and exaggerated apprehension and a proper degree of wholesome fear."

Charles Rayner, the Petroleum Advisor of the Department of State, told a Congressional investigating committee in 1944 that "World War II has been and is a war based on oil," meaning that petroleum was both the lure and the lubricant of the various clashing war machines. One need not take the statement as exclusive truth any more than one should assume that a naval officer's characterization of the same war as a fight for control of the sea is an adequate explanation. Nevertheless, the statement does give an indication of the enormous importance oil assumes in the strategic thinking in the State Department. A more comprehensive picture of the place of petroleum in the formation of the national interest is offered in a memorandum, "Petroleum in International Relations," published by a State Department official, John A. Loftus, in 1945:

Another major category of problems concerns the support given by the Department on behalf of the United States Government to American nationals seeking to obtain or to retain rights to engage in petroleum development, transportation, and processing abroad. This is the traditional function of the Department with respect to petroleum. It has continued to be significant, though of temporarily diminished importance, during the war period. As normal economic conditions return this function will come to be of very great importance. Recently significant exploration concession rights have been obtained by American companies, with the assistance of the Department, in Ethiopia and Paraguay. In Iran the negotiations which were apparently near to culmination last fall have been temporarily suspended for political reasons. In China there are great possibilities for the post-war period. Large, potentially productive areas in Colombia are yet to be concessioned out to private enterprise; and in Brazil, where there may be very great potentialities of petroleum production, no concessions at all have yet been granted. In both Colombia and Brazil there is a fair probability of basic legislation being enacted which would permit the obtaining of concessions by private companies on a mutually satisfactory basis. The foregoing cases involve areas where concession rights are being sought. There are other critical situations where concession rights are in jeopardy and where the Department's vigilant attention is required. Furthermore, there are other areas where after the war there is a genuine possibility of securing an amelioration of the unfavorable discriminatory conditions under which American nationals were able to obtain rights before the war.

In the postwar period the most successful piece of petroleum diplomacy was the CIA-sponsored coup against the Iranian nationalist premier, Mohammed Mossadeq, in 1954. Mossadeq came to power on May 1, 1951, and three days later seized the British-owned Anglo-Iranian Oil Company. In a fiery speech the wispy premier announced that Iran was taking rightful possession of "a hidden treasure upon which lies a dragon." Oil companies in the West boycotted the nationalized oil company, and Iran lost the major source of its foreign exchange. The newly elected Eisenhower Administration had come to the view that Mossadeq must go. It began its campaign against Mossadeq with economic pressure. "There is a strong feeling in the United States," the President wrote the Iranian, ". . . that it would not be fair to the American taxpayer for the United States Government to extend any considerable amount of economic aid to Iran so long as Iran could have access to funds derived from the sale of its oil products if a reasonable agreement were reached."

Exactly five weeks later, Mossadeq having rejected this offer, Kermit Roosevelt, a grandson of President Theodore Roosevelt, formerly a history professor and OSS agent and at the time CIA's principal covert operative in the Middle East, arrived in Iran to direct a coup against Mossadeq. His mission was to replace him with General Fazollah Zahedi, who, despite his suspected Nazi sympathies during the war, was considered far more willing to cooperate with the oil companies and the State Department. Assisting in the operation was Brigadier General H. Norman Schwartzkopf, famous twenty years earlier as the New Jersey State Police officer who investigated the Lindbergh-baby kidnapping and later as the weekly narrator of the radio program "Gangbusters." With the help of five U.S. agents and seven Iranian intelligence operatives, Roosevelt plotted the coup from a Tehran basement. An admiring CIA colleague called it "a real James Bond operation."

Shortly after the U.S. agent's' arrival, the Shah dismissed Mossadeq, but Mossadeq's supporters rioted and forced the Shah to flee the country. On August 19, 1953, while his chief, Allen Dulles, was conferring with the Shah in Rome, Roosevelt was recruiting street mobs to oppose the Mossadeq supporters and the pro-communist Tudeh Party, which was also demonstrating against the impending coup. With the help of substantial sums, which Roosevelt used for hired demonstrators to whip up the growing anti-Mossadeq mobs, and the support of the Iranian army, heavily dependent on U.S. equipment, the insurgents were able to turn the tide against the intractable premier and to drive him from office. The U.S. Military

Assistance Mission in Iran took an active part in the operation. Major General George C. Stewart, director of military assistance, later told the House Foreign Affairs Committee:

> When this crisis came on and the thing was about to collapse, we violated our normal criteria and among other things we did, we provided the army immediately on an emergency basis, blankets, boots, uniforms, electric generators, and medical supplies that permitted and created an atmosphere in which they could support the Shah. . . . The guns that they had in their hands, the trucks that they rode in, the armored cars that they drove through the streets, and the radio communications that permitted their control, were all furnished through the military defense assistance program . . . had it not been for this program, a government unfriendly to the United States probably would now be in power.

Once installed as premier, Zahedi concluded an agreement for an oil consortium which was highly favorable to U.S. companies. The details of the consortium agreement are still classified by the National Security Council. ("Making them public," Secretary Dulles explained to Congress, "would adversely affect the foreign relations of the United States.") But the basic nature of the agreement is known. The British lost their former monopoly on Iranian oil. U.S. companies, including Gulf and Standard Oil of New Jersey, received a forty-per-cent interest in the consortium, which was negotiated for the United States by such oil-company executives on loan as Herbert Hoover, Jr., of Union Oil, and Howard W. Page, vice-president of Jersey Standard. By 1967, U.S. firms which before World War II had controlled about 10 per cent of the Middle East oil reserves now controlled 59 per cent.

The United States government continues to provide a variety of services to the major oil companies,* on the ground that anything that increases American access to petroleum is in the national interest. Many of the privileges won for the industry, such as the oil depletion allowance, have been procured and defended on the ground that without them insufficient oil would be produced for the national defense. Most of the partnership activities of the State Department and the oil companies are better-kept secrets than the activities of the Defense Department, although tireless readers of such industry publications as *Petroleum Intelligence Weekly* and *World Petroleum*

---

* The relationship between the federal government and the major oil companies with primary operations abroad is not entirely cooperative by any means. The domestic oil companies have had sufficient power to secure the imposition of import quotas on oil and other restrictive policies which protect them at the expense of the "majors."

will glean some hints as to how the government and the oil companies work together. In 1966, for example, the American International Oil Company signed an agreement with the Indian government to establish India's largest fertilizer plant at Madras. The Johnson Administration held up shipments of food under the Food for Peace program at a time of serious famine in India as pressure to induce the Indians to make a deal satisfactory to the oil company. The pressure worked, and the Indians were forced to abandon their program for public ownership of the fertilizers' industry and to give effective control of the operation to foreign companies. As the New York *Times* wrote at the time: "Much of what is happening now is the result of steady pressure from the United States and the Internation Bank for Reconstruction and Development, which for the last year have been urging a substantial freeing of the Indian economy and a greater scope for private enterprises."

In 1960 the oil-producing countries established the Organization of Petroleum Exporting Countries, which has grown more bold and more powerful in the last ten years. OPEC is able to get better prices for crude petroleum and to demand a greater share in oil revenues for the producing countries. The organization makes it more difficult for the oil companies to enlist the State Department in such gross power plays as the Indian fertilizer deal. The oil companies are becoming reconciled to the growing nationalization of the oil fields themselves, although they believe that they will be able to fight successful rear-guard actions for years to come. In this new phase of petroleum development, transportation, refining, and world pricing become even more critical, and these for the most part remain firmly in the hands of the companies. The U.S. and the World Bank, which is managed by Americans and is largely dependent upon U.S. government and private capital, have long discouraged producing companies from building their own refineries, pipelines, and transportation facilities on the ground that the foreign companies can do it much more efficiently. That, of course, is true, but the result, indeed the desired result, from the point of view of the companies, is to keep the producing companies dependent.

As the oil companies become more "multinational," in the sense that their producing and marketing activities become truly global, the government-business partnership is changing. The oil companies themselves, as Robert Engler has put it in *Politics of Oil,* are reaching for a form of world government in which they can rationalize and protect their world-wide activities. Increasingly they are beginning to look like governments themselves. They employ large and competent staffs which specialize in such sovereign functions as intelligence, negotiations with governments, and propaganda. Intelligence analyses prepared by oil companies tend to be more competent, more analytical, and less ideological than similar reports from the official "intelligence community," probably because the companies do not have to defend the past in quite the same way the State Department does.

Increasingly, the "majors" are coming to perceive that their interests and their traditional view of the "national interest" are no longer precisely the same. Monopolistic control of markets, prices, refineries, and transportation facilities and market sharing agreements are a more effective guarantee of stable growth and continued profits in foreign countries than direct pressure from Washington.

8

Changing Patterns of Imperialism: Capitalism, Expansionism, and War

I T IS ONLY a little more than one hundred years since the first serious analytical efforts to identify and to explain the economic drives behind imperialism and how they lead to war. Before John Hobson and his Marxist interpreters, the idea that empires seek to expand their domain, power, and influence through war was taken as a fundamental fact of political life, a phenomenon so universal and so obvious that it required no analysis. The debates on imperialism of the last century have been dominated by Marxist thought. Hilferding, Lenin, Kautsky, Luxemburg, the neo-Marxists of our own day, Baran, Sweezey, Magdoff, O'Connor, as well as the non-Marxists such as Hobson and Schumpeter, all discuss imperialism in terms of economic determinism: Does capitalism produce wars?

The debates on imperialism have generated considerable confusion. In part this is due to the fact that the word is asked to serve too many purposes and thus ends up as debased currency, like "revolution" and other fashionable political words that politicians of every stripe like to make their own. It can mean, for example, domination of one nation by another, in which case it would be appropriate, say, in describing the invasion of Czechoslovakia, to use John Foster Dulles' favorite term "Soviet imperialism," an expression more recently taken up by Mao Tse-tung. It can also be used, as Lenin used it, to describe a stage of capitalist development, in which case it is not necessary to argue that capitalism leads to imperialism because it *is* imperialism. The term is also used, frequently with a "neo" in front of it, to describe a wide range of exploitative relationships between rich, developed capitalist nations and poor, dependent, nonindustrialized countries. Sometimes imperialism is simply equated with foreign investment.

But the confusion also stems from a failure to make certain crucial distinctions in discussing the relationship of capitalism to imperialism and the connection between imperialism and war. According to Leninist theories of imperialism, the modern capitalist nation is driven by internal economic "contradictions" to expand economically and militarily abroad, to dominate weaker peoples, and ultimately to go to war to protect its crucial overseas privileges. The anti-Leninists argue either, like Schumpeter, that capitalism, far from needing war, actually inhibits the warlike impulses of nations, or, like Kautsky, that the contemporary capitalist world, despite the pressures to fight imperialist wars, has an even stronger interest in so regulating its affairs that the cycle of international competition and war Lenin predicts will not occur.

The heart of the debate is the Leninist contention that the capitalist system is inherently expansionist and feeds on war. On the basis of this analysis Leninists make two assertions. First, the overthrow of capitalism is the key to the problem of war. Second, in a socialist world there would be no war. Most of this chapter will deal with the first assertion. But we will begin by briefly considering the second.

The Leninist argument that imperialism, war, and capitalism all live or die together is credible only if one accepts a narrow definition of imperialism and war. Some Marxist theorists define imperialism to mean only those forms of exploitation peculiar to advanced capitalism. Others define war as armed struggle carried on by capitalist states. Such definitions can form the foundation of unassailable theories but they do not explain much. Lenin himself recognized that "imperialism existed before the latest stage of capitalism," but he argued that certain characteristics of "finance capital" which had not existed before the twentieth century explained the peculiar dynamics of modern imperialist wars. It is possible to have a serious debate over whether the economic needs of the contemporary capitalist state are pushing it *toward* or *away* from war. But those who proclaim the faith that wars cease when capitalism is overthrown have left history and politics for religion. Patterns of exploitation, territorial and economic expansion, and war existed before modern capitalism. There is nothing in Marxist theory to explain why in some altered form they should not survive it. Even more to the point, the history of communist states, as the people of Czechoslovakia,

Poland, and Hungary will testify, does not support the simple faith that the overthrow of capitalism brings an end to invading armies or economic exploitation of the weak by the strong. The invasion of Czechoslovakia in 1968 was executed and justified to the world in terms remarkably similar to the American invasion of the Dominican Republic three years earlier.

Nevertheless, there are important differences between socialist imperialism and capitalist imperialism (although less difference between socialist wars and capitalist wars). The Soviet Union under Stalin sacked the countries of Eastern Europe right after World War II and continues to engage in forms of economic warfare with other communist countries. However, as P. J. D. Wiles, in his exhaustive study *Communist International Economics,* observes:

> economic imperialism in any direct sense has practically ceased with Stalin. On the contrary, the U.S.S.R. has moved from the tribute-exacting to the post-imperialist paying out period in one decade. She has never "sent a gunboat." Debt collection and property protection rank miles behind politics for her.*

Thus her foreign aid programs, by and large, have far fewer economic strings to them than U.S. programs, but not a ruble is given without some political return. Yet the Soviets have developed on the foundation of a substantially not-for-profit economy and public ownership of the means of production a national security bureaucracy that looks remarkably like the American, and despite profound differences in economic policy, behaves much like its counterpart too.

Lenin used to argue that if socialist states had to go to war it would be to defend themselves against the remaining capitalist powers. The abolition of war could come about only after the world revolution had ended the capitalist system everywhere. But in the fifty-year history of socialism in Russia, Soviet troops have invaded some socialist states and have threatened to invade others. Indeed, since 1945 Soviet armies have been used only against socialist states. All of this suggests that, whatever else the connection between capitalism and war may be, expansionism, exploitation, and war cannot be automatically ended by getting rid of capitalism.

(2)

BUT IF THE overthrow of capitalism is not sufficient to end the cycle of expansionism and war, is it, nevertheless, a necessary precondi-

* (New York: Frederick A. Praeger, 1969), p. 521. For a description of the difference between communist and capitalist techniques of imperialism and economic warfare, see chapters 16 and 17.

tion? This is the question with which the remainder of this chapter will be concerned. The Leninist theory, which we shall now describe, proclaims the inevitability of war under capitalism. Any social theory bold enough to speak in such terms has an enormous burden of proof to bear. Nonetheless, Lenin's theory of imperialism cannot be easily or comfortably dismissed merely because certain parts of the theory are obviously wrong or inapplicable to the present day or because the whole body of Leninist theory, even as revised, hedged, and refurbished by latter-day disciples, fails to add up to a provable prophecy. The theory must be taken seriously if it proves no more than a tendency. In the nuclear age a social system about which there is even a strong suspicion that it breeds war is plainly unacceptable.

In our analysis of the relevance of capitalist theory to the American experience we shall start, where Lenin started, with the theories of John A. Hobson. Imperialism, he said, is "the use of the machinery of government by private interests, mainly capitalists, to secure for them economic gains outside their country" which would not otherwise be available. Thus gains achieved through imperialism are what the Marxist economist Maurice Dobb calls "privileged investment"—i.e., "investment in projects which carry with them some differential advantage because they are backed by the power of the state."

Hobson argued that imperialism was a consequence of the failure of English capitalism to make an adequate distribution of income to the working class. There were inadequate markets at home because the impoverished worker had no money to buy consumer goods. Therefore, since investment in the British economy was not profitable, the entrepreneur looked abroad for more attractive opportunities. Hobson pointed out that between 1871 and 1911, the years of the greatest colonial expansion, British overseas investments grew in value from 785 million pounds to 3,500 million pounds. "The economic root of Imperialism," Hobson wrote, "is the desire of strong organized industrial and financial interests to secure and develop at the public expense and by the public force markets for their surplus goods and their surplus capital. War, militarism, and a 'spirited foreign policy' are the necessary means to this end." Colonialism was thus a way, Hobson argues, for these "strong financial and industrial interests" to invest their idle funds without redistributing wealth in the domestic economy.*

For Hobson, a British liberal, imperialism was a matter of deliberate choice; the capitalists who ran the Empire believed, erroneously, he thought, that rapid foreign expansion was the easiest way to solve their political and economic problems. Imperialism

* J. A. Hobson, *Imperialism: A Study* (London: Allen and Unwin, rev. ed., 1902), p. 106.

was determined by the "power of the imperialist forces within the nation to use the national resources for their private gain." But there were no iron economic laws that led to this policy. Indeed, Hobson's whole purpose in developing his theory was to argue for income redistribution and market expansion inside England as a substitute for foreign investment. Imperialism, he argued, could and should be ended because it leads to war.

Karl Kautsky, the German Marxist, came to a somewhat similar conclusion by a different route. Drawing on Rudolph Hilferding's *Finanzkapital,* published in 1910, Kautsky argued in the pre–World War I years that the concentration of economic power and the controlling position of banks over capitalist economies had created a wholly new international situation. The rapid trend toward monopolization, the need to export capital, and the rise of protectionism all indicated that the international economy was moving away from free trade and toward competitive imperialism. Like Hobson, he believed that the new imperialism was self-defeating. The burdens of the arms race, which were an inevitable aspect of imperialism, interfered with the development of a productive economy and hence slowed down the accumulation of capital. Through imperialism, capitalism was "digging its own grave." By this time in his life a pacifist and a reformer rather than a revolutionary, Kautsky held out a vision of a less self-defeating imperialism that would possibly lead to peace not war. It was "at any rate conceivable," he argued, that "the joint exploitation of the world by internationally united finance capital in place of the mutual rivalries of national finance capitals" might take place.* In short, the rationalization of the world economy by giant cartels, or, to use the contemporary term, multinational corporations, might serve to snap the link between capitalism and militarism. The hope for peace rested on the possibility that the capitalists might come to see their own true interests.

Lenin angrily rejected any such possibility. For him the phenomenon of imperialism as an inevitable stage of capitalism was an essential foundation stone of a revolutionary theory. He began by adopting Hobson's basic approach and he argued that the capitalists, the new British ruling class, were using imperialism to escape the "contradictions" of their domestic economic system. He quoted Cecil Rhodes as saying in 1895:

> I was in the East End of London [a working-class quarter] yesterday and attended a meeting of the unemployed. I listened to the wild speeches, which were just a cry for "bread! bread!" and on my way home I pondered over the scene and I became

---

* Quoted in George Lichtheim, *Imperialism* (New York: Frederick A. Praeger, 1971), pp. 105 and 106.

more than ever convinced of the importance of imperialism.
. . . My cherished idea is a solution for the social problem, i.e.
in order to save the 40,000,000 inhabitants of the United King-
dom from a bloody civil war, we colonial statesmen must acquire new lands to settle the surplus population, to produce
new markets for the goods produced in the factories and mines.
The Empire, as I have always said, is a bread and butter question. If you want to avoid civil war, you must become imperialists.*

But Lenin differed with Hobson in his unwavering judgment that
capitalism could never rid itself of imperialism and indeed that
imperialism was itself a historically determined stage of capitalism,
the "highest" and final stage. Lenin's thesis was that the formation
of monopolies and the concentration and centralization of capital
under the control of investment banks in developed capitalist economies necessarily leads to a capital surplus which cannot be invested
profitably at home because unions drive wages up. Monopolies are
formed to protect profit margins by investing surplus in economically
underdeveloped areas of the world where wages are low. The power
of the state is invoked to protect the "privileged investment" of the
monopoly capitalists.

In Lenin's theory the need for systematic continuous expansion
in underdeveloped areas occurs only when the industrial sector of
an economy becomes concentrated in the hands of a few owners,
and banks begin to dominate "all the economic and political institutions of contemporary capitalist society." Then the pressures to
find cheap raw materials to feed the mushrooming industrial machine and to secure new outlets for profitable investment become
irresistible. Profit margins are higher in underdeveloped areas abroad
than at home because labor costs in colonial areas can be kept at
subsistence level by the judicious use of the army and the police,
while in the advanced industrial countries it has become impossible
to maintain sweatshop conditions because of public pressure and
the increasing use of labor-saving machines.

In Lenin's theory, the competition of capitalist nations to carve
up the exploitable world would lead inevitably to war, for, as he argues, capitalist powers divide up the world on the basis of a "calculation . . . of strength," and since "the relative strength of the
capitalist powers" is always changing, some country is always ready
to fight to protect its position of dominance, or to challenge the
top dog. This explanation for the inevitability of war under capitalism has come to be known as the theory of uneven development.

Lenin's theory, as George Lichtheim has pointed out, had a dual

* Lenin, *Imperialism* (New York: International Publishers, 1939).

function. It was designed to explain the extraordinary upsurge of European and American foreign investment at the end of the nineteenth century and it also provided an analysis of the structural changes in the world economy associated with "finance capital" or "monopoly capital." In addition, it served the purpose of explaining why the revolution had not happened. Marx had predicted that the accelerating misery of the worker under capitalism would make him a revolutionary, for he would have nothing to lose by revolution but his chains. In the two generations since Marx's death, contrary to his predictions, wages had risen and working conditions had substantially improved. "Monopolistically high profits," Lenin explained, make it economically possible for the capitalists "to corrupt certain sections of the working class, and for a time a fairly considerable minority, and win them to the side of the bourgeoisie of a given industry or nation against all the others." Out of the "enormous superprofits" which the "powerful world plunderers armed to the teeth [America, Great Britain, Japan]" exacted from the colonial world, "it is *possible to bribe* the labor leaders and the upper stratum of the labor aristocracy." Imperialist adventures abroad preserve the position of the capitalists at home. In short, Lenin argued, the welfare imperialism of Austen Chamberlain (and, he would have added, Harry Truman and Lyndon Johnson) works, at least for a while.*

If Lenin's theory was designed, in part at least, to explain the delayed revolution, one of Joseph Schumpeter's principal motivations for writing *Imperialism* in 1919 was to explain the catastrophe that had just brought the empires of Europe close to ruin and to defend capitalism from the charge that the system itself was responsible for the carnage. Schumpeter based his theory on a historical analysis of empires of the past, including the Egyptian, Frankish, and Arabian. The problem, as he saw it, was not to explain why empires go to war but why they go to war for ultimately self-defeating purposes. In short, Schumpeter is interested in why great nations act contrary to their own interests and in particular why the capitalist classes in charge of modern nations seem so ready to play out the irrational, self-destructive role assigned to them in Lenin's theory (which, by the way, in 1919 he had yet to read). His definition of imperialism is "the objectless disposition on the part of a state to unlimited forcible expansion." †

Schumpeter's analysis of imperialism begins with an inquiry into the interests of the ruling class: "There is but one way to an understanding: scrutiny of domestic class interests, the question of who

---

* Lenin's arguments on welfare imperialism are also in *Imperialism.*
† Joseph Schumpeter, *Imperialism and Social Classes,* trans. Heinz Norden (New York: World Publishing Co., 1968), p. 51.

stood to gain." The ruling class, he says, "was always inclined to declare that the country was in danger when it was really only class interests that were threatened." This is, of course, the same analysis the Marxists make. Where Schumpeter diverges from the Marxists is in his way of looking at domestic interests. "Our analysis of the historical evidence," he writes, "has shown . . . that non-rational and irrational, purely instinctual urges towards war and conquest play a very large role in the history of mankind." Men in charge of societies act out of personal or class interests, but they often interpret these interests irrationally. Just as Marx had said that the exploited classes suffered from "false consciousness" and so misconceived their true stake in revolution, so Schumpeter suggests that the capitalist ruling classes, suffering from a similar sort of false consciousness, fail to understand their real interest in peace. The capitalists have a vested interest in peace because war interferes with moneymaking. "A purely capitalist world," Schumpeter argues, "can offer no fertile soil to imperialist impulses," because the capitalists can get richer through free trade than they can through war. The race to accumulate absorbs the energy of the ruling class and leaves little left over for war and conquest. Imperialism is contrary to the "inner logic" of capitalism.*

Why then in 1914 did the most advanced capitalist nations hurl major portions of their populations at each other in a war fought, in good part at least, over colonial expansion? Imperialism in the modern capitalist state, Schumpeter insists, is "atavistic." It originates from "past rather than present relations of production." The martial spirit, the love of glory, and the weakness for the holy war all played an important role in keeping rulers of past ages in power. The ideology of capitalism, he argues, is pacifism. In a purely capitalist world, he asserts, "wars of conquest and adventurism in foreign policy are bound to be regarded as troublesome distractions." Wars persist only because the institutions of precapitalist society survive. "Created by wars that required it, the machine now created the wars it required." In this brilliant formulation, Schumpeter captures the essence of an alternative theory of imperialism. "The gain of the capitalists as a class cannot be a motive for war" in an open world of free trade, but vestigial institutions from an autocratic past, such as the army or aristocracy or militant church, can still push a nation into imperialism.† Schumpeter argues, contrary to Marx, that the state, which promotes and manages wars, is not the executive committee of the bourgeoisie but is a distinct entity with interests of its own which do not always coincide with the true interests of the ruling capitalist class. "The bourgeoisie seeks to win over the state for itself

* *Ibid.*, p. 53.
† *Ibid.*, p. 64.

and in return serves the state and state interests that are different from its own." *

(3)

THERE IS MUCH that these four thinkers, Hobson, Lenin, Kautsky, and Schumpeter, have to teach us about contemporary imperialism. Anyone trying to make sense of American expansionism and militarism is in debt to all of them. But he must borrow selectively. Schumpeter's insight that the state has interests different from the capitalist class as a whole or the major corporations in particular is borne out, as we discussed in Chapter 7, by the American experience. His understanding of the imperialist habit of mind and bureaucratic momentum make his work extraordinarily relevant. At the same time, the portrait he paints of the modern capitalist state —nonexpansionist, free trading, peace-loving, disturbed only by old soldiers who refuse to die—is as faithful a reproduction of contemporary reality as a faded daguerreotype. Despite Schumpeter's prophecy and contrary to his advice, neither capitalists nor capitalist states have interpreted their real interests as avoiding "such things as protective tariffs, cartels, monopoly prices, forced exports (dumping), an aggressive economic policy, an aggressive foreign policy generally. . . ." It is almost as if the State Department had taken Schumpeter's list of evils to be avoided as its guide.

Lenin's theory of imperialism has been criticized for inaccurately reflecting the period he was studying. Some historians have cast serious doubt on Lenin's major premise that the principal imperialist countries were in fact in the grip of monopoly capitalism at the beginning of the twentieth century. As James O'Connor points out, "in the most powerful imperial country, Great Britain, there were few trusts or cartels of any consequence in 1900." † The investment in the colonies was not under the control of the big banks, as Lenin's theory pictured it, but enterprises such as the British East Africa Company raised their capital from small investors such as retired military officers. Nor, as Robinson and Gallagher have shown, did the African colonies turn out to be particularly profitable, either as trading partners or major absorbers of capital. Indeed, as Lichtheim has pointed out, "the bulk of British investment, before and after 1914, went to the developed industrial areas of Western Europe,

---

* *Ibid.*, p. 25.

† See D. K. Fieldhouse, "Imperialism: A Historiographical Revision," *Economic History Review*, XIV, 1961. (Cited in K. T. Fann and Donald Hodges, eds., *Readings in U.S. Imperialism* [Boston: Porter Sargent, 1971], p. 34.)

North America, South Africa, and Australia–New Zealand, leaving the dependent tropical empire starved of investment capital." *

Contemporary critics correctly point out that the principal U.S. foreign investment is not in the poor countries, as Lenin predicted, but in the rich countries. Neither is foreign trade with the Third World crucial to the U.S. economy in quantative items. In 1968 total U.S. exports amounted to $34 billion, about 4 per cent of the Gross National Product, according to the New York University economists S. M. Miller, Roy Bennett, and Ahmed Rhazaoui.† The same economists estimate that about one-third of these exports went to low-income countries. The Third World has been getting a declining share of U.S. exports since 1955.

As of 1966 the total accumulated investment of all rich countries in poor countries (at book value) was $28.4 billion. Four out of every ten dollars of this investment was in oil. In recent years, as Miller et al. have found, "investment in low-income countries is a sharply declining percentage of the annual investments of all high-income countries." The United States appears to follow this pattern. In 1968, 31.4 per cent of all U.S. overseas investment was in low-income countries while at the beginning of the decade more than 36 per cent of total overseas investment was in the Third World. Profits repatriated from U.S. investment in poor countries in 1968, according to *Survey of Current Business,* were $2.9 billion, about 4 per cent of the profits from the domestic operations of U.S. corporations.

While these profits were often crucial to particular corporations they are not, so the critics of Leninist theory argue, of a magnitude to be critical to the survival of the economy as a whole. In other words, the managers of the U.S. corporate economy could sacrifice the whole investment, if they chose, in the interests of curbing militarism and avoiding war without courting collapse of the whole economy, provided they were willing to expand investment in the public sector in the United States and to enlarge the domestic market by substantially raising the income of the poor (which Hobson had said was the only alternative to imperialism). Thus the contemporary critics of Leninist theory argue, much as Hobson did, that using the state to promote and back up imperialist investment in weak economies is a matter of choice for the United States. The United States, they argue, does not need the poor countries. Relations with the Third World are sufficiently marginal to the operation of America's trillion-dollar economy that Americans could pay higher prices for raw materials and invest on more generous terms

* Lichtheim, *op. cit.,* p. 117.
† "A Neo-Imperialism Critique: Do the Rich Nations Need the Poor?" an unpublished paper.

without interfering with American prosperity. Some companies would suffer. Consumers might pay a few cents a pound more for coffee. But the U.S. economy would hardly collapse if the United States adopted a policy toward foreign trade and investment which was, in the recent words of a Washington *Post* editorial writer, "more reflective of its ideals and its long-term interests." Gunnar Myrdal points out that the rich countries exploit the poor nations precisely because they are not dependent upon them.

Neo-Leninist critics such as Harry Magdoff argue that such a quantative analysis of American imperialism is misleading. It is the most technologically advanced and most politically powerful corporations that depend most heavily upon the machinery of the state to open up the rest of the world to American business. It is these corporations, as we have seen, which exercise a decisive influence on U.S. policy in many areas. Moreover, as Baran and Sweezy have argued, the crucial drive toward foreign economic expansion is not the falling rate of profit, as Lenin thought, but the inability of advanced capitalist economies to absorb economic surplus. Surplus, in Marxist theory, is socially wasteful production.

In a capitalist society surplus accumulates at a fast rate because corporations continually seek to lower costs and maximize profits. There is an increasing problem of absorbing the surplus in the home economy, as James O'Connor argues, because huge subsidized corporations which feel no competitive pressure to be more efficient tend increasingly to be capital-saving, since their managers "suppress new technologies to preserve the value of existing productive capacity." This idle capital cannot be invested in such a way as to increase the domestic consumer market because the population does not have the purchasing power or the confidence in the future to keep buying consumer goods at a sufficiently accelerating rate. There are also political limits on the government's ability to absorb surplus by investing in public housing, health, or other welfare activities which compete with already existing services and commodities in the private sector. Therefore, the only solution to the maintenance of a growth economy is to keep expanding the market until it is global in its reach. High military expenditures are indispensable to the solution of the surplus problem in two ways. First, as Luxemburg pointed out, the military budget is itself a device for absorbing almost infinite investment. Weapons never glut the market because every few years weapons systems are declared obsolete and replaced by even more expensive models. Second, a powerful military is an indispensable instrument for opening up the global market to American firms.

We come now to the single strongest argument for the proposition that the American economy cannot survive without the American

empire: The United States is in many crucial respects a "have-not nation." Americans constitute 6 per cent of the world population and consume each year more than 50 per cent of its resources. Many of the most critical resources are no longer produced in abundance within the continental United States. In 1966, for example, the United States produced 35,000 tons of manganese ore and imported over 2,365,000 tons. Manganese is essential for the production of steel. Eighty to 90 per cent of bauxite, without which aluminum cannot be made and hence without which no airplane can be produced, comes from foreign sources. Almost 100 per cent of colombium, chromium, and cobalt, all used in amounts varying from ten to 2,800 pounds in every jet engine, must be imported.*
It has been estimated by mining experts that by 1980, 50 per cent of U.S. iron-ore needs will have to be met by imports and by the year 2000 about 75 per cent. The United States, which in the 1920's used to be a net exporter of minerals, has in the postwar period been forced to import an increasingly major portion of its critical mineral requirements. This has been due not only to the population rise but to the dramatic changes in technology and consumption rates. The electrification of America has led to a heavy dependence on copper, which is used as the primary conductor of electrical current. The United States consumed in 1967 about 18 pounds per person while world-wide per capita consumption was 3.2 pounds. Although the United States is the world's largest copper producer, it is a net importer of this crucial metal since domestic production costs are so high.

According to Charles C. Park, Jr., former Dean of Mineral Sciences at Stanford University, "90 of the minerals most essential to the nation's industrial complex" must be imported by the United States. In 1954, a staff report of the President's Commission on Foreign Economic Policy analyzed the problem in the following terms:

> This transition of the United States from a position of relative self-sufficiency to one of increasing dependence upon foreign sources of supply constitutes one of the striking economic changes of our time. The outbreak of World War II marked the major turning point of this change.
> Both from the viewpoint of our long-term economic growth and the viewpoint of our national defense, the shift of the United States from the position of a net exporter of metals and

---

* Harry Magdoff, *The Age of Imperialism* (New York: Monthly Review Press, 1969), p. 52. See also Charles F. Park, Jr., *Affluence in Jeopardy* (San Francisco: Freeman, Cooper and Co., 1968); Gabriel Kolko, *The Roots of American Foreign Policy* (Boston: Beacon Press, 1969); and the 1962 report of the President's Materials Commission (The Paley Report).

minerals to that of a net importer is of overshadowing significance in shaping our foreign economic policies.

In the early 1950's the International Development Advisory
Board concluded that about three-quarters of the minerals deemed
strategic enough to stockpile under government programs came
from the underdeveloped world. Those who argue that the raw material dependency of the United States is a key factor in shaping its
foreign policy can cite not only the objective needs of U.S. industry
but also the frequent expressions of alarm by leading political figures
that our economy is to a great extent at the mercy of political developments in the poor, raw-material-producing countries. "The
loss of any of these materials through aggression," concluded the
International Development Advisory Board, "would be the equivalent
of a grave military setback." The Rockefeller Brothers Fund report
puts it this way:

> Nevertheless, the economic situation of the industrialized
> nations remains precarious. If Asian, Middle Eastern and Afri-
> can nationalism exploited by the Soviet bloc, becomes a destruc-
> tive force, European supplies of oil and other essential raw
> materials may be jeopardized.

"If by a show of aid they succeed in extending the communist rule
throughout Asia and Africa," Vice-President Richard Nixon warned
a conference on private investment in 1957, "the Kremlin will have
won. It would control their immense wealth in oil, uranium, copper
and many other materials essential for the economic life of the free
world. And the Western world would be forced to surrender without
firing a shot."

Military bureaucrats like to stress the important contribution
which the military machine makes to America's economic requirements. In 1969, for example, the Navy testified before the House
Armed Services Committee:

> There are about 30 selected metals and minerals critical
> enough to the security of the Nation that they are stockpiled
> and specifically reported by the Department of the Interior. We
> are dependent upon other countries for a major portion of these
> materials—over 63 percent. This dependency is growing. Some
> percentages of foreign dependencies are:

Beryllium (ore)	100	Manganese (ore)	99
Chromite	100	Mica (sheet)	99
Columtium	100	Platinum	99
Tin	100	Rutile (i.e., titanium)	99
Tantalum	99	Antimony	95

Asbestos	95	Zinc	60
Cobalt	92	Lead	55
Nickel	91	Mercury	50
Aluminum	89	Copper	41
Silver	82	Tungsten	38
Fluorspar	74	Iron (ore)	34
Cadmium	60		

The freedom of the seas that these facts of life demand is only assured if we can assure that no potential enemy is strong enough to take it away.

There is no doubt that the U.S. standard of living depends upon maintaining mineral concessions, marketing arrangements, and trade agreements which will insure that coffee stays on the grocery shelf at prices housewives can afford and, more important, that the flow of manganese, copper, and bauxite to American factories is uninterrupted. An ever-expanding consumer economy in a country with serious deficiencies in natural resources can only be maintained by an ever-extending global reach. Even such non-Marxist observers of America as Claude Julien, the foreign editor of *Le Monde,* are pessimistic about American foreign policy for just such reasons. "Founded on the economic empire," he concludes, "the American way of life would probably not survive a withdrawal within national boundaries." *

(4)

THE NEO-LENINIST argument that America has no choice but to pursue expansionist policies, both economic and military, is formidable. Those who deny its force usually point out, as S. M. Miller does, that the total dollar value of nonferrous metals imported from low-income countries in 1967, for example, was only $2.3 billion. How could an item of such relatively small value in comparison with the GNP account for America's interventionist policies? Since, however, these metals are crucial components of the nation's industrial output, such a comparison of figures does not dispose of the issue, particularly since the costs of militarist policies are distributed widely throughout the society, and the short-term benefits, as we have seen, accrue to the biggest and most powerful corporations. The ex-

* See Claude Julien, *The American Empire,* trans. Renaud Bruce (New York: Random House, 1971).

pressions of alarm of government officials and industry leaders about the need to assure uninterrupted access to strategic materials located abroad seem much more convincing.

Nonetheless, there are some problems not only with the neo-Leninist theory but with the implications that are often drawn from it. It is often assumed in Marxist writings that a socialist America would be less dependent upon strategic raw materials from abroad. But any government, whatever its political ideology and whoever owns the means of production, will face the same choice as the present one. A society dedicated to growth will make the same demands on resources whether it is capitalist or socialist. One can argue that it was capitalism that created the unbridled appetites we now associate with civilization, and that the profit system through advertising helped to make consumption the prime civic virtue. But the socialist world is now also committed to ever-expanding growth, and, in the Soviet Union, conspicuous consumption is a badge of social achievement. There is nothing to suggest that a socialist government along the Soviet or even the Chinese model would seek to wean the American people away from the American way of life. Clearly, there is no reasonable prospect that the United States will reduce its claim on the world's resources under the system of state capitalism now evolving. Because the essence of American capitalism is growth, the adoption of a "zero-growth" economy or policies aimed at reducing consumption seem inconsistent with that system. But if the price for ending imperialist policies is to cut wasteful consumption, then the solution must be more radical than socialism as it has been preached. Only a government prepared to sell the American people on a very different value system or one prepared to coerce them into austerity can hope to reduce the national dependence on foreign resources. These are the most crucial problems facing the next generation of Americans and they transcend questions of profit and private ownership.*

Another assumption in the neo-Leninist analysis of raw materials which is frequently echoed by businessmen is that the United States can only preserve its access to vital raw materials if it succeeds in preventing revolutionary or nationalist governments from coming to power in producing countries. For this reason, it is argued, the United States will continue to intervene militarily throughout the Third World. But the assumption that once raw-material-producing countries leave the "Free World" they will deny the United States

---

* Whether some form of community ownership under which decentralized political entities own or have control over productive resources is a good idea, which I happen to think it is, is a question to be decided on its own merits—i.e., whether it is sound domestic policy. It is misleading to use foreign policy to make the case for the necessity of socialism.

their minerals on ideological grounds is not borne out by recent history. No revolutionary regime which has come to power in recent years has proposed cutting off trade with capitalist countries. Indeed, the Soviet Union, Cuba, and Eastern European regimes have pressed the United States to buy their raw materials. Even North Vietnamese officials have told American visitors that they would welcome trade after the war. (It should not be forgotten that Algeria has become a major trading partner of its former brutal colonial master.) Trade with the communist world has been limited because the United States has practiced economic warfare against regimes that were ideologically repugnant to her, such as Castro's Cuba, in the hope of weakening or overthrowing them. But while revolutionary regimes are quite prepared to sell vital raw materials to the United States, they are not prepared to give them away or to subsidize U.S. industries. They want what they regard as a fair price and on ideological grounds they oppose the exercise of economic power on their own territory by foreign corporations. What all this means is that corporations doing business with revolutionary movements can no longer have the same control that they could exert on dependent countries in the past. They must now either accept lower profits, or, more likely, pass the added costs of doing business on to the American consumer. But even revolutionary regimes in poor countries depend upon foreign exchange. They cannot charge anything they like since few countries have a monopoly on any raw material and all are to a great extent dependent upon the international market. No one has made a plausible argument why American capitalism should collapse if the costs of certain raw materials go up. Some corporations may be unable to get used to doing business in anything but the grand manner of Cecil Rhodes, but their demise, surely a social benefit, would hardly cause an economic ripple. The Ford Motor Company has a huge assembly plant in Rhodesia which it would certainly not like to have nationalized. But if the oppressive white minority were ever overthrown by a revolutionary regime, Ford would survive. Indeed, so dependent upon foreign technology and foreign-controlled market arrangements is any poor country, whatever its political ideology, that Ford would probably be invited to stay, although under less favorable terms. If the Ford Motor Company can enter a joint venture to produce trucks in communist Russia it can do business in revolutionary Rhodesia. The economic giants, which exercise important influence on U.S. national security policy, are precisely the institutions with the resources to adjust to doing business in revolutionary societies. That they would prefer to deal with a Prime Minister who is on their payroll or a stockholder, or to work with graduates of Eton rather than former guerrillas is obvious. But that IBM, Standard Oil, and General Motors can and will do business with the most militant revolutionaries is beyond doubt. A case in point is the billion-dollar natural gas deal El Paso gas concluded with the socialist government of Algeria at a time when the United States had no diplomatic relations with that government. Ironically, the deal was negotiated by Clark Clifford, one of the influential architects of U.S. Cold War policy.

The long-term situation poses a different problem. For the first time in human history the exhaustion of critical raw materials has become a plausible possibility. The industrial regions consume 77 per cent of the world's coal, 81 per cent of the world's petroleum, and 95 per cent of the world's natural gas. Competition among the industrial nations for access to energy sources and critical metals will sharpen in all events because escalating demands are outrunning dwindling supplies. (Such proposals as the development of synthetics or the cultivation of the ocean bed offer no panaceas as these processes themselves require massive consumption of energy.) If Third World countries under revolutionary regimes were to undertake major industrialization programs by diverting a much greater share of their own energy sources and critical metals to their own use, obviously the problems of the developed countries, particularly the United States with its enormous requirements, would become very serious indeed. American studies of raw materials, such as the Levy Report on oil prepared for the World Bank, argue that producing countries should not and probably will not develop their own industrial system to exploit their own resources.* And, as we have seen, U.S. policy does nothing to encourage such development. There is no doubt that there is a fundamental conflict between Third World countries wishing to industrialize and the present industrial powers, particularly the United States, which wishes to continue the dependence of poor countries on the international oil companies, U.S. mining interests, and U.S. financing. But the poor countries have little capacity to use their own resources even if they were to embark on an ambitious industrialization effort. For the foreseeable future they have no choice but to sell raw materials to finance their imports and their efforts at industrialization. It will be a long time before the competitive claims of the poor for scarce resources will be felt. But the competition for resources among the rich is growing intense.

The real basis of the Leninist argument that capitalist states cannot control their imperialist impulses is politics, not economics. It is possible to envisage a form of capitalist economy in the United

---

* Report by W. J. Levy, Inc., to the International Bank for Reconstruction and Development, "The Search for Oil in Developing Countries: A Problem of Scarce Resources and Its Implications for State and Private Enterprise," 1960. See also Edith T. Penrose, *The International Petroleum Industry* (Cambridge: M.I.T. Press, 1968), especially Chapter 3.

States adequate for maintaining prosperity and a reasonable standard of living that did not depend upon the continuation of the most egregious imperialist practices of the past. It would be government policy to encourage U.S. firms to divest their investment in poor countries and to supply technological knowhow to help countries build up their own productive resources. More generous marketing and pricing arrangements for the Third World would be adopted. Military interventions would be abandoned. The defense budget would be drastically cut and investment in American society would rise dramatically. The hundreds of billions needed to rebuild our cities, to clean up the rivers, lakes, and air, to provide education and health care for all, and to eliminate hunger would be spent. The tax structure and other fiscal policies would be revised to encourage a rapid redistribution of income to build up an American market. Government policy would encourage American factories to export products that met real needs of the majority of the earth's population —cheap, simple, durable necessities of life—and would discourage the current destructive practice of regarding the rest of the world as a place to unload goods that cannot be sold here. Industries that cannot compete with foreign countries, including defense industries, would be assisted to convert to something more productive. Waste and inefficiency, whether in missile plants or shoe factories, would not continue to be subsidized.

An American economy reconstructed along such lines would not end American imperialism. The sheer power and size of the United States would still give Americans enormous advantages in dealing with weaker countries and these advantages would continue to be exploited, at least to some degree. But such changes would have an extraordinary impact upon the whole world and would open up the possibility of building a more rational world economy in which the poor do not continue to get poorer. All such changes, as radical as they may appear, are theoretically possible within the framework of the present American economic system.

If the United States does not move in this direction the reason will not be iron laws of economics but political inflexibility. It will mean that the managers of the American economy are incapable of perceiving their own long-term interests. Like those who struggled against Franklin Roosevelt's emergency resuscitation of capitalism, the current generation of managers appears ready to court economic and social disaster by clutching privilege too long. The Leninist theory states that the ruling class is fated to commit economic suicide by failing to accommodate the system fast enough to cope with its growing contradictions. The contradictions in the American economic system are there for anyone to see—a growing fiscal crisis, an employment crisis, a productivity crisis, a balance of payments crisis, a trade crisis, and the specter of world depression triggered by the very protectionist devices used to manage these crises. What indications are there that the national security managers and the corporate managers are prepared to deal with these crises without imperialism and without war?

(5)

IT IS IMPORTANT to distinguish the issues of imperialism and war. If we define imperialism in its broadest terms—domination of the weak by the strong—it appears to be an inevitable part of the human condition. Indeed, even Hobson's definition with which we started the discussion—the use of state machinery to advance national economic interests—is broad enough to be applicable to many different economic and political systems. Even if all the anti-imperialist policies he recommends or those just outlined above were followed, a great nation such as the United States would still exhibit some expansionist tendencies. There appears to be an unbreakable link between the concentration of great power in the nation-state, irrespective of economic system, and the impulse to dominate and control other nations. This impulse manifests itself in special ways under capitalism because under that system certain attitudes and needs have been developed and the techniques of domination have been perfected. But it is impossible to conceive of any reforms within the structure of the capitalist nation-state (or within the socialist nation-state for that matter) that promise to end the economic exploitation of weak, dependent peoples by stronger peoples who are technologically advanced and are free of the historic self-doubts of the colonized. Excesses can be curbed, gross injustices corrected, and present unfavorable trends in the economic relations between the Third World and the advanced industrial countries can be reversed. But as long as international society is composed of nation-states of varying size and power, imperialism in some form will remain.

The link between imperialism and war, however, is another matter. There are important trends now discernible in the United States and in international society that lend credibility to Karl Kautsky's predictions in the second decade of our century. Kautsky, it will be recalled, raised the prospect of an "ultra-imperialism," an imperialism of peace, as an alternative to Lenin's vision of inevitable, cataclysmic war. His prediction of the "joint exploitation of the world internationally united finance capital in place of the mutual rivalries of national finance capitals" is coming to pass in the age of the multinational corporation. Although the postwar period is perhaps the most dynamic expansionist era in the history of capitalism, the wars between capitalist nations which Lenin prophesied have never seemed more remote. The number one nation talks about initiating an era of negotiation and a generation of peace and the communist powers declare that war is not inevitable. In large measure such moderate talk and cautious action are the consequences of the atomic bomb and the realization that nuclear war is self-defeating. The elites of the Great Powers, despite attempts at atomic diplomacy and talk of preventive war, saw this almost as soon as the mushroom cloud lifted over Hiroshima. But the idea that the use of conventional military power for traditional imperial purposes may also be self-defeating is now gaining currency among America's leading corporate managers. This recrudescence of "business pacifism" dates from the Vietnam War, or, to be more accurate, from the moment when the financial community perceived it to be a failure.

The Vietnam War forced the managers of the American corporate economy to ask themselves for the first time in a serious way whether territorial control and political influence abroad is worth the price of war. The debacle in Southeast Asia is a watershed in American history because American leaders under pressure began to calculate the costs of imperial wars. Until Vietnam, America's wars, as Eliot Janeway has put it, "seem to have paid not only somebody, but usually almost everybody." The lesson that Norman Angell tried to teach in 1909 in his book *The Great Illusion,* namely that war does not pay, was never taken seriously in the United States because it was plainly not applicable to the American experience. As we saw in Part I, World War II showered the American people with benefits—economic prosperity, a scientific and industrial explosion, a sense of national purpose, not to mention much of what was left of other people's empires. World War I weakened the European victors and World War II brought them to the edge of bankruptcy, but the United States benefited from both. Even the staggering human tragedy of the Civil War had produced an economic boom. In the postwar period the Korean War, as Eliot Janeway has analyzed it, was "the last of the long line of America's wars to prove an unquestionable plus for the economy," * although the United States achieved only a stalemate at best. But the war in Vietnam was an economic crisis for America instead of an economic opportunity.

The inescapable reality that the Vietnam War is an economic "loser"—that the expenditure of more than $90 million a day for six years has purchased neither peace nor prosperity—has shattered the business consensus in support of high defense budgets and military

* *The Economy of Crisis* (New York: Weybright and Talley, 1968), p. 3.

interventionism. A Louis Harris poll taken immediately after President Nixon's invasion of Cambodia in May 1970 revealed that 78 per cent of top executives in the five hundred largest firms thought that the President's policies had contributed to the biggest drop in the stock market since the 1929 crash. More than a third of these businessmen, a group which traditionally supports any President in a war and certainly any Republican President, expressed active opposition to the Nixon policy and another 17 per cent expressed doubts. American businessmen began to express the same distrust about the management of the U.S. economy that European bankers had previously manifested in the recurring monetary crises of the 1960's. The President of DuPont and the Chairman of International Business Machines spoke of the disastrous economic effects of the war, which, the DuPont chief executive declared, was "tearing at the whole fabric of our social and political and economic life." The Urban Coalition, a group composed of some of the same liberal businessmen who not so many years ago enthusiastically endorsed the concept of a permanent war economy and high government investment overseas through foreign aid, now favor a $24 billion cut in the military budget. Their enthusiasm for foreign aid is muted as well.

The testimony of Louis B. Lundborg, Chairman of the Board of the Bank of America, before the Senate Foreign Relations Committee is a good illustration of the new skepticism in the business world about militarist policies:

A good part of the progressive deterioration in this position over the years since 1964, the year before the major acceleration of the Vietnam war, may be accounted for by the large increase in foreign exchange outflows associated with military expenditures. These rose from less than $3 billion in 1964 to nearly $5 billion in 1969. This, however, is not the only measure of the impact of the war and the subsequent inflation on the balance of payments. The more important impact and the one which is likely to have the most long-lasting effects is on our competitive position in international and domestic markets, reflected in the rapid rise in the rate of importing of goods and services. . . .

When we survey the very real needs in our economy in the areas of housing, urban transit, environmental pollution, etc. it is clearly evident that we do not need to create war-related demand for resources in order to maintain full employment. Our problem now is one of establishing meaningful priorities to meet the quality-of-life demands of our citizenry.*

* Louis B. Lundborg, "Statement to the U.S. Senate Committee on Foreign Relations," April 15, 1970. In Seymour Melman, *The War Economy* (New York: Oxford University Press, 1970), p. 175.

Aviation Week and Space Technology, one of the leading trade journals of the high-technology weaponeers, condemned the Nixon war policy because it was giving "preparedness" a bad name in the country and was leading to what it termed an "assault with broad axe and butcher knife" on the defense budget. Although oil and copper companies sold huge quantities of their products to the American forces in Vietnam, they discovered that the state was less able to protect their interests than before the war. Because of widespread fears of "another Vietnam" the Nixon Administration was far more acquiescent in the expropriations of U.S.-owned strategic resources in Peru and Chile than it undoubtedly would have been in the pre-Vietnam era. Corporate managers are also aware that the war machine is the biggest single devourer of scarce metals.

It would be foolish to exaggerate the changes in perception and calculation of interests that are taking place among businessmen. Obviously some firms, particularly shipping, construction, helicopters, and small arms, have benefited substantially from the war and would be quite happy to merchandise future wars. But the corporate giants are concerned ultimately about the investment climate in the United States, where they have about one trillion dollars invested. The domestic fiscal crisis that plagues every large city, the inflation that fuels the growing consumer revolt, the recurring bomb threats that periodically empty buildings and delay airplanes, the violence of the inner city, the mounting drug crisis, and the general air of dissatisfaction in the country are traceable in large measure to what are now generally known as "distorted priorities" and the consequent failure of the nation to deal with its real problems. The failure of a government absorbed in foreign wars to invest in social infrastructure in the United States seriously affects the American investment climate.

The new American corporate managers are more sophisticated than the primitive capitalist of a generation ago. They are, if anything, more expansionist. "American business cannot long afford to ignore these emerging and developing lands," a former Vice-President of General Foods writes in a how-to-do-it book on foreign investment, "if we do, we will wake up one day to find that the best 'plums' have been taken up by more thoughtful investors from these other parts of the world."

But increasingly they recognize that economic power is a much more practical instrument than military power for expanding markets and securing access to raw materials. While the most advanced sectors of American industry are quite prepared to sell sensors, computers, and other esoteric devices necessary for the "electronic battlefield" which is supposed to make painless low-key military intervention in poor countries practical, businessmen are increasingly skeptical about the ability of the military to protect their interests. They recognize better than the military managers, since they have no career investment in counterinsurgency, that fighting wars, even small wars, in primitive economies against a backdrop of Great Power conflict and nuclear weapons is uneconomic. They know that the more technologically complex military systems become, the more vulnerable they are to sabotage by guerrilla forces. Capital-intensive war may solve political problems for politicians who are understandably reluctant to conscript voters for interminable battles in the mud of Asia or the mountains of Brazil. But unless it meets with instant success, high-technology combat soon incurs costs that outweigh the benefits.

Finally, corporations that are increasingly dependent upon foreign operations have image problems. If the U.S. government pursues the same basic strategy in other countries facing insurgency that it tried in Vietnam, it will reflect badly on American corporations abroad. Bureaucratic homicide engenders anti-Americanism, which complicates life for corporate managers—unfriendly local banks, customer resistance, even smashed windows. Thus, American businessmen are beginning to see that strong government economic support is much more useful in their competitive battles than military support. They note that the Japanese, German, and Dutch businessmen have prospered despite the loss of their colonies and military empires. The most powerful U.S. corporations are beginning to understand that even nationalization is not the end of the world. Let the poor countries take over a majority interest in their own natural resources or even all of it. What if Chile owns the copper? It will still have to be processed and shipped. U.S. firms are still in a position to make huge profits by supplying these essential services. Typically, the same U.S. firms that own natural resources in poor countries also control essential processing, transportation, and marketing facilities. Oil-producing countries can organize, as they have, to get better prices each year for crude petroleum but they are still at the mercy of the foreign oil giants, most of them American, that have the tankers, refineries, and pipelines—the key for turning an intrinsically worthless viscous substance into revenue.

Recognizing all this, corporate managers are seeking to minimize their relationship with the U.S. government when they operate abroad. Having found that even with the whole panoply of weapons at its disposal the State Department cannot prevent nationalization, they prefer, in an increasing number of cases, to develop their own strategies. Many U.S. firms are vigorously trying to project a "multi-national" image. Recent articles in trade journals warn executives not to confine their social contacts to the "American community," to stay away from the embassy, and even to avoid hotels identified as "American" either because of their ownership or clientèle. Obviously, corporation executives still go to Washington to seek all sorts of assistance from the U.S. government, especially when nationalization is under way, but contingency planning against future nationalization is based increasingly on the economic power of the corporation rather than on the military power of the state.

(6)

IS THE RISE of the multinational corporation the fulfillment of Kautsky's vision of an imperialism of peace? The managers of these giant corporate units are becoming aware that their interests and the interests of the national security managers clash. Guided as they are by exclusively economic criteria, the corporate managers are coming to see that the pursuit of the national interest through military power threatens corporate property and corporate profits. In his study of the leading high-technology industries in the United States, Michael Maccoby finds that the managers are coming to see themselves as a self-conscious class with a new transnational ideology. The nation-state is obsolete. Patriotism is old-fashioned and glory is much too expensive to purchase at the cost of sound money and corporate expansion. Multinational corporations no longer need the state to open up or guarantee markets. They do better on their own. Indeed, as we have seen, the shrewd executive believes that national identification is an encumbrance. States are territorial; capital is international. Hence corporations can penetrate foreign economies under the banner of international economic cooperation while the state must continually defend itself against charges of colonialism and imperialism.

George Ball, Herman Kahn, and other celebrators of the multinational corporation proclaim the dawn of a new era in international relations. The corporation has outgrown the state, ushering in what Robert Heilbroner calls a "businessman's peace" in which "pragmatism and production take precedence over national pride and vainglory." The "cosmocorp," as George Ball calls it, transcends national rivalries and hence has made war a thing of the past. National economies are now so entangled with one another that no one can afford to go to war.*

The multinational corporation is a structure for rationalizing the whole world economy and in this lies its extraordinary power. The basic idea on which it rests is the internationalization of production. In earlier eras the exchange of goods was the basis of world com-

* The ideology of multinational corporations is discussed in Robert Heilbroner, "The Multinational Corporation and the Nation-State," *The New York Review of Books*, February 11, 1971.

merce. Now it is the spread of productive facilities themselves. In 1966 the U.S. exported $43 billion of goods and services to various parts of the world but the value of goods and services produced by U.S.-owned facilities abroad came to $100 billion, or two and a half times as much. Kenneth Simmonds estimates that 71 of the top U.S. industrial corporations employ on an average about one-third of their total payroll overseas. Sixty-two of the top one hundred American firms have factories in at least six foreign countries. Professor Raymond Vernon estimates that nearly half of the 500 largest companies listed by *Fortune* "have extensive overseas investments in plants, mines, or oil fields" and a score or two have a third or more of their total assets overseas.

International production is for the most part under the management of a relatively small number of multinational corporations. Most of them are American. But Judd Polk of the International Chamber of Commerce now calculates that the rate of capital outflow from the industrialized nations of Europe and Japan is about the same as that of the United States. Thus, for these nations too, the export of commodities is giving way to the export of production itself. Professor Howard Perlmutter argues that if the present trends continue it will not be long before three hundred corporations (of which two hundred will be American) will dominate the world economy, much as the top fifty or a hundred U.S. corporate giants dominate the U.S. economy.

Are multinational corporations really multinational? In what sense is a U.S. company with substantial productive facilities located abroad a truly multinational corporation? With few exceptions, the top management remains in American hands. As Robert Heilbroner notes, there are "a few harbingers of true internationalism" in the presence of a Canadian president of Standard Oil of New Jersey, a Venezuelan on its board, and a Frenchman as president of IBM World Trade Corporation. But a study by Kenneth Simmonds reveals that only 1.6 per cent of the 1,851 top managers of U.S. companies with large overseas payrolls are non-Americans. Do these figures not suggest that much of the euphoric rhetoric about the "denationalized" corporation is merely public relations?

The answer is no. It is already clear that a U.S. company managing a substantial portion of its productive assets overseas develops a relationship with the U.S. government quite different from that of a domestic company, whether or not Americans, Italians, or Venezuelans are in charge or Americans own most of the capital. The identity and loyalties of the corporation will be substantially shaped by the requirements of the corporation, not the national loyalties of the owners and managers. Corporate managers ask not what their corporation can do for their country but what their country can do for their corporation.

For the last decade two different answers have been given by two different categories of industry. The first category depends crucially upon the federal government for its survival. Within this category are the defense industry, older industries such as steel, shoes, and textiles, and of course the railroads and the airlines. All of these industries are favorably subsidized in one form or another. They are not efficient enough to survive without special government protection and support, whether in the form of import quotas, military contracts, or special loans. The second category is symbolized by the electronics industry. Helped by government through military contracts to get started, the high-technology companies long ago outgrew their dependence upon government and, unlike the just mentioned industries, have struck out on their own to conquer the global market. True, the U.S. corporate takeover in Europe spearheaded by the technologically advanced corporations was encouraged by the government in two ways. First, the national security managers were prime movers behind the Common Market. (It was not until the mid-1960's that government managers began to perceive that there were conflicts developing between the corporate interests of U.S. firms in Europe and the state interests of the number one nation.*) Second, the federal government encouraged the flow of capital to Europe in the late 1950's and early 1960's by failing to adopt domestic economic policies that could sustain a growth rate in the American economy high enough to satisfy the dynamic industries.

But conflicts between the interests of the U.S. government and the interests of the multinational corporations have developed. The most obvious source of tension has been the balance of payments crisis, which we have already discussed. This is one of the reasons why the managers of multinational corporations have been against the Vietnam War. The war, which more than any other factor is responsible for the gold drain, created a crisis which the U.S. Treasury attempted to solve by placing restrictions on investment by U.S. corporations abroad. The Voluntary Capital Restraint Program of 1965 was followed by a program of mandatory controls in 1968. The U.S. government asserted the right to compel foreign companies in which a U.S. company had as little as a 10-per-cent interest to declare dividends so that earnings could be repatriated to the United States. U.S. companies were forbidden to transfer capital to their subsidiaries in Europe. The attempt by the U.S. to make laws which in effect regulate corporations located abroad has angered both foreign governments and the multinational corporations themselves. Although the

---

* On conflicts between multinational corporations and the U.S. government, see Jack N. Behrman, "Multinational Corporations and National Sovereignty," in *World Business* (New York: The Macmillan Co., 1970).

managers of the large corporations operating abroad are aware that the U.S. government has three powerful weapons to secure compliance with national policy—the Internal Revenue Service, the Antitrust Division, and the Office of Defense Procurement—about half of the U.S. businesses polled in a confidential survey in October 1965 indicated that they "must be free to do whatever is necessary to compete effectively and profitably." A substantial number of firms responded that their "first responsibility" was to "our shareholders and employees," not the U.S. Treasury. In the ensuing years corporate managers have come to see the conflict between profits and patriotism in even clearer terms. At a recent meeting of top managers of multinational corporations some of the ideologists of the "cosmo-corp" exhorted the Americans in the audience to take a much greater interest in politics so that the foreign policy of the United States could be brought into line with the interests of the multinational corporations.

U.S. corporations operating abroad as multinational enterprises now seek maximum freedom from U.S. government control and surveillance. At one extreme are international pirate companies, such as Bernard Kornfeld's Overseas Investors Services, which seek to elude all governments. But all U.S. corporations with substantial European operations and assets are aware that they cannot afford to comply enthusiastically with the U.S. Treasury when it is engaged in a trade war or some other economic battle with local governments, for in the last analysis it is these governments which can tax or even confiscate profitable enterprises in which they have made enormous investments.

Those U.S. corporations which have substantial assets invested abroad, employ foreigners, depend upon foreign governments for regulation and protection, and concentrate increasingly on the global rather than the U.S. market, find that they are forced to dissociate themselves publicly from nationalist economic policies designed in Washington. When the Nixon Administration at the behest of such noncompetitive domestic industries as wool, cotton, and synthetic textiles "closed the gold window" and imposed a ten-per-cent surcharge on many imports, multinational corporations could not afford to echo Secretary of the Treasury Connally and dismiss the angry reactions abroad as the rantings of "economic crybabies." Being able to do business abroad in a nonhostile climate is much more important to them than any patriotic regard for the "strength" of the dollar. It is also clear that they are not prepared to sacrifice economic opportunity abroad to save weak industries at home or to save jobs.

Another crucial area of conflict between the number one nation and businesses aspiring to control a world market is the transfer of technology and strategic items. We have previously mentioned cases where corporations were ingenious in circumventing or flouting U.S. regulations against shipping strategic metals to communist countries. In a number of other situations, however, the U.S. government has succeeded in forcing the multinational corporations to forgo commercial opportunities in order to serve some political objective of the State Department. Thus in 1968 the Treasury refused to grant an export license to a U.S.-owned Belgian company to export farm equipment to Cuba. In 1964 IBM-France was prevented from selling computers needed for the French nuclear program as part of a diplomatic campaign to induce the French to halt their nuclear weapons program and to sign the test ban. Ford–South Africa has been stopped from shipping armored trucks to the South African government. The State Department warned Standard Oil of New Jersey not to let its Canadian affiliate sell oil to ships taking Canadian wheat to China and, according to the Toronto *Daily Star,* received an equally threatening note back from Jersey, the world's largest multinational corporation. "If you want to start a first-class international row, just keep pressing the matter."

Multinational corporations are increasingly concerned about the conflicting regulations of the American and the host governments. The latter attempt to enforce policies that will maximize local participation in the firms, maintain employment levels, and prevent U.S.-owned corporate giants from putting all local competitors out of business. Being used as an instrument of the U.S. Treasury causes anti-American resentment and makes U.S. corporations with substantial assets abroad more a target for retaliation. As Seymour Rubin, former counsel to AID has observed, tensions between a multinational corporation and the host government increase whenever corporate managers are "thought to be obeying the dictates of their governmental policy makers rather than those of an impersonal profit and loss statement." *

For these reasons corporations operating abroad are more and more seeking to free themselves from the jurisdiction of the nation-state, particularly in the area of antitrust. What the managers of the multinational corporation would like is to be free of all regulation except for minimal surveillance by an international agency, which some of them are calling for on the assumption that it would be weaker and less obnoxiously "political" than national governments in Washington, Paris, or Bonn.

The vision of the multinational corporation is thus in direct conflict with both the pretensions of the number one nation, the source

---

* Seymour Rubin, "The International Firm and the National Jurisdiction," in Charles P. Kindleberger, ed., *The International Corporation: A Symposium* (Cambridge: M.I.T. Press, 1970), p. 179.

of much of their economic strength and talent, and the aspirations of local governments seeking to maintain control of their own territory in the face of overwhelming economic penetration. Clearly, the weaker the government, the more pressing this problem. George Ball candidly put his finger on the dilemma the multinational corporation poses for host countries, particularly for poor countries: "How can a national government make an economic plan with any confidence if a board of directors meeting 5,000 miles away can by altering its pattern of purchasing and production affect in a major way the country's economic life?" *

It is crucial to the vision of the "cosmocorp" that it be free to rationalize the world economy in the most efficient manner possible free of uneconomic political constraints. It will transfer technology from one country to another only if that will improve the consolidated balance sheet. Usually it will have business reasons for keeping technology out of the hands of potential commercial competitors, but if there are business reasons for making it available, the "cosmocorp" cannot afford the patriotic concern that the technology might also be adapted to military purposes and be used against the United States. Like the U.S. companies that sold scrap iron to Japan on the eve of World War II, the managers of the multinational corporations believe that business and politics are separate departments.

In response to this challenge the nation-state in general and the number one nation in particular are asserting the prerogatives of sovereignty in stronger terms than ever before. We have recounted the increased activities of American state capitalism abroad and the extravagant claims to regulate U.S. corporate activities beyond the territory of the United States. The U.S. government is continually seeking to make corporations serve political ends not only as participants in economic warfare, defenders of the dollar, and guardians of Fort Knox, but also as "cover" for intelligence operations and even, as in the case of Continental Airlines in Laos, as integral parts of military operations.

The competition is still in an early stage, and who will win it is by no means clear. The multinational corporation has certain crucial advantages. Because the nation-state is obviously obsolete in many ways the "cosmocorp" appears ideologically progressive. In the nuclear age the nation cannot defend the population. Fighting imperial wars is uneconomic and this fact cannot ultimately be kept a state secret. The major world problems are international in scope and cannot be solved by a single nation. The multinational corporation, however, can be an instrument of peacemaking and economic development. The rationality of the marketplace will overcome the

* Quoted in Heilbroner, *op. cit.*

foolishness of the battlefield. This ideology, which, as we have seen, has much truth behind it, is likely to appeal to the best educated, most innovative, and idealistic people of the developed world who will more and more prefer to identify with the corporation rather than the state. The state, in the United States or elsewhere in the capitalist world, may well suffer a "brain drain" as patriotism is swept out of fashion. In a world of scarcity it is hard to oppose the orderly division of the planet into markets and production units based on the dictates of efficiency instead of national pride. If the number one nation proves incapable of re-establishing rules for the international economy to take the place of the Bretton Woods arrangements, the structural inadequacy of the nation will become even clearer and the corporations will grow bolder in asserting sovereignty.

Yet the nation still holds the strongest cards. The basis of political power is still territoriality. Stephen Hymer and Robert Rowthorn argue that multinational corporations are beholden to the state because they need it to "deal with the problems of the business cycle, social security, unemployment, unbalanced regional growth, labor unrest, attacks on property and order, etc." In short, they say, "multinational corporations require multinational states." * But since such states are not on the horizon, corporations must put up with the nation-state with all its deficiencies. Yet it is by no means clear that the corporations are incapable of dealing with many of these problems themselves. They already maintain large private security forces and run their own welfare programs.

In its struggle to maintain the control over the corporations which the corporate managers are seeking to escape the government has two powerful domestic allies. One is dependent industry, that vast and growing sector of the U.S. economy that requires federal subsidies for survival. The industries are a strong force for nationalism. Not only do they need economic protection from foreign competition but their interests are tied in so many ways to the state that they must celebrate it. If "national security" ceases to be an important public issue, then domestic oil producers, domestic watchmakers, and steel companies, all of which derive important economic privileges by invoking these magic words, will suffer.

The second ally is organized labor. Multinational corporations transfer their labor-intensive operations abroad to take advantage of low wages. Skilled and semiskilled operations are located in Europe; operations requiring little or no skill are located in twenty-cents-an-hour areas such as Hong Kong and Taiwan. The major U.S. labor unions are mounting a campaign to control the internationalization

---

* Stephen Hymer and Robert Rowthorn, "Multinational Corporations and International Oligopoly: The Non-American Challenge," in Kindleberger, *op. cit.,* p. 81.

of production. A United Electrical Workers pamphlet is typical of labor's complaints: "A rising tide of important products made in factories owned by U.S. corporations overseas and by foreign owned corporations is eroding jobs. . . ." * Corporations which "flee" to low-wage countries should be punished. Quotas should be established for their goods. The transfer of technology developed in the United States to other countries so that they can be more competitive with American industry should be stopped. The United Auto Workers is attempting to keep pace with the internationalization of the auto industry (nine companies with factories located around the world produce four-fifths of all the cars in the world) by establishing World Auto Councils for international collective bargaining.

The organized labor movement does not have a common position on the multinational corporation but they all agree that it is a major problem. The option of corporations to shift production abroad weakens labor's bargaining position. Because the flight of capital and talent will have increasingly adverse effects on American workers, most labor bureaucrats are likely to press for a nationalist foreign policy. Thus, in addition to the traditional reasons organized labor has had to support a national security public works program, it will now have added incentive to support the policies that strengthen the hand of government in its fight with the corporation. Those policies, by definition nationalist, stress national security, external threats, and the need for government control.

If the outcome of the competition is uncertain, one important effect of it is not. The growing power and internationalist ideology of the corporations means that the number one nation no longer has the discretion traditionally associated with national sovereignty. Schumpeter's analysis of the modern capitalist is vindicated. The interest of the leading corporations is indeed in peace, and, increasingly, the corporate managers are coming to see it. That being so, the power of the corporations will serve as a restraining influence on military adventurism.

Yet the pressures to use military power continue to be strong. Many international conflicts that have traditionally caused wars are now coming to the surface. The trade war with Japan is beginning to take on racist overtones. Whisperers in the Pentagon, adjusting to the *rapprochement* with China, now echo Chou En-lai's warnings about Japanese revanchism. The competition for markets in the next generation is likely to be more intense than anything Lenin envisaged. The growing panic caused by the realization that the total natural resources of the earth are finite in quantity provides an incentive for war more powerful than the greed that drove the nations

* For further information on the United Electrical Workers, see Robin Murray, "The Internationalization of Capital and the Nation-State," *The New Left Review*, May–June 1970, p. 84.

of Europe to fight over Africa a century ago. But despite these developments, the interests of the most powerful economic structures in developing a rational, peaceful system for exploiting the earth's wealth seem so strong, and the self-defeating nature of war so clear, that Kautsky's imperialism of peace may indeed be at hand.

Only those attracted to the politics' of pique could fail to prefer Kautsky's vision to Lenin's in an age when the "cataclysmic wars" predicted by the founder of Bolshevism would bring not world revolution but world annihilation. But an imperialism of peace, while infinitely preferable to an imperialism leading to nuclear war, is still imperialism, and the human costs of imperialism, however peaceful, are staggering. It is clear that we need a new definition of the word more suited to describing and criticizing the phenomena that characterize the strange new age we are in.

The essence of imperialism, regardless of the economic system from which it proceeds, is the unjust bargain. Human beings are used to serve ends that are not their own and in the process they pay more than they receive. The effort by two hundred multinational corporations (or twenty or two thousand) to rationalize the world economy is part of an imperialist pattern of a new dimension. James Ridgeway has recently calculated ownership patterns of the earth's mineral resources. He predicts that the mineral resources of the earth will soon be under the control of four centers of power: the predominantly American multinational corporations, the predominantly European multinational corporations, the Soviet state enterprise, and the Chinese state enterprise.* If the attempt of a few hundred corporate managers in multinational private and state enterprises to determine how and where the resources of the whole earth shall be developed is successful, these members of the new international managerial class will for practical purposes be the first world conquerors in history.

While it is claimed by the apologists for the multinational corporation that the peaceful division of the world is the most "rational" way to exploit resources, expand productivity, and promote the good life for the greatest number, the interests of the great corporate units conflict with the basic human needs of a majority of the world's population. The supreme value pursued by the new breed of corporate managers is efficiency. This is an improvement, to be sure, over glory, *machismo,* and the excitement of winning, which, it will be recalled, are so important to the national security managers. For those who can make a contribution to the rationalized world economy there will be rewards. But the stark truth is that more than half of the population of the world is literally useless to the managers of the multinational corporation and their counterparts in Soviet and Chi-

* Research from an untitled manuscript to be published by E. P. Dutton in 1972.

nese state enterprises, even as customers. There are not enough twenty-cents-an-hour jobs to employ even a small fraction of the world's poor and the drive toward greater efficiency will eliminate many of those that now exist. We saw in the last chapter how corporations respond to their own economic needs, which transcend territory, and not to the needs of people living in any specific territory. Thus Henry Ford can go to England and threaten to close the Ford factories there and put thousands out of work if labor legislation suiting the corporation's needs is not passed. Corporate managers feel little responsibility for maintaining employment or local prosperity and, increasingly, there will be no political authority capable of imposing such responsibility.

The result will be to accelerate the process of lopsided development. An international technological elite and to a lesser degree anyone of use to them will prosper, and the useless (as defined by the criteria of the corporations) will starve. Even if a massive global welfare program to prevent famine were possible (and the world reaction to the monumental catastrophe that befell the Pakistanis and the Biafrans and the daily routine of death and suffering in Calcutta give scant encouragement), the waste of human potential would be monumental. Human beings cannot develop within a framework that gives that opportunity only to the privileged few who know how to be "efficient," according to someone else's criteria.

The rational world economy envisaged by the corporate managers has no room for those who do not share their vision or know how to contribute to it. Some can continue to produce raw materials at low wages to be consumed by others who can make more efficient use of them. Others can perform service tasks. But most of the earth's poor will be outside that economy, just as they are outside the money economy today. The new imperialism does not *need* an international underclass, as theorists of imperialism used to argue. On the contrary, their very existence complicates the establishment of the rational world economy. But the new imperialists have no idea what to do with this underclass other than to encourage it not to breed so fast. And in the process of rationalizing the world economy they break the power of local leaders, who may have noneconomic reasons to care what happens to the useless, and they smash the fragile bonds of local cultures that at least offer roots and a touch of dignity to the losers of the earth.*

* The defense of the multination corporation and foreign investment as instruments of peaceful development rests entirely on the absence of rational alternatives. See, for example, Raymond Vernon, *Sovereignty at Bay* (New York: Basic Books, 1971), especially pp. 170–91. The most crucial intellectual and political task of the 1970's is the development of an alternative vision of a world economy based on the values of just distribution of economic and political power and the priority of human growth over economic growth.

III

IMPERIAL
DEMOCRACY

9

The Public Mood:
Isolationism Old and New

WALTER LIPPMANN begins his classic study *Public Opinion* by recounting the story of an island on which Englishmen, Frenchmen, and Germans were living in 1914. The island was totally cut off from communication with the outside world except for the mail steamer, which came once in sixty days. On one such bi-monthly visit, the news arrived that the Great War had started six weeks before. "For six strange weeks," Lippmann observes, the English and the French, on the one hand, and the Germans, on the other, "had acted as if they were friends when in fact they were enemies." The point is a familiar one. Governments shape the attitudes of their populations on foreign policy issues by imposing official standards for judging friends and enemies. The loyal citizen is expected to subordinate his personal definition of "friend" and "enemy" to the political judgment of his government.

The citizen who insists upon the right to decide for himself who is his enemy soon finds himself in violation of the selective service laws and possibly in confrontation with the laws of treason. In an un-soldierly moment President Eisenhower once expressed the absurdity of the state's claim to pick friends and enemies for its citizens: "People want peace so much that some day governments had better get out of the way and let them have it." In no other area of political life is the government so fully in control of the life of the average citizen. By speaking certain code words into a telephone or pushing a button, the President of the United States can mark a whole nation of foreigners for nuclear annihilation and insure that one hundred million Americans, perhaps more, will die minutes later. Whether this power is ever exercised is solely a matter of his personal discretion. It is subject to no effective political restraint.

Indeed, the nature of foreign policy—the abstractness of the issues, the remoteness of its objects, and the secrecy with which it is conducted—means that on almost any matter the national security managers have an extraordinarily free hand. In Part I, we attempted to follow the thought processes of the national security managers in defining the national interest. In Part II, we explored the single most important external influence of their decisions, the owners and the managers of big business. In Part III, we shall be looking at the role of the public.

There is a public mood that develops around foreign policy issues, a set of attitudes, prejudices, hopes, and fears. Pollsters try to capture the shifts in mood and politicians try to manipulate them. The national security managers, as the Pentagon papers make clear, constantly talk to one another about the need to "educate" the public. In many cases this word, with all its noble traditions, is merely a euphemism for outright deception; in others, "education" is a code word for more subtle propaganda, the reinforcement of stereotypes, the stimulation of fears, and the quieting of disturbing doubts. We shall look in some detail at the "education" process and see how it works. But just as it would be naïve to accept the traditional civics-book view that the managers of American foreign policy are responding to the desires of the American public instead of shaping these desires, it would be equally misleading to conclude that the public has no influence on foreign policy or that it is infinitely "educable." Nowhere is the mysterious interaction between leader and led more elusive than in the area of foreign policy.

(2)

IN THE COURSE of diplomatic negotiations, it is not uncommon for statesmen to argue for some concession by insisting that the people back home will accept nothing less. The experienced negotiator knows that popular pressure on foreign policy issues is usually a myth, for hundreds of polls confirm what dictators, kings, presidents, and foreign ministers have known for centuries—that the public is ill informed on foreign policy issues and for the most part apathetic. In nondemocratic societies, it is assumed as a matter of course that foreign policy is an elite preserve and that the citizen's role is to pray for peace and to contribute sons and tax money whenever the government decides to go to war. In democratic societies such as the United States, the role of public opinion in the formation of foreign policy is much more complex, for where traditional myths of popular government exist, leaders do not dare to commit the nation to war without enlisting a minimum level of public support. No major foreign policy decision in the United States has ever been made in response to a spontaneous public demand. But frequently—the Spanish-American War is one example—popular support for decisions taken by a handful of government officials is swiftly and skillfully engineered. Occasionally elections are lost or thought to be lost on foreign policy issues.

In a democracy, the apathy of a citizen with respect to an issue increases in proportion to his distance from it. As hard as it is for parents to work up sufficient interest in their children's education to agitate for decent schools, it seems far more futile for citizens to concern themselves with the great issues of war and peace. American political apathy is summed up in a familiar bit of folk wisdom, "You can't fight city hall." How much more hopeless a prospect is a fight with the Pentagon or the White House.

Until foreign policy issues impinge directly on the personal life of an American citizen, as when his son is drafted or the military base at which he works is closed, the foreign involvements of his government touch him somewhat less than a television drama or a football game. He may follow a war or a negotiation in the newspaper or on television to see who is winning. He is unlikely to know much about the issues at stake or to care deeply unless he feels his country to be spectacularly triumphant or humiliated. He has no sense of personal responsibility for the overwhelming issues of war and peace because he believes that he has no way of influencing them. A survey conducted by Leonard Cottrell and Sylvia Eberhart in the summer of 1946 revealed that over half of the respondents counted on a nuclear war in ten years.* When asked whether they were worried about the prospect, typical answers were: "What's the use?" "I'm not worried. It wouldn't do me any good," or, "No, I don't care. I got everything I need. From the morning when I get up, I pick apples and I get a dol-

---

* Leonard Cottrell and Sylvia Eberhart, *U.S. Attitudes on Nuclear War* (New York, 1946); and also Lester Markell, ed., *Public Opinion and Foreign Policy* (New York: Harper and Row, 1949) and Bernard Cohen, *The Press and Foreign Policy* (Princeton, N.J.: Princeton University Press, 1963).

lar a bushel. So why should I worry about that bomb?" A Roper poll conducted seven years later found that somewhat over half of the respondents thought that another world war was certain within three years. Throughout the postwar period, a succession of polls has revealed the same pervasive pessimism about long-term prospects of peace, although in recent years, the fear of war appears to have receded. Whenever the question is put, respondents are also pessimistic about their own chances of surviving a nuclear war, but they do not sound as if the prospect of their own death in a nuclear catastrophe has really penetrated their consciousness. For most Americans, the fear of losing a job or of being mugged on the street is much more real.

Public-opinion polls also reveal pervasive ignorance of foreign affairs throughout the U.S. population. Martin Kriesberg estimated on the basis of studies conducted in the early postwar period that 30 per cent of the electorate are "unaware of almost any given event in American foreign policy," 45 per cent are "aware but uninformed," and about 25 per cent reveal "knowledge of foreign problems." Despite the great official concern with communism during the last generation, a majority of Americans, according to the repeated findings of many polls, cannot accurately identify many countries with communist governments. The same low level of information of foreign affairs exists elsewhere. A survey conducted by the Canadian Peace Research Institute, for example, in the early 1960's, showed that 25 per cent of business and union leaders in Canada thought Austria, Thailand, or Egypt had communist governments. At no time in the postwar period could more than a tiny minority of Americans give an accurate account of the history of the dispute over Berlin, identify the ownership of Quemoy or Matsu, or describe the legal effect of the Geneva Accords of 1954 on Indochina. President Eisenhower's nominee to be Ambassador to Ceylon, a better-than-average-educated department-store executive named Maxwell Gluck, could not identify the Prime Minister of that country when a Democratic-controlled Senate committee, sniffing blood, pressed him on the matter.

The low level of information and concern about foreign policy and national security isues on the part of the general population explain in part why the elite who make national security policy and write about it have a much freer hand than in domestic policy. The Iowa farmer has firm views about farm prices, police protection, drugs, and inflation, and the steelworker has his own ideas on unemployment and equal job opportunity because these issues intersect with personal experience. Politicians on either end of the political spectrum who present these issues in ways too much at variance with such personal experience risk being written off either as "pointy-headed intellectuals," to use George Wallace's contribution to the American political

vocabulary, or as heartless Neanderthals. On foreign policy, however, there is rarely a fund of personal experience on which the voter
can draw and therefore he is peculiarly vulnerable to authority. As
Gabriel Almond concluded in his 1950 study *The American People
and Foreign Policy,* "The American foreign policy mood is permis-
sive; it will follow the lead of the policy elites if they demonstrate
unity and resolution." *

Presidential signals produce significant changes of mood. In December 1946, only 22 per cent of the public, according to the American Institute of Public Opinion, thought that foreign policy problems
were the most important. Four months later, after President Truman's
dramatic enunciation of the Truman Doctrine, 54 per cent thought
foreign policy was the paramount issue. Analysts of public-opinion
polling note that the responses differ markedly if they are prefaced
with "The President thinks. . . . Do you agree?" The ordinary
citizen is ready to oppose the judgment of the commander-in-chief on
a matter of national security only when the credibility of the President
has been seriously compromised by events. (In the case of LBJ it was
his furtive personality as much as events that aroused public suspicion
and hostility.) Thus, during the escalation of the Vietnam War the
President could count on getting a huge majority for anything he did,
including starting the bombing (in the summer of 1966, 70 per cent
of the population favored bombing storage dumps in Hanoi and
Haiphong) and stopping the bombing. Even in the period of his declining popularity, President Johnson was usually able to mobilize
about two-thirds support for any major move, whether it widened or
limited the war. On the eve of the Cambodian invasion of April 1970,
only 7 per cent of the respondents said that they would favor sending
American boys into Cambodia. Immediately after President Nixon
announced the invasion, 50 per cent approved the action even though
53 per cent believed that the invasion would widen the war instead of
shortening it. After each major move of escalation, immediate support for the President increased, although long-term opposition to the
war deepened.

Most Americans do not resolve foreign policy issues on their own
merits because they lack the information and, above all, the self-
assurance to make the judgments. What they say to Gallup and Harris and what they do in the voting booth are in reality votes of confidence in the leadership of the country. The more serious the crisis,
the more dependent the voter feels. "Don't change horses in mid-
stream" is a powerful slogan any leader can use to keep power, but it
is never so effective as in a national crisis prompted by an external
threat. In a climate of fear, people close ranks behind the leader until

* Gabriel Almond, *The American People and Foreign Policy* (New York:
Frederick A. Praeger, 1960), p. 88.

he becomes totally discredited. In March 1945, a month before the final Nazi collapse, Hitler would have done very well had a Gallup poll been taken in Germany.

There are only two ways to get sustained public attention and concern on foreign policy issues. The first is to dramatize a crisis and the second is to link the national security issue to domestic issues. In Chapter 10, we shall discuss the management of the "educational" dimension of foreign affairs crises and the relationship of actual events to the "lessons" that are taught about them. Here, we shall briefly recount some of the national security issues that have aroused the greatest public concern. Although in every major crisis—the Berlin confrontation, the U-2 crisis, and the invasions of Lebanon and the Dominican Republic—the President's mail is overwhelmingly favorable and the public-opinion polls look like votes of confidence, the public mood has been distinctly more "dovish" than the foreign policy consensus developed by the national security managers. By this, I mean that the public has been less disposed to pay the price of a foreign policy based on force. In 1945 and 1946, for example, public pressure for demobilization was so strong that Marshall, Acheson, and Forrestal were afraid the sudden shrinking of the army would undermine U.S. negotiations around the world. The minute the war ended, Americans wanted their sons and husbands back. Foreign policy issues quickly receded in importance. It was not until two years later, when the crisis atmosphere had been dramatized by the Truman Administration, that Americans were again willing to accept conscription and the permanent deployment of substantial troops abroad.

The only weapon system that elicited a strong public reaction was the ABM. The Johnson Administration's Sentinel program encountered heavy public opposition because the missiles were scheduled to be placed in suburban areas of large cities. The public became nervous. The missiles might make the city more of a target than it already was. They might misfire. There might be a nuclear accident. A missile emplaced in the North Dakota wilds that one might read about occasionally in the Sunday supplements was one thing, but a missile in the backyard was quite another. Like the family fallout shelter, which elicited a similar negative public reaction when President Kennedy tried to push a mass civil defense program in 1961, the ABM was an ugly reminder of the hopelessness of nuclear war which most Americans preferred not to have. The opposition to the Vietnam War also developed because the American people were not prepared to pay the price of victory, or even the price of avoiding defeat. There is an obvious correlation between the casualty rates and the mounting opposition to the war. This was also true in the Korean conflict. In addition, however, there were other costs associated with the Vietnam War. The internal dissension, the depth of student opposition, the "credibility gap," the drug problem in Vietnam, and the breakdown of discipline in the armed forces all contributed to the unprecedented three-fourths majority for a quick withdrawal that developed in 1971. For the first time, more than 50 per cent of the respondents thought the war to be not only a "mistake," but also "immoral." Even in the South, a region that has traditionally supported America's wars with enthusiasm and has contributed far more than its fair share to the armed forces, by the beginning of Nixon's third year in office, a majority was for getting out of Vietnam by the end of that year despite the President's clear contrary intention.

The conventional wisdom inside the national security bureaucracy during most of the Cold War has been that the public is more "hawkish" than the government and that the less educated are more jingoist than the college-educated population. Visitors to the White House in the Johnson and Nixon Administrations who questioned the war policies being pursued would receive lectures on the dangers of a "right-wing backlash" if the United States promptly withdrew from Vietnam. White House associates recall that Lyndon Johnson was far more worried during the Vietnam War escalation about public attacks from the right than from the left. But this does not suggest that the public was more committed to the obliteration of Vietnam than the national security managers, or even that Johnson thought so. It does suggest that the Administration was genuinely worried that demagogic appeals could be used to stir up the public. To condemn the party in power for not fighting hard enough is irresistible for the opposition, because no matter how unpopular a war, voters expect victories. President Kennedy would tell critics who questioned some of his tough policies that the mood of the electorate was tougher still. In my second term, he would hint, I will take political risks for peace.* Political scientists pictured the public as a sleeping beast that must be frightened into supporting foreign policies it could never understand, but which, once aroused, was extraordinarily fierce. For example, as Professor Thomas E. Bailey put it, "The more ignorant the citizen, the more bellicose and jingoistic. . . ." Yet, as we shall see, the national security managers talking to one another worry far more about the latent pacifism and isolationism of the public than about its jingoism.

(3)

WHETHER THE PUBLIC is more jingoist in outlook than the national security managers raises the most profound questions about the na-

* See Kenneth O'Donnell, "LBJ and the Kennedys," *Life,* August 7, 1970, pp. 44–48.

ture of the American system. If the ignorance, fear, and primitive passion of the majority has the effect of pushing the government toward military adventurism and nuclear war, perhaps we should look upon democracy as a dangerous luxury. Perhaps secrecy and unlimited presidential power in foreign affairs are necessary to protect the nation from the people. From de Tocqueville to Walter Lippmann a succession of observers of the American scene have insisted that popular government is "the least suited to the conduct of foreign affairs." Ambitious politicians ready to pander to the prejudices of the mob are, they argue, given to overreacting or underreacting to foreign crises. Only specialists in national security sufficiently insulated from the shifting passions of the crowd, sufficiently skilled in shaping public opinion so that they need not fear it, can take the long view of foreign affairs. If the mood of the crowd really counted for much in the conduct of foreign policy, so the argument goes, the nation would swing wildly from isolationism to preventive war.

The argument bears a hard look. The proposition that people are readier to support war the lower they are on the social, income, or educational scale is supported by the flimsiest of evidence. In 1950, Gabriel Almond reviewed the public-opinion literature of the time and found that "unskilled and semi-skilled labor, domestic servants, and farmers are the least informed group in foreign policy matters, the least interested in international issues, the most pessimistic about efforts to maintain peace, and the most inclined toward nationalist and isolationist attitudes." Twenty years later, pollsters and columnists discovered the "hard-hat," the lower middle class construction worker, who feels so crowded by rising prices, declining real wages, the angry demands of the militant blacks, and by the mocking manners of college students, that he wants to get out of Vietnam by bombing it into the Stone Age. The "hard-hat" and the lower middle class "middle American," who comprise the single biggest bloc in what President Nixon liked to call his "silent majority," are supposedly vulnerable to the demagogic appeals of a Curtis LeMay (the Air Force general who ran for Vice-President on the George Wallace ticket in 1968) or of a politician on the Hitler model who is able to make the public forget their domestic frustrations by appeals to military adventurism and martial glory.

The public-opinion polls, as inadequate as they are, simply do not support the view that the well-educated and well-fixed are more pacifistic in outlook than the poor grade-school dropout. The surveys confirm the unsurprising fact that the poor tend to be more ignorant of foreign policy matters than the college-educated man of affairs and to feel little motivation to become informed. One unskilled worker summed up a prevalent feeling in reply to an interviewer. "Foreign affairs: that's for people who don't have to work for a living." However, Milton Rosenberg, Sidney Verba, and Phillip Converse,* public-opinion analysts at the Universities of Chicago and Michigan, have found that as regards the Vietnam War, at least, the passions of the poor may lead to more sensible opinions than the schooling of the rich.

> Vietnam opinion polls have rather consistently shown that college-educated people (about 30 per cent of the public now) have been, relatively speaking, "hawkish," in their attitudes, while, at the other end of the spectrum, people whose education did not go beyond grade school (the bottom 20 per cent of the population now) are distinctly "dovish." Indeed a very disproportionate number of the nation's grass roots "doves" are concentrated here.

Even when blacks who have special reasons for being against the Vietnam War are removed from the sample, these analysts point out, grade school whites "still remain more dovish than any other group of comparable size in population."

It is true, as a 1971 study conducted by Potomac Associates suggests, that the uneducated are readier to accept conspiracy as an explanation of foreign policy problems—i.e., Communists and "sell-outs" in the State Department, masterminds in the Kremlin, etcetera—and to favor blunderbluss policies.† But this does not tell us very much. Once threats are identified for them by their leaders, unsophisticated people will normally favor direct rather than subtle means of dealing with them, particularly if they are told that they work. Tell a man that he is locked in mortal combat with an enemy who is out to kill him and offer him a choice of ridding himself of this threat by pushing the button of "preventive" war or adopting some more pacific but vaguer solution, and you are likely to get a "bellicose" response. But, fortunately, people in the real world have more common sense than polls often suggest.

Election campaigns bear out these findings. A small number of retired generals preaching "preparedness" and hinting at preventive war have gone down to defeat in Congressional elections. The enormous majorities which Lyndon Johnson piled up against Barry Goldwater in 1964 were due in large measure to LBJ's success in tagging the Republican candidate with Johnson's own Vietnam policy, then in the final planning stages, and in painting him in the public mind as a nuclear nut. In these elections, the poor and the uneducated voted

---

* *Vietnam and the Silent Majority* (New York: Harper and Row, 1970), p. 55.

† This 1971 poll by the Gallup Organization shows that the top and bottom of the income scale are most ready to support a compromise end of the war. Manual laborers in the $7,000–$15,000 income range are the most hawkish. Albert Cantril and Charles Roll, *Hopes and Fears of the American People* (A Potomac Associates study) (New York: Universe Books, 1971).

consistently for what they were told was the "peace candidate." To-day, in the wake of the Vietnam disillusionment, the pollster Louis Harris concludes on the basis of extensive interviews that "peace is the single most powerful idea in the United States today."

But with all America's wars, peace has always been a powerful idea in this country. The foreign policy issue has not been a choice between peace and war but between approaches to peace. For much of American history, the preferred solution was cultivated isolation-ism and the avoidance of entangling alliances. In the postwar period, the so-called 'internationalist' consensus has held that preparation for war, military alliances, and "negotiation from strength" are the only means of preserving peace and that "weakness invites war." The new foreign policy mood emerging from the Vietnam War reflects not so much a new interest in peace as a goal as it does a profound war weariness and a growing feeling that wars for peace do not make much sense. If we wish to understand something about the changing public mood on issues of war and peace, it is hopeless to put much faith in available poll data. The results are based on small samples and loaded questions. Results vary significantly when the wording is changed to hint of a different "right" answer. (Thus, it hardly suggested the depth of isolationist sentiment in the country when only one per cent of the college-educated respondents in a 1947 National Opinion Research Center poll said they approved "of this government keeping to itself and not having anything to do with the rest of the world.") Polls are useful for measuring immediate reactions to specific events. They are much less useful for capturing the mood or thought processes of the electorate.

Is there nothing then to be said about the popular mood on foreign policy issues beyond such political maxims as "The public doesn't like wars except when we win them and they don't cost much"; "The pub-lic will follow the commander-in-chief almost anywhere"; and "The American people do not like to lose wars or suffer humiliation"? To say anything sensible about what goes on under the skin of a single individual is a considerable analytic achievement. When that number is multiplied by millions, the risks of degenerating into high-sounding gibberish are considerable. Nevertheless, there is a cluster of recurring attitudes toward the outside world that seem to be at the heart of public opinion on foreign affairs. These attitudes are cultivated in varying degrees by the government and are fed by the communications media.

The key to understanding the public mood, in my view, is to grasp the real nature of American isolationism. It is the well-spring of our peculiar brand of patriotism. "Nothing is more embarrassing in the ordinary intercourse of life," wrote Alexis de Tocqueville in 1835, "than this irritable patriotism of the Americans." Through much of our history, the myth of American exceptionalism has pervaded the whole society, imparting special meaning to personal lives. "Know that this is the place where the lord will create a new Heaven, and a new earth in new Churches, and a new Commonwealth together," the settlers of Massachusetts Bay Colony announced on landing. "Many hundred years must roll away," John Adams declared, "before we shall be corrupted. One pure, virtuous, public spirited, federative republic will last forever, govern the globe and introduce the perfection of man." The myth of exceptional virtue has persisted to our day, reinforced by grade-school texts, veterans' encampments, election speeches, and comic strip heroes. America stands above the nations, her destiny of power manifest and her claim of virtue unassailable.

Erich Fromm has traced the rise of what he calls "group narcissism" over the last several hundred years.* The myth of collective superiority of a nation or race compensates for feelings of personal inferiority or worthlessness. An individual gains self-esteem because he is a member of a master race or a number one nation, or is a product of a superior culture. The more rootless or dissatisfied he feels in his personal life, the more he clings to his group identity and the more he separates himself from the rest of mankind through the celebration of his own race or nation. Patriotic sentiments are often based on gratitude for community recognition and success. Sometimes they are based on a deep love of tradition. But jingoism, which is a caricature of patriotism, is more often an expression of personal failure. As Fromm points out, those who fail by the standards of their own society are the most likely to fall prey to group narcissism, a pathological condition political leaders carefully cultivate as a source of tremendous power. Hitler and Stalin promoted the myth of collective superiority and mass-produced the *folie à deux* for the very people whose personal lives belied it. The German unemployed and the lower middle class were caught up in Hitler's neo-Wagnerian drama. The sweating Stakhanovite, returning from a ten-hour day to share a corner of a room, was induced to believe that he was the new superior "Soviet man." In the twentieth century, group narcissism is far more socially acceptable than individual narcissism. Thus, Fromm observes, an individual who declares that he and his family are the only clean, intelligent, honest people in a society in which all the rest are corrupt, lazy, dirty, incompetent, or predatory, is generally thought to be offensive and probably crazy. But the same sentiments can be expressed with respect to a group and receive tumultuous applause from every member of the group and amused tolerance from outsiders.

All nations preach the ethic of national superiority but the United States has made a religion of it. The protected shores and material riches, the experiments in political liberty and the endlessly repeated personal success story all gave the myth a certain plausibility. As the bulging cattle boats stuffed with immigrants attested, the United

* Erich Fromm, *The Heart of Man* (New York: Harper & Row, 1964).

States was not just a place to live or a series of plots on which one's ancestors had settled hundreds of years before. It was a nation where you could *choose* to live, and people chose it not merely because it was a piece of good real estate but because it was the embodiment of an idea.

On the other hand, like all true believers, Americans have felt periodic twinges of doubts. The educated classes looked to Europe for culture. Frontier life of the nineteenth century was too rude and commercial life of the twentieth century too consuming. From Henry James to Jackie Kennedy, worshipers of style have turned their backs on America. The First World War taught Americans that they could not escape the intrigues and wars of the older powers and, try as they might, they could not convert them into moral crusades. The Great Depression taught them that they were not immune from catastrophe and created a strong suspicion that economic salvation could be purchased only at the price of war.

In the postwar period, self-doubt in America grew as the great social problems—racial injustice, hunger, inadequate housing, bad medical care, collapsing social services in the city—began to surface and no magic solutions were invoked. Among those who could claim to participate in the Affluent Society, the doubts were the greatest. It became a literary cliché to describe the quiet desperation of the aspirin-popping, success-jaded suburbanite. Beginning in the 1950's, political leaders deplored the "loss of spirit" in the land. "We have no message to send to captive peoples to keep their faith and hope alive," John Foster Dulles wrote in 1950. By the end of the decade, a Committee on National Goals had been organized by the Eisenhower Administration, charged with articulating the American purpose in the hope of recapturing it. (The Secretary of the Commission was William P. Bundy, who within five years would become the chief bureaucrat in charge of planning how to "turn the screw" on North Vietnam.) By the end of the 1960's, the quest for the Dream had degenerated into a flag war. The American flag, worn as a lapel button, bumper sticker, or T-shirt had become the principal symbol of the division of America. The old patriots brandished the flag like a gauntlet inviting dissenters on the war to return to the fold or go into exile: "America: Love it or Leave it." The young patriots began shredding the flag and wearing it in the form of belts, hats, and accessories to bell-bottom trousers, as if their claim to a piece of America depended upon making a full-scale assault on the national religion.

(4)

IT IS PRIMARILY in relationship to the outside world that the citizen is conscious of himself as an American. There is an elusive connection between national purpose as articulated and promoted by the managers of foreign policy and individual purpose, between national security and personal security. For the average citizen, national security policy is a package of fears, dreams, and diversions.

One of the legacies of America's geographical isolation and her lack of visible enemies manning pillboxes on the frontier is that there is very little correlation between individual feelings of personal safety and the state of national security, as measured by the official criteria of the government. Only in moments of extreme crisis that are dramatized by presidential television appearances, such as the Cuban missile crisis of 1962, does the citizen make a connection between national security and personal insecurity. It is ironical that the national mood is more relaxed today than in the early postwar years when the United States was incomparably the most powerful nation on earth and the sole possessor of the atomic bomb. Yet, if we are to believe the polls, Americans, by and large, feel safer today despite the fact that the Soviet Union has three or more megaton bombs targeted on each major U.S. city. One can only conclude that ordinary people use psychological rather than rational measurements for security. The crisis atmosphere of the early 1960's, promoted by a government seeking to raise the military budget, has subsided because the government now is exploring détente with the Soviet Union and China. Yet, though the U.S.S.R. is far more formidable an adversary than twenty years ago, most people do not know what the policy of the Soviet Union is, or how strong it is. They do not even have a very clear idea where it is. It is not the Soviet Union as a real political entity, much less the two hundred million real human beings who live there, that intrudes into the American consciousness. It is the Soviet Union as a symbol. So also for North Vietnam, China, or for that matter, France. To a large extent, these symbols are defined for people by their government.

Walter Lippmann made the point many years ago that the human mind fastens on "stereotypes" as a way of making sense out of the hopeless complexity and confusion of the real world. The more remote the object, the simpler the stereotype. In a time of anxiety, the political pressures mount to create stereotypes and to turn them into scapegoats. The picture Hitler drew for the German people of the six million Jews of Europe bore no relationship to reality, but it was powerful enough to incite a civilized nation to commit genocide. The German dictator was able to make the German people project their self-doubt and self-hate onto an external "enemy" who became all the more "dangerous" because he was living in their very midst. For Americans in 1946, the stereotype of the Soviet Union, Stalin, and communism played a somewhat similar role. For many people, these abstractions became convenient explanations of deep feelings of social and psychological distress. (Even the flesh-and-blood character Joseph

Stalin became a stereotype, a Genghis Khan-like world conqueror, which he never was, instead of the mass murderer of his own people, a fact most Americans did not appreciate until years later.)

For the American people, the immediate postwar years were marked by unprecedented feelings of insecurity, which for individuals and nations alike reinforce isolationist tendencies. This insecurity, in my view, had much less to do with the reality of Russian power—much of Russia was still in ashes—than with the bureaucratic revolution in the United States and the staggering social and political upheavals that accompanied World War II. Old values were crumbling. Small-town America was disappearing from whole regions of the country. For many Americans, the life of the farm, the close family, and the rooted community were over. Thanks to the melting pot of military service, the racial migrations of the war years, and the revolution in communications and transportation, the United States for the first time in its history was a continental society. The atomic bomb brought a credible picture of national catastrophe to Americans for the first time in almost a hundred years and contributed to the general anxiety. But more pervasive than the prospect of a common death under a mushroom cloud was the fear of what the new common life would be.

With the breakdown of old associations—family, church, community, and small business—Americans began to identify more and more with the state in Washington to give purpose and meaning to individual lives. To be sure, the old Jeffersonian ideology persisted. As necessary as they were in supplying social security checks, farm supports, and government contracts, bureaucrats in Washington were still felt to be meddlers when it came to domestic affairs. But in the world of national security, bureaucrats became statesmen, protectors of the land, and spokesmen for the nation. They expressed what it meant to be an American at a time when American identity was becoming more and more of a confusing notion. America was not a state in Aristotle's sense—i.e., a territory small enough to be "visible as a whole" to one man's eye—even though Jefferson had once dreamed of turning his purchased empire into a series of "ward republics" where face-to-face politics could flourish. Nor was America a national state, homogeneous in race, language, and outlook. With its leadership no longer in the exclusive hands of a white Anglo-Saxon Protestant elite but with its shores now barred to free immigration, America represented neither the nineteenth-century nationalism, which was based on homogeneity of national type, nor a real melting pot in which miscegenation was encouraged. The uneasy compromise between deep-seated racism and slowly evolving minority rights did not add up to either a coherent or inspiring national identity. Nor by the mid-twentieth century did American represent a powerful political idea. Other nations such as Britain and Sweden had drawn ahead of the United States in social services without sacrificing democracy. The United States was no longer the exclusive, or even the preferred political model for colonial people. The American system was given universal credit for its unparalleled capacity to develop technology and to create wealth under certain conditions, but unlike the days of Franklin, Adams, and Jefferson, mid-century America no longer promised the perfectability of man. What characterized America was now its power, and the citizen's sense of belonging was somehow related to the vicarious exercise of national power. More and more an American came to mean someone who identified with the struggle against America's enemies. Americanism became defined in terms of un-Americanism.

Through his American identity the citizen could try to recapture the spiritual bonds and kinships with his fellow citizens even as he was becoming more and more isolated from them in his day-to-day existence. Anticommunism came to serve as a kind of glue to hold a rapidly fragmenting society together. When the glue began to crack under the pressures of the Vietnam War, it was not easy to find another national purpose to take its place. At the height of the Cold War, Archibald MacLeish bemoaned the military cast of American rhetoric with its emphasis on "fighting for freedom." Freedom, he warned, is not something you defend but something you use. Yet the idea of a common defense against a hostile external world was perhaps the only discernible principle of unity in competitive mid-century America.

For the citizens of the number one nation foreign policy also offers dreams of glory. This is a phenomenon we notice readily in other countries. It did not take American observers long to figure out that Mussolini was building a successful political career for himself by creating an official fantasy life for the Italian people. The Mediterranean would again become an Italian lake, the glories of Rome would be revived. Like Hitler, Stalin, and scores of lesser dictators, Mussolini was in the business of selling pride to his own people. But so also are the managers of American foreign policy. National security is primarily defined in terms of reputation for having more power than all other nations and a willingness to use it. From the much-publicized Bikini atomic tests of 1946 to the saturation bombing of the Vietnam War, the United States government has offered its citizens a continuing power fantasy. A worker or a farmer or a frustrated businessman who may feel powerless in his personal life, through presidential exhortations, Pentagon propaganda, and daily TV reporting is given a symbolic share in the greatest power in the world. An illustration of the power fantasies of the powerless in national security matters is provided by an interview with a sixty-seven-year old Virginia farmer conducted in the course of a Social

Science Research Council survey in 1946. The farmer had never finished grade school, read no newspapers or magazines, but occasionally listened to someone else's radio. In 1945 his total income was under five hundred dollars. When asked about the atomic bomb, he replied, "If they had enough atomic bombs, they could use them to clean out a nation. The man that made that bomb was a man after my own heart. I love him. I don't care if he was a nigger. I'd love his neck." *

Obedient, almost worshipful of law and order in his personal life, the powerless can become a lawful, vicarious killer simply by switching on the 6:30 news and listening to the daily body count. To kill, preferably with advanced technology, for many Americans, offers a certain thrill if one is not made to feel unduly concerned about the victim. This, at least, is the profitable analysis made by the promoters of television bloodletting, the creators of sadistic comic strips, and the producers of cinematic carnage. The spontaneous wave of sympathy for Lieutenant Calley rather than for those he shot is an indication of how much more easily a nation of winners can identify with the executioner than the victim. In their study of American and foreign movies, Leites and Wolfenstein noted that although there is much killing in American films, murder does not have the emotional impact of many foreign films because the drama does not involve the audience in the life of the victim. He is a dehumanized lump of flesh. The pleasures of vicarious violence are ruined by twinges of guilt. In American society racism serves the function of dehumanizing victims so that their deaths will look more like a game than a tragedy. From the monkey-like Indians of the old westerns to the "twenty-one Oriental human beings" Calley was convicted of killing, America's victims appear in American eyes to deserve their fate because they are less than human. The contempt ordinary law-abiding Americans in three wars have felt for Asians and the cruelty they have visited upon them has not been matched in our Occidental wars.

One of the most important political uses of foreign policy is the relief of boredom. Imperial fantasies enliven dull days. Not only do they provide the citizen something big and powerful with which to identify, they also offer excitement of competition. What game can compare with the competition of two nuclear powers for the control of the world, particularly when one side represents good and the other evil? So crucial is the game aspect of foreign affairs in domestic life that most peace proposals of the last generation have consisted of suggestions for transforming the competition rather then ending it. A succession of "peace races," "competitions for coexistence," and "aid wars" have been proposed as a substitute for military confrontations.

* Cottrell and Eberhart, *op. cit.,* p. 43.

The space program has been explicitly defended as a way of channeling America's aggressive energies into nonlethal activities.

Public interest in the world's second-most-expensive game was at its height when President Kennedy blew the opening whistle in 1961 and announced the national goal of being the first to place a man on the moon before the decade had ended. By the time the mission was accomplished, however, public attention had flagged somewhat, partly because the novelty had worn off, but mostly because the Russians had made it clear that they were no longer in that particular race. So, too, such public enthusiasm for supplying aid to the "developing countries" as there was evaporated when Americans began to suspect that this was another race the Soviet Union was willing, perhaps even happy, to let the Americans win.

(5)

IT HAS BECOME fashionable in the postwar period to interpret modern American history in terms of the continuing tension between the pulls of "isolationism" and "internationalism." According to the standard syllabus of American diplomatic history, the American people "came of age" in World War II, rejected their isolationist past, and embraced a new "internationalism" based on a commitment to the higher manifest destiny of "world responsibility." There is considerable confusion in all this terminology between state behavior and popular attitude. Before World War II, the predominant public mood was indeed profoundly pacifist, antimilitarist, and noninterventionist. It was best characterized as a "live and let live" attitude. Since the United States could not reform the corrupt nations of Europe, it should stay out of their way. The historic suspicion of large standing armies and military adventurism that has always coexisted in this country with a deep fascination with and respect for military power had not yet been overwhelmed by the crisis atmosphere of the Cold War. Yet all during the interwar period, the United States intervened, politically and militarily, in Latin America and China, and was heavily involved in the economics of Europe. When World War II came, the public hope that the United States could remain aloof from Europe's struggles, avoid entangling alliances, and rely on the dollar to project American power was shattered. The historic apathy toward maintaining large standing armies and big military establishments dissolved. Americans showed a new readiness to support the appeals of their government for a world-wide military force and for a highly interventionist foreign policy. Indeed, there was no area of the world where Washington bureaucrats did not seek to project their influence.

But there was no change in the fundamental isolationist attitudes of the American people.

All populations of nation-states are isolationist to varying degrees. The very meaning of belonging to a nation implies a legal and spiritual separation from the rest of humanity. American isolationism has been especially strong because of a series of geographical and historical accidents. A succession of foreign observers have noted that domestic isolationism is deeply imbedded in the American grain. "In their intense and exclusive anxiety to make a fortune," de Tocqueville writes, "they lose sight of the close connection which exists between the private fortune of each of them and the prosperity of all. . . . The discharge of political duties appears to them to be a troublesome impediment which diverts them from their occupation and business." Bryce, Dickens, and Herbert Spencer, and in our own day Erich Fromm and D. W. Brogan all stress the peculiarly single-minded obsession with the immediate and the close-at-hand that characterizes the American. The Russian political scientist M. Y. Ostrogorski, writing in 1910, observed:

> Of all races in an advanced stage of civilization, the American is the least accessible to long views. . . . Always and everywhere in a hurry to get rich, he does not give a thought to remote consequences; he sees only present advantages. He is pre-eminently the man of short views, views which are often "big" in point of conception or of greed, but necessarily short.*

The British political scientist Richard Titmuss recently devised an ingenious method of measuring altruism in a society by determining whether blood is freely given or sold to those who need it for survival. The United States, by this measure, is still very much a society dedicated to the proposition that God helps those who help themselves. The very definition of an isolationist society is one where each man is expected to look after himself.

In the postwar period, swarms of Americans have gone abroad, a good many of them soldiers. American power has been engaged over vast regions of the earth. But this phenomenon can be described as "internationalism" only in an Orwellian sense. Americans are never more isolationist than when they go abroad to kill foreigners. Using foreign lives and property as a backdrop for projecting American power is the epitome of national egoism. "We fight in Vietnam today," Lyndon Johnson used to say, "so that we will not have to fight in San Francisco tomorrow." As Assistant Secretary of Defense John T. McNaughton, Jr., once stated in a secret memo published in *The Pentagon Papers,* only about ten per cent of the reason why the

---

* Quoted in Almond, *op. cit.*, p. 399, from M. Y. Ostrogorski, *Democracy and the Party System in the U.S.* (New York: Macmillan, 1910).

United States was in Vietnam had to do with helping the Vietnamese people. Most of the reasons had to do with preserving and expanding American power and prestige.

The "internationalist" versus "isolationist" debate is really an argument about little more than military strategy. The "internationalists" who have determined the foreign policy consensus for a generation have one view of geopolitics. The "isolationists" have had another. Both were principally concerned with promoting the American national interest. The "internationalists" have believed that America's "vital interests" lay with Europe and that to maintain a noncommunist Europe it was necessary to project American power on a global scale. They successfully promoted the experience of World War II as a national lesson. The United States had to fight in the war because she had failed to play the key role in the politics of the prewar world to which her power entitled her. Thus, the United States had been an accomplice in the appeasement of dictators. The remedy was to build alliances and forward defenses to keep war from American shores. Superior military power deployed far from the United States was the price of continued safety for the American public. "No more Munichs!" exclaimed the recently converted former isolationist Michigan Senator Arthur Vandenberg in early 1946. "America must behave like the *number one world power* which she is."

Ohio Senator Robert Taft and former President Herbert Hoover, on the other hand, believed that military interventionism, symbolized by sending a permanent U.S. army to Europe, would bring war to American shores rather than avoid it. Hoover proposed making "this Western Hemisphere the Gibraltar of Western Civilization" and predicted that communism would wear itself out on the steppes of Asia. For Taft, who took a similar line, the issue was not isolationism but "the degree of participation in world policies. . . ." He believed that the Acheson "total diplomacy" of a global forward defense and world-wide containment of communism would militarize the American society and bankrupt the economy. The purpose of U.S. foreign policy was not to reform the world but to achieve "the peace and liberty of the United States." This could be done by maintaining our dominance in the Western Hemisphere. (For peculiar historical reasons "isolationists" have also had a much stronger commitment to China than the "internationalists.") The "internationalists" such as New York Governor Thomas E. Dewey took no issue with the "isolationists'" objectives. They were not arguing for world government or internationalism as an end in itself but as an instrument of American protection. "What would we do," the Governor orated, "as an island of freedom in a Communist world, outnumbered fourteen to one, with oceans which would no longer be our protecting moat but a broad highway to our front door?"

What is called the new "internationalist" attitude of the public is, in reality, evidence of a successful educational campaign to enlist support for the prevailing military strategy. After a prolonged bipartisan chorus of authoritative pronouncements along the lines of the just quoted remarks of Governor Dewey, the American people came to believe that "peace is indivisible" (anywhere in the world that catches the attention of the State Department), that "aggression unchecked is aggression unleashed," and that therefore the safety of our shores demands far-flung military deployments, a network of alliances, bases, clients, police actions, and other imperial paraphernalia. From 1951, the year of the so-called Great Debate when the Taft-Hoover forces failed to prevent the stationing of a permanent six-division army in Europe, the "internationalist" strategy for protecting American power was substantially unopposed for almost twenty years. The remnants of the old "isolationist" tradition with its heavy reliance on international law, conciliation, and disarmament, which had so long been personified by Idaho Senator William Borah, were discredited. By 1951, to believe as Borah did that the danger to the republic stemmed from the excessive war-making power of a trigger-happy executive rather than from communism or any other external threat was to find oneself in the politically unenviable position of being praised in *Pravda.*

Not until the excesses and failures of the Vietnam War penetrated the American consciousness did the public begin to question the basic assumptions of the "internationalist" strategy, which many now came to see was simply a more palatable name for "interventionist." The "new isolationism" which Presidents Nixon and Johnson alike profess to see on the horizon and which both decry does not portend a greater emotional withdrawal from the world, but only a growing disenchantment with a politico-military strategy that does not appear worth its political, economic, or moral costs. Indeed, there may be developing in the United States, particularly among young people, the first signs of a genuine internationalism in which U.S. citizens are beginning to identify with people in other countries as human beings instead of stereotypes. The sense of reality that could come in the wake of imperial failure might open the possibility for real relatedness with distant peoples and cultures that was never possible in the era of "the arrogance of power."

Thus, the fact that the public has been willing to support those foreign policy initiatives which their leaders label as "internationalist" says almost nothing about the depth of popular isolationist feeling. The public, as we have seen, is ready to follow in any direction in foreign policy—even to disaster. There are better indications of the persistence of isolationist feeling; one is the widespread suspicion of foreign aid except among sophisticated constituencies who understand its self-serving uses. Most of the country is suspicious of "hand-outs," "give-away diplomacy," and "globaloney." Sensitive to the depth of such predictable feelings of parochialism, successive admin-istrations have tried to sell aid programs as expenditures for national security or for the stimulation of the U.S. economy. As Jerome Bruner observed in his study of public opinion in wartime, *Mandate from the People,* "public support for international issues stands or falls with our conceptions of the *quid pro quo."* Generosity with no expectation of reciprocation is a rare private virtue. It is almost never a public virtue anywhere, and in a society like the United States, which is built on the exchange transaction, compassionate giving on a group basis without expectation of gain or avoidance of some loss is almost unknown.

Another symptom of American isolationism is our boundless optimism. Dean Acheson once noted that Americans like to call problems "headaches" as if taking a powder was all that was neces-sary for a fast cure. Foreign observers throughout our history have commented on the national faith in progress, and particularly in progress through technology. American optimism is one of the most attractive national characteristics in many respects, but in foreign affairs it conceals a lack of relatedness and understanding. When America, in the tradition of many empires before her, acts as the bull-dozer in the china shop, paving over ancient societies as in Indo-china, it is because she barely notices that they are there.

(6)

DURING the entire Vietnam War, only a tiny fraction of the Ameri-can population ever demonstrated real concern over the homicidal impact of the war on America's ally, South Vietnam, not to mention the "faceless Vietcong." When *American* deaths in battle exceeded one hundred a week, it became a matter of national torment, but the millions of Vietnamese who were burned, blasted, or made home-less were shrugged off as natural calamities of war. If the vindication of American pride could have been purchased at a price somewhat short of genocide, it is reasonably clear that a majority of Americans would have supported the policy. But, it should be emphasized, that does not mean that public sentiment forced the war.

Perhaps the best index of the strength of isolationist sentiment in the United States is the degree of group narcissism found among Americans. In the Social Science Research Council survey conducted in the summer of 1946, only 15 per cent of the respondents were satisfied with the way other countries of the world were behaving, but almost two-thirds were at least fairly well satisfied with the way the United States was acting. Such self-criticism as was revealed was aimed at what was thought to be excessive American altruism. "We are too soft"; "You can call any American a sucker"; and the United States has "tried to see everybody's point of view" were typical answers. Over half of the respondents could not think of a single mistake the United States had made, and about 30 per cent were sure that their government had made none.

Such chauvinist sentiments are, of course, common in other countries, although they appear to vary with size and power. Military weakness has an astonishing way of encouraging people to see other points of view. Power and self-righteousness are constant companions. A pecular characteristic of the United States, however, is the supreme ease with which chauvinism is rationalized. In a *Fortune* magazine survey of January 1947, only 4.2 per cent thought that the United States "must do the best we can for the rest of the world, even if what we do isn't always the best thing for America." About 8 per cent thought that we "must look out for our own interests first, last, and all the time, and not care too much about what happens to the rest of the world." But 32.5 per cent believed that there was no conflict between American interests and the interests of humanity at large since Providence had conveniently arranged things so that "what is best for the world is best for America."

American self-righteousness is buttressed by a remarkably innocent belief that such opposition to the United States and its policies as may exist in the world is due to the ignorance, depravity, or moral weakness of foreigners. Such attitudes are shared in full measure by America's leaders and have been cultivated by them. But moralizing about international politics, an American proclivity which critics such as George Kennan and Hans Morgenthau have noted and lamented, evidently touches a responsive chord in the American consciousness. "Ours must be the world's moral leadership or the world won't have any," Senator Arthur Vandenberg wrote in his diary in 1946, but almost any of his Michigan constituents could have said it. A succession of Presidents have viewed themselves as moral teachers on a global scale, and have received mass applause for it. For William McKinley, the Spanish-American War was nothing less than a stern duty to "uplift and civilize and Christianize" the Filipinos. As he moved into Central America, Theodore Roosevelt proclaimed America's "responsibility for the moral welfare of others which cannot be evaded." Woodrow Wilson vowed that he would send troops to Latin America to fulfill his obligation to "teach the South American republics to elect good men."

The anticommunist crusade which is so often identified as the dominant theme of postwar American foreign policy evoked a strongly positive public response during the Cold War precisely because it played on deep-seated isolationist attitudes. The former United Nations Secretary-General Trygve Lie once wondered why the strongest nation in the world with a discredited Communist party was obsessed with communism when Norway, close to the Soviet frontier, with a small army and a substantial Communist Party, was able to take a much more relaxed view about sharing the world with the Soviet Union. America's obsession with communism goes back to the Russian Revolution and the Red Scare of the 1920's. According to Robert Murray, who made a comprehensive study of the period in 1919, witnesses testified before a Senate committee that

> the Red army was composed mainly of criminals, that the Russian revolution had been conducted largely by former East-Side New York Jews, that Bolshevism was the Anti-Christ. . . . Newspaper editors never tired of referring to the Russian Reds as "assassins and madmen," "human scum," "crime-mad," and "beasts". . . Newspapers climaxed this sensational reporting with gigantic headlines: "RED PERIL HERE!," "PLAN BLOODY REVOLUTION," and "WANT WASHINGTON GOVERNMENT OVERTURNED."

By the 1930's, the Red Hysteria, the Palmer Raids, and scare headlines about Lenin's impending takeover were memories, but the fear of contamination was so great that the city of Cambridge passed an ordinance forbidding the public library to carry any book containing the magic words "Lenin" or "Leningrad." The rebirth of the vigilante movement, with the formation of the House Un-American Activities Committee in 1938, the Smith Act, state sedition trials, and contempt proceedings of the McCarthy era is familiar history.

It is tempting to offer a rational explanation of this irrational phenomenon. Communism was a direct challenge to the free enterprise system in the United States. Therefore, the nation mobilized to throw off this ideological virus much as the body mobilizes to throw off germs. The trouble with such an explanation is that it does not do justice to the intelligence of America's leaders. There were times, no doubt, particularly in the early months of the Russian Revolution, when the American government may have been genuinely alarmed at the prospect of world revolution. But for most of the period during which anticommunism has been official policy, U.S. officials have made sober and accurate assessments of Soviet power, although they have consistently communicated a much more alarmist picture to the public. They have known that the Soviet Union was neither able nor interested in promoting a revolution in the United States, and that the future of General Motors could be threatened far more by capitalists in Japan and Europe than by anything in the latest Five Year Plan.

For most Americans, the real essence of the Soviet threat is that the Soviet Union has professed an alternative system for organizing large industrial societies. The trend toward détente with the Soviet Union at a time when the U.S.S.R. is the chief supplier of an army engaged in killing Americans has been accompanied by the news that U.S. and Soviet societies are "converging." Even though the Soviet Union is far more dangerous a military rival than in the days of Stalin and in the process of becoming "more like us" is imitating United States interventionist policies in the Middle East and elsewhere, thus increasing the risks of war, the Soviet Union is perceived as less of an ideological threat than in the past. And that makes a crucial difference.

Why should the managers of U.S. foreign policy care about an ideology that seems to confuse, bore, or depress Americans more than they do about missiles or disputed territory? Why should the American people care what kind of government the Vietnamese or the Indonesians have? The answer, it seems to me, is that Americans, for all our contrary rhetoric, are made uncomfortable by diversity. The very existence of alien ideologies with significant followings is a threat. The substance of the ideology is less important than its existence. Thus, the "godlessness" of communism is offensive to many Americans, not because they are in anguish over the prospect of two hundred million Russian souls in hell, for most Americans do not believe deeply in hell themselves, or because God cannot take care of Himself in fending off the attacks of the League of the Militant Godless, but rather because official atheism is a direct attack on official piety. As Adlai Stevenson put it in the 1952 campaign, "Religious faith remains in my opinion our greatest national resource. . . ."

For Americans, the validation of the American system comes through its acceptance by others. We judge the worth of our society by the extent to which it is imitated and praised abroad. This sort of "other directedness" is profoundly isolationist. Perhaps the classic statement of the missionary-isolationist was Senator Kenneth Wherry's 1940 election pledge to the people of Nebraska: "With God's help, we will lift Shanghai up and up, ever up, until it is just like Kansas City." The insatiable desire for "prestige" abroad is a manifestation of what Karen Horney called the "neurotic need for affection" which she, along with other observers, believed to be basic to the American character.*

Why should American self-esteem depend upon the evaluation that foreigners make of our culture? It is far more than a matter of

* See Karen Horney, *The Neurotic Personality of Our Time* (New York: W. W. Norton and Co., 1937).

dollars and cents, for those who seem to care the most whether foreigners drink Coca-Cola, read the *Reader's Digest,* buy "Bonanza" for the local television, or welcome the Holiday Inn own no stock in any of these enterprises. They simply regard foreigners who reject American ways as extremely threatening. Resistance to the spread of American influence is felt to be an attack on America. A man is a success in America when he senses that he is admired and loved by a requisite number of people. Hence, as Horney suggests, in our culture, the "normal individual of our time" has "an intensified need for affection as a remedy." The neighbor, child, or business associate who dresses differently, cuts his hair differently, or believes differently is considered by most Americans to be withholding loyalty, respect, or affection. He is, in short, a living reproach. So also are foreign countries which implicitly criticize American ways by rejecting them.

In its older form, isolationism was a way of controlling the threat of ideological contamination by means of physical separation. The United States would keep to itself and thus avoid the corruption of the Old World. But now everyone recognizes that commerce, communication, and the technology of warfare make separation a physical impossibility. The new isolationist who calls himself "internationalist" still pursues the illusion of a perfect security that will permit America to remain pure and unchanging in a world in revolution. Aware of the practical difficulties, the new isolationist still cherishes the dream that power can be used to convert, by force if necessary, those foreigners who have fallen into un-American habits of mind, for there is no real safety for America except in a world that conforms to an American vision. The roots of the new isolationism are as old as the Republic.

IO

The Manipulation of Public Opinion

Though the world of national security is an elite preserve, it is evident that those who make foreign policy decisions always have one eye on the public reaction. Although such decisions are seldom made in response to public opinion, the national security bureaucracy is constantly taking the public's pulse. There are even rare cases when official tactics are directly influenced by a public outcry. The wave of demonstrations that greeted President Nixon's invasion of Cambodia no doubt prompted him to announce a date for the military withdrawal a few days later.

In most cases, however, the American public is just another audience to be discreetly handled, much like the Soviet government, the Chinese Communists, or the Israeli Cabinet. A typical internal statement on handling the public as an "audience" is the memorandum Assistant Secretary of Defense John T. McNaughton wrote to Secretary McNamara on September 3, 1964:

> Special considerations during the next two months. The relevant audiences of U.S. actions are the Communists (who must feel strong pressures), the South Vietnamese (whose morale must be buoyed), our allies (who must trust us as "underwriters"), and the U.S. public (which must support our risk-taking with U.S.

lives and prestige). During the next two months, because of the lack of "rebuttal time" before election to justify particular actions which may be distorted to the U.S. public, we must act with special care—signaling to the DRV that initiatives are being taken, to the GVN [Government of South Vietnam] that we are behaving with good purpose and restraint.*

Handling the problem is accomplished by a variety of performances, each designed to create the right mood for the moment. In mustering public support for national security policy, national security managers find it necessary alternately to frighten, flatter, excite, or calm the American people. They have developed the theater of crisis into a high art.

For the national security manager, public opinion is simply one more problem that demands skillful management. A hostile public can restrict diplomatic flexibility and foreclose "options." A strong "national will," as the Joint Chiefs of Staff never tire of pointing out in top secret memoranda, is a crucial element of national power, an important chip in the game of nations. A policy cannot be safely pursued if it totally ignores significant shifts in public mood. Thus, no President in 1971 would deliver the kind of pep talk Lyndon Johnson used to deliver to the nation during the escalation of the Vietnam War in 1965—not even Lyndon Johnson. Several planners say privately of the Vietnam War that their greatest miscalculation was excessive confidence in their ability to manage public opinion.

Nevertheless, the impact of adverse public reaction to the direction of policy is depressingly slow and weak. The Vietnam conflict dragged on more than a year after a clear demonstration that over 70 per cent of the public was for an immediate end to the war through the withdrawal of all U.S. troops. Both President Johnson and his successor used to brag in public speeches about their willingness to risk unpopularity in the pursuit of the "right" course. In a series of "deep background" laments, Lyndon Johnson used to describe himself for a few favored reporters as a modern Abe Lincoln, ready to take on the criticism and anger of the ungrateful crowd in order to protect its true interests.

However, a hostile public reaction has an immediate psychological effect on national leaders. While the public lacks the power to translate its mood into quick political change in the area of foreign policy, its power to make leaders feel uncomfortable is communicated instantly. Elias Canetti, in his monumental work *Crowds and Power,* notes that the difference between rich men, celebrities, and rulers is that while the first collects money and the second a chorus of admir-

* Neil Sheehan et al., *The Pentagon Papers* (New York: Bantam, 1971), p. 311.

ing voices, the third collects men. Above all, says Canetti, the ruler wants "living men, whom he can make die before him, or take with him when he dies." * Satisfying the collector's instinct is a necessity for all those afflicted with the psychological need to rule. In the early days of the Vietnam War Lyndon Johnson used to carry around in his pocket the latest public-opinion polls and would show them compulsively to every important visitor. Expressions of public support were, in 1965, almost irrelevant to keeping his office or to pursuing his policy, for essentially the same policy was pursued long after the support evaporated. He was collecting people, gathering them into his camp, much as kings and dictators use plebiscites, parades, and mass meetings for the same purpose. Thus, symbols of public adulation became crucial morale boosters for leaders who do not enjoy exercising power unless they are loved, or at least admired. The unfavorable primary results from New Hampshire in 1968, which undoubtedly had a profound effect on LBJ's decision not to run for re-election, did not mean that the President was in serious danger of losing his office, but only that he was losing his crowd. Perhaps that was enough.

In the area of foreign affairs, the crowd, as the President and his advisers view it, is both a nuisance and a necessity, a source of power and a limitation on its exercise. National security managers who write about public attitudes demonstrate a magnificent contempt for the crowd. Unlike the President, who draws power and personal satisfaction from being "President of all the people," professionals in statecraft whose personal constituencies extend no further than the seventh floor of the State Department or E-ring of the Pentagon find dealing with the public only a nuisance. Diplomats resent Congressional inquiries into foreign policy issues as an invasion of their privacy. On crucial matters, they protect that privacy by invoking "executive privilege," a tradition under which national security managers have a right to decide when the peoples' representatives have a need not to know. Extensive secret military operations were carried on in Laos for over five years before Congress or the public were able to obtain any information about them at all.† George Kennan, one of the most sophisticated foreign service officers, reveals something of the professional's annoyance at having to keep Congress and the public informed on foreign policy strategy. When asked in early 1948 by a journalist about "what he viewed as our failure to expose adequately to members of Congress the strategic realities underlying the Marshall Plan proposal," Kennan replied that he had "entered a profession which I thought had to do with the representation of United States

---

* Elias Canetti, *Crowds and Power* (New York: The Viking Press, 1962), p. 397.

† Laos operations are described in Hearings Before the Senate Subcommittee on U.S. Security, *Agreements and Commitments Abroad*, Vol. 1, 1971.

interests vis-à-vis foreign governments . . . and never understood that part of my profession was to represent the U.S. government vis-à-vis Congress." Kennan confided to his diary his annoyance at Congress's effort to interfere in what he plainly regarded as the private affairs of the State Department;

> . . . my specialty was the defense of U.S. interests against others, not against our own representatives. . . . I resented the State Department being put in the position of lobbyists before Congress in favor of the U.S. people. . . . it was up to them to inform themselves just as it is up to us to inform ourselves. . . .*

The foreign policy professional prides himself on being a cool calculator. As we discussed in Part I, this self-image scarcely takes account of the rampant irrationality that pervades the national security bureaucracy. But as he weighs options, assesses risks, and conjures up scenarios, the crisis manager sees himself, nevertheless, as a supreme rationalist, fallible, of course, but confident that he has mastered the techniques for managing problems in an imperfect world. The public, on the other hand, is emotional, undependable, and far too irrational to be entrusted with delicate matters of state. Moreover, as Arthur Sylvester, then the Pentagon's chief public affairs officer, once declared in what is known in the State Department and the Pentagon as a famous bad performance, there are occasions when the government has a positive duty to lie to the people.†

Dean Acheson has spelled out the official rationale of the national security manager as to why the public must be deliberately confused for its own good. We are not talking here about the deliberate lie concerning specific factual matters such as whether U-2 planes do or do not fly over the Soviet Union, whether the United States has troops in Laos, or whether the Gulf of Tonkin episode, the closest thing to the official *casus belli* of the Vietnam War, ever took place in the way the Secretary of Defense testified that it did. Official lies have been employed in each of these situations and in many others. More significant than the instant historical rewrite for which public relations officials have an irresistible weakness is the calculated exaggeration. Arthur Vandenberg once told President Truman that he would have to "scare hell out of the country" if he expected to get public support for rearmament and an interventionist policy. Charles Bohlen writes that some top State Department officials at the time of the Truman Doctrine thought that the United States may have "exaggerated" the Soviet threat a "bit" to arouse the public. Acheson concedes that the

* George Kennan, *Memoirs (1925–1950)* (New York: Bantam, 1969), p. 428 n.
† William Rivers, *The Opinion Makers* (Boston: Beacon Press, 1967), p. 154.

purpose of NSC-68, the top-secret policy memorandum prepared before the Korean War in 1950 which outlined the future U.S. rearmament program, was to "bludgeon the mass mind of 'top government,'" and to provide a basis for "preaching" to the public. The paper established the basic Manichean theme of U.S. foreign policy —that, in Acheson's words, the Kremlin's design was "world domination" while the American aim was "an environment in which free societies could exist and flourish." In his memoirs written almost twenty years later, Acheson comes close to admitting that NSC-68 and the public campaign based upon it were misleadingly simple, but he defends exaggeration and scare tactics as necessary instruments of policy:

> The task of a public officer seeking to explain and gain support for a major policy is not that of the writer of a doctoral thesis. Qualification must give way to simplicity of statement, nicety, and nuance to bluntness, almost brutality, in carrying home a point. It is better to carry the hearer or reader into the quadrant of one's thought than merely to make a noise or to mislead him utterly. In the State Department, we used to discuss how much time that mythical "average American citizen" put in each day listening, reading, and arguing about the world outside his country. Assuming a man or woman with a fair education, a family, and a job in or out of the house, it seemed to us that ten minutes a day would be a high average. If this were anywhere near right, points to be understandable had to be clear. If we did make our points clearer than truth, we did not differ from most other educators and could hardly do otherwise.*

Thus, the national security managers believe that the public is so passive that it can be aroused to give positive support to a foreign policy initiative, particularly if it is a risky one, only if it is presented in the context of a crisis and then only if the crisis is deliberately oversold. Overselling is so standard a technique that a substantial literature has developed on the subject. George Kennan, Walter Lippmann, and a number of political scientists have worried in print about the dilemma of the foreign policy manager who, having made his point "clearer than truth," creates his own "right-wing backlash" which then prevents him from ever making conciliatory moves in the future. The fact is that "preventive war," the prescription of the right wing, was much more in line with the rhetoric of Acheson, Dulles, and early John F. Kennedy than were the ambiguous policies they actually followed. Once having identified the problem of security as a death struggle with an enemy out to "bury" you and to "rule the world," it is hard to defend moderate or conciliatory strategies for resisting such

* Dean Acheson, *Present at the Creation: My Years in the State Department* (New York: W. W. Norton and Co., 1969), p. 375.

a menace. This is the essence of the problem national security managers face in manipulating public opinion: How do you dramatize a crisis without tying your hands for the future? Although many managers would put it more delicately, almost all would agree with General Maxwell Taylor's response to a television interviewer when he was asked whether the people had a "right to know" about major foreign policy decisions: "A citizen should know those things he needs to be a good citizen and to discharge his functions. . . ." * But what does he need to know to "discharge his functions" as the national security managers see them?

(2)

THE TRADITION of news management in the United States goes back to the days of George Washington. Every leader tries to present events to the public in such a way as to elicit what he thinks is the right response. If a leader wishes to avoid war, he will minimize foreign crises; if he wishes to "prepare public opinion" for war, a recurring phrase in the Pentagon papers, he will sound the note of alarm. Thus, an area such as Formosa or Korea or South Vietnam can be declared one day to be empty of "vital interests" for the United States and on the next can be transformed by the State Department mimeograph into a "vital bastion of the whole Free World." In each of the above cases a Secretary of State once wrote off an area as being "outside the defense perimeter" of the United States only to change his mind (and his rhetoric) in response to future events.

The man who developed the art of playing public opinion like a giant console was Franklin D. Roosevelt. Clare Booth Luce's 1944 campaign diatribe, "He lied us into war because he did not have the courage to lead us" is unfair only if one believes that FDR had no alternative to lying. As a statement of history it is lamentably accurate. Each step of the descent into war was shrouded in mystery or actual deception. All the American people needed to know to be good citizens was contained in public announcements of discrete decisions after they were made, such as the exchange of destroyers for bases, the occupation of Iceland, the orders to shoot Nazi submarines "on sight." The public statements, particularly in the 1940 campaign, including FDR's famous pledge never to "send your boys into a foreign war," bore no relationship to the thinking inside the Administration, where it was assumed the United States must eventually enter the war and that for it to do so the public must be "prepared."

Almost as soon as World War II was over the Truman Administra-

* Maxwell Taylor made this statement to Bernard Kalb in a CBS broadcast of June 17, 1971.

tion began to worry about how to manage public opinion. During the war the Soviet Union had been built up as a "gallant ally." Despite a strong residual anticommunism which continued to be expressed in some local newspapers and particularly in the Catholic press, the mass media, with the encouragement of the Roosevelt Administration, were picturing the Soviet Union as a country of babushkas, smiling peasants, and waving grain presided over by an austere but kindly Uncle Joe. Hollywood turned out such later Cold War embarrassments as *Mission to Moscow,* the story of how the multimillionaire U.S. ambassador Joseph Davies was captivated by an avuncular Stalin, and *North Star,* a minor extravaganza of the steppes written by Lillian Hellman. Russian Relief, Soviet-American Friendship, and similar causes attracted New York and Washington society. The impact was registered in the public-opinion polls. A succession of wartime surveys revealed that a majority of Americans had positive feelings toward the Soviet Union and were optimistic about Soviet cooperation in the postwar world.

By August 1946, according to the SSRC survey cited in Chapter 9, only 25 per cent of the respondents believed that we could "count on Russian government to be friendly with us." By this time the disputes with the Soviet Union over Eastern Europe and the U.N. had been well publicized. But the Truman Administration was worried that the public did not take the Soviet threat seriously enough. Public pressure for demobilization was intense. Forrestal records in his diary that the State Department, particularly Acheson, then Under Secretary, expressed "great embarrassment and concern" about this at Cabinet meetings. In a diary entry for 1946, Forrestal gives a picture of public relations planning at the highest level:

> I said I thought the President should get the heads of the important news services and the leading newspapers—particularly Mr. Sulzberger of the New York Times, Roy Roberts, Palmer Hoyt, the Cowles brothers, John Knight, plus Roy Howard and Bob McLean of the AP—and state to them the seriousness of the present situation and the need for making the country aware of its implications abroad. I said these were all reasonable and patriotic men and that I was confident that if the facts were presented we would have their support in the presentation of the case. The President agreed to do so.
>
> I also suggested that the heads of the broadcasting systems be called in . . . Secretary Ickes suggested that the State Department arrange a nation-wide hook-up to present the impact of the overrapid demobilization on our foreign policy. . . .*

* Walter Millis, ed., *The Forrestal Diaries* (New York: The Viking Press, 1951), p. 129.

Forrestal devoted much of his time to seeing, as Kennan put it in a celebrated dispatch from Moscow, "that our public is educated to the realities of the Russian situation." Kennan himself was worried about "hysterical anti-Sovietism" as well as the naïve treatment of Stalinism cultivated during the war, but the Secretary of the Navy increasingly saw himself as Paul Revere, and it was in this spirit that he circulated Kennan's views about the Soviet threat in the higher reaches of government, and persuaded the foreign service officer to publish them in an even tougher form as the famous "X" article in *Foreign Affairs*. Years later Kennan regretted the article as oversimple and alarmist.

Thanks to Forrestal's intervention, Kennan's views on the Soviet threat and his military-sounding prescription for dealing with it substantially shaped the public image of the Soviet Union. "My reputation was made," Kennan writes in his memoirs. "My voice now carried." A few months later Forrestal and Harriman proposed "the need for countermeasures" against communist propaganda "in our own country." Recalling that the Nye Committee in the 1930's "staffed by Communist attorneys" (an apparent reference to Alger Hiss) "had much to do with the curtailment of our own armaments industry," Forrestal predicted "the recurrence of attacks such as the Nye investigation, to prove that the Army and Navy and American business were combining on a neo-fascist program of American imperialism." Because such countermeasures, including the highly developed Pentagon public relations effort recently documented in such books as Senator William Fulbright's *The Pentagon Propaganda Machine* and the celebrated CBS-TV program "The Selling of the Pentagon" were so skillfully employed, the predicted attacks were inaudible for more than twenty years.

To enlist public support for the Truman Administration policy of "total diplomacy" against the Soviet Union, Secretary of State Dean Acheson carefully cultivated a widespread belief in communism as a monolithic world force. This campaign involved the use of very loose language by men who prided themselves on their precision. In the Greek civil war, for example, as in Vietnam almost twenty years later, the State Department pictured the conflict as a "red tide of aggression" sweeping over hapless Greece from the outside.* Acheson called the insurgency a "thrust by the Soviet Union" when, in fact, there was no evidence that the Soviet Union was behind it, and we know from Milovan Djilas that Stalin attempted to stop it. Interven-

---

* See Richard J. Barnet, *Intervention and Revolution* (New York: New American Library, 1968), Chapter 6, and also Harry Truman, *Memoirs* (New York: New American Library, 1965), Vol. 2. President Truman cites "intelligence reports" (p. 121) to the effect that the Greek rebels were "under Soviet direction."

tion in an internal conflict such as that in Greece or in Vietnam elicits charges of imperialism around the world because the United States has of course no legitimate mandate to put down revolutions in other people's countries. Public support within the U.S. can be mustered and some foreign criticism silenced, if the revolution can be made to look like an international war and the insurgents can be labeled secret agents of the Kremlin or of the Chinese or of someone else. Despite the fact that insurgents by definition live in the country where they are fighting, the State Department has been reasonably successful in painting many of these conflicts as invasions. Once this is accomplished, memories of Hitler are evoked and the dispatch of an American expeditionary force becomes plausible. Thus through the use of judiciously careless language, State Department propagandists have been able to package every military intervention to look like another in America's long line of defensive crusades.

In fairness to Acheson it must be said that he and the other top managers of the American foreign policy did believe in the threat of a monolithic world communism. They thought that the Soviet Union was looking for "situations of weakness" to exploit anywhere in the world. But what they told the American people was "clearer" than the "truth" which they perceived. The invasion of Korea was seized upon as "proof" that world communism was on the march, when the State Department's own intelligence sources concluded that it was a limited, local engagement. For the political analyst the moves of the Communists in Korea were mysterious.* It was a most inopportune time for the Soviets to launch an invasion, because they were boycotting the United Nations and did not yet have a deliverable atomic bomb.

If we are to believe Khrushchev's memoirs, the invasion was the initiative of Kim Il Sung, the North Korean Premier. Stalin, who apparently had been told that the people would greet the invaders as liberators (much as Kennedy would be told similar nonsense about the Cubans eleven years later), reluctantly acquiesced. Whatever the facts, the Korean invasion provided no clue whatever to Soviet intentions in Europe. Yet Acheson was able to use the Korean War as a crucial event for the management of public opinion toward Germany. Acheson believed that a German army was a necessary political device to integrate a new West German state into a tight "Atlantic Community," but before Korea this was too subtle an idea for the public, especially since it involved an enemy that had been crushed and disarmed just five years before. As McGeorge Bundy candidly comments in his edited record of Acheson's career, *The Pattern of Responsibility,* "it was the shock of Korea which shifted the position Acheson

---

* Kennan, *op. cit.,* p. 524, and Edward Crankshaw, ed., *Khrushchev Remembers* (Boston: Little, Brown and Co., 1970), pp. 367–73.

was ready to take publicly. . . ." * Under the impact of this crisis the Truman Administration was able not only to reverse its China policy and to make a military commitment to Chiang Kai-shek on Formosa, it was also able to use Korea to muster the necessary support for German rearmament.

(3)

THE VIETNAM WAR is the classic case for studying news management, not only because the national security managers felt a need to mislead the public on an unprecedented scale but also because so much information about that process has become available. We know that there were huge discrepancies between what the managers of the war learned about the basic nature of the conflict and what they taught the public, including Congress. In the Eisenhower and early Kennedy era Ngo Dinh Diem, the man the United States had found to run South Vietnam, was extolled in CIA-inspired articles in the *Reader's Digest* as "The Biggest Little Man in Asia" and the hero of "Vietnam's Democratic One-Man Rule." The top managers of the U.S. counterinsurgency program knew even in the late 1950's that fighting for Diem and fighting for freedom were not exactly the same.

But by the early 1960's the deception escalated. President Kennedy was fighting what Ralph Stavins calls a "private war." In March 1961 President Kennedy instructed various national security agencies to "make every possible effort to launch guerrilla operations in Viet-Minh territory at the earliest possible time."

The covert actions against Laos and North Vietnam which were stepped up in 1963 were ostensibly for the purpose of stopping infiltration into South Vietnam. From 1964 on the United States publicly charged that the war was instigated and promoted by Hanoi. Yet President Kennedy had been told in 1962 by his close personal friend, Michael Forrestal, then serving as a White House assistant, that "the vast bulk of both recruits and supplies come from inside South Vietnam itself." The Special Group for Counter-Insurgency set up by President Kennedy concluded on April 5, 1963, that "we are unable to document and develop any hard evidence of infiltration after October 1, 1962." The State Department counterinsurgency specialist on Vietnam during this period has observed: "Throughout this time no one ever found one Chinese rifle or one Soviet weapon used by a VC." † What became the public theory of why and how the war

---

* (Boston: Houghton Mifflin, 1952), pp. 32 and 77.
† Ralph Stavins, "Kennedy's Private War," *The New York Review of Books*, July 22, 1971.

was being fought was contradicted by the managers' own internal evidence. "Aggression from the North," a theory used to explain why the South Vietnamese government was at war with its own people and to justify a massive U.S. "counter" intervention was, in the same official's words, "completely phony." *

The second major discrepancy between private information and public pronouncements concerns the "dominoes theory." It was commonplace to proclaim in public that the "loss" of Vietnam would mean a world-wide shift in the balance of power and that a failure to fight in Vietnam would mean fighting some day in San Francisco. Indeed, some of the same rhetoric was used in the highly classified internal dialogue. Vice-President Lyndon Johnson, for example, told John F. Kennedy after his 1961 trip to Saigon that if the United States abandoned Vietnam, it would have to "throw in the towel in the area and pull back our defenses to San Francisco and a 'fortress America' concept." Yet when the CIA was asked whether the rest of Southeast Asia would "necessarily fall if Laos and South Vietnam came under North Vietnamese control," the answer, although hedged in the self-protective language which intelligence analysts (along with investment advisers and other paid prophets) habitually use, was negative:

> With the possible exception of Cambodia, it is likely that no nation in the area would quickly succumb to Communism as a result of the fall of Laos and South Vietnam. Furthermore, a continuation of the spread of Communism in the area would not be inexorable.

Three Presidents based their public case on the dominoes theory and demanded extraordinary American sacrifices on that basis, for surely the public could not be convinced that Vietnam alone was worth fifty thousand American lives. It is possible to find internal documents in the Pentagon papers in which the national security managers seek to persuade each other that all Asia "would go down the drain" in the event of a communist victory, but these were not reasoned analyses. As we have seen, there is a strange process of autosuggestion which makes men believe their own propaganda even when it is belied by impressive and expensively procured evidence. This happens because officials are unwilling to let facts stop them from what they

---

* In his memorandum to the Secretary of State of June 29, 1965, George Ball calls the Vietcong "largely an indigenous movement" and the conflict in South Vietnam "essentially a civil war within that country." In his memorandum to the President a few days later he makes the same points, which were of course the exact opposite of public propaganda and much internal discussion. He correctly predicts that the dispatch of U.S. ground troops will turn the war into a fight between the United States and "a large part of the population of South Vietnam, organized and directed from North Vietnam. . . ."

have already decided to do. As William Bundy put it in a secret 1964 memorandum (quoting Maxwell Taylor), "There was a danger of reasoning ourselves into inaction."

The national security managers were always aware that to do what they had decided to do in Vietnam would require a massive "public education" campaign. According to the official Pentagon study, Secretary of State Rusk, at the Honolulu Conference in June 1964, expressed the worry that "public opinion on our Southeast Asia policy was badly divided in the United States at the moment, and that therefore, the President needed an affirmation of support." In a briefing paper for the Secretary, Assistant Secretary of State William P. Bundy called for an "urgent" public relations campaign "to get at the basic doubts of the value of Southeast Asia and the importance of our stake there." A few days earlier, Bundy had drafted a model Congressional resolution similar in language to the one actually presented to Congress for enactment a few months later at the time of the Gulf of Tonkin incident.

The participants at the Honolulu meetings concluded that it was essential to obtain a Congressional resolution "prior to wider U.S. action in Southeast Asia," not so much because it would produce real unity in the country but because it would produce the appearance of unity. To project unity was an essential part of U.S. planning because even in 1964, the war managers knew that public distaste for operations in Indochina would encourage the Vietnamese to keep resisting. Public opinion must be marshaled, the planners reasoned, for public morale is either a weapon which can be used to intimidate an enemy or a fatal chink in the national armor. The draft Congressional resolution, which was "surfaced" at the time of Tonkin, was designed, according to a Bundy memorandum, "as a continuing demonstration of U.S. firmness and for complete flexibility in the hands of the executive in the coming political months." The world must know, as the official Pentagon historian noted, "of the firm resolve of the United States Government in an election year to support the President in taking whatever action was necessary. . . ."

The day after the election William Bundy drafted a memorandum on handling world and U.S. public opinion during the projected escalation of the war:

Bien Hoa [a U.S. base which had recently been attacked by the VC] may be repeated at any time. This would tend to force our hand, but would also give us a good springboard for any decision for stronger action. The President is clearly thinking in terms of maximum use of a Gulf of Tonkin rationale, either for an action that would show toughness and hold the line till we decide the big issue. . . .

Three weeks later, the Vietnam Working Group, which had been charged with writing up the "scenarios" for escalating the war, had prepared the following program for handling world public opinion:

A. A White House statement will be issued following the meeting with Ambassador Taylor, with the text as in Tab B, attached.

B. Ambassador Taylor will consult with the GVN promptly on his return, making a general presentation (in accordance with the draft instructions) as stated in Tab B, attached. He will further press for the adoption of specific measures as listed in the Annex to Tab B.

C. *At the earliest feasible date, we will publicize the evidence of increased DRV infiltration. This action will be coordinated by Mr. Chester Cooper in order to insure that the evidence is sound and that senior government officials who have testified on this subject in the past are in a position to defend and explain the differences between the present estimates and those given in the past. The publicizing will take four forms:*

1. *An on-the-record presentation to the press in Washington, concurrently with an on-the-record or background presentation to the press in Saigon.*

2. *Available Congressional leaders will be given special briefings. (No special leadership meeting will be convened for this purpose.)*

3. *The Ambassadors of key allied nations will be given special briefings.*

4. *A written report will be prepared and published within the next ten days giving greater depth and background to the evidence.*

D. Laos and Thailand

The U.S. Ambassadors in these countries will inform the government leaders (in general terms) of the concept we propose to follow and of specific actions requiring their concurrence or participation. In the case of Laos, we will obtain RLG approval of an intensified program of (U.S. armed) reconnaissance strikes both in the Panhandle area of Laos and along the key infiltration routes in central Laos. These actions will not be publicized except to the degree approved by the RLG. It is important, however, for purposes of morale in SV, that their existence be generally known.

Thailand will be asked to support our program fully, to intensify its own efforts in the north and northeast, and to give further support to operations in Laos, such as additional pilots and possibly artillery teams.

E. Key Allies

We will consult immediately with the UK (DC) Australia, New Zealand (Bundy) and the Philippines. (Humphrey?)

1. UK. The President will explain the concept and proposed actions fully to Prime Minister Wilson, seeking full British support, but without asking for any additional British contribution in view of the British role in Malaysia.

2. Australia and New Zealand will be pressed through their Ambassadors, not only for support but for additional contributions.

3. The Philippines will be particularly pressed for contributions along the lines of the program for approximately 1800 men already submitted to President Macapagal.

F. We will press generally for more third country aid, stressing the gravity of the situation and our deepening concern. A summary of existing third country aid and of the types of aid that might now be obtained is in Tab C, attached.

G. Communist Countries

1. We will convey to Hanoi our unchanged determination (and) our objectives, and that we have a growing concern at the DRV role, to see if there is any sign of change in Hanoi's position.

2. We will make no special approaches to Communist China in this period.

3. We will convey our determination and grave `concern to the Soviets, not in the expectation of any change in their position but in effect to warn them to stay out, and with some hope they will pass on the message to Hanoi and Peiping.

H. *Major statement or speech. Depending on U.S. public reaction, a major statement or speech may be undertaken by the President during this period. This will necessarily be required if a reprisal action is taken, but some other significant action, such as the stopping of the flow of U.S. dependents, might be the occasion. Such a statement or speech would re-state our objectives and our determination, why we are in South Vietnam, and how gravely we view the situation. It should in any event follow the full publicizing of infiltration evidence.**

Throughout the prosecution of the Vietnam War, the war managers tried to package events in certain ways purely for the purpose of influencing public opinion. These recurring devices give a much better picture of what they really think moves the American people than what they tell visiting political scientists. The most effective device

---

* These documents appear in *The Pentagon Papers*, p. 375.

for enlisting initial public support for an American war is to shed American blood in small quantities. In the early planning documents on the escalation of the Vietnam War, John T. McNaughton and others used to talk about the symbolic importance of an American blood sacrifice. Not only was it necessary to risk losing your own citizens to convince the enemy of America's "will and determination," it was necessary to "spill American blood" to commit the American people. Canetti observes that the blood sacrifice is an essential ritual in any war:

> Rulers who want to unleash war know very well that they must procure or invent a first victim. It need not be anyone of particular importance, and can be someone quite unknown. Nothing matters except his death; and it must be believed that the enemy is responsible for this. Every possible cause of his death is suppressed except one: his membership of the group to which one belongs oneself.*

Long after it ceased to be a fight for freedom, the war continued to be a struggle to redeem the sacrifices of the Americans who had already died in Indochina. While the best way to dramatize a "vital interest" in an obscure country which most Americans could not come within five thousand miles of locating on a map is to report that an American has died there in the line of duty, once Americans are there in large numbers they themselves constitute an obvious "vital interest." Further prosecution of the war can be defended as necessary operations to protect American troops, and indeed, the air war in the North, as well as invasions of Cambodia and Laos during the Nixon Administration, were explained to the public in exactly this way. When support for the war precipitously declined, President Nixon tried to convince the public that the object of the fighting was to get American prisoners back. The managers operate on the assumption that the public is most vulnerable to emotional appeals that touch its isolationist nerve. Indeed, only such appeals can cut through the apathy and boredom with which most citizens regard the dull mysteries of foreign affairs. President Kennedy understood what it took to excite the public. "People forget this when they expect me to go on the air all the time educating the nation," Schlesinger quotes him as saying in 1961. "The nation will listen only if it is a moment of great urgency. They will listen after a Vienna [the disastrous summit meeting with Khrushchev which set off the 1961 Berlin crisis]. But they won't listen to things which bore them. That is the great trouble." †

---

* Canetti, *op. cit.*, p. 138.
† Arthur Schlesinger, Jr., *A Thousand Days* (Boston: Houghton Mifflin, 1965), p. 722.

Fear is the strongest emotional stimulant. Before the Vietnam War fear was most successfully packaged in support of increased military budgets. It still is an annual ritual for the Pentagon to leak top secret intelligence about horrible new Soviet weapons. In the Truman Administration, Pentagon officials used to warn the public regularly about the coming "year of maximum danger," the fateful moment when it was calculated that the Soviets would have enough atomic bombs to try a first strike on the United States. But when it came to the Vietnam War, it was harder to play on fear, for the stubborn fact always remained that the enemy was a fourth-rate power with no capacity whatsoever for hurting Americans who stayed out of their country. The dominoes "theory" was designed to transform Vietnam into a respectably frightening enemy. When President Johnson or Secretary Rusk talked about dominoes, one could almost see the victorious Vietnamese in junks and sampans sailing under the Golden Gate bridge.

The national security managers understand that the next best thing to fear for eliciting the right response from the American public is guilt. The Puritan ethnic is still strong in America, and appeals to "stand by our friends" and to "honor our commitments" can shame people into supporting wars that make them feel queasy. President Johnson dramatized a rather ambiguous letter of qualified support which Eisenhower had sent to Diem in 1956 offering assistance to refugees and economic aid under certain circumstances into a sacred pledge to fight to the death. He did this not only to calm the people by suggesting that there had been no change in policy over the years, but also to make them feel shame for the growing impulse to "bug out on our friends." "We have promises to keep," he would constantly remind his audience. Perhaps the most extreme use of the tactic of guilt was Johnson's denunciation of the war critics as "racists" who were interested only in helping white people in Europe but not yellow people in Asia.

The picture of the average American which the national security manager carries around with him in his head, then, is of a private, apathetic fellow, with fundamentally peaceful and decent instincts, who is moved not by reason but by theater. The greatest compliments the managers pay the people are their efforts at public deception, for most of the operations that are covertly undertaken offend public morality and would, if known in time, elicit widespread public opposition. The moral sensibilities of the general public are not wholly different from those of the managers, who are, after all, products of the same culture. (Indeed, the thing which struck me about the internal discussion of foreign policy issues in classified documents to which I had access when I worked in the government was that with all the assumptions of superior knowledge on which they were based and with all the effort to "educate" and "prepare" the public they reflected, the level of analysis was surprisingly similar to the public's discussion.) But in one important aspect there is a difference that has obviously impressed the managers themselves. Many Americans do have a sense of fair play and would be shocked by the knowledge that their government was engaging in secret wars, sabotage, and assassination. That is precisely why governments resort to covert activities. If the Johnson Administration had had to explain to Congress or to the public in 1963–64 why it was bombing Laos, opposing conferences for a peaceful settlement in Indochina, conducting raids against North Vietnam, kidnaping North Vietnamese citizens, and parachuting in sabotage teams, it might well have been forced to stop. Americans will support the most terrible retribution against America's enemies, but they do not favor the waging of aggressive war.

(4)

NEIL SHEEHAN, after reviewing the forty-seven-volume Pentagon study of the war, has written:

> To read the Pentagon papers in their vast detail is to step through the looking glass into a new and different world. This world has a set of values, a dynamic, a language and a perspective quite distinct from the public world of the ordinary citizen and of the other two branches of the Republic—Congress and the judiciary.
>
> Clandestine warfare against North Vietnam, for example, is not seen, either in the written words of the senior decision-makers in the Executive Branch or by the anonymous authors of the study, as violating the Geneva Accords of 1954, which ended the French Indochina War, or as conflicting with the public policy pronouncements of the various administrations. Clandestine warfare, because it is covert, does not exist as far as treaties and public posture are concerned. Further, secret commitments to other nations are not sensed as infringing on the treaty-making powers of the Senate, because they are not publicly acknowledged.*

The world of covert operations is free of public morality. There are restraints of prudence but not of compassion or justice. For McNamara, the CIA "Plans for Covert Action Into North Vietnam" in 1963, which included "a wide variety of sabotage," was an "excellent

* Introduction by Neil Sheehan, *The Pentagon Papers.*

job" that raised no issues of legality or simple humanity. Such questions could be avoided because no one needed to take responsibility for hidden operations.

Once a war surfaces, however, it must be presented as defensive effort. It was for this reason that the Johnson Administration, while preparing to take the American people into war, even considered what McNaughton termed "deliberately provocative actions." The dispatch of DeSoto PT boat patrols and destroyer probes was designed to elicit a reaction from North Vietnam which could then serve as a *casus belli* for the United States. Unlike that of rulers everywhere, who may have esoteric reasons for fighting wars, many of them too complicated or unpalatable to explain to the people, the public passion for war is aroused only in response to a threat. Unless a war is perceived as defensive, the public will regard it as frivolous, dishonorable, or excessively dangerous.

The Vietnam War offers an unparalleled illustration of the uses of secrecy. In contrast to covert operations, which are nonevents staged by nonpersons, never, if possible, to be officially acknowledged, secret operations are well advertised. That important secrets exist is carefully broadcast; only the substance is obscure. Secrecy is a particularly effective device for manipulating public opinion because it intimidates the uninitiated and elicits feelings of awe and guilt. "If you only had access to the cables, you wouldn't say the things you do," is the standard ploy which the national security manager has used so effectively against prying reporters, impertinent professors, and even dispirited Senators trying to get the facts. None of the above wish to say or write anything that might embarrass secret negotiations, give aid and comfort to an enemy, or risk being contradicted by tomorrow's official communiqué. For the public, the mystique of secrecy is powerful. Although officials from time to time make admissions that give much of the game away, such as Lyndon Johnson's published remark that 98 per cent of official secrets are printed in the New York *Times* within a matter of days, most people believe that there is an enormous gulf between what they know and what their leaders know. This is a peculiarly immobilizing belief.

How true is it? The gap between what the managers know and what the citizens know is greatest with respect to the activities of the U.S. government itself. By the judicious use of the "cover story" the U.S. government can confuse its own public and "world opinion," making each think, for example, that combat soldiers and espionage agents sent to Vietnam and Laos before the war officially escalated were aid technicians and experts in flood control. Lyndon Johnson was able to create the impression by sending a small army of diplomats around the world on a crash "peace campaign," that the United States was interested in negotiating a compromise settlement to the war when it was really interested in advertising a "flexibility" which in truth did not exist. The government knew much more than it told the public or than what could have been discovered in the press at the time about such matters as what the *Pueblo* was doing when it was captured, what U.S. diplomats were telling the Dominican politicians and generals when the Marines landed in 1965, and whether U.S. planes bombed a Soviet merchant ship in June 1967. Former chief Pentagon public affairs officer Phil G. Goulding has written in his book *Confirm or Deny* that when he denied that the last of these events happened on June 3, 1967, he "told an untruth to the American people. . . ." His apology is interesting:

> Worse than that, I also misinformed some 235 million people of the second most powerful nation in the history of the world, the Union of Soviet Socialist Republics. . . . Misleading the puny-armed French a couple of years earlier on our supersonic reconnaissance plane's taking snapshots of their atomic plant was one thing, but walking the Soviet Union down the garden path was another.*

It is also true that the government has access to a far greater mass of information about what other governments are doing and thinking than is available to the public. About four billion dollars a year is spent by the Pentagon alone for its world-wide intelligence and communications network. Thousands of people spend their lives gathering what is called "raw intelligence" for the policymakers in Washington. In the CIA headquarters in Langley, Virginia, and indeed at every embassy and substantial military headquarters around the world, there are men and women sitting behind rows of steel desks cutting and pasting the New York *Times, Le Monde, Die Frankfurther Allgemeine, Nhan Dan, Pravda,* and the *Rand Daily Mail.* From other sources, some of them can tell you more than you would ever want to know about the eating habits, preferences in women, and secret ambitions of Indonesian generals, Congolese parliamentarians, and Ceylonese police officials. A tiny minority of this global army of intelligence gatherers employ esoteric or clandestine means to get information. These techniques are the most jealously guarded secrets of the national security bureacracy. So closely held are they that an official deemed to have a "need to know" about such things as electronic surveillance and the identity of espionage agents is initiated into these mysteries in an elaborate rite which involves having a code word whispered into his ear. Nevertheless, sometimes even these secrets will out. When he was Special Assistant to the President for National Security Affairs, McGeorge Bundy was embarrassed to

---

* (New York: Harper & Row, 1970), p. 139.

find his picture on the cover of the *New York Times Magazine* hold-ing a sheaf of papers stamped with a magic word hitherto known to no more than a hundred people. But he was no more surprised than the CIA agent in "deep cover" in the Black Forest of Germany who received a visit from an Internal Revenue Service employee demand-ing the payment of back taxes.

The nub of the secrecy issue is this. Should the fact that the citizen and his representatives in Congress share only a fraction of the in-formation about the outside world that is available to the national security bureaucracy seriously inhibit them from making independent critical judgments about policy? The managers of the Vietnam War continually pleaded with critics not to come to the conclusions about the conflict to which ordinary common sense was leading them be-cause the real situation was much more complicated. "You don't know the whole story," they would say. Of course, that was true, as the Pentagon papers have shown, but the vital pieces of information that were missing would have confirmed the doubts, not allayed them. Moreover, a careful reader of *Le Monde* would have had a far more accurate picture of North Vietnamese strategy than was available in the secret papers of America's war managers. Yet until the recent disclosures dramatized the dangers of secrecy, most Americans, in-cluding members of Congress, were intimidated into silence by the prospect of confronting the information iceberg. Even within the up-per reaches of the national security bureaucracy itself, the top man-agers used secrecy as a weapon to neutralize bureaucratic opposition. During one of the pauses in the bombing of North Vietnam Robert McNamara sent a top-secret cable to the military deliberately mis-informing them that the pause was merely for the purpose of assess-ing the damage that had been done and had no political significance, when, in fact, it was a crucial element in a political "scenario" which the military were known to oppose.

(5)

ON NO ISSUE is the national security manager more perplexed as to how to manage the public mood than on the issue of peace. All other things being equal, peace is more popular than war. The popular preference for peace, as we have seen, worried Truman and his ad-visers, for they thought "wishful thinking" would seriously weaken the nation. They went to considerable lengths to disparage the idea that peace without tension was possible and to brand as a popular confusion the notion that acting peaceful was the best way to insure peace. In a mortal struggle such as the one in which the United States was locked with the Soviet Union, they insisted, preparing for war is the safest road to peace.

In order to combat the enormous Soviet propaganda campaign that equated "peace" and the Stalinist foreign policy, the U.S. officials sought to discredit the word. Those who wanted just "peace" were made to feel as if they were either heirs to Neville Chamberlain's umbrella or dupes of the Communists. The American position was "peace with justice," a goal that might well involve fighting a series of righteous wars. It was the Communists with their Stockholm Peace petition, which had reportedly garnered the signatures of five million hapless victims, who were trumpeting "peace" as an end to itself. Those who listen to cries of peace, Administration officials warned, will wake up some day to find themselves slaves. So successful was this campaign to discredit the "peace" slogan that by the early 1950's any organization using the word was suspect. According to Arthur Schlesinger, there were those in the Kennedy Administration as late as 1961 who objected to naming the new overseas volunteer agency the "Peace Corps" "on the ground that the word 'peace' had been expropriated by the Communists. . . ." *

That suspicion of the word "peace" had persisted so long is evidence of the success of the early Cold War propaganda, for by 1961, the nation had just been through eight years of a President who yearned to be the symbol of peace. Dwight D. Eisenhower believed that he had been elected, in large part, to put an end to the Korean War, and this he proceeded to do. In later years, he came to believe that he had been able to accomplish this by threatening the Chinese with the atomic bomb, but there is very little independent evidence that such a threat was either communicated or believed. The fact is that the new Republican President made a compromise settlement, in effect a ratification of the military stalemate, which his Democratic predecessor could have made but did not dare to make. Once having brought the war to an end, Eisenhower spent the rest of his term seeking to calm the American people on the issue of war and peace even as his predecessor had felt the need to stir them up.

At the very beginning of his term, Eisenhower wanted to take the initiative on the peace issue. "Look, I am tired—and I think everyone is tired—of just plain indictments of the Soviet regime," the new President told his speech-writer Emmet Hughes. "I think it would be wrong—in fact, asinine—for me to get up before the world now to make another one of those indictments. Instead, just *one* thing matters: what have *we* got to offer the world? What are we ready to do to improve the chances of peace?" Hughes recalls in his memoirs that Eisenhower, "the blue eyes agleam and intent," went on to out-

* Schlesinger, *op. cit.*, p. 606.

line the speech he would deliver (much watered down) on April 16, 1953, under the title *The Chance for Peace.*

Here is what I would like to say.

The jet plane that roars over your head costs three-quarters of a million dollars. That is more money than a man earning ten thousand dollars a year is going to make in his lifetime. What world can afford this sort of thing for long? We are in an armaments race. Where will it lead us? At worst, to atomic warfare. At best, to robbing every people and nation on earth of the fruits of their own toil.

Now, there could be another road before us—the road of disarmament. What does this mean? It means for everybody in the world: bread, butter, clothes, homes, hospitals, schools—all the good and necessary things for decent living.

. . . Let us talk straight: no double talk, no sophisticated political formulas, no slick propaganda devices. Let us spell it out, whatever *we* really *offer* . . . withdrawal of troops here and there by both sides . . . United Nations–supervised free elections in another place. . . . *And let us say what we've got to say so that every person on earth can understand it.**

The history of the Eisenhower years is the story of the tension between a President with a deep distrust in war as an effective instrument of policy and a Secretary of State who believed that military bluff was the most important element of policy. While Eisenhower was seeking to catch the world's imagination by making peace offers, Dulles was disparaging any compromise settlement on Korea, as he told Hughes, "until we have shown—before all Asia—our clear superiority by giving the Chinese one hell of a licking." Eisenhower, a war hero who could only enhance his reputation by talking peace, and who was genuinely committed to finding some dramatic formula that would satisfy the deep longing for peace shared by ordinary people everywhere, had picked a Secretary of State who genuinely believed that even talk of peace was dangerous.

John Foster Dulles "and all his sophisticated advisers," as Eisenhower called them, cultivated a peculiarly belligerent style with such celebrated Dullesian verbal salvos as "massive retaliation," but the Dulles policy was in most respects a continuation of Acheson's. When it came to the public relations of peace, there was considerable continuity in approach from one administration to the next. State Department professionals have always been aware that the idea of peace has remained a popular goal despite all the efforts to equate the word with communism. Accordingly, much effort is devoted to placing

---

* Emmett Hughes, *Ordeal of Power* (New York: Atheneum, 1963), p. 113.

what is called the "onus" for resisting sound approaches to peace on the other side. (In the planning of disarmament documents, particularly, a process in which I participated in the early 1960's, the best thing one could say in defense of a particular proposal was that it would "shift the onus.") But although the national security managers are anxious to win points in the "contest for world opinion" by being armed with plausible, if non-negotiable proposals, they are nervous about peace negotiations that have some prospect of reaching an actual agreement. That is not because the State Department wishes to avoid all agreements with America's principal adversaries. In the Dulles era, while the Secretary in public speeches was disparaging the very idea of reaching any accommodation with Communists as hopelessly naïve because Lenin's pupils, as atheists and opportunists, could never be trusted, he was quietly negotiating the Austrian State Treaty and other agreements. But the path of negotiation was perceived by Dulles and other national security managers as littered with booby traps. The greatest risk was euphoria. The managers' nightmare was a summit conference that would kindle such hopes for peace among the American people that popular support for armaments expenditures might decline and pressure might mount to make unwarranted concessions.

In the Kennedy era, the national security managers were concerned that talk of peace undercut the effort "to stiffen the national will" for the confrontation with Khrushchev. After the Cuban missile crisis a peaceful settlement began to look more attractive to the President, and his rhetoric changed drastically in a speech at American University in June 1963. Two months later, a Partial Test Ban agreement was negotiated with the Soviet Union. The opponents of the test ban treaty argued that this limited agreement would "lull" the public into a false sense of security and create "irresistible pressures" to make new concessions to the Soviet Union. The Joint Chiefs of Staff, General Maxwell Taylor had reported to the Senate Foreign Relations Committee, have the "most serious reservations" about a test ban because of "the fear of a euphoria in the West which will eventually reduce our vigilance." Earlier, Admiral Lewis Strauss expressed the standard view of the Dulles era: "I am not sure that the reduction of tensions is necessarily a good thing." *

But Kennedy overcame these objections. His rhetorical treatment of the peace issues in his last months in office was totally different from the tone of the first hundred days. Kennedy had come into office promising to "get the country moving again." His concern, as he expressed it throughout the campaign, was the low state of American "prestige" around the world, which he attributed directly to the dis-

---

* Schlesinger, *op. cit.,* p. 911.

astrously low Eisenhower defense budgets. This was the attraction he held for men such as Bundy and Rostow. The Roman rhetoric of the Inaugural Address, with its heavy emphasis on "paying any price, bearing any burden" in the "long twilight struggle," was an elegant throwback to the tough line of the Truman Administration.

Eisenhower had spent his last two years in office after the death of John Foster Dulles following the advice of James Haggerty, his press secretary, that he should leave the White House as the "man of peace" and thus bequeath the Republican Party a good "image" for the 1960 campaign. Appear more often at the United Nations. Take more world trips. Try a summit meeting with Khrushchev. This was the substance of Haggerty's advice and Eisenhower tried it all. Kennedy knew that the policy, without Ike's authority to defend it, was vulnerable, particularly since Nixon, the Republican candidate, was uncomfortable playing a surrogate "man of peace." In the first two years of the Kennedy Administration, the rhetoric of struggle continued to be the dominant note. However, when the Test Ban Treaty was ratified by the Senate in September 1962, public-opinion polls showed that 80 per cent of the public was in favor of it. In his speeches around the country in the last few weeks of his life, Kennedy sounded the peace theme and was surprised and pleased by the applause he received for it.

By the 1964 campaign, it had become conventional wisdom in the Democratic Party that being a man of peace was worth votes, particularly since Goldwater, the Republican candidate, seemingly wished to be known as a bombardier. Four years later, the mood of the country was one of such war weariness that Richard Nixon, who had made his reputation as a hunter of Communists—in the State Department, at Dienbienphu, and in a Soviet model kitchen—now proclaimed that the "era of confrontation" was about to pass into history to be replaced by a still mysterious "era of negotiation." By the end of his first term, the political climate had so changed from the days of the Truman Administration that Nixon was credited with having staged a political coup by announcing a forthcoming visit to Communist China.

(6)

LET US now look at some of the basic techniques by which news management is accomplished. It only needs to be added that "the inherent right of the government to lie—to lie to save itself . . ." in Arthur Sylvester's celebrated phrase, is exercised in many different ways. In his book *Confirm or Deny,* former Assistant Secretary of Defense for

Public Affairs Phil Goulding gives several examples of outright lies "to protect the national interests" and several more of making events clearer than truth. Some events are ordered to be "played in low key"; others are magnified. In both cases, the government seeks to convey an impression in the public mind different from its own assessment for the purpose of promoting some policy. President Nixon used the executions which occurred in North Vietnam in connection with a forced land-reform program after the first Indochina War to warn critics of his war policy that they would have a "bloodbath" on their hands if the United States pulled out of Vietnam, thereby creating the false impression that the executions were reprisals against those who had opposed them in the war. By his third speech on the subject the deaths had escalated from one hundred thousand into "millions."

Another technique is the official "leak." In an affidavit presented in connection with its court battle to publish the Pentagon papers, the Washington *Post* alleged that its reporters had been shown classified documents on numerous occasions. This is, of course, standard procedure. The obvious purpose is to lend credibility to a news angle which the government is eager to promote. A reporter able to hint at "authoritative sources" is much more likely to print the story as the government would like to see it. However, many leaks come from sources trying to counteract official policy rather than promote it. The military services make liberal use of the "leak." These usually involve "secret intelligence" about new Soviet weapons. Sometimes, they are designed to whip up a little war fever. Admiral Robert Carney, for example, gave a "backgrounder" in March 1955 in which he permitted himself to be identified only as a "high Administration official." Based on secret intelligence, he predicted war with the Chinese Communists in the Formosa Straits within a month. His initiative led to a presidential counterleak to the effect that there would be no war. Brigadier General Robert Scott was another high officer in the Eisenhower Administration who tried to leak information designed to prove the need for a fatter Air Force budget. The Administration managed this problem by tapping his telephone and playing him the recordings.* In the Kennedy Administration, enemies of Under Secretary of State Chester Bowles regularly fed columnists the "news" that he was about to be fired and thereby helped to bring it about. But most leaks are for the purpose of explaining or defending official policy, not undermining it.

A third technique is the pseudo event. To influence public opinion in the right way, it is sometimes necessary, as the national security managers see it, to keep certain news off the front page or to bury it.

---

* See William Rivers, *The Opinion Makers* (Boston: Beacon Press, 1967), p. 146.

News managers share James Reston's judgment that Americans are a "distracted people, busy with the fierce competitions of modern life." Just as it is hard to get their attention at any time except in a crisis, it is easy to distract them further. The President can always get headlines by holding a news conference, even though he may have nothing of substance to say. He can announce the appointment of an ambassador or speculate about a rise in the cost of postage stamps. He can talk about the future, and it will take precedence over events that are actually happening in the present. Thus, Nixon's sensational announcement about a projected trip to China seven months hence drowned out the news of new proposals by the North Vietnamese and the NLF in Paris, which was precisely one of its purposes.

A less subtle technique is direct contact with the owners and managers of the press. Stanford journalism professor William L. Rivers describes how this worked in the Kennedy Administration:

> The boldest and most successful instrument of Kennedy's press policy was known somewhat cynically around the White House as "Operation Publisher." It began before the Inauguration, when Kennedy invited North Carolina publishers to dinner and talked to them about his problems and policies. Then he began bringing publishers from all over the nation to the White House for confidential two-hour luncheons.
>
> "Operation Publisher" was extraordinarily useful. How adroitly the President used the meetings was made clear by a Republican publisher's description of the luncheon he attended: Everything is handled in such an informal manner you feel at ease. The President asked us for our opinions on a number of matters. He told us he liked to have as much background as possible before making a decision. The President speaks so frankly about things that you get a feeling that he trusts you and is taking you into his confidence.*

Not all attempts by the Administration to manage foreign policy news are so civilized. According to Schlesinger,

> [Kennedy] retained an evidently inexhaustible capacity to become vastly, if briefly, annoyed by hostile articles or by stories based on leaks (presumably those that did not emanate from the White House). When this happened there would be complaints to the staff, calls to reporters, searches for the sources of stories, and even the cancellation for a time of the *New York Herald Tribune*.†

* *Ibid.*, p. 164.
† Schlesinger, *op. cit.*, p. 718.

It was in the largely self-generated crisis atmosphere of the Kennedy Administration that Defense Department officials began to talk about news as "part of the arsenal of weaponry." The President himself, having successfully persuaded the New York *Times* not to print their scoop on the upcoming Bay of Pigs invasion, told the American Newspaper Publishers Association a few days after that fiasco that the press should continue to censor itself in the interests of national security. (Sometime later, according to Schlesinger, he changed his mind.)

During the brief reign at Camelot, every newspaper in the country treated the Kennedys as glamorous copy. Readers learned that the White House gently swayed to the music of Lester Lanin as the handsome, sophisticated, exquisitely tailored New Frontiersmen and their enchanting wives danced into the night in the East Room. The energetic President with the attractive wit and the winning smile arrived. No one would guess that he had spent his day speed reading through thousands of pages of documents and personally calling the key bureaucrats throughout the government. The newspapers portrayed him as a man who worked hard and played hard, a man fully in charge. To his credit, Kennedy did not take the Kennedy myth as seriously as his admirers. He told a press conference that he was reading more and enjoying it less. Flattering copy about his image did not compensate for news stories with unfavorable slants or which did not get the point. Merriman Smith, veteran White House reporter, was impressed by how much energy the Kennedy Administration spent reacting to newspaper stories: "How they can spot an obscure paragraph in a paper of three thousand circulation two thousand miles away is beyond me. They must have a thousand little gnomes reading the paper for them." *

Newspaper editors and publishers would receive calls from the White House, occasionally from the President himself, blasting them for their "errors" and suggesting ways to make amends. Sometimes the White House retaliated against an individual reporter. When David Halberstam began to write the truth about the Diem regime, Kennedy personally called the publisher of the New York *Times* in an attempt to have him recalled from Vietnam. In the early days of the Kennedy Administration, one of the senior editors of *Fortune* was working on an "inside" article about the White House staff which purportedly identified McGeorge Bundy as a secret "soft" who did not want to resume nuclear testing. So concerned about getting a bad image for a good decision was Bundy that he and the President called the editor in and rewrote the article with him over a weekend.

Lyndon Johnson devoted at least as much energy as the Kennedys

* Rivers, *op. cit.*, p. 160.

to cajoling, overwhelming, flattering, and occasionally threatening members of the press. Two nationally syndicated columnists, William S. White and Drew Pearson, close personal friends, wrote glowingly of his daily triumphs, but the President's continuing larger-than-life performance became less and less convincing against the background of an escalating war. Johnson began to be in serious political trouble when the "credibility gap" itself became news.

(7)

THE NATIONAL security bureaucracy has other less obvious ways of influencing public opinion than such direct attempts at news management or such official public relations activities of the Pentagon as red carpet tours of military installations, "national security seminars," and television commercials. The State Department has a small official public information program which conducts briefings for civic groups. School children may obtain "simplified" accounts of how the United States got into Vietnam, and a number of other places too, all of which have a fairy-tale quality about them. Anyone can arrange a private showing of the film "Why Vietnam," a celluloid White Paper, by calling the State Department.

The subtlest forms of manipulation are covert. The Central Intelligence Agency, despite the clear legal prohibitions on conducting propaganda activities within the United States, has made U.S. opinion a prime target, but it has concentrated on influencing elite opinion rather than the general public. Using the cover of other agencies, it has financed the distribution of thousands of free books to libraries throughout the United States. Articles in scholarly magazines such as *Foreign Affairs* are written by Agency personnel without identification. One that came to light was George Carver's article on "the faceless Vietcong" published in the April 1966 issue of *Foreign Affairs*. The CIA has also financed scholarship and scholarly books at such leading universities as Massachusetts Institute of Technology. Much of the academic work on counterinsurgency, internal war, modernization, and other academic formulations of official policy concerns was covertly initiated by intelligence agencies or openly funded by the Pentagon. It is impossible to assess how influential these agencies were in defining the limits of the scholarly debate on crucial foreign policy issues, but some of the most widely discussed and widely used social science texts of the 1950's and 1960's had official money behind them. This fact was neither known nor its significance appreciated by most of the scholarly community. The reason it is hard to assess the importance of official national security agencies in guiding the scholarly debate on the great issues of war and peace—counter-insurgency, the nature of Soviet policy, the origins of the Cold War, Chinese-Soviet relations, the risks of the arms race versus the risks of disarmament—is that scholars who did not get checks from the CIA or "Aunt Ida," as some Cambridge professors affectionately called the Department of Defense–sponsored Institute for Defense Analysis, frequently came up with equally good rationales for official policy. This is a subject to which we will return.

A few years ago, the first of what appears to be a new generation of "whistle-blowers," to use Ralph Nader's term, revealed to the public that the CIA had been funding the National Student Association and several other ostensibly private religious, civic, labor, and educational organizations that were dealing with foreign affairs during the 1950's and early 1960's. The former NSA officials who revealed that the well-financed student organization had been living off the Treasury for years by means of secret conduits and dummy foundations had decided that there was something inconsistent about their roles as students and as espionage agents. The incident, like the disclosure of the Pentagon papers by another "whistle-blower" a few years later, aroused momentary indignation because of the deception that was revealed. Some people were particularly outraged that innocent students had attended international conferences as unwitting mouth-pieces for the CIA or that literature professors who innocently supplied propaganda for the agency-financed *Encounter* magazine had been used, duped, and finally made to look foolish. The clandestine CIA activities of the 1950's involving the molding of elite opinion have, it seems to me, a deeper significance.

Shortly after the disclosures in *Ramparts* magazine first revealed the connections between the CIA and NSA, I interviewed a veteran intelligence agent who had been engaged in undercover work since 1941. He was now thoroughly disgruntled, and talked about the CIA, which had just thrown him out, as "the most dangerous organization in the world." On closer examination, it was not the objectives of the Agency that bothered him, or even its methods, but its current management. When I pressed him about the NSA affair, expecting at least a little righteous indignation, I received a very different, and to me, quite enlightening, response. He began by saying that we didn't need those college kids to act as spies. They weren't very good at it, and the information they turned up was practically worthless. The operation served an educational function. Its purpose, which the disgruntled agent thoroughly approved, was to implicate—his word may have been "enlist"—key members of the elite in fighting the Cold War. By making businessmen abroad, students, missionaries, foundation officials, etcetera, a part of the intelligence apparatus, by having them act as information gatherers and occasionally as bit players in agency operations, he said, we made them conscious of the continuing struggle with communism. When we made a student "witty," we recruited him for life.

The recruiting pattern bears him out. The Harvard Law School was a key source of talent for the Agency and a number of promising students who were tapped by Professor Robert Amory, later Deputy Director of the CIA, usually stayed close to the Agency in some form or another. In the crisis atmosphere of the 1950's, the Agency had little trouble identifying and enlisting future opinion makers, for these were usually student leaders or, in the vernacular of the 1950's, "big men on campus." They also went after lesser figures with special talents. As a major in Russian language and literature at Harvard, I narrowly missed going to Washington to work for the Agency. (My final reluctance had nothing to do with being against the CIA, its objectives, or even its methods, which in 1950 I assumed, along with most of the rest of my generation, were necessary. Frankly, I was put off by the elaborate psychological test, which kept asking whether I wanted to be a beekeeper, to eat exotic foods, or to spy on my friends.)

The CIA clandestine operations in the United States concerned with the manipulation of elite opinion were managed by Cord Myer, Jr. Mr. Myer was one of the founders of the World Federalists and a genuine idealist of the Woodrow Wilson mold. His principal associates in designing the program were also liberals who thought that the visible part of the U.S. foreign policy establishment was too conservative, stodgy, and inflexible to meet the "dynamic challenges" of the 1950's. The CIA has an undeserved popular image as a nest of reactionaries interested in establishing right-wing dictatorships through assassination and other grisly methods. These methods are certainly used. Ambassador Colby reported to the Senate Foreign Relations Committee that the "Phoenix" program had assassinated over twenty thousand "Vietcong infrastructure." (On examination, it appears that the only working definition of "Vietcong infrastructure" is someone killed by the "Phoenix" program.) But not infrequently, the CIA has supported moderate socialists, occasionally even revolutionaries, as in Algeria. There are plenty of thugs on the payroll, foreign and native born, but the management is genteel, rather scholarly, and reads the *New Republic*.

The real reason why the CIA resorted to deception to move public opinion is rooted in what it conceived to be its liberal ideology. In the early Cold War it was hard to get Congressional support for any foreign organization or U.S. organization dealing with foreign affairs that had a political line left of Congressman Richard Nixon. Senators from the Midwest would have been outraged if they had been asked to support "socialistic" magazines such as *Encounter*, "left-wing" labor unions in Europe and Latin America, and organizations such as the National Student Association, which all through its years of CIA financing was denounced from time to time on the floor of Congress as "communistic." The solution was not to ask. As the defenders of the policy made clear in the inquiries following the *Ramparts* disclosures, the CIA student program was part of the "excellence" race with the Soviet Union. Once the Soviets devised the great international student conference as an arena of the Cold War, it was a matter of national pride that the U.S. field a first-rate team. Natural selection might have yielded stumbling football players or fraternity glad hands, no match for articulate NKVD agents who had the effrontery to pose as students. Moreover, an overt program would become enmeshed in domestic politics. A junket to Vienna or Sofia at government expense to take part in a conference would have been almost as good a piece of patronage for a Congressman as an appointment to Annapolis. So the managers of the CIA took the responsibility for "educating" the country on their own and in the process revealed their contempt for the American people, representative government, and the very liberal ideology they thought they were pursuing.

(8)

IT WOULD BE a serious mistake to think that all manipulation of public opinion on foreign affairs emanates from the government. True, as we have seen, the government is behind somewhat more of it than appears on the surface. Nonetheless, the foreign policy consensus of the last generation could not have been held together without the crucial parallel influences of the press, organized religion,* the intellectual establishment, and popular culture, all of which are in important respects independent of the government. Each of these topics deserves a book in itself and none will be done justice here. But it would be misleading to end a discussion of public opinion without briefly considering the role each plays in the manipulation process.

We might begin by defining more precisely what we mean by manipulation. When the government practices this art, it is clear that government officials are using various brands of propaganda to enlist support for their own policies. What does it mean to say that a newspaper or a church manipulates public opinion on national security issues? It means using emotional appeal, political influence, or threat to encourage public support for official policies that could not

* The role of organized religion in promoting and dissolving the foreign policy consensus will be taken up in the next chapter, "Foreign Policy and Electoral Politics."

be elicited through rational argument alone. I am aware that one man's logic is another man's emotional appeal; that it is possible to disagree as to what is irrational, and that, indeed, all politics involves some element of magic. But the conscious attempts to mold opinion by irrelevant and illogical argument, by appeals to fear, hate, and guilt, as well as the various motives behind such efforts, are not too hard to identify. It is this that we shall now briefly do.

The press is subject to a number of continuing pressures to support, or at least not to criticize radically, the foreign policy of the United States. First, newspapers are in the business of selling news. News is produced by newsmakers, the most important of whom are the top officials of the government. The White House correspondent who covers the President, the top newsmaker of them all, is limited as to what he can say in criticism of the Chief Executive. He can call him "cranky," "angry," sometimes even "unsure of himself." However, unlike editorial writers who operate at a safe distance, he cannot call him a liar or a planner of an aggressive war, even when the use of such strong language would be honest reporting. (There are few editorial writers today who would call the President a man with the soul of Uriah Heep in the body of a baboon, as the *Tribune* described Lincoln more than a hundred years ago. Whether the advance in civility has not been purchased at too great a cost is an open question.) A correspondent indiscreet enough to use honest intemperate language will lose "access" to officials, which is much like a surgeon losing his knife. Washington correspondents who funnel most of the national political news to the public maintain continuing social contact with the men they cover at dinner parties, embassy receptions, and cocktail parties. Social convention, business, and politics all insure that the Washington correspondent will give the high official more respectful attention than he deserves. The correspondent is aware that "irresponsible" correspondents and columnists become targets of official whispering campaigns. "I had not been in Washington a fortnight," Anthony Howard, Washington correspondent for the London *Observer* recalls, "before I was drawn on one side by what is known here as a 'high source' and solemnly assured that Walter Lippmann was 'senile.'" * (Lippmann at the time probably was the most influential critic in the country of the Johnson Vietnam policy.)

Second, reportorial laziness is an important government asset. With the conspicuous exception of a few correspondents such as David Halberstam and Malcolm Brown, most of the early years of the Vietnam War were reported as official fairy tales in which the "faceless" Vietcong were being humanely eliminated, while, under the guidance

* Rivers, *op. cit.*, p. xv.

of U.S. pacification officers, democracy was firmly taking root in the provinces. It was years before American newspaper readers learned that Saigon was an obscene snarl of corruption, venality, and prostitution, that one-fourth of the population were refugees, that whole populated areas designated as search-and-destroy targets were marked for forceable relocation or death, that U.S. soldiers were killing their officers. A few stories in a few newspapers gave this "other side" of the war, but most of the reportage mirrored what the government wanted broadcast simply because it was based on government handouts. It is much easier to go to a briefing than to visit a supposedly "pacified" village—and a great deal safer.

In many other foreign policy areas, government communiqués and press releases prepared by public relations offices are good ways to fill up empty news columns with a minimum of effort. Some of this canned news is supplied by right-wing dictators who spend hundreds of thousands of dollars each year to market benign images. Obviously, the worse the reality the more expensive the image. Thus, the infamous Dominican dictator Trujillo employed distinguished Americans with impeccable liberal credentials such as Morris Ernst and Franklin D. Roosevelt, Jr., as image polishers. In the relatively rare instances where there were takers for outright bribes, Trujillo bribed in the grand manner. According to Irwin Ross's study *Image Merchants,* the Dominican Republic Information Center paid the International News Service $6,000 every three months to distribute propaganda under the guise of news. To bribe the head of the Mutual Broadcasting Corporation, Alexander Guterma, cost $750,000.*

Third, just as the government can get attention by dramatizing crises so editors and publishers sell newspapers by black headlines. A crisis with black and white heroes against a background of mounting violence makes especially good copy, particularly if it culminates in a clean victory. To write about complexities, subtleties, or nuances of negotiation taxes a reporter's skill and may open him to the charge of being unduly sympathetic to America's adversaries. It is for that reason, among others, that the television networks have never had an analysis in depth of the negotiating positions of the various sides of the Vietnam War. When I tried to bring up the subject on an NBC "special" right after the Tet offensive of 1968, the producer kept passing me notes to say something juicy about the CIA in Laos. She was against the war, but she knew that she would receive no plaudits for a serious, probably dull, discussion of the issues. The program would be counted a success only if it made "hard news" in the Monday morning edition of the New York *Times.*

---

* See Irwin Ross, *The Image Merchants: The Fabulous World of Public Relations* (Garden City, N.Y.: Doubleday and Co., 1959).

The opportunities for the introduction of the hidden bias in modern news reporting are unlimited. *Time* can elevate a political personality to the pantheon of "the tough-minded," "the distinguished," "the dynamic," "the muscular," "the electric," one who always gives "straight, hard answers," or consign him along with favorite targets of the past, such as Harold Stassen, to an ash heap made up of people with "clammy hands" and "ill-fitting toupees" who "fish cough drops out of their mouth." (Of course, the loaded phrase can be used in the service of every political point of view. Some of the most dynamic, tough-minded people in *Time* have ended up in Pravda as "jackals.") Newspapers are also adept at turning headlines into editorials. Perhaps the best example of an Orwellian headline was the following from the Honolulu *Star-Bulletin* of June 2, 1968: VIET CROPS SAVED IN DEFOLIATION PROGRAM.

Robert Cirino, reviewing a great number of journalism studies, persuasively documents the obvious in his book *Don't Blame the People* *—i.e., that the overwhelmingly predominant bias in American journalism, Vice-President Agnew to the contrary, is conservative, in favor of the status quo, and strongly supportive of U.S. foreign policy. He analyzes the hidden bias in newspaper headlines, and surveys various content analyses of *Time, Life* and *U.S. News* and the slanted enthusiasms of TV reporters. It is safe to say that not many Republicans and few generals are caught fishing cough drops out of their mouths or adjusting their toupees.

Until *Life* magazine began to turn against the war in the twentieth year of active U.S. military involvement in Indochina the mass media consistently presented the story of the conflict as a continuation of the great American crusade that began in World War II. Rereading back issues of *Look, Saturday Evening Post,* and in more sophisticated guise, the *New Yorker* for the 1950's and early 1960's is an education in how to paint the world clearer than truth. The United States is the inevitable victim. All nations but one play "power politics." The struggle is between "freedom" (us) and "totalitarianism" (them). There is enough doubt in the outcome of this giant game to provide suspense. At the height of the Cold War screaming headlines on the world-wide red menace sold newspapers. Anxious citizens wanted to be told when and where World War III would break out. But while the mass media helped feed the climate of fear through uncritical reporting of official alarmism, newspapers, magazines, and TV also kept alive the myth of victory.

At the height of the Berlin crisis in 1961 *Life* printed a cover story on fall-out shelters with Edward Teller's reassuring but irresponsible assertion that "99 per cent can be saved." One of the high water

* Los Angeles: Diversity Press, 1970.

marks of the Cold War was the October 27, 1951, issue of *Colliers,* then a magazine with a circulation in the millions, which was devoted in its entirety to a "history" of World War III. The Korean War had been dragging on for more than a year. The editors of *Colliers* decided to boost morale and their own sagging sales by presenting a blueprint for American victory: A "you are there" dispatch by Edward R. Murrow from the cockpit of the B-36 that dropped the atomic bomb on Moscow; Hanson Baldwin's description of the invasion of Russia; "I Saw Them Chute into the Urals" by Lowell Thomas; a description of the political re-education of the Soviet Union by Arthur Koestler —"With the defeat of Communist imperialism the victors also won responsibility for humanity's last chance at salvation. They met this challenge with glorious vision"; cartoons by Bill Mauldin and copious illustrations of occupied Russia being rehabilitated by generous victors. The war begins with a Soviet attack on Yugoslavia which is met by U.S. "saturation A-bombing of the U.S.S.R. . . . on legitimate military targets only." Three years later the Soviet Union "degenerates into a state of chaos and internal revolt." That the United States had a right to destroy the Soviet Union under these circumstances was never questioned.

By the same token, information which disturbs the fantasy that the United States has both power and virtue on its side is much harder to get published. Eyewitnesses to the My Lai massacre offered confessions and a packet of bloody photographs to mass magazines for over a year before Seymour Hersh broke the story. No one would print them. The public was not ready for this, editors would say. Daniel Ellsberg offered the Pentagon papers to a major TV network a year before they were disclosed. Top executives read them, noted that they held the greatest story of the decade, and handed them back. When they were finally published, the attention was focused on the sensational circumstances of their revelation, not their extraordinary substance, for although the public had now gotten used to massacres, it was not yet ready to face the planning of aggressive war. No government official attempted to censor, threaten, or silence the press on these occasions. It was not necessary.

Why, then, if the government has perfected the techniques of news management and the press has such strong incentive to support the Administration's foreign policy, did so much criticism erupt over the Vietnam War? The most important single answer is television. TV, and to a lesser extent the photo magazines such as *Life* and *Look,* is the only news medium that successfully depicts acts in addition to communicating words. Network camera crews were encouraged by the Pentagon to show the American people the reality of combat in the hopes of inspiring patriotic support at home. Instead, because the true character of the war could not be disguised, TV coverage inspired disgust. Most important, the acts Americans saw committed on their screens made the stream of words emanating from the White House seem hollow, even insulting. (One of McNamara's subordinates has advanced the thesis that the national security managers were more obtuse about the war than the average citizen because they worked straight through the Huntley-Brinkley show and stayed out too late at parties to catch the eleven o'clock news.) There have always been foreign policy critics in America but they have usually been drowned in the foreign policy consensus. It took a failure of the magnitude of Vietnam to undermine that consensus and to validate observations and arguments that critics had been making for years. Even so, during most of the war years there was a discrepancy between what correspondents and cameramen were reporting and the conclusions editorial writers and TV commentators were drawing.

When it became politically acceptable to be against the war, corruption, dope-peddling, and internal dissension in Saigon suddenly became news. Peace demonstrations received noticeably more sympathetic treatment. TV programs on militarism and the excesses of the Pentagon began to appear. TV film footage on the war now received more pointed treatment.

Once again the mass media were reflecting and reinforcing a changing public mood. More important, they were registering the shift in opinion of the business and financial elite, who by 1968 had turned against the war. The attacks on the "Eastern establishment press" begun by Vice-President Agnew in 1969 for their criticism of Administration foreign policy were concentrated on the networks, the Washington *Post,* and the New York *Times,* not only because these are the most powerful of the media (the *Post* and the *Times* syndicate their news coverage and columnists all over the country) but also because they made irresistible targets for a populist defense of the Nixon war policies for which the intended audience was the "silent majority." Despite the networks' disclaimers that they have not been intimidated by Agnew's attacks, treatment of the war became noticeably more sympathetic to the Administration. For the most part the media accepted the Nixon definition of "winding down the war" despite the escalating (and largely unreported) air war throughout Indochina.

It is, of course, an oversimplification to suggest that the press is always subservient to the government. Most reporters try to get news even if it does not reflect favorably on the government and some editors will print it. As we have noted, the television cameras graphically captured the horror and stupidity of the Vietnam War, and occasionally a David Brinkley or a Walter Cronkite would betray a trace of anger. The New York *Times* and other newspapers editorially opposed the war policy for a number of years, although no major newspaper, so far as I am aware, proposed setting a date and getting out before this obvious solution was proposed by Senator Charles Goodell in 1970. (Some months earlier, when I proposed something similar in a speech to a group of Senators, the Washington *Post* wished to reprint the speech but insisted on excising the part at the end about setting a date and cutting off funds, as that was such a "far-out" idea it would undercut the credibility of the rest.)

Occasionally, there are great pitched battles between a newspaper and the government over foreign policy. Two such historic occasions involved the publication of secret documents. Three days before Pearl Harbor, the Washington *Times Herald* printed the secret war mobilization plans. The newspaper's purpose was to show that Roosevelt, whom the publisher regarded as a Dutchess County Communist, was pretending to offer peace when he was really planning war. The source of the leak was a general who thought the news would wake up the country and produce bigger Army Air Corps appropriations. The go-between was Senator Burton K. Wheeler, a leading isolationist, who thought the publication would have the opposite effect. Almost thirty years later, the New York *Times* published the secret Pentagon study of the Vietnam War, including planning documents. By this time, much of the press was smarting at the realization of how much it had been deceived during the long years of the war. Yet even though the publication involved the issue of the freedom of the press, a matter on which even the most reactionary publishers tend to sound like Tom Paine, a surprising number of newspapers across the country supported the government's efforts to suppress the publication. Most of the editorial outrage that was expressed was focused on the deception of the press and the public rather than on the shocking substance of the papers. To read the editorial advice given on that occasion, one might conclude that the press was telling the policymakers, "Next time you plan an operation like the Vietnam War, take us into your confidence."

Indeed, the impulse of every newspaper columnist and television personality, however eager they sometimes are to expose the peccadillos of graft, corruption, and conflict of interest, is not to question the basic purposes or motives of official policy. This has to do not only with the press's dependence on government for news production, but more important, with the fact that most members of the press and most readers of newspapers are patriotic. Reporters do not feel comfortable writing about their own government in the same vein in which they write about other governments. As foreign correspondents they may well be sensitive to the power struggles behind the scenes and take a skeptical view of all official pronouncements but in reporting on their own government, they give officials the benefit of the doubt. (It is worth comparing U.S. and French reporting on Vietnam. A Martian would never believe it was the same war. It is safe to predict that the French reporting rather than the American will be the basis of the historical record.)

Until the Vietnam War became an acknowledged failure it would have shaken the world view of the average American to suggest that the United States did not always act out of the most generous or noble motives, or, indeed, that it did not always have legal and moral right on its side. The bloodiest events can be reported as long as responsibility for them is not assigned to American officials. But it spoils breakfasts to read that your sons are committing war crimes in pursuit of an illegal, immoral, and endless war, and when newspapers spoil breakfasts, subscriptions are canceled. That is why editorial writers burn with righteous rage over every atrocity of the enemy, real or imagined, but go to great lengths to preserve the myth of American innocence, for they have every interest in not disturbing the peace of mind of their readers and their advertisers. Thus, for example, at the time of the U-2 incident, when Khrushchev had announced that a U.S. plane had been shot down deep in Soviet territory on an alleged espionage mission, and the Eisenhower Administration had admitted the facts but offered a "cover story" about collecting weather information, much of the American press, according to Professor William L. Rivers's survey, "devoted the next two days to predictable editorials such as this one published in the New York *Mirror:*"

THE WORD IS "MURDER"

Premier Khrushchev personally ordered the rocket-destruction of an unarmed U.S. aircraft which had drifted into Soviet air space, probably because its pilot became unconscious when its oxygen equipment failed. . . . Khrushchev has revealed himself and his beastly character to the full; he is a pig in human form.*

When President Eisenhower admitted that the plane was indeed on an espionage mission and Khrushchev, reporting that the pilot was still alive, began to excoriate the United States, most newspapers, as Rivers puts it, "began to echo the demand of the New York *Journal-American* that U.S. citizens 'form up' behind their government."

(9)

ONE OF THE crucial questions about the Cold War consensus is this: How did it happen that there was no strong anti-imperialist impulse among America's intellectuals? How is it that so many national se-

* Rivers, *op. cit.*, p. 150.

curity assumptions that became safe to challenge after the breakup of that consensus in the Vietnam War were absolutely untouchable only a few years earlier? How is it that our most brilliant political and social critics could not bring themselves to challenge the "motives" of their own leaders, as if the study of human behavior involves anything less? How is it that as brilliant and courageous a scholar as Hans Morgenthau could write as late as 1967 about U.S. global military intervention, including the Vietnam War: "Only the enemies of the United States will question the generosity of these efforts, which have no parallel in history"? * Why were there no respected intellectual leaders of the anti-imperialist tradition of William Graham Sumner, Carl Schurz, and the Anti-Imperialist League to speak out against imperialism and militarism? †

There are two obvious answers, both of which are valid, but which, standing alone, are inadequate. The first is McCarthyism. There is no doubt that the climate of fear which the Wisconsin Senator capitalized upon and helped to promote produced ideological conformity, self-protective blindness, and the prudent avoidance of controversy. But what was it about the intellectual climate of America that permitted McCarthyism to flourish and caused his attackers to question only his "methods" and not his "objectives"? (The typical liberal position which I myself remember taking in college was in fact to endorse his objectives. We took our lead from Adlai Stevenson, who said that J. Edgar Hoover was the man to do what McCarthy was attempting.) Again, there are the obvious answers which we have already mentioned. The Truman Administration itself advanced much the same analysis of the world struggle with communism as McCarthy did, and the reckless speeches of Attorney General J. Howard McGrath confused dissent and disloyalty with the same abandon. It was not lost on young academics looking for tenure that men such as Harlow Shapley, the distinguished astronomer, were being harassed for their political views and that some were being dismissed. In an era of loyalty oaths and traveling Congressional witch-hunts, when great universities congratulated themselves on not firing leftist English professors, young men attracted to the social sciences understandably sought safe niches, safe subjects, and safe views. The same pressures existed in the mass media and the entertainment industry with fewer protections. This was the era of the TV blacklist and the "Hollywood Ten" hearings.

The second obvious pressure for ideological conformity was the increasing dependence of a new class of intellectuals and academics

---

* Quoted in Noam Chomsky, *American Power and the New Mandarins* (New York: Random House, 1967), p. 32.

† For an account of anti-imperialism, see E. Tompkins, *Anti-Imperialism in the United States* (Philadelphia: University of Pennsylvania Press, 1970), and Robert L. Beisner, *Twelve Against Empire* (New York: McGraw-Hill, 1968).

on the government. We discussed in Part I the impact of the bureau-cratic revolution on government-university relations. Grants, consult-antships, interesting travel assignments, and the summons to Washington for White House task forces, State Department advisory committees, and other ego-boosting activities were all reserved for "responsible" academics. The "responsibles," their prestige enhanced by flattering attention from Washington, rose to the top of their pro-fessions in the universities. There they were in a position to influence what younger men learned and taught. The men in charge of those areas of the social sciences most relevant to current policy, such as "Russian Studies," "Chinese Studies," or "National Security Studies," were the most religious in staying within the bounds of official ortho-doxy.

However, the influence of government on the intellectual and scholarly community extended far beyond those who lived in fear of receiving a subpoena or in hope of receiving a check. The state helped to set intellectual fashions for thinkers who never had any contact with the Department of Defense or the CIA or, for that matter, the Communist Party.* The mobilization of the university in war led to a reassessment of the very purposes of intellectual effort. As Zbigniew Brzezinski, one of the celebrators of the new intellectual man, puts it:

> . . . the largely humanist-oriented, occasionally ideologically-minded intellectual-dissenter, who sees his role largely in terms of proffering social critiques, is rapidly being displaced either by experts and specialists, who become involved in special gov-ernment undertakings, or by the generalists-integrators, who be-come in effect house-ideologues for those in power, providing overall intellectual integration for disparate actions.†

Intellectuals have come to see their role as supporting and rationaliz-ing power, much as Julien Benda noted more than a generation ago, not only because of the familiar external blandishments but also be-cause they find the practice of what is called the new pragmatism in-herently fascinating. The thrill of manipulating the environment, whether it be a new pacification technique for Vietnam, a new propa-ganda approach for Eastern Europe, or a new set of policy options for the National Security Council, is irresistible for those whom Noam Chomsky calls "the new mandarins"; a generation of bright, driven men has found it infinitely easier and more rewarding to try to man-

---

* It is worth noting, however, that a large number of Cold War ideologues had experimented with various forms of Marxism-Leninism in the 1930's. Once having switched sides, they brought to the anti-Communist struggle some of the Manicheanism and paranoia of Stalinism; a taste for ideological orthodoxy inherited from the Party, along with the outrage of the betrayed, and the zeal of the convert.

† Chomsky, *op. cit.,* p. 30.

age the world than to understand it. Moral questions about when and
how to use power have baffled the best minds since the dawn of history. It is hard to find right answers, harder still to convince others.
But the techniques of using power can be developed and demonstrated with a virtuosity that all will admire. The drive for excellence
can be satisfied by a well-worked-out bombing pattern as easily as by
a new input-output model or a new approach to nation-building. One
need only listen to the testimony of Leonard Sullivan, Deputy Director for Southeast Asia Matters, Office of Defense Research and Engineering, to appreciate that this professional killer is embarked on
an intellectual adventure:

> These developments open up some very exciting horizons as
> to what we can do in five to ten years from now: when one
> realizes that we can detect anything that perspires, moves, car-
> ries metal, makes a noise, or is hotter or colder than its surround-
> ings, one begins to see the potential. This is the beginning of the
> instrumentation of the entire battlefield. Eventually we will be
> able to tell when anybody shoots, what he is shooting at, and
> where he was shooting from. You begin to get a "year 2000"
> vision of the electronic map with little lights that flash for differ-
> ent kinds of activity.*

The worship of power and technique was advertised by the "new
mandarins" as "pragmatism," although there was little in the works
of William James or John Dewey to support the amorality and in-
strumentalism to which the term was applied. If politics was the art of
the possible, the only relevant intellectual activity was the science of
the possible. That meant helping men of power to keep it.

* *Congressional Record,* Vol. 115, No. 136 (August 11, 1969), p. S59593.

I I

Foreign Policy and Electoral Politics

Modern American democracy is sustained by two crucial myths. The first is bipartisanship, "Politics stops at the water's edge." In his Farewell Address, George Washington lamented the "baneful effects of the spirit of party" on our foreign relations, although, as Frederick Dutton has pointed out, that very statement was timed to affect the outcome of an election. In the postwar era the "bipartisan foreign policy" worked out by John Foster Dulles, Senator Arthur Vandenberg and the nonpartisan (but largely Republican-voting) national security managers of the Truman Administration, has become, in Kenneth Crawford's words, the "Jehovah of our political tradition." The most casual glance at recent history, however, reveals that some foreign policies are more bipartisan than others. Since the end of the war, some aspect of foreign policy has been injected into every presidential election.

The second myth is that while the handling of the crucial issues of war and peace are entrusted for a period of years to the President and whatever advisers he chooses to help him, the voter has a chance every four years to ratify or to overturn what they have done and even to give some guidance for the future. Thus the President's enormous powers over foreign affairs are subject to a quadrennial check. The President's fear of the voter's displeasure acts as a restraint on the exercise of his lordly discretion. This myth makes it possible to reconcile the sharp increase in presidential prerogatives in foreign relations of recent times and the democratic tradition.

In *Democracy in America* de Tocqueville declared in an often-quoted passage that democracy and effective diplomacy are antithetical:

> As for myself, I do not hesitate to say that it is especially in the conduct of their foreign relations that democracies appear to me decidely inferior to other governments. . . . Foreign politics demand scarcely any of those qualities which are peculiar to a democracy; they require, on the contrary, the perfect use of almost all those in which it is deficient. . . . Democracy can only with great difficulty regulate the details of an important undertaking, persevere in a fixed design, and work out its execution in spite of serious obstacles. It cannot combine its measures with secrecy or await their consequences with patience. These are qualities which more especially belong to an individual or an aristocracy.

The conflict between popular government and aggressive statesmanship, between democracy and empire, is an ancient one. Sometimes, as the historian William A. Williams argues, there is a broad base of support, even some grass-roots initiative, for expansionist policies, as in the agrarian movements of the turn of the century. Sometimes jingoist movements arise, such as the Goldwater-LeMay wing of the "radical right," which press the President toward more adventurous policies than he wishes to undertake. But the historical record shows that the President's view of the national interest typically involves more expense, more taxation, more danger, and more casualties than the public wants to accept. This is surely what Dean Acheson means when he writes that "the limitation imposed by democratic political practices makes it difficult to conduct our foreign affairs in the national interest. . . . " The conflict between democracy and the "national interest" (as revealed to the executive) has been resolved in favor of the latter.

We have noted that a prime consequence of the bureaucratic revolution was the shift of power over national security affairs from Congress to the President. Although the changes in World War II were dramatic, this process had been going on for a long time. According to Woodrow Wilson, the "most striking and momentous consequence" of the Spanish-American War was "the greatly increased power and opportunity for constructive statesmanship given the President by the plunge into international politics and into the administration of distant dependencies. . . ." * When foreign affairs

* Quoted in Dean Acheson, *A Citizen Looks at Congress* (New York: Harper Bros., 1957), pp. 50–51.

play a prominent part in the politics and policy of a nation, Wilson concluded, "its Executive must of necessity be its guide: must utter every initial judgment, take every first step of action, supply the information upon which it is to act, suggest and in large measure control its conduct." Every postwar President has been a Wilsonian not only in his belief in America's moral duty to bring a reformist vision to the world, but also in his view that the President must have the power to run the crusade his own way. The modern President counts among his major triumphs the preservation of the presidential prerogatives in foreign affairs. In 1951, for example, when the so-called "Great Debate" was taking place in Congress over how many divisions the President had a right to assign permanently to Europe, the White House carried on a high-pitched campaign to prevent the efforts of isolationists led by Taft and Wherry to "tie the President's hands." For Truman the issue at stake was not so much the numbers of troops in Europe but the powers of the Presidency. No modern President wants to be known as the man who weakened the office, and each has endeavored to pass on its awesome powers intact.*

Thus the President, being beyond the reach of public opinion for four years in his conduct of foreign affairs, and largely independent of Congress as well, can be influenced only by the quadrennial referendum. Do elections give voters a meaningful choice on foreign policy issues? Are foreign policy issues important in national elections? What guidance do elections give the winning candidate for the exercise of his enormous powers over foreign affairs and how responsive is he to the popular will in foreign policy?

When aspiring candidates consult experts in winning elections, they usually are told that foreign policy issues do not move voters unless they are combined in some fashion with "bread and butter" economic issues. People are interested in the size of the defense budget and whether a new bomber will be built because jobs are at stake. They are interested in tariffs. But only a tiny fraction of the electorate is interested in whether NATO has a "forward defense," whether the United States supports Pakistan or India, whether the United States sends military assistance to Latin American dictators or invites South Africa to participate in NATO maneuvers. On any of these issues the President may receive some unfriendly mail or public criticism from small segments of "elite" opinion, meaning a selected population with some special reason to care deeply about the outcome, but there will be no public mandate. Such matters are not presented as domestic political issues in the context of elections. Indeed, a review of the presidential elections from 1940 to the present reveals that at

---

* This theme runs throughout Truman's memoirs. Lyndon Johnson in his memoirs reveals that shortly after taking office he came to regard the Senate, whose majority leader he was for so many years, as a "threat" to the exercise of presidential power.

no time have clear-cut foreign policy alternatives been presented to the electorate by the major parties in such a way as to permit voters to influence future policy. In short, while foreign policy *themes* have played an important role in presidential elections, foreign policy *issues* have been blurred in such a way as to preclude meaningful choice.

In 1940 FDR promised that "your boys are not going to be sent into foreign wars" but he made it clear that the industrial might of America would be dedicated to the defeat of the Axis. Wendell Willkie, the Republican candidate, was also an "internationalist" who, like Roosevelt, believed that it would be necessary to enter the war but hoped that the day could be postponed. The impending war was the primary public concern, but there was no foreign policy issue presented, since both candidates essentially agreed. The real issue was between Roosevelt's experience and the attractions of a fresh face.

In 1944 the war again dominated the election. This time too the choice was a matter of personality and tradition. Should a President attacked by his opponent as a "tired old man" be given a fourth term in the midst of a war in preference to a young man, Thomas E. Dewey, who claimed the ability to pursue the old man's war plans with greater vigor?

In 1948 the election did present the voters with some foreign policy choices on which to express opinion but only because of the presence of the third-party candidate, Henry Wallace. The former Vice-President ran on a platform which condemned the policy of containment, the Truman Doctrine, and rearmament. Because the Wallace movement was infiltrated with Communists and the candidate was successfully tarred as a "dupe," he attracted only about a million votes. The other forty-six million Americans who voted for Dewey or Truman had no foreign policy choices because none were presented. Truman explains in his memoirs:

> One of the things I tried hard to keep out of the campaign was foreign policy. There should be no break in the bipartisan foreign policy of the United States at any time—particularly during a national election. I even asked that a teletype machine be set up on the Dewey train so that the Republican candidate personally could be informed on all the foreign developments as they progressed. . . .*

In the midst of the campaign Truman decided to send Chief Justice Fred Vinson as a special emissary to Stalin "to overcome any damage the Wallace campaign may have caused in stirring up the feeling . . .

---

* Harry Truman, *Memoirs: Vol. 2: Years of Trial and Hope* (New York: New American Library, 1965), p. 211.

that this administration was not doing all it could in the interest of peace." But news of the impending mission was leaked to an unfriendly newspaper and Truman, worried about being branded an "appeaser," canceled the mission. Dewey did not attack the main lines of the Truman foreign policy, but he did challenge the sincerity of the Administration's commitment to Israel. He also exploited the issue of Communists in government, but the question whether Truman or Dewey was the more vigilant in rooting Stalinists out of the State Department hardly gave the voters a chance to express their view on what the global role of the United States ought to be.

In 1952 the Communists-in-government issue had become hotter. Richard Nixon had launched his political career on Whittaker Chambers' pumpkin papers and the subsequent conviction of Alger Hiss for lying about them. The hunt for subversives was bipartisan. The Republicans produced the Mundt-Nixon law on controlling subversive activities and Hubert Humphrey proposed outlawing the Communist Party. The Republicans charged the Truman Administration with losing China, inviting the attack in Korea, and pursuing the "negative, defeatist" policy of containment. Foreign policy themes dominated the 1952 election. Eisenhower's greatest appeal beyond his promise to bring a new morality to a Washington of corrupting deep freezes, dubious fur coats, and sleazy "five per-centers," all allegedly the result of twenty years of Democratic rule, was his reputation as soldier-statesman. "I will go to Korea," he announced, but like Richard Nixon sixteen years later, he gave no hint of how or on what basis he would settle the Korean War. The only choice on foreign policy offered the voters was a rhetorical one: "liberation" (of Eastern Europe) versus "containment." Dulles never spelled out how he planned to rescue the "captive peoples" without a world war and when pressed by reporters to explain what he had in mind, the future Secretary made it clear that it wasn't much.

In 1956 Dwight D. Eisenhower could have been re-elected irrespective of platform or opponent. As it happened, two foreign policy crises—the Soviet suppression of the freedom fighters of Budapest and the Anglo-French–Israeli invasion of Egypt—at the height of the campaign, probably won Eisenhower extra votes on the "don't change horses in mid-stream" theory. In the campaign Stevenson did differ with the Administration on the matter of nuclear testing and did make use of a somewhat softer rhetoric on foreign policy. But with the exception of the testing issue there was once again little substantive choice for the voter.

The 1960 election campaign was dominated by the atmospherics of foreign policy. John F. Kennedy's major theme, suggested to him by Walt Rostow, was getting the country "moving again." It was clear to anyone listening to Kennedy campaign rhetoric that most of the movement he had in mind was abroad. The great issue, he would repeat throughout the campaign, was America's falling prestige. The Eisenhower Administration, made up of miserly old men, had stinted on the nation's defense and allowed a dangerous "missile gap" to develop. The torch must now be passed to the young and vigorous who would fight the Communists with the courage and subtlety so lacking in the quiet clubhouse atmosphere of the Eisenhower White House. Here was a clear foreign policy difference with the Eisenhower Administration, which maintained (correctly, as it turned out) that there was no missile gap. But the Republican candidate, Richard Nixon, pressed by Nelson Rockefeller, endorsed a military program identical to the one John F. Kennedy asked for and largely obtained once in the White House. On July 23, 1960, Nixon and Rockefeller issued a joint statement proposing "more and improved bombers, airborne alert, speeded production of missiles and Polaris submarines, accelerated dispersal and hardening of bases, full modernization of the equipment of our ground forces, and an intensified program for civil defense." *

The second of the famous TV debates between Kennedy and Nixon concerned foreign policy. The emphasis was on such emotion-laden issues as whether American prestige was falling or whether Eisenhower should have apologized to Khrushchev for flying a U-2 over his country. Although these issues aroused a certain amount of passion, neither offered the voter a chance to vote on the future. However, two policy alternatives were raised. One was insignificant and the other was a piece of pure theater. The first involved the decision to defend the tiny islands off the Chinese mainland, Quemoy and Matsu, from an attempt by the Chinese Communists to occupy them. (Nixon: Yes; Kennedy: No.) The second concerned an invasion of Cuba. According to Nixon's own account, *Six Crises,* the darkest hour of the 1960 campaign was when he was trapped by circumstances and his opponent into appearing "softer" on Castro than Kennedy. The Democratic candidate, who had been secretly briefed that plans for a covert operation against Castro were under way, argued forcefully that the United States should take strong measures to rid the hemisphere of the Communist "only ninety miles away." Nixon, who was privy to the plans, was forced, in order to protect them, to take a public position that an invasion of Cuba would be illegal and would offend world opinion.

> I was sure then, and I am now, that the position I had to take on Cuba hurt rather than helped me. The average voter is not interested in the technicalities of treaty obligations. He thinks, quite properly, that Castro is a menace, and he favors the candi-

* Theodore White, *The Making of the President, 1960* (New York: Atheneum, 1961), p. 228.

date who wants to do something about it—something positive and dramatic and forceful—and not the one who takes the "statesmanlike" and the "legalistic" view.*

The campaign of 1964 was billed by the Goldwater forces as the first in modern times to present the voter with a choice instead of an echo. Goldwater was a religious anticommunist. He believed that freedom, which as an abstract matter he held to be the highest human value, was imperiled by Soviet communism. Goldwater's advisers, including Professor Stefan T. Possony, William Kintner, Robert Strausz-Hupe, Warren Nutter, David Abshire, and active-duty Air Force Generals such as Dale O. Smith and Brigadier General Robert C. Richardson III instructed him in the virtues of tactical nuclear warfare, the dangers of negotiation, and the plausibility of victory by means of the hydrogen bomb. Goldwater's rhetoric was totally different from Johnson's. It was easy to paint him as "trigger-happy" because he would suggest such things as defoliating jungle trails with nuclear weapons. As an Air Force reserve major general his inclination was to build his campaign around the attacks on Robert McNamara that were then the favorite topics of the day at U.S. officers' clubs around the world. Most of his alternative policies were vague, although the voter instinctively felt that, whatever one could say of him, Goldwater was not a "me-too" candidate. There was indeed a choice. Whenever the choice became explicit, however, as when the Republican candidate suggested that battlefield commanders should have discretion to use nuclear weapons, the public became alarmed. It was all right to be fanatical about Communists, but it was another thing to be cavalier about nuclear weapons when the American people were also under the gun.

Lyndon Johnson successfully exploited Goldwater's Strangelovian image to make himself appear a man of peace by contrast—without sacrificing his reputation for toughness. The irony of the campaign of course was that Johnson adopted the Goldwater policy. Indeed, the contingency planning actually conducted and put into effect by the Johnson Administration in Vietnam was extraordinarily similar to the following recommendations prepared for Goldwater in early 1964 by one of his top foreign policy advisers. The only difference is that the Goldwater adviser's recommendations were somewhat more modest.†

1. An American summons to Hanoi to discontinue the operations against South Vietnam.

---

* Richard M. Nixon, *Six Crises* (Garden City, N.Y.: Doubleday and Co., 1962), p. 356.

† I am indebted to Karl Hess, former Goldwater adviser, for this information about the Goldwater campaign of 1964.

2. Demonstrative American overflights for reconnaissance, showing-the-flag purposes, and leaflet missions.
3. Naval patrols in North Vietnam waters, first to show the flag, later to carry out a quarantine and finally, if necessary, to establish a blockade.
4. Aerial harassment of the main supply routes into South Vietnam, including those leading through Laos. This could be undertaken with bombs and land mines plus the landing from the air of demolition squads.
5. Overflight along the Chinese–North Vietnam borders.

During the campaign Goldwater was flooded with such advice from his Air Force friends as the following (from a memorandum of conversation between Air Force Generals Dale Smith and Robert Richardson): "We must resolve to use nucs as necessary in the Far East, just as in Europe, but this may not be a good campaign line at this time." In 1964 the voters thought they were exercising a choice on the issue of war and peace in Vietnam and were wrong. On the issue of nuclear policy the campaign also presented an important choice, and on this point the voters were not deceived. Lyndon Johnson had come to believe that it was prudent to arrange limited arms control agreements with the Soviets and to exercise some restraint in nuclear matters. But Goldwater, who believed that the most reckless policies actually lessened the risks of war, was a Cold War caricature.

The foreign policy issue of 1968 was of course Vietnam, and that issue was decided before the conventions. The McCarthy candidacy had helped to persuade Johnson not to run. The convention split over the Vietnam plank—i.e., whether to have an unconditional bombing halt as an inducement to the enemy to negotiate a settlement. The Johnson forces won at the convention, which was a scene of great frustration, fury, and pitched battles between Mayor Daley's police and antiwar demonstrators. Frederick Dutton gives a good summary of the rest of the campaign:

> Nixon, Humphrey, and Wallace, each in his own way, pledged an end to the war in Southeast Asia and a sweeping reappraisal of America's priorities abroad and at home. Nixon claimed to have a plan (never revealed during the campaign) for an early end to the war. And, by coincidence or otherwise, the incumbent Democrats, after long refusing to de-escalate the Vietnam conflict, suddenly called a bombing halt five days before the election. A close Nixon friend just as quickly got the American-maintained South Vietnamese government to indicate some well-publicized reservations about the move, all on the weekend before the U.S. balloting.*

* Frederick G. Dutton, *Changing Sources of American Power* (New York: McGraw-Hill, 1971), p. 167.

The "close Nixon friend" was Mrs. Claire Chennault. When I had occasion to talk to the former Vice-President a few months after the election, he said flatly, "Thieu and Ky lost me the election."

In the last few days of the 1968 campaign, there were sharp and sudden shifts of opinion. As Theodore H. White reports in *The Making of the President 1968,* "regional poll-masters were finding . . . a seven-point change in Michigan; a three-point shift to Humphrey in Ohio was moving that state to the doubtful column. . . . In California Nixon's ten-point lead of mid-October was melting. . . ." * Louis Harris, whose final poll predicted Humphrey as the winner, attributed the sudden shift to "the women's vote." The bombing halt "has gotten to them," Harris told White. The women were for peace. If the election had been held on Saturday or Sunday, the Nixon campaign leaders believe that they might have lost. But by Tuesday it was clear that the bombing halt would not lead to a quick end of American battle casualties.

Thus foreign policy issues are used as campaign vehicles to create political moods. None of the elections just reviewed, with the exception of 1964, was a referendum, for no clear-cut choices were presented. In 1964, where such a choice was presented, the Johnson voters ended up with the Goldwater policy on the most crucial foreign policy issue. Indeed, as the Pentagon papers reveal, Johnson's huge popular mandate for peace was considered by the national security managers to be a crucial prerequisite for escalating the war. Had the mandate been less, Johnson might well have been more cautious.

(2)

However, the fact that quadrennial elections do not serve as clear-cut votes on foreign policy issues does not mean that elections are without influence on the President and the national security managers. On the contrary, elections are kept very much in mind in the making of policy. Daniel Ellsberg has expressed the view that the continued escalation in Vietnam despite pessimistic intelligence prognoses was due primarily to the fear shared by three Presidents that defeat in Vietnam "this year" would lose an impending election. The memory of the "loss of China" and the political capital this provided political opponents haunted the Democratic administrations of the 1960's. It was a memory also bound to affect their Republican successor, for he had made much of the rhetoric of the "China sell-out" in advancing his own career. Having campaigned against Adlai Stevenson by

* Theodore White, *The Making of the President, 1968* (New York: Atheneum, 1969), p. 446.

charging him with membership in "Dean Acheson's College of Cowardly Communist Containment," Nixon was loath to give any opponent the chance to brand him as a man who accepted defeat.

In the Cuban missile crisis of 1962, to take another example, domestic political considerations were very much in the forefront. In his account, Roger Hilsman, who was in charge of intelligence in the State Department at the time, concludes that the country may not have been in mortal danger as a result of Khrushchev's placing some missiles in Cuba, "but the Administration certainly was." * A Republican Senator, Kenneth Keating, who had received reports from refugees about the Soviet military buildup, began charging the Administration with reckless disregard of the national security. The Administration, which was particularly vulnerable on Cuba, was well aware that the issue could be used to its serious disadvantage in the upcoming Congressional elections. Even though, as Secretary McNamara reported to the "Ex Comm," the group charged with managing the crisis, the missiles in Cuba did not change the military balance, accepting them risked political humiliation. Robert Kennedy, his brother's closest political adviser, told him in the midst of the crisis, ". . . if you hadn't acted, you would have been impeached." †
The sensitive manager understands that public outcries and the threat of punishment at the polls do not come from a spontaneous popular reaction to national security decisions but from the political exploitation of these decisions by skillful adversaries—a China Lobby with enough money to haunt every office in Congress, a political opponent with enough demagogic appeal to tag the Administration with the "loss of China," "twenty years of treason," or "bugging out of Vietnam."

The unorganized public mood obviously affects the climate in which the national security managers operate. The conduct of foreign policy has had a different feel since the strong anti-Soviet feelings of the early Cold War years have subsided. Nevertheless, shifts in mood have little impact on specific decisions until voters are politically organized. Relatively small numbers of voters are ever organized for foreign policy issues, for the fundamental fact remains that most people feel incompetent and irrelevant when it comes to foreign affairs. Thus a week after President Kennedy's extraordinary American University speech with its dramatic change in tone of the treatment of U.S.-Soviet relations, the White House received fifty thousand letters, of which 896 had to do with the speech and 28,232 concerned a freight rate bill pending in Congress.

---

* Roger Hilsman, *To Move a Nation* (New York: Dell Publishing Co., 1967), pp. 196–198.

† Robert F. Kennedy, *Thirteen Days* (New York: W. W. Norton, 1969), p. 45.

The real influence of the public is exerted through the political coalitions that constitute the major parties. While the public at large has a marginal and unfocused interest in foreign affairs, certain key groups, essential for getting out the vote at election time, do have strong financial or ideological interest in particular foreign policy choices. The dominant majority party during the last forty years has been the Democratic Party, an implausible but remarkably persistent coalition of interests: organized labor, organized ethnic minorities in the cities, New Deal industrialists, the "Deep South," and the Farm Vote. The Democrats cannot win if there are serious defections from this coalition. The Republicans win only if there are.

The organizers of each of these coalitions have had strong commitment to the anticommunist consensus at the heart of American foreign policy. They were able to mobilize opinion and votes for a strong anticommunist and interventionist foreign policy only because such policies served their own parochial interests as they saw them.

Let us take organized labor. Samuel Lubell tells the story of David Dubinsky's sitting in a limousine behind a police escort on the way to a Roosevelt campaign rally, reminiscing about the old days when he was a pollwatcher for the Socialists in New York. "I slept for three nights with my wrists strapped to the ballot box so Tammany leaders wouldn't throw the box into the river. Now look at me! In a limousine! With a police escort!" The story captures part of the history of the transformation of organized labor. The arrival of the "labor statesman" who was courted at the White House and consulted on a variety of national issues meant that labor was now "on the team." On national policies that did not directly or immediately mean lower take-home pay for workers it was politically prudent and personally satisfying to help the President. It cost nothing to support the White House on foreign policy.

But beyond this there were specific reasons why the generation of labor leaders who took over the major unions after World War II were strongly anticommunist. Many of them, such as Dubinsky and Walter Reuther, were veterans of successful fights against Communists in their own unions. Samuel Lubell describes the transformation of a United Auto Workers local after one such struggle:

> When I first visited Chrysler Local Seven of the United Automobile Workers a few days after Roosevelt's third term victory, the scene was one of belligerent activity. . . . boards bristled with photographs of police clubbing strikers and of tear gas riotings. . . . the union's educational director . . . began boasting freely of how class conscious the auto workers were and how ready they were to vote Roosevelt a fourth or a fifth term. He wore a lumber jacket. . . .

Returning eight years later, after Truman's victory, the whole atmosphere of the local had changed. The strike photographs had come down from the bulletin boards and had been replaced by idyllic snapshots of the union's annual outings and sporting events. An honor roll listed fifty-nine union members who had been killed in the war. . . . The "class-conscious" educational director was gone—ousted in the UAW-wide fight against Communists which Walter Reuther led. On their desks, the new officers had propped the slogan, "UAW Americanism for Us." They were wearing green jackets and green silk legion caps.*

Stalin's foreign policy was a convenient political weapon for intra-union struggles.

Second, old trade unionists—many with roots in the non-Leninist socialist tradition and others, such as Jay Lovestone, scarred in fights with Stalin—were passionate haters of the Soviet system. They understood that the tight regimentation of Russian society under the Communist Party had crushed the possibility of a free labor movement. (It is worth remembering that on his visits to the United States and Britain Khrushchev would get into fights with labor leaders a few hours after being toasted by bankers.) Third, many union members had other pressures on them to be anticommunist. Many were exposed to the teachings of the Catholic Church on communism. Others came from Eastern Europe and identified with the peoples of the Soviet satellites. Finally the Cold War meant big military contracts and big military contracts meant jobs. Thus super-Americanism was a politically useful note for labor officials to sound within the unions.

The American Federation of Labor became the most ideologically militant political force in American life. Under the influence of Jay Lovestone's conspiratorial view of the world and his unrelenting hard line, the AFL took positions on the Vietnam War and trade with communist nations that were clearly against the economic interests of its members. The Indochina conflict, for example, was the largest single force propelling the inflationary economy that reduced the real wages of workers each year that the war dragged on.

(3)

IN THE CITIES the Democratic Party under Franklin D. Roosevelt successfully mobilized the Poles, Czechs, Lithuanians, and other ethnic minorities whose parents had come to the United States in the

---

* Samuel Lubell, *The Future of American Politics* (Garden City, N.Y.: Doubleday and Co., 1956), pp. 190–91 ff.

waves of immigration that ended just before World War I. Samuel Lubell makes a persuasive case that the source of traditional isolationism was ethnic, not regional. It was not the fact that the Middle West was far from Europe that made it anti-interventionist but that in 1940 German-Americans and to some extent Irish-Americans did not like the idea of going to war to fight Germans or to save Englishmen. Roosevelt's majorities dipped in German and Italian neighborhoods and rose in New England, where people did identify with their British forebears.

A crucial reason, in my view, for the decline in popular control over foreign policy is the decline in importance of ethnic politics. The President has a much freer hand in making national security decisions than his predecessors a generation or two ago because the restraints imposed by ethnic loyalties are much weaker.

In 1914 Woodrow Wilson declared, "We definitely have to be neutral, since otherwise our mixed populations would wage war against each other." Such a statement would be inconceivable today. It is now fashionable to talk about the "ethnics"—lower middle class, largely blue-collar workers of Eastern European origin. But the term is something of a misnomer. Lower-middle-class second- and third-generation Americans appear to have some common aspirations and common anxieties. They are patriotic and fiercely resent the affluent college student who spits on the flag, for their parents chose America because they thought it was better than other places. Having struggled for a house and a car and a little respectability, they don't like to see respectability getting a bad name. But they hardly identify with the countries of their origin in the way their grandparents did two generations ago. "Big Bill" Thomson used to run for Mayor of Chicago against King George V. German-language and Swedish-language newspapers were powerful political forces. Today there are few issues on which sizable blocs of voters can be aroused as Poles, Germans, Czechs, or British. True, organizations of Eastern Europeans still meet, hold rallies, and demand that Congress re-enact the "captive peoples resolution." But all the Czech voters in Chicago could not move the Johnson Administration to more than a mild protest at the Soviet invasion of Czechoslovakia in 1968. Nor was the Czech community organized to put pressure on the Administration. Despite the advent of jet aircraft, Czechoslovakia was farther away for Czech-Americans than for their parents a generation ago.

The last election in which ethnic concern with a foreign policy issue played a crucial role was the election of 1946. This was the election in which the Republicans won Congress for the first time in sixteen years. The "class of 1946" in the Senate included some of the most celebrated archconservatives of the postwar era—Indiana's William Jenner, California's William Knowland, and, of course, Wisconsin's Joseph McCarthy. In the House the Republicans picked up fifty-five seats. As Peter Irons has noted in his study of that campaign, a number of the traditionally Democratic districts that suddenly began sending conservative Republicans to Congress had heavy Polish and other Eastern European constituencies. In 1946 Republicans campaigned vigorously on the "sellout" of Poland at Yalta by the Democrats. Senator Arthur Vandenberg met in London on January 29, 1946, with Adam Tarnowski, the Minister of Foreign Affairs of the exiled anticommunist "London Poles," and told him that "the next as well as future elections will demonstrate that the American Poles will better appreciate where their vital interests lie and will give their ballots to the Republicans." To insure this result Vandenberg and other prominent Republicans raised the Polish issue at every opportunity, publicly and privately. A letter Vandenberg received from a fellow Republican of Polish extraction lays out the strong ethnic component in the electoral strategy pursued by the Republicans in 1946:

> Just now there lies before our party a truly marvelous opportunity to regain its lost ground. . . . America is populated by scores of national minorities. The Poles constitute only one of the major groups. . . . We have here Lithuanians, Letts, Estonians, Finns, Rumanians, Yugoslavs, Ukrainians, Hungarians, Czechoslovaks, Bulgarians, Greeks, Italians, Swedes, Danes and Norwegians. . . . A courageous stand of the Republican leaders in the UNO recognizing the right of all these nations to independence, is bound to win the good will of the corresponding minorities in America.
>
> If we want to win the elections in 1946 and 1948—we cannot afford wasting energy in attempting to get votes controlled by the PAC [the CIO Political Action Committee]. We must win the elections by taking away the votes of those Democrats who comprehend the suicidal trend of the present administration's international policy. . . .

The Republican successes with the ethnic minorities in 1946 helped to popularize anticommunism as an electoral issue. The message was not lost on the Truman Administration which began to denounce Soviet policy in Eastern Europe after the election with greater vigor and sharpness. Thus, by 1948 it seemed pointless to punish the by now strongly anticommunist Truman Administration for the loss of Poland under his predecessor, and once again Polish districts swung to the Democrats. Americans of Slavic origin continued to be politically active, but the influence of the ethnic minorities of Europe on foreign policy was over.

There was no longer, as in World War I and World War II, any sizable group of Americans who identified with the potential enemy. Most of the immigrants from what was now the Soviet Empire were bitterly anti-Russian as well as anticommunist. Many of them identified with such long-gone (or never-were) political entities as Ruthenia, Moldavia, and the Ukraine, and unlike many Germans and Italians of the 1930's, who were taken with Hitler's and Mussolini's imperial fantasies, they derived no satisfaction from the expansion of Russian power. Indeed, they saw the only possibility of freedom for their own people in the defeat and break-up of Stalin's domain.

The one great exception which suggests that the reports of the demise of ethnic influence on foreign policy are premature is the role of the organized Jewish vote on issues affecting Israel. Here is the one case in the postwar generation of a group with fresh ties to a foreign country. It is a unique case because the American Jews were citizens of the United States many years before the state of Israel existed. They can be considered immigrants only in a spiritual sense since very few American Jews have ever lived in Israel. Nevertheless, the emotional pull of Israel for American Jews, coming hard upon Hitler's genocidal nightmare, was in some ways stronger than the nostalgia of the Irish, the Germans, and the Poles for the "old country," a place, after all, which they or their parents had rejected, usually for very good reasons. Moreover, the organization of American Jews was superb. The United Jewish Appeal, the "Bonds for Israel" rallies, the educational campaigns of the American Jewish Committee and the American Jewish Congress gathered millions of dollars as they built ethnic pride. The location of large numbers of Jewish voters in New York, the state (until recently) with the largest number of electoral votes, gave organized Jewry a powerful voice in the councils of the Democratic Party. Wealthy Jews were important contributors to Democratic campaign chests.

Jewish influence on foreign policy is a result of the large Jewish immigrations of the late nineteenth century. In the early part of the century Jews were much less successful. In 1840 President Van Buren, at the behest of American Jews, made a diplomatic intervention to protest ritual murder accusations against Jews in Damascus, but in 1857, despite mass meetings in New York and elsewhere, President Buchanan refused to intercede with the Vatican to rescue an Italian Jewish boy who had been kidnaped by papal authorities. Beginning in 1897, however, American Jews were sufficiently organized politically to prevent the passage of bills designed to eliminate the flow of Jewish immigration. When the Immigration Act of 1924 was finally passed, its discriminatory provisions were expanded so as not to single out the Jews.

In his essay "Racial Problems and American Foreign Policy," Professor Paul Seabury summarizes "the success of Jewish-Americans in influencing foreign policy in the era since World War I":

> Their aims have been two-fold: to gather U.S. support for the establishment of the independent state of Israel, and since World War II, to gain admission to the United States for displaced Jews. . . . Like most minority groups, Jewish-Americans have exerted their influence primarily through the electoral process. During the 1948 presidential campaign, the Jewish community successfully pressured both political parties to adopt Zionist planks in their party platforms. In a few local elections with a large Jewish minority, candidates of both parties were forced to outbid each other in their enthusiasm for the new state of Israel, which frequently became the major issue of the campaign.
>
> The overwhelming success of the "Jewish" position in recent years on the various Middle East questions has been attributed to the simple fact that there are few Arabs in the United States and quite a large number of Jews.*

While the above summary is essentially accurate, it leaves a number of things out. There was one conspicuous failure of organized Jews in recent times. Arthur Morse has documented in his *While Six Million Died,* if anything, too delicately, the deaf ear which the Roosevelt Administration turned to the pleas of Jewish leaders to rescue the Jews of Europe.† It is true that in 1948 American Jews had a crucial role in setting the policy of the Truman Administration toward Palestine. The President had an adviser in the White House, David K. Niles, whose full-time job was liaison with the Jewish community. Most Presidents since that time have had someone on their personal staff to play that role. But it is not accurate to suggest that American Jews have been able to write U.S. foreign policy in the Middle East. That policy is the result of the play of competing forces. Indeed, U.S. Middle East policy is one of the very few cases where strategic interests as defined by the national security managers, commercial interests as defined by the major corporations operating in the area, and domestic political interests as defined by those in the business of winning elections do not neatly coincide.

Harry Truman reports in his memoirs that "some of our diplomats" thought that the Arabs "on account of their numbers and because of the fact that they controlled such immense oil resources, should be appeased. I am sorry to say that there were some among them who were also inclined to be anti-Semitic." Pressures from big business and the military, as we noted in Part II, were, for the most part, in

---

* In George W. Shepherd, Jr., ed., *Racial Influences on American Foreign Policy* (New York: Basic Books, 1970), pp. 66 ff.
† New York: Random House, 1968.

support of conservative Arab governments willing to deal generously with the oil companies.

At the same time the concern of Jewish leaders with Israel has been used to enlist their support on other foreign policy issues. For example, Lyndon Johnson once called in a group of Jewish leaders and told them that if they wanted a strong commitment to Israel, they had better support the Vietnam War. Under Nixon, less dependent upon the traditionally Democratic Jewish vote he is unlikely to get in any event, diplomatic pressure has been exerted upon the Israelis to accept a Middle East settlement which is not to their liking. At the same time the opinion of American Jews on Middle East issues seems to be becoming more sophisticated. Some of the Jewish organizations, such as the American Jewish Committee and the American Jewish Congress, seem somewhat less ready than in the past to give a blanket endorsement of the official Israeli line. The Jews remain, however, the last ethnic force with significant influence in the setting of U.S. foreign policy.

(4)

CLOSELY RELATED to ethnic politics is the politics of religion. Indeed, the influence of the Roman Catholic Church on American foreign policy has been exerted largely through the ethnic minorities. In Polish parishes, for example, priests in the early postwar days endlessly denounced the "betrayal" of Yalta and organized letter-writing campaigns to reverse the decision. Philip Murray, the President of the CIO in 1946, was incensed to discover, he wrote to friends, that the pastor of his church had given school children the job of distributing copies of the right-wing Catholic paper "Today's World," which attacked the CIO for being soft on the communist "rape" of Eastern Europe. The Association of Catholic Trade Unionists played a key role in fighting the Communists in the United Electrical Workers and Transport Workers, using access to government files to identify the Party members. As Richard Ward's study of labor politics puts it, "ACTU's Detroit chapter was instrumental in the spring of 1946 in defeating the leftist Thomas-Addes-Leonard ticket against Walter Reuther" for the leadership of the United Auto Workers. Two years later, in response to a national call by the Catholic hierarchy, priests across the country urged their parishioners to write their friends and relatives in Italy imploring them to vote against the Communists.

The Roman Catholic hierarchy in the United States remained bitterly anti-Soviet throughout the war despite the alliance with Stalin. The Paulist publication "Catholic World" was running editorials in

1942 and 1943 insisting that there could be "no alliance with atheism." Typical was this editorial comment in May 1942: "The Soviet brand of Communism is atheist, materialist, anti-God, anti-Christ, and I think anti-human. . . . To me the Russian leaders seem more cruel than the Czars and the Russian people in a worse plight than they were under the old regime." The "chief obstacle to the rebuilding of civilization after the war," the same paper concluded the following year, "will probably be Communism." By 1944: "Fascism is not and never was as dangerous as Communism." The same year Monsignor Fulton J. Sheen, an influential Catholic spokesman, was demanding that the United States enforce the "moral law" against Russia in Poland or "face twenty-five years of barbarism" at the end of which Russia would end up owning Europe. Representative Wasielewski of Wisconsin declared on Polish Constitution Day (May 3) 1945, "As the last outpost of the Western World, Poland has been repeatedly called upon to protect and preserve Christian civilization." *

The official position of the Roman Catholic Church was laid down in 1937 in Pope Pius XI's encyclical *Atheistic Communism*. "Communism," the Pope declared, "is intrinsically wrong, and no one who would save Christian civilization may collaborate with it in any undertaking whatsoever." His successor, Pius XII, the wartime Pope, was, if anything, even more strongly anticommunist. His closest collaborator in the United States, Francis Cardinal Spellman, was warning by 1946 that the Communists were "digging deep inroads into our nation." By 1949 he delivered a sermon from the pulpit of St. Patrick's Cathedral warning that the United States was in imminent danger of "Communist conquest and annexation." To punctuate the Cardinal's prophesy, New York priests arranged for the distribution of thousands of copies of a comic strip pamphlet *Is This Tomorrow?* picturing communist mobs setting St. Patrick's Cathedral on fire and nailing the Cardinal to the door.

The fight of the Roman Catholic Church and Soviet communism was a real one. The Soviets were guilty of inhuman behavior in Eastern Europe, including police torture and the forcible repatriation of thousands of escapees from Soviet terror. But the Church had managed to overlook similar official brutality in Spain, Greece, and many other places. The real conflict arose over the clear Soviet intention to break the political power of the Church in Eastern Europe, a policy they largely succeeded in carrying out. No doubt many Catholic

* The material on anti-Soviet sentiment among Catholic leaders is from Fred J. Cook, *The Nightmare Decade* (New York: Random House, 1971), pp. 143–45. I am also indebted to Peter Irons for making available material from his files from the Pilsudski Institute, editorials from various Catholic periodicals, and data from his study of the role of the Catholic Church in the Congressional campaign of 1946.

clergymen believed that America was in mortal danger from the Communists, but their immediate interest was in enlisting the United States as an ally of the Church in the global struggle with communism.

The way to do that was to indoctrinate the millions of Catholic voters on whom the Democratic Party depended. When Catholics deserted the Democrats in large numbers in 1952, the issue of communism—in Washington, in Europe, and in Korea—was paramount. Probably no group of Americans was so deeply aroused emotionally about foreign policy issues as Catholic parishioners at the height of the Cold War.

The impact of Catholic voting strength was felt on foreign policy in a number of ways. It provided ideological support for the Truman policy of supporting centrist Catholic parties in Western Europe and for the Eisenhower rhetoric of liberation of Eastern Europe. An important figure in the early postwar period was Father Edmund Walsh, regent of the Georgetown University School of Foreign Service, perhaps the largest supplier of Foreign Service Officers. Walsh had been head of the Papal Relief Mission in Russia in the 1920's and was so disillusioned with his experience that he dedicated the rest of his life to fighting communism. Friend and counselor to James V. Forrestal, whose paranoia on the subject of communism matched his own, Walsh was the man who suggested to Joseph R. McCarthy that communism was the issue on which the Senator could make a splash. To his credit, unlike less fanatical political opportunists, he later denounced McCarthy's methods. Perhaps the most important influence of the Roman Catholic hierarchy on a foreign policy issue was the Church's role in the 1950's with respect to Vietnam. When the CIA picked Ngo Dinh Diem to make a try at creating an independent South Vietnam after the Geneva Accords of 1954, Cardinal Spellman was an enthusiastic backer, since Diem was a devout Catholic. Spellman was strongly for sabotaging the Geneva settlement which he looked upon as a "surrender." "If Geneva and what was agreed upon there means anything at all, it means taps for the buried hopes of freedom in Southeast Asia."

The advent of John XXIII and his encyclical *Pacem in Terris,* the death and retirement of Cardinal Spellman and his generation, and the fresh winds of the ecumenical movement brought about a change in the Church's impact on foreign policy.* By the time of the escalation of the Vietnam War it was evident that the Pope was not wholly pleased with American policy. Within the United States hundreds of

* For an account of new trends in Catholics' foreign policy thinking, see *Pacem in Terris, An Encyclical Letter of John XXIII* (New York: American Press, 1963), and Francine D. Gray, *Divine Disobedience* (New York: Alfred A. Knopf, 1970).

priests, including a sprinkling of bishops, denounced the war from the pulpit and on the streets. Father Robert Drinan was elected to Congress as an antiwar candidate. The most militant wing of the peace movement was dominated by revolutionary priests such as Philip and Daniel Berrigan, who preached symbolic violence against draft records as the means of stopping real violence against human beings in Indochina. Like its historic enemy, the Church was no longer a monolith, and that promised to have a profound effect on American foreign policy.

American Protestantism, because it has been split and is much less well organized, has had a less obvious impact on foreign policy. On the right fringe are fundamentalist groups which in the prewar period were sufficiently anti-Semitic and anticommunist to applaud Hitler's efforts. In the postwar period, with the change of enemy these former isolationists became the most ardent interventionists. Men such as Dr. Fred Schwarz, the Reverend Billy James Hargis, and the Reverend Carl McIntyre preached global conversion by means of the Bomb. Their crusades were well financed by such fierce anticommunists as the dog-food millionaire H. L. Hunt and some of the oil-rich Texans. Their political power was considerably greater than their numbers. When *Life* magazine wrote a somewhat critical story on Dr. Fred Schwarz's Anti-Communist Crusade, Arthur Schlesinger recalls, "the outcry from Schwarz's backers, some of whom were national advertisers, induced *Life*'s publisher, C. D. Jackson, to fly to a Schwarz rally in the Hollywood Bowl and offer a public apology." *

Some remnants of the strong prewar pacifist strain in American Protestantism survived the war. Many of these antimilitarists were conservative on domestic issues. Some, such as the Quakers, opposed the draft, NATO, the arms race, indeed the whole direction of American foreign policy. A larger number of Protestant parishioners, less committed pacifists, were willing to support the main outlines of the policy but yearned for softer rhetoric, more tries at negotiation, and a greater emphasis on using America's "moral power" rather than physical strength.

The most powerful Protestant organization dealing with foreign policy was the Federal Council of Churches of Christ in America (now known as the National Council of Churches). The crucial figure in developing its positions on foreign policy was John Foster Dulles, Chairman of the Council's Commission on a Just and Durable Peace from 1941 to 1947. According to Ernest Lefever's study *Protestants and United States Foreign Policy 1925–1954,* Dulles, "more than any other person, was responsible for shaping the mind of the Protestant Churches respecting the postwar world." There is little doubt that the Council's work in the early postwar period made it

* Arthur Schlesinger, Jr., *A Thousand Days* (Boston: Houghton Mifflin, 1965), p. 754.

easier for Protestant Republican voters of the Midwest, by tradition isolationist and somewhat pacifistic, to support the interventionist bipartisan foreign policy. At the same time the Council did not always fall in line behind official policy. Despite Dulles' strong personal endorsement of the Truman Doctrine, the Federal Council "neither supported nor opposed" it. In its statement "Cross-Roads of American Foreign Policy," the Commission on a Just and Durable Peace opposed using aid "as a tool for fostering political alliance" and stressed the American obligation "to seek a comprehensive settlement of all our conflicting interests with Russia." These compromises with Dulles' own views, then already formulated, suggest how strong the prewar pacifist tradition still was in the mainstream of American Protestantism. As the Cold War grew more bitter and the rhetoric escalated, the antimilitarist note grew weaker, but it revived dramatically in the Vietnam War. An organization under the aegis of the National Council, Clergy and Laymen Concerned about the War in Vietnam ran newspaper ads and other campaigns to dramatize the destruction and atrocities for which Americans were responsible. Still, though the leading denominations passed resolutions against the war, political organization by Protestant denominations to bring the war to an end was sporadic and ineffective.

(5)

ONLY A WORD needs to be said about the role of business in the coalition which the Democrats seek to preserve and the Republicans seek to tear apart, for the business interest in foreign policy was dealt with at length in Part II. The support of business is crucial not because businessmen represent votes but because they represent money, and in an election, particularly in the TV era, money means votes. While the Republicans continue to be the party of big business, attracting campaign contributions from the owners and managers of automobile, oil, and steel companies, the Democrats have attracted the new generation of missile and electronics entrepreneurs. William D. Phelan, Jr., has studied the political ties of five of the defense companies that experienced the most dynamic economic growth in the 1960's. Each of the following companies increased its revenues by more than five hundred per cent: Litton Industries, Ling-Temco-Vought, Gulf & Western, Teledyne, and McDonnell Douglas. Phelan suggests that the following information about these companies is not wholly irrelevant:

The chairman and chief executive of Litton is Charles B. Thornton, a member of the Defense Industrial Advisory Council, longtime associate of McNamara, and close friend of President Johnson. The top man at L-T-V is James J. Ling, one of Humphrey's leading supporters, a business ally of several of Johnson's longtime Dallas backers, and the holder of corporate control over several subsidiaries in whose management Abe Fortas and his law partners have been particularly active. Perhaps the most powerful outside director at Gulf & Western is Edwin L. Weisl, Johnson's most loyal backer in New York. Cyrus Vance went to the Defense Department from Weisl's law firm. The top man at Teledyne, Henry G. Singleton, has long associations with both Thornton and Howard Hughes, an influential man in Johnson's background during much of his career. Teledyne's co-founder and a powerful director is George Kosmetsky, the dean of the business school at the University of Texas.

Finally, McDonnell Douglas is well-connected to the Missouri branch of the Democratic Party. In addition to ties to Clark Clifford and Stuart Symington, it at one time included among its directors James E. Webb, until recently head of NASA, and a close advisor of both Johnson and the late and very powerful Senator Kerr of Oklahoma.

When one scores five out of five, desultory muckraking becomes structural revelation. As we have seen, all the biggest corporate winners have had powerful political contacts at high levels in the government and in the Democratic Party. This does not signify corruption so much as the realities of the military-industrial system.

In the 1960 presidential race the Democrats, using erroneous intelligence estimates leaked by the Air Force, cried "missile gap" and distributed hundreds of thousands of copies of a booklet calling for "an impressive additional expenditure of about $4 billion a year on our strategic forces." John F. Kennedy personally played the preparedness theme to the hilt: "I am convinced that every American who can be fully informed as to the facts today would agree to an additional investment in our national security now rather than risk his survival and his children's survival, in the years ahead." The Kennedy advisers, who had shrewdly estimated that the number of voters opposed to survival was small, came ten years later to see that such demagogic appeals undermined national security. In 1968 Richard Nixon, speaking a few hundred yards from a General Dynamics plant, charged the Democrats with a "security gap." This time the public was more skeptical, mostly because of their disillusionment with the Vietnam War. Nevertheless, in the same election at least one U.S. Senator, Joseph Clark of Pennsylvania, was helped to defeat by the efforts of a union upset about his interest in cutting the defense budget and closing down defense installations.

Most Congressmen and Senators, who have little personal knowledge of defense matters, have generally concluded that the political climate in the country demanded continued support for high-level defense expenditures. Many of them have found it convenient to run against Khrushchev or Mao on a "preparedness" platform. The combined influence of unions and the modern weapons industry on the Democratic Party has made it the party of the arms race. The two Democratic Presidents of the 1960's each came to national prominence on the preparedness issue. Lyndon Johnson as head of the Subcommittee on Preparedness was the most powerful advocate in the Senate throughout the 1950's for big defense budgets. John F. Kennedy's most compelling theme in the 1960 election was rearmament. Samuel F. Downer, financial vice-president of Ling-Temco-Vought, one of the ten largest defense contractors, once summed up the political advantages of big military budgets in these words:

> Its selling appeal is defense of the home. This is one of the greatest appeals the politicians have to adjusting the system. If you are President and you need a control factor, you can't sell Harlem and Watts, but you can sell self-preservation, a new environment. We are going to increase defense budgets as long as those bastards in Russia are ahead of us.* The American people understand this.

(6)

WHAT ARE the possibilities of a new coalition dedicated to a foreign policy of peace? There are some favorable signs. The most obvious is the change in the public mood characterized by the defenders of the old foreign policy consensus as the "new isolationism." As we argued in Chapter 9 it is as misleading to call the new skepticism of military interventionism "isolationism" as it is to call the advocates of preventive war, counterinsurgency, big military budgets, and retaliatory economic policies "internationalists." All traditional foreign policy attitudes are rooted in isolationist assumptions. We are, however, beginning to see in this country, particularly among college-trained young people and a small fraction of the Vietnam veterans,

---

* The U.S. intelligence community which spends billions each year on reconnaissance satellites and other esoteric devices for gathering such information has consistently disputed the self-serving claims of munitions makers and disappointed Air Force generals that the Soviets are "ahead" in the arms race. They have been consistently "behind," although because of the superfluity of killing on both sides both terms long ago lost their meaning.

some fundamentally new attitudes about international politics.

Most of the change in attitude, however, is of a traditional character. A number of public-opinion polls reveal a deep and widespread aversion to another military involvement. In the areas of the Middle West where anticommunist propaganda was most successful ten years ago, "never again" sentiments are strong. They extend not only to the obvious—another land war in Asia—but to other wars that not so long ago were thought to be sacred commitments. A majority of Americans, it now appears from the Potomac Associates survey and Oliver Quayle polls, would be reluctant to aid NATO allies such as Germany or fight for Israel. The figures have little predictive value. It is impossible to assess how quickly such attitudes would change after just one presidential TV address in an atmosphere of crisis. But they do show that as of the present there has been a major shift of opinion. Even more significant is the shift in elite opinion. The Council on Foreign Relations conducted a survey of "leading citizens in thirty-four cities" which shows a significant rise of "new isolationist" sentiments and skepticism about America's wisdom and even her motives among the group that has been the most articulate supporters of the foreign policy consensus.

Within each of the bastions of the Democratic Party which we have discussed there are changes in attitude. Some union officials are beginning to see relationships between war, inflation, the decline of real wages, and the collapse of social services. The changes in attitude among the churches has been gradual but important. We have also noted the rise of the new business pacifism. Now that the President with the most impeccable anticommunist credentials calls for an era of negotiation, it is hard for traditional anticommunist groups to organize politically around that issue. One of the most significant developments of the Nixon era is the collapse of the strident right wing on foreign policy. Although conservatives have expressed their opposition to Nixon over his China policy, most have continued to support him, not only because they have no alternative but also because their support for a "low profile" foreign policy has been purchased by protectionist economic policies and the dedication to "law and order" at home. The remnants of the old "China Lobby" were powerless to keep Nixon from turning his back on twenty-five years of rhetoric.

If the political strength of the prowar forces in American society is declining, is it also true that the strength of propeace forces is increasing? Not necessarily. There is indeed strong support for a "low profile" interventionist policy, but the same people who will cry "never again" with respect to a war will continue to support high defense budgets. They are prepared to continue as spectators of the game of nations even as the players change. Neither "peace" candidates nor the "peace movement" have yet been successful in raising those basic issues of national security which must be understood before people will dare to vote for a real "change of priorities." What is security? How much of the earth's resources should we consume? On the scale of threats that imperil our children's future, where do you put the Soviet invasion of Europe? A Chinese invasion of India? The *extra* missiles that the Soviets will build next year? The peace candidates are unable to touch people deeply on fundamental peace issues because they are either unaware of the painful economic choices involved or are unwilling to state them candidly. The "peace movement" of the 1960's failed in part because a small but visible segment of it projected an image of hating America (or Amerika, as it was written) and of celebrating the triumph of America's enemies. Now the Vietnamese, as far as I am concerned, were not and never have been enemies of any American who did not travel to their country to kill them. But most Americans still delegate the job of deciding who the enemy is to the President, even when he fails to follow constitutional procedures for doing it. They understandably look askance at people who propose policy alternatives and hold aloft a Vietcong flag, and they are not attracted to people who obviously hate their own country. There is much to hate *about* America, and nothing so much as American militarism from which so many other evils flow. But no one who hates *America* or appears to hate it can change this country. A peace movement can be successful only if it articulates a new brand of American patriotism. This does not mean merely being unashamed of the flag, which, after all, was there before Vietnam and the Cold War, but proclaiming a new concept of the national interest in which the citizen's stake in foreign policy is clearly articulated. A political party that was truly prepared to promote these domestic economic and social policies necessary to build a foreign policy of peace would keep analyzing all foreign policy issues in terms of two questions: Who benefits? Who pays?

But an effective peace coalition would need to do more than that. Even as it was redefining what the national interest really is—for steelworkers, welfare mothers, teachers, army officers, children, old people, bankers, migrant farmworkers—it would reach toward genuine internationalism and world community. The rhetorical basis has already been laid. Even national security managers admit that the nation-state is obsolete. Despite the extraordinary efforts of national governments to exert something close to a monopoly on foreign relations, the advances in transportation and communications make this impossible. There is genuine international consciousness growing, and it is not all at the service of the multinational corporation. Young Americans are now able to understand and to empathize with the problems of their generation in other countries far better than their parents could. As traditional loyalties to the nation break down, new transnational bonds, associations, and even classes are in the making.

A politically effective peace party would have to articulate a new role for America—neither number one nation, a meaningless and obscene goal in a world on the brink of famine, nor a self-pitying helpless giant. It would have to be honest with the American people about how little national security there is to be purchased in the modern world through military power. It would have to develop a vision of a new world economy based on fairer distribution of resources and power across the planet and to discuss candidly what sacrifices in standard of living Americans must make and what isolationist assumptions we must give up to make such a vision a reality.

12

A Generation of Peace?

THE DISASTROUS ADVENTURE in Indochina has compelled the most searching re-examination of America's role in the world since the eve of World War II. Henry Stimson's recruits and their disciples, relatives, and business associates, men schooled in the war against Hitler who promoted the extravagant imperial creed of global responsibility and perfected the techniques of expansionism, are leaving the stage at the very moment when the foreign policy consensus they labored so long to create is cracking. The remarkably consistent policies they pursued for a generation no longer seem to most Americans quite so noble or inevitable as at the height of the Cold War. That the United States is indeed an empire, more powerful and extended than any in recent history, once a subversive idea whispered by radicals left and right, is now widely recognized. A small library of books on American imperialism and American empire have appeared in the last few years, including a number which defend the American empire as the last best hope of earth.

Public attitudes toward allies and enemies so carefully cultivated for so long by national security officials are changing. The two official nightmares of the State Department, a Communist China on the rampage and a Soviet invasion of Europe, dissolve as President

Nixon announces that he will visit Peking and concludes a compromise agreement with the Soviet Union on the access routes to Berlin, receiving for both the plaudits of the American Legion. Other sacred tenets of American policy, such as free trade and the international monetary arrangements concluded almost thirty years ago at Bretton Woods, are suddenly scrapped. Respectful clients such as Japan have become formidable commercial rivals. The extravagant rhetoric of "Atlantic Community" that clothed the dream of a great white wealthy Western alliance is gone. The foreign aid program is defeated in the Senate. Protectionism and economic isolationism are the order of the day. It is no longer controversial to suggest that the resources of the United States are limited or that playing the role of "the policeman of the world" strains American society.

Do the recent dramatic changes in rhetoric, attitudes, and policy mean a decisive break with the past? Are we moving into the generation of peace proclaimed by President Nixon? Can the United States renounce militarism and war as primary instruments of policy and accommodate its fears and appetites to the postimperial world?

The historical record is not encouraging. It is not easy to find examples of empires that broke their own expansionist cycle by voluntarily dismantling their imperial structures. Most empires have stopped expanding only when they were defeated, usually by a combination of internal decay and external attack. As a general rule, empires fail to recognize until too late that their outward thrust has already been stopped. They insist upon playing out their defeat to its final tragic act. True, in our own time Britain, France, Japan, and Germany have abandoned their territorial empires, but in each case the decision to liquidate their colonial holdings was the consequence of severe reverses. For Japan and Germany the decision was imposed by the victors in two world wars. France lost her empire through a series of military defeats, by Hitler in 1940, by Ho Chi Minh in 1954, and by the Algerians in 1958. Ostensibly a victor in 1918 and 1945, Britain suffered such grievous economic losses in both wars that she could not afford to keep her empire. Most of the former colonial powers are now seeking, with considerable success, to compensate for their loss of empire by means of economic rather than politico-military expansionism.

In neither economic nor human terms is the American defeat in Vietnam comparable to any of the catastrophes that have befallen the nineteenth-century empires. It has been a political and social shock as well as a warning. It has compelled changes in style and technique, even in some of the rules of the game. But significant as these changes are, we are still basically in the same game. The day the last American soldier and airplane leave Southeast Asia the American empire will still be the strongest on earth. The United States is struggling to maintain itself as the number one nation in a revolutionary world. We still prefer to make the world safe for the United States as it is rather than to remake a United States that feels comfortable at peace and can afford peace.

How different the new foreign policy establishment will be from the old one will depend upon how fast the rules of the game change and which lessons are accepted as the new orthodoxy. Among some of the top military the lessons of Vietnam are limited indeed. The untroubled advocates of mass bombardment believe that the Vietnam catastrophe is the product of a failure of will, a sentimental unwillingness to kill enough people fast enough. More sophisticated critics in the Counter-insurgency Division of the Joint Chiefs of Staff believe that the lesson of the war is that Vietnam was a poor place in which to intervene. They reject neither the analysis of the world that brought six hundred thousand troops to Vietnam in the first place nor the essential con-tours of the strategy under which they fought there. The failure was an accident of history and geography. Thailand, they say, is quite another matter; unlike South Vietnam, neither the country nor the government was invented by the United States. The Philippines, too, are a good place to try counterinsurgency warfare because, as one officer put it, "the country is surrounded by water, so it would be im-possible for an insurgent movement to receive outside aid."

Some of the civilian managers who lived through the escalation of the Vietnam War have had a somewhat more radical learning experi-ence. They question the old Cold War myths about "monolithic com-munism." They appear to have learned that the Soviet Union is not engaged in an ideological crusade but is developing into an impressive, though still moderately cautious, imperial power. For some this be-lated discovery is unaccountably a source of comfort. From this new perspective they conclude that one need not intervene everywhere—some dominoes are more important than others. A war with guerrillas in, say, Thailand need not necessarily be equated with a war with the Soviet Union or China. There is a greater willingness to accept the existence of local politics and local issues and less readiness to see the Kremlin's hand in every revolutionary movement. In addition, the post-Vietnam national security managers now conclude that the ob-sessive fear of falling dominoes in the Kennedy-Johnson days was exaggerated. Cuba and Vietnam may have been exceptions, not models. In most countries the insurgents appear to face overwhelm-ing odds in their attempts to topple even the most reactionary gov-ernments. This reversed analysis of the world leads to injunctions of caution to avoid "overcommitments" and at the same time some agonizing self-doubt about "neo-isolationism."

The official lessons of the Nixon Administration's foreign policy are reflected in the defense budget and the "Nixon Doctrine." The

United States will "lower its profile" by encouraging "indigenous" troops to fight each other with American weapons or where possible by resorting to automated war through the technology of the "electronic battlefield." The goal is to maintain the present American position in the world through more judicious management of military power without involving the American people in an interminable, ambiguous war in which large numbers of Americans continue to get killed week after week.

The new strategy is the product of the belated recognition of the costs of empire. The United States has been seriously weakened in a number of ways by its national security policy. Money and energy diverted from the domestic economy to the arms race has made it impossible to confront crises of health, nutrition, housing, transportation, and the environment. The failure to solve pressing domestic problems that are tearing at American society has made Americans increasingly insecure at home without purchasing any added protection from abroad. The costs of empire include uncontrollable inflation, decline in real wages, the deterioration of domestic industry, mounting unemployment, and, of course, the balance of payments crisis. America's heavy industry, mobilized for military production, is no longer able to compete with foreign nations for civilian markets, including the American market. Ironically, the quest for an empire which was supposed to expand American influence has left the American economy more and more vulnerable to the decisions of foreigners. Those who hold the American dollars and the American gold that have been poured out to support the empire are now in a position to exert control over jobs, prices, and interest rates in the United States or else force the United States into extreme economic isolation. By the standards of *realpolitik* America's imperial overreach has resulted in a real loss of power.

Because the managers of American foreign policy have been made aware of these realities, the rules of the game are indeed changing. The Nixon Administration appears to have abandoned the policy of "world responsibility," the great theme of U.S. foreign policy from World War II to Vietnam, in favor of a neo-Metternichean vision of shared responsibility. The setting for the era of negotiation, as Henry Kissinger sees it, is a world of multiple superpowers—at least three, U.S., U.S.S.R., and China. Formal and informal agreements to recognize "primary responsibility" for each in its own area of the world—i.e., spheres of influence—will now be negotiated regardless of the intensity of conflicts over ideology. Limited arms agreements will be sought. The Administration will follow its own advice and speak more softly in the world, all the while following "America first" economic policies.

Thus, the passing of the war generation in the wake of the Vietnam tragedy signals a new foreign policy consensus in the making. As dramatic as some of its elements appear, however, there is nothing to suggest that the new consensus will enable the United States to catch up with the twentieth century. The strategy changes but the basic goals remain. The new strategy is infinitely preferable to nuclear brinksmanship, globalism, and blind anticommunism, but a strategy of peace remains only a pious hope unless it is rooted in institutional change. Unless a strategy grows out of deep changes in the goals and values of a society, it is vulnerable to being swept aside by events. Whether the Nixon Doctrine or some Democratic equivalent works will depend entirely upon what foreigners do. If they are willing to accept the present distribution of power and resources in the world and the rules of the game as laid down by the United States, we will have peace, provided the managers of American foreign policy do not once again overreach themselves. But it seems more likely that before a generation of peace comes to pass other nations will feel strong enough to challenge the revised concept of American supremacy, thus raising the specter of war.

It has been the thesis of this book that war is primarily the product of domestic social and economic institutions. Of course, wars are triggered by external events. Of course, there are such things as real conflicts and real threats. But it is the institutions in a society with the power to decide which are the most important threats and what should be done to meet them that determine whether a nation goes to war. For more than a generation American society has been organized for war rather than peace. It is still organized for war.

During the years in which the principal activity of the United States government has been preparing and fighting wars there has been a substantial decrease in citizen loyalty. In addition to overt subversive acts such as draft-card burnings, insulting officials, and bombing buildings, there is the far more common phenomenon of symbolic subversion. The counterculture of the 1960's deliberately mocks the manners, pieties, and myths of the nation's rulers and those who still trust them. There is an immense gulf between the values of the national security managers and the values of their children's generation. Many of the younger generation are repelled by the old imperial goals and have great trouble identifying with a state that pursues them. Despite efforts to modernize the imperial creed and to develop a new orthodoxy, the disillusionment and anger of college and high-school students has helped to undermine the spirit of the foreign policy elite. It is hard for leaders to dismiss the mounting attacks on the conventional definition of the national interest among the younger generation because they involve far more than a militant few—indeed, a number of their own children. They are aware that they no longer have an explanation of what is happening in the world that is credible to the next generation and yet they cannot come to terms with the values celebrated by that generation. In some form these values are increasingly shared by young people who have never burned a draft card or joined a commune. The new generation did not grow up in Hitler's world. The national security lessons etched in their consciousness are not Munich and the Rhineland but Hiroshima and Vietnam. The threats they fear are not a second Hitlerian sweep across Europe by the Soviet Union but nuclear war, ecocide, and famine. For a tiny but growing group of Americans the ecological death of Lake Erie is as traumatic an event as Pearl Harbor was for their parents. In gross capsule form, the emerging values that threaten current definitions of the American national interest are these: Mindless growth is obscene; the taking of human life is not a casual act; competition is destructive; technology does not liberate; freedom is preferable to order; hierarchies crush; the world is one.

(2)

WHAT CAN we conclude from our attempt to trace the roots of war in American society? What kind of institutional changes are necessary? What is possible?

It is frustrating but true that there is no single revolutionary stroke that will cut the roots of war. They are deeply entwined around every institution, including our schools and family life. The number one nation is dedicated to winning. In kindergarten games and high-school football contests, in power plays in offices and board rooms of great corporations, in the inevitable academic rivalries of universities, and of course in the struggles of politics, the overriding objective is to win. The myth of competition and the glory and excitement of victory are fundamental to the American way of life. No nation honors its winners more or is more confused as to what to do with its losers. This is a country where being called "aggressive" is a compliment.

But just because there is no simple explanation for America's inner drives toward war and no single dramatic remedy, we need not conclude that we must necessarily succumb to the cycles of expansionism, war, domestic repression, internal decay, and final collapse which have marked the decline and fall of our imperial predecessors. If the analysis of this book is even partially correct, then certain practical steps to reduce the threat of war become obvious. American society must be organized for peace. We are not saying that if American society were organized for peace, there would be no war. Obviously other nations also have it in their hands to plunge the world into war. But unless American society is organized for peace, the continuation of our generation of war is inevitable. The number one nation is in the strongest position of all to set the tone for international relations and to create the climate under which other nations deem it practical or impractical to organize themselves for peace. An America organized for peace would be far stronger—in terms of economic strength, domestic tranquillity, and citizen loyalty—than the American empire.

In this book we have analyzed the three main roots of war: The first is the concentration of power in a national security bureaucracy which increasingly comes to play by its own rules without regard to what it does to the country it is supposed to be defending. America cannot be organized for peace until the excessive power of that bureaucracy is broken. There are three ways it can be done. The first, and most important, is to shrink the military bureaucracies in size so that the balance of power in government once again passes to those agencies which are in the business of building and healing instead of killing and destroying.

The second is to re-establish some form of popular control over the national security managers so that they will no longer be free to play out their imperial fantasies at the expense of the American people. Congress must reassert the constitutional prerogatives it gave up so long ago in the area of foreign affairs. There should be a constitutional limit on the President's right to commit troops abroad without a declaration of war. As long as it remains fashionable for Administration officials to lie to Congressmen and Senators and to invoke the doctrines of executive privilege and prior luncheon engagements to avoid Congressional inquiry, Congress's role will continue to be that of impotent critic and obedient moneybag. One subpoena issued to a recalcitrant Secretary of Defense to compel testimony on one of our secret wars could do more to restore constitutional balance than weeks of hand-wringing. Congress is now aware that it can reassert its rightful constitutional powers only if the mystique of secrecy is dispelled. The presumption that because the world is dangerous the President must have the power to act secretly and hastily has been the source of tragic error. The fact that the world is dangerous is the best argument for slowing down the process of decision-making and opening it up to public scrutiny and debate.

The third structural change in the national security bureaucracy would be to change the system of rewards and to introduce the notion of personal responsibility for official acts. The system as it now operates rewards the warmakers. Those who strive for peace other than by military means do so at great personal risk; those who engage in bureaucratic homicide do so with impunity. There must be a new operational code for the national security managers that rewards peacemakers instead of warmakers. It is in this connection that serious discussion of the issue of war crimes in Vietnam is so important.

The second great root of war is embedded in our capitalist economy (ever more state capitalist) and the business creed that sustains it. The primary reason military power is projected abroad is to buy influence, which has been thought essential to the maintenance of the American standard of living. The growth game—attempting to solve problems of poverty, unemployment, and maldistribution by an ever increasing GNP—requires the production of more goods each year than Americans can afford to buy and the consumption of more materials than we can produce domestically. The system works only if the government stimulates profitable private wants instead of satisfying unprofitable public needs. The pressures to expand domestic production beyond the wants of the American people makes the economy increasingly dependent upon foreign investment. For more than twenty years the United States has been unable to manage its economy in such a way as to maintain "acceptable" employment levels without massive war production. There has been no serious effort to convert admittedly unnecessary and wasteful military production to peaceful purposes because no one has yet proposed a plan for doing it within the framework of the present U.S. economy.

The dependence of the American economy upon foreign raw materials or upon war production means that certain foreign policy options are for all practical purposes foreclosed. The United States cannot disarm, significantly lower the defense budget, or relax economic warfare against commercial competitors, nor can the American businessmen halt the restless, exploitative search for economic opportunity abroad unless the economy is managed in a very different way. It is theoretically possible within the framework of the capitalist system for the government to stimulate the economy by making massive sums available for investment in social services—health, education, transportation, and environmental rescue. It is also theoretically possible to redistribute income in this country so that millions more Americans could afford to buy American products. The incentive system could be changed in such a way that the man with venture capital would find it profitable to invest in meeting social needs instead of stimulating and satisfying private wants, which are becoming more and more trivial and providing increasingly less satisfaction. (When you already have an electric waxpaper cutter, what is left?) But as long as the American economic imperative is growth, the pressures toward economic expansion and military presence abroad will be irresistible. The United States has staggering problems of maldistribution of wealth which must be solved before this country can afford a significantly less interventionist foreign policy. As long as social conflict in the United States is managed by economic growth instead of solved through fairer distribution, American foreign policy will remain in an imperial straitjacket. But regardless of economic system, an America that continues to gobble up fifty per cent of the earth's resources each year while millions starve will never find peace. Whether such far-reaching reconstructive changes can be accomplished under some modified form of private ownership or mixed economy can only be answered by making the attempt.

The third great root of war is the vulnerability of the public to manipulation on national security issues. People do not perceive where their true interests lie and hence are easily swayed by emotional appeals to support policies that cost them their money, their sons, and their own lives. Because they have been willing to accept uncritically the myth of the national interest—i.e., the definition advanced by the national security managers—they exercise almost no control over the commitments the managers make in their name. Supposedly the beneficiaries of national security policy, they become its hostages. There can be a foreign policy which really protects the interests of all Americans only if those interests are articulated in the political process. Before Americans can safely conclude that any particular policy advanced by the national security managers is really in the interest of workers, welfare recipients, salesmen, suburban families, ghetto streethangers, farmers, teachers, pensioners as well as the owners and managers of Standard Oil, First National City Bank, General Dynamics, or the Army, Navy, and Air Force, they must ask Schumpeter's nasty question: Who benefits?

To make the changes in American society needed to permit a new foreign policy will require the politicization of foreign policy issues. Until the majority of people who do not directly benefit from it come to see in concrete terms how they are being hurt by American foreign policy, they will continue to give uncritical support to expansionist policies wrapped in the flag and promoted through fear. If people are not able to see the connection between esoteric questions of foreign policy and their personal lives—their jobs, their families, their chances for personal survival—the making of national security policy will continue to be an elite preserve and it will continue to be made for the benefit of that elite. But without a program to reconstruct the American economy and American society no political party can get the votes for a foreign policy of peace. There will be no foreign policy of peace until the deep but inarticulate aspirations for peace of the American people are awakened and expressed, and their practical economic and personal interest in an economy of peace makes itself felt in the political process. Neither political party now reflects those aspirations, for each is controlled by forces in our society which have benefited or have thought they benefited from permanent war. We can have a chance for a generation of peace only if the American people demand it and are prepared to build a society rooted in the politics of peace.

Index

Acheson, Dean, 34, 49, 54, 58, 61, 63, 73, 114, 121, 132, 162, 261, 269
Adenauer, Konrad, 57
Agnew, Spiro, 301
Air Policy Commission, 181
Air War: Vietnam (Harvey), 14
Alcorn, Robert H., 32
Almond, Gabriel, 245, 248
America as a Civilization (Lerner), 20
American Federation of Labor, 39–40, 318
Amory, Robert, 295
Angell, Norman, 255
Arbenz, Jacobo, 157
Arendt, Hannah, 21
Armaments, expenditures for, 52, 173, 216
Atomic bomb, 17

Bailey, Thomas E., 247
Baker, Charles B., 174
Baldwin, Hanson, 19, 300
Ball, George, 19, 62, 107, 229
Baruch, Bernard, 36, 176
Bay of Pigs, invasion of, 66, 77, 98, 292
Beam, Jacob, 112
Bissell, Richard, 18
Bohlen, Charles, 100, 269
Bomb, atomic, 17
Borah, William, 260
Boston Panama Company, 192

Bowles, Chester, 51, 59, 112, 290
Brazil, foreign investment in, 196
Breech, Ernest R., 148
Brown, Harold, 127
Brown, Irving, 41
Bruce, David, 32
Bruner, Jerome, 261
Brzezinski, Zbigniew, 395
Bukharin, Nikolai, 40
Bundy, Harvey H., 53
Bundy, McGeorge, 62, 63, 70, 72, 78, 97, 102, 274
Bundy, William P., 91, 102, 107, 252, 277
Bureaucracy, national security, 54, 77, 79, 110; conflicts in, 124; critics within, 113; growth of, 24, 44, 53; inertia of, 97; influenced by business, 178–179, 181–182; language of, 110, 129–131; loyalty in, 62; lying of, 127; in Pentagon, 90; power of, 138; war role of, 24–27, 80–82, 96; warfare within, 123
Bush, Vannevar, 42
Business: aided by government money, 167–168, 181, 183; attacks of, on radicals, 175; control of, over mineral resources, 237; executives of, in government posts, 179; exploitation by, of small countries, 149, 196; government regulations of, 233; government support of, 151; influence of, on U.S. foreign policy, 170, 176, 180; interests

Business (*continued*)
of, in Vietnam War, 227; interests of, in world oil, 200–202; investments of, abroad, 170–172, 188, 194, 196, 215, 228–229; lobbying in government by, 184; multinational, 229–231, 234–237; and patriotism, 232; power of, over government, 178; sales of strategic goods abroad, 187; with socialist and revolutionary societies, 221
Byroade, Henry C., 29

Cambodia, invasion of, 80, 226, 245, 266
Canetti, Elias, 267
Cannon, Warren M., 199
Capitalism, 144; crises of, in U.S., 223–224; and imperialism, 210–211; system of expansion of, 207
Carney, Robert, 290
Carter, William, 35
Carver, George, 293
Central Intelligence Agency: news management of, 293–295; role of, in politics abroad, 202; war role of, 38–41
Chennault, Claire, 315
Chomsky, Noam, 305
Cirino, Robert, 299
Clark, Granville, 53
Clay, Lucius, 161
Clayton, William, 54, 139
Cleveland, Harlan, 19
Clifford, Clark, 49, 83, 114, 182, 222
Cohen, Benjamin V., 152
Cold War, 34, 100, 187, 257, 303, 327
Colonialism, 20
Common Market, 169
Congo, 18

Cooper, Chester, 83, 90, 113, 120, 278
Copeland, Miles, 18
Corwin, Edward, 38
Crowds and Power (Canetti), 267
Cuban missile crisis, 253, 288
Czechoslovakia, invasion of, 208

Davis, Norman, 26
DeCornoy, Jacques, 14
Dill, Sir John, 27
Djilas, Milovan, 273
Dobb, Maurice, 209
Dominican Republic, invasion of, 208, 246
Dominoes theory, 132, 144, 160
Donovan, William J., 31
Douglas, McDonnell, 328
Downer, Samuel F., 329
Downs, Anthony, 119
Draper, William, 53
Drinan, Robert, 326
Dubinsky, David, 40, 317
Duce, James Terry, 199
Dulles, Allen, 77, 202
Dulles, John Foster, 54, 56, 58, 62, 65, 73, 157, 161, 252, 287, 326
Dutton, Frederick, 314

Economics: of defense spending, 166; free enterprise system of, 143
Economy: capitalist, 210; impact of war on, 192; inflationary, 109; postwar, 146; stabilization of, 145; U.S. policy of, 170; war, 18, 37, 40, 45, 226; world, 238
Eichmann, Adolph, 15
Eisenhower, Dwight D., 28, 33, 77, 126, 159, 286, 289, 303, 311
Eisenhower Doctrine, 38

Ellsberg, Daniel, 107, 300, 315
End of Empire, The (Strachey), 188
Engler, Robert, 204
Espionage, 31, 120
Executive Life (Whyte), 119
Expansionism, 17, 138, 208–209, 214, 219

Fall, Bernard, 104
Finletter, Thomas K., 180
Flannagan, John W., Jr., 46
Foreign aid, 154–156
Foreign policy, U.S.: bureaucracy of, 51; as campaign issues, 315; and defense spending, 163; influences of big business on, 143, 144, 151–152, 154, 180; Jewish influence on, 321–322; managers of, 55–56, 64, 67, 72; and national crises, 142; news management about, 275, 278; presidential power in forming, 309; propaganda of, 270; Protestant influence on, 326; public opinion of, 242–243, 267–270
Forrestal, James V., 30, 53, 154, 162, 325
Foster, William, C., 181
Frankfurter, Felix, 53
Fromm, Erich, 251
Fulbright, William, 273

Galbraith, John Kenneth, 79, 112, 122
Gardner, John, 44
Gelb, Leslie, 88
General Motors, 36
Geneva Convention of 1949, 121
Gluck, Maxwell, 244

Goldwater, Barry, 249, 313–314
Gompers, Samuel, 40
Goodell, Charles, 302
Goulding, Phil G., 284, 290
Gross National Product, 24–25, 215
Guerrilla warfare, 79

Halberstam, David, 292
Halsey, William F., 46
Harriman, Averell, 54
Harris, Louis, 250
Harvey, Frank, 14
Heilbroner, Robert, 183, 230
Henderson, Leon, 35
Herod, W. R., 147
Hersh, Seymour, 300
Heydrich, Reinhard, 15
Hillenkoeter, Roscoe, 29
Hillman, Sidney, 39, 40
Hilsman, Roger, 31, 85, 89, 316
Hiroshima, Japan, 17
Hiss, Alger, 63
Hitler, Adolph, 16, 84
Hobson, John A., 209
Ho Chi Minh, 73, 104
Hofstadter, Richard, 140
Holman, Eugene, 140
Honduras, 155
Hoover, Herbert, 259
Hoover, J. Edgar, 304
Hopkins, Harry, 28, 35, 85
Horney, Karen, 264
House Un-American Activities Committee, 78, 263
Howard, Anthony, 297
Hudson, Michael, 121
Hull, Cordell, 26, 185
Humphrey, Hubert, 112, 311

Imperialism (Schumpeter), 151, 212

Imperialism: American, 20–22, 223; capitalist, 210–211; economic, 209; ideological conformity in, 304; Leninist theories of, 207, 214

Industry: expansion of, 45, 169; steel, 174; technological advances of, 174–175

Inflation, 109, 173

Inside Bureaucracy (Downs), 119

Iran, 202

Isolationism, American, 250, 258

Iwo Jima, battle of, 46

Janeway, Eliot, 225

Jingoism, 251

John XXIII, Pope, 325

Johnson, Lyndon B., 19, 49, 62, 77, 83, 86, 87, 108, 247, 249, 276, 283, 313, 323

Johnson, Robert, 104

Joint Chiefs of Staff, 27, 114, 123, 161

Julien, Claude, 219

Kahn, Herman, 229

Kautsky, Karl, 210, 224

Kaysen, Carl, 32

Kennan, George, 101, 112, 268

Kennedy, John F., 19, 49, 66, 77, 85–88, 142, 246, 311

Kennedy, Robert, 62, 79, 128

Khrushchev, Nikita, 82, 303

Kidron, Michael, 195

Kissinger, Henry, 60, 336

Knox, Philander C., 200

Kolko, Gabriel, 179

Komer, Robert, 85

Korean War, 246, 274

Kornfeld, Bernard, 232

Labor: advocates defense spending, 166; and multinational corporations, 235–236

Langer, William L., 32, 44

Lay, James, 29

Leahy, William, 28, 189

Lebanon, invasion of, 246

Lefever, Ernest, 326

LeMay, Curtis, 248

Lenin, Vladimir, 211

Lerner, Max, 17, 20

Leuchtenburg, William E., 141

Lewis, John L., 40

Lichtheim, George, 18, 211

Lilienthal, David, 33

Ling, James J., 328

Lippmann, Walter, 47, 101, 247, 253, 270

Lockheed Corporation, 142

Lodge, Henry Cabot, 67, 87, 102

Long, Augustus, 200

Lovestone, Jay, 40, 318

Lovett, Robert A., 49, 53, 78, 181

Lubell, Samuel, 317

Luce, Henry R., 18

Lundborg, Louis B., 226

Luxemburg, Rosa, 163

MacArthur, Douglas, 23

Maccoby, Michael, 229

MacLeish, Archibald, 255

Macomber, William, 64

Magdoff, Harry, 194, 216

Manhattan Project, 41

Manpower Act of 1946, 27

Marcuse, Herbert, 32

Marshall, George C., 28, 29

Marshall Plan, 152

Marxism, 212–213

McCarthy, Joseph, 100

McCarthyism, 263, 304

McClelland, David, 70, 73

McCloy, John J., 49, 53, 63, 181

McCone, John, 181
McNair, Lesley J., 46
McNamara, Robert, 60, 90, 97, 118, 119, 187, 282, 285, 316
McNaughton, John T., 81, 90, 97, 103, 107, 258, 266, 280
Mead, Margaret, 43, 71
Mellon National Bank, 147
Melman, Seymour, 173, 183
Military: aid, 34, 106, 156; bureaucracy, 31, 44; economic power of, 167; espionage, 31; expenditures of, 163–166, 172, 174, 181, 183, 226; network of bases, 30; permanent organization of, 43; population, 30; postwar planning for, 28
Military-industrial complex, 35
Miller, S. M., 219
Millis, Walter, 28
Mitchell, General Billy, 15
Monnet, Jean, 57
Monroe Doctrine, 25
Morgenthau, Henry, 161
Morse, Arthur, 322
Mossadeq, Mohammed, 202
Mumford, Lewis, 38
Murray, Philip, 323
Myer, Cord, 295
My Lai massacre, 300
Myrdal, Gunnar, 216

Nagasaki, Japan, 17
Nasser, Gamal Abdel, 18
National Security Council, 103
National security managers: as advisers to presidents, 78, 83; advocating use of violence, 109; approach of, to foreign policy, 120; backgrounds of, 54, 59, 62, 68; influence on, by business, 182; morality of, 64, 68, 70; motivating of, 125, 304; news

National security managers (*continued*)
management by, 271, 290; official lying by, 126, 269; operational code of, 95–99; plan Vietnam War, 90–91; power of, 71, 89; predilection of, for violence, 116–117; relations with presidency, 77; urge expansion of military, 165; use massive coercion, 144
NATO, 309
Nazis, 16
Neustadt, Richard, 93
Ngo Dinh Diem, 275, 325
Nitze, Paul, 50, 53, 78, 122
Nixon, Richard M., 60, 77, 170, 218, 226, 245, 289, 311, 312, 328, 330, 334
Nixon Doctrine, 336–337
North Vietnam, 80; bombing of, 102, 103, 110, 113; coercion used on, 104; desire of, to trade with U.S., 221

O'Connor, James, 214
Oil companies, 199
Oppenheimer, J. Robert, 111

Pace, Frank, 166
Pacifism, 47
Page, Howard W., 203
Park, Charles C., 217
Paterson, Thomas, 153
Patterson, Robert, 53
Patton, George S., 47
Pearl Harbor, 26
Pentagon papers, 242, 276, 285
Perlo, Victor, 167
Petras, James, 192
Peurifoy, John, 190

Pham Van Dong, 60, 73
Phelan, William D., Jr., 327
Piel, Gerard, 42
Politics: of anti-communism, 311; of appeasement, 99; CIA role in, 202; of coercion, 101, 104; and ethnic organizations, 319–324; of expansionism, 138, 145, 150, 169, 171, 219; international, 96, 98, 106, 121; lying in, 126; use of pressure in, 204; of protectionism, 158; Catholic influence in, 323–325
Polk, Judd, 230
Polls, public opinion, 243–244, 248–249, 250, 268
Pornography of Power (Rubinoff), 72
Potsdam, treaty of, 161
Power: balance of, 96; of business over government, 178; capitalism and, 144; economic, 141, 173; and morality, 306; presidential, 242; as war motivation, 97
Presidency: advisers to, 77, 78; effect of, on foreign policy, 91–93; powers of, 92, 309
Propaganda, 43, 102, 103, 108, 270, 293–295
Public Opinion (Lippmann), 241

Radford, Arthur, 122
Ramparts, 294, 296
Randall, Clarence B., 190
Rayner, Charles, 201
Reinsch, Paul S., 189
Reuther, Walter, 40, 41, 317
Revolution, 60, 74
Richardson, John, 89
Ridgeway, James, 237
Rivers, William L., 291
Rockefeller, David, 178

Rockefeller, Nelson, 34, 143, 185, 312
Roosevelt, Franklin D., 26, 27, 38, 271, 318
Roosevelt, Kermit, 202
Root, Franklin R., 196
Ross, Irwin, 298
Rostow, Eugene V., 69
Rostow, Walt Whitman, 19, 53, 74, 79, 105
Royall, Kenneth, 33
Rubinoff, Lionel, 72
Rusk, Dean, 21, 49, 53, 54, 98, 118

Salinger, Pierre, 61
Schlesinger, Arthur, Jr., 32, 64, 78, 88, 109, 286
Schumpeter, Joseph, 151, 212, 214
Schwartzkopf, H. Norman, 202
Scott, Robert, 290
Shapley, Harlow, 304
Sheehan, Neil, 282
Sheen, Fulton J., 324
Simmonds, Kenneth, 230
Simpson, Smith, 124
Sloan, Alfred P., 161
Smith, Merriman, 292
Smith, Walter B., 29
Somervell, Brehon, 36
Sorenson, Theodore, 88
Souers, Sidney, 29
South Vietnam, 102, 131, 159
Spanish-American War, 243
Speer, Albert, 16, 84
Spellman, Francis Cardinal, 325
Spencer, Herbert, 258
Stalin, Joseph, 253–254, 318
Standard Oil Company, 162–163
Stassen, Harold, 51, 59, 112
State Department: managers of, 55–56; role of, in Vietnam, 89
Steinhardt, Lawrence, 158
Stettinius, Edward, 35

Stevenson, Adlai, 304
Stewart, George C., 203
Stimson, Henry L., 31, 53
Strachey, John, 188
Strauss, Lewis, 288
Sullivan, Leonard, 306
Sylvester, Arthur, 269 289

Taft, Robert A., 51, 154, 259
Tarnowski, Adam, 320
Taylor, Maxwell, 53, 76, 79, 80–
  82, 104, 271, 288
Technology of war, 16, 17
Terror, war uses of, 14
Tet offensive, 114
Times (New York), 302
Times Herald (Washington), 302
Titmuss, Richard, 258
Tokyo, fire raid on, 15
Truman, Harry S, 16, 17, 54, 56,
  68, 84, 164, 309, 310–311, 322
Truman Doctrine, 25, 38, 41, 161–
  162, 189, 245
Twining, Nathan, 123

Udall, Stewart, 38
United Fruit Company, 157
United Nations, 66
United States government: anticommunist movements of, 263;
  and big business, 168, 176–178,
  181, 193; business creed of, 142,
  144–150; diplomacy of, 25–26;
  economic coercion of, 153, 159;
  espionage activities of, 31, 120;
  expansion policies of, 18–19;
  foreign policy of, 51, 64–66,
  138, 140; imperialism of, 20–
  22; industrial expansion and,
  169; military-base network, 30;
  military population, 30; power

United States government
  (*continued*)
  expansion of, 150; secrecy of,
  282, 284; State Department, 25,
  27, 55–56, 89; territorial acqui-
  · sition by, 17; war expenditures
  of, 34, 36, 52, 96, 164, 225
United States Steel Corp., 36, 174

Vance, Cyrus, 328
Vandenberg, Hoyt S., 29
Vandenburg, Arthur, 259, 262, 320
Vanderbilt, William, 31–32
Vernon, Raymond, 146
Vietnam War, 64; business benefits
  from, 190; casualties of, 261;
  critics of, 110–113, 300; as cause
  of economic crisis, 182, 225;
  escalation of, 88, 97, 101, 105,
  113, 129, 325; expenditures for,
  96, 225; failures of, 260; as inflation cause, 173; managers of,
  73, 85–87, 90–91; negotiations
  about, 99; news management
  about, 275; officials lying about,
  127; opposition to, 246–247,
  252; Pentagon study of, 302;
  secrecy about, 283
Vincent, John Carter, 112

Wallace, George, 244
Wallace, Henry, 35, 51, 101, 310
War: and balance of power, 69;
  bureaucratic management of,
  24–27, 80–82; and big business,
  35–37, 45, 141, 227; casualties
  of, 44, 61, 261; contingency
  plans for, 23, 79; counterinsurgency, 24, 79, 157; economy, 18,
  37, 45, 109, 139, 160; escalation
  of, 88, 105; expenditures for, 34,

War (*continued*)
36, 52, 96, 164, 225; guerrilla,
79; and imperialism, 224; labor's
role in, 39–40; Leninist theories
of, 207, 211; managers of, 73,
83–87; military-industrial complex of, 35; mobilization, 36–37,
175; and morality, 64, 68–69,
111, 127; motivation for, 47, 97,
99, 101, 125, 132, 211, 213, 236;
negotiations, 98, 250; opposition
to, 122, 252; presidential power
in, 93; propaganda, 43, 102, 103,
108; revolution, 60, 74; as solution to political problems, 91;
Spanish-American, 243; technology in, 15, 16, 33; uses of terror
in, 14; role of universities in, 42–
43; weapons programs for, 246.
See also Cold War; Vietnam
War; World War II
Weisl, Edwin L., 328
Welch, Leo D., 19, 200
Welles, Sumner, 26
Westmoreland, William, 111
Wheeler, Burton K., 302
Wherry, Kenneth, 264
White, Theodore H., 70, 315

Whyte, William H., Jr., 119
Wiesner, Jerome, 181
Wiles, P. J. D., 208
Williams, William Appleman, 146
Willkie, Wendell, 310
Wilson, Charles E., 164
Wilson, F. M. Huntington, 177
Wilson, Woodrow, 23, 47, 65, 262,
319
World Bank, 204, 222
World War II: and business expansion, 141; casualties of, 44; economic motivations for, 160; and
election of 1948, 310; expenditures for, 36; industrial expansion after, 45; military-industrial
complex of, 35; promoted national unity, 46; U.S. benefits
from, 225; U.S. economy during,
40

Yalta conference, 27

Zahedi, Fazollah, 202

Some other books published by Penguin
are described on the following pages.

Richard J. Walton

COLD WAR AND COUNTERREVOLUTION

This is a radical re-evaluation of President John F. Kennedy's foreign policy. Basing itself squarely on the available evidence, *Cold War and Counterrevolution* reveals that Kennedy was a hawkish counterrevolutionary whose vigorous anti-communism prevailed over his sympathy for the oppressed peoples of the world. Although he had political skill and several great achievements to his credit, Kennedy's chief legacy was the miscalculations of Cuba, Berlin, and Vietnam. As this courageous book makes clear, it is not too early to subject that legacy to strict historical scrutiny. Between 1962 and 1967, Richard J. Walton as the Voice of America's principal United Nations correspondent.

Stephen E. Ambrose

RISE TO GLOBALISM

A searching review of American foreign policy between 1938 and 1970. American involvement in World War II, the Cold War, the Korean conflict, the Berlin crisis, the invasion of Cuba, and the war in Vietnam are among the events that Professor Ambrose surveys as he relates them to the larger themes of America's rise to, and maintenance of, her enormous global power. Yet going far beneath these vast currents, he looks at traits of the American character—economic aggressiveness, racism, fear of communism—and shows how they have helped shape the nation's foreign policy. It is this probing beneath the surface of history that makes *Rise to Globalism* a uniquely valuable work. Stephen E. Ambrose is Professor of History at the University of New Orleans.

Ralph Lapp

THE WEAPONS CULTURE (Rev. Ed.)

A prominent member of the scientific community traces the spread of the nation's military establishment and explores its impact on our society. He describes the emergence of America's present defense posture from World War II to today's concern with the Red Chinese nuclear potential, and probes the other factors that have nurtured the growth of the defense establishment: domestic politics, brinkmanship, anxiety about powerful enemies, and military and economic greed. The central question the author examines is whether the United States can honorably maintain an adequate nuclear defense without becoming the world's number-one aggressor and without warping its national character. Ralph Lapp, who has contributed a new introduction, is a consulting physicist at the Nuclear Science Service.